American Ethnic and Cultural Studies

JOHN C. WALTER & JOHNNELLA E. BUTLER
SERIES EDITORS

American Ethnic and Cultural Studies

The American Ethnic and Cultural Studies series presents critical interdisciplinary, cross-disciplinary, and comparative studies of cultural formations and expressions of racialized peoples in North America. Focusing on African Americans, American Indians, Asian Americans, Chicanos/as, and Latinos/as, and on comparative works among these groups and racialized Euro-Americans, the series also explores new and changing configurations of race and ethnicity as shaped by gender, class, and religion in global and domestic contexts. Informed by research in the humanities, arts, and social sciences; transnational and diasporic studies; film studies; legal studies; public policy, environmental, urban, and rural studies, books in the series will aim to stimulate innovative approaches in scholarship and pedagogy.

Color-Line to Borderlands: The Matrix of American Ethnic Studies
EDITED BY JOHNNELLA E. BUTLER

Color-Line to Borderlands

The Matrix of American Ethnic Studies

EDITED BY JOHNNELLA E. BUTLER

UNIVERSITY OF WASHINGTON PRESS   SEATTLE   LONDON

LIBRARY OF CONGRESS CATALOGING-IN-PUBLICATION DATA

Color-line to borderlands : the matrix of American ethnic studies / edited by Johnnella E. Butler.

    p.   cm.—(American ethnic and cultural studies)

Includes bibliographical references and index.

ISBN 0-295-98090-7 (cloth : alk. paper)— ISBN 0-295-98091-5 (pbk. : alk. paper)

    1. United States—Ethnic relations—Study and teaching.   2. Pluralism (Social sciences)—Study and teaching—United States.   3. Minorities— Study and teaching—United States.   4. Ethnicity—Study and teaching— United States.   I. Butler, Johnnella E.   II. Series.

E184.A1 C54   2001   305.8'0071'173—dc21   00-068320

E pluribus unum.

As social conditions become more equal, the number of persons increases who, although they are neither rich nor powerful enough to exercise any great influence over their fellows, have nevertheless acquired or retained sufficient education and fortune to satisfy their own wants. They owe nothing to any man, they expect nothing from any man; they acquire the habit of always considering themselves as standing alone, and they are apt to imagine that their whole destiny is in their own hands.

—*Alexis de Tocqueville,* Democracy in America

I'm trying to give you something to track your spirit with.

—*Nana Peazant in Julie Dash's film,* Daughters of the Dust

In the sharing of our varied stories,
We create
Our community of a larger memory.

—*Ronald Takaki,* A Larger Memory: A History of Our Diversity, with Voices

Contents

III Changing and Emerging Paradigms

Acknowledgments

THE EDITOR AND CONTRIBUTORS ACKNOWLEDGE THE GEN-erosity of The Ford Foundation in funding projects under the direction of Johnnella Butler that have supported both the conceptualization and the production of this book. We also appreciate the support of the National Endowment for the Humanities for its help in funding an extensive faculty development project, titled "Teaching U.S. Pluralism: American Studies and American Ethnic Studies," directed by Johnnella Butler and Betty Schmitz at the University of Washington. Special

Special thanks go to Michael Foote, a most patient, thorough, and excellent research assistant.

Introduction: Color-Line to Borderlands

JOHNNELLA E. BUTLER

A border is a dividing line, a narrow strip along a steep edge. A borderland is a vague and undetermined place created by the emotional residue of an unnatural boundary. It is in a constant state of transition.

—*Gloria Anzaldúa,* Borderlands/La Frontera

Borders are policed on both sides. Someone who walks between and in and out of national and institutional borders draws attention to the arbitrariness of divisions and to the vested interests of gatekeepers.

—*Shirley Geok-Lin Lim,* Among the White Moon Faces

W. E. B. DU BOIS OBSERVED IN *THE SOULS OF BLACK FOLK* that the problem of the twentieth century is the problem of the color-line, and he proposed a "merging" for the Negro "to attain self-conscious manhood, to merge his double self into a better and truer self. In this merging he wishes neither of the older selves to be lost."[1] Here, as in many other places in *The Souls of Black Folk*, published forty years after the abolition of slavery, Du Bois signals the borderlands. For example, in "Of the Sons of Master and Man," he argues that "only by a union of intelligence and sympathy across the color-line in this critical period of the Republic shall justice and right triumph."[2] In "Of the Training of Black Men," Du Bois speaks again of moving across the color-line, when he states that among the functions of the Negro college is the charge to "help in the solutions of problems of race contact and co-operation." He encourages all Americans to seek the "higher individualism which

xi

the centers of culture protect; . . . a loftier respect for the sovereign human soul that seeks to know itself and the world about it; that seeks a freedom for expansion and self-development; that will love and hate and labor in its own way, untrammeled alike by old and new."[3] He also knows that "truth" is "above the Veil," above the racial line that seeks to maintain the ignorance perpetuated by a racialized existence, and that to be above the Veil one has to move across the color-line. Du Bois ends that chapter with this reflection:

I sit with Shakespeare and he winces not. Across the color line I move arm in arm with Balzac and Dumas, where smiling men and welcoming women glide in gilded halls. From out the caves of evening that swing between the strong-limbed earth and the tracery of the stars, I summon Aristotle and Aurelius and what soul I will, and they come all graciously with no scorn nor condescension. So, wed with Truth, I dwell above the Veil. Is this the life you grudge us, O knightly America? Is this the life you long to change into dull the red hideousness of Georgia? Are you so afraid lest peering from this high Pisgah, between Philistine and Amalekite, we sight the Promised Land?[4]

Removing racism and valuing difference while developing connections among apparent differences would allow us to have a nation that could achieve its optimal possibilities, that could "sight the Promised Land." Du Bois thus signals the breaking of binaries and the generative dialectics that would characterize a pluralistic nation that seeks a cooperative, relational coexistence for its many diversities.[5] Indeed, Du Bois's life may be read as one spent in the borderlands. Although he does not offer a precise appreciation of Africa in *The Souls of Black Folk*, he indicates its significance to humanity. One might view Du Bois's life as a journey through the borderlands of African and Western civilizations, immersed in the dialectics generated by disparate cosmologies, existences, and conflicts. In this respect he might well be viewed not only as the father of Black Studies but also of Ethnic Studies.

Ethnic Studies, Higher Education, and the Borderlands

The genesis of this book and of Ethnic Studies in general reflect the current transitional period in higher education and in the nation. In regard to human relations in the United States, we live in a borderlands that maintains policed yet unmarked color-lines implicit in our actions and our folkways. Thus as a nation we frequently seek legal and often vicious retreats to the color-lines when the indeterminacy of the borderlands challenges racialized, gendered, and classed self-concepts. Ethnic Studies in its various forms—African

American Studies, Asian American Studies, Chicano/a Studies, Latino/a Studies, comparative and ethnic-specific U.S. American Ethnic Studies, and American Indian Studies—has drawn higher education, usually kicking and screaming, into the borderlands of scholarship, pedagogy, faculty collegiality, and institutional development. This book seeks to further the discussions about Ethnic Studies in the academy, toward the aim of the institutionalization of Ethnic Studies. These discussions—charged with disciplinary and budgetary turf battles, with conflicting judgments about the value and practice of interdisciplinary and multidisciplinary studies, and most problematically with the racism, prejudices, and biases ingrained in much of America's national identity—nonetheless are transitional and potentially transformative conflicts and discussions. Both I and the fourteen contributors to this volume intend for the discussions to be transformative, moving administrators, faculty, students, and the nation at large closer to the goal of crossing boundaries, perhaps even agreeing to do away with boundaries, toward the generative goal of merging and creating anew ways of being and doing for the betterment of humankind.

In 1992, The Ford Foundation agreed to my proposal to restructure remaining funds in a departmental grant to implement the major in American Ethnic Studies at the University of Washington to fund a two-day symposium on Ethnic Studies in the United States. This seemed a logical step, for the department had instituted its major, had begun search processes for several additional key positions, and had submitted a proposal to the administration to develop a graduate program. Other programs and departments across the nation were similarly working to institutionalize Ethnic Studies—either ethnic-specific programs (such as African American Studies, Asian American Studies, Chicano/a Studies, Latino/a Studies) or comparative programs with ethnic-specific concentrations, with Native American Studies either standing alone or tentatively aligned with Ethnic Studies because of the sovereign status of Indian nations. By spring of 1993, I organized an Ethnic Studies symposium.

In addition to University of Washington faculty members from the Department of American Ethnic Studies, eleven directors and chairs and four faculty from key departments and programs from across the nation convened on April 23–24, 1993, at the University of Washington-Seattle to discuss the state and the institutionalization of the emerging discipline of Ethnic Studies.[6] Before the conference, I identified topics for four sessions, through phone conversations, written correspondence, and suggested readings from the participants. In addition, the American Ethnic Studies department, with the assistance of the Dean of the College of Arts and Sciences, planned a reception during the symposium for community leaders, University of Washington faculty and administrators, and meeting participants. Leaders of community organizations showed both their interest and support of Ethnic Studies through their attendance and their requests for an immediate follow-up to discuss ways the department at the University of Washington could lend support to their efforts and how they could assist the department. Norm Rice, then Seattle mayor, gave a rousing welcome, connecting the missions of academic programs to community involvement. The following four topics and commentary structured the two-day conference agenda:

1. *The Methodology and Structure of Ethnic Studies.* Participants discussed whether Ethnic Studies is a discipline or a field that incorporates disciplines and interdisciplinary and comparative methodology. The topic covered the interdisciplinary and comparative nature of Ethnic Studies, distinguishing between multidisciplinary and interdisciplinary; the ways in which Ethnic Studies curricula reflect these methodologies; and a discussion of the need to identify the bases of comparative Ethnic Studies. Commentary examined what the U.S. groups of color share: that is, what is similar and dissimilar in their experiences that can provide a basis for comparative analysis. Finally, conference participants discussed what distinguishes Ethnic Studies from the inclusion of the study of U.S. people of color in the "traditional" disciplines (on undergraduate and graduate levels).

2. *Institutional Structures for Ethnic Studies.* This topic examined the relationship between interdisciplinary and comparative units and ethnic-specific units. The issue expanded to include the possibility of desired, productive relationships between such ethnic-specific professional organizations as the Asian American Studies Association, the National Council for Black Studies and such organizations as the National Association for Ethnic Studies and the American Studies Association, which attempt to provide a professional home for all the variations.

3. *Hiring for Ethnic Studies and for "Traditional" Departments.* Conference participants explored ways to assist university administrations in identifying and hiring minority faculty without hampering the growth of Ethnic Studies programs and departments. We also examined the problem of traditional departments hiring faculty of color with expertise in race theory and ethnic and race content whose positions have no structural connections with Ethnic Studies. Often such positions block filling the academic needs of Ethnic Studies. In many cases Ethnic Studies departments or programs are told that they cannot "duplicate" areas of study supposedly covered in the traditional departments. This point is related to the first agenda topic

in that it demands that Ethnic Studies faculty define the field of study and its parameters, scope, and depth.

4. *Strategies for Developing Graduate Study.* Symposium participants also identified the generative strategies for further developing undergraduate and graduate programs (this involves faculty development for Ethnic Studies faculty as well as for faculty who wish to include Ethnic Studies content in traditional departments); and for securing funding for graduate student support as well as for discretionary expenses, lecture series, endowed positions, community outreach activities, and so on.

Participants indicated little concern about enrollment in courses and majors. Representatives from all Ethnic Studies units reported healthy enrollment and student interest, and most long-established units reported steady enrollment and increasing student interest (e.g., the Department of American Ethnic Studies at the University of Washington has averaged 150–200 students per year enrolled as majors from 1993 to 1999). Many Ethnic Studies students graduate with either single or double majors and continue with graduate studies in the humanities and social sciences, law, medicine, public policy, social work, education, and management, among other fields. Other students with Ethnic Studies majors find employment after graduating, as do majors in other humanities and social science fields.

Conference participants expressed overarching concern for and interest in identifying ways to connect—through scholarship, pedagogy, and institutional structures—the differences between and among mainstream and marginalized groups, scholarship, and teaching. They viewed this connection as key to the transformation of the U.S. higher education in meeting the "dizzying array of changes that are reconfiguring our society."[7] At the end of the symposium participants envisioned compiling a report for The Ford Foundation to address the following topics:

1. The educational mission of Ethnic Studies, including what functions Ethnic Studies programs and departments can, do, and should perform within higher education and in the surrounding communities of which colleges and universities are a part.

2. Curriculum design and content, including what constitutes an acceptable Ethnic Studies curriculum and what its courses should cover.

3. Governance, including who could or should control Ethnic Studies.

4. Professional certification, including what kind of qualifications faculty teaching Ethnic Studies courses must possess and what kind of research they must do and publish to be hired or promoted to tenure.

5. An overview statement, including the mission and objectives of Ethnic Studies.

6. A discussion on integrative methodology and what makes the form it takes unique to Ethnic Studies, including orality, comparative cultures, insiders' perspectives, dispelling of false invocations of the objective and the subjective, and working with and investigating the connections, boundaries, borders, and places in between disciplines, U.S. people of color, and Whites.

7. Use of a terminology that encompasses dichotomies, syntheses, and generative tensions.

8. The identification and use of the insider's perspective, including teaching and doing scholarship and research from the point of view of the people studied.

9. The relationship to Women's Studies, Gay and Lesbian Studies, and American Studies.

10. Connecting Ethnic Studies to communities and examining its relationship to communities.

11. A broad discussion of Ethnic Studies programs and their structures.

12. Ethnic studies' contributions to pedagogy and scholarship.

13. Stated opposition to simplistic descriptions and uses of "learning styles."

14. The rationale and need for institutional funding and funding from outside sources.

15. The development of future Ethnic Studies programs.

16. The roles of national professional organizations to function as "learned societies" in the endorsement of accepted venues of publication in Ethnic Studies scholarship, in developing graduate studies programs, and in guiding the continued development and review of undergraduate programs.

17. Ensuring a "future for our past" through the cultural preservation of national resources.[8]

It soon became clear, however, that the growth of Ethnic Studies programs and departments and the numerous topics to be covered warranted a book rather than a mere report. Most of the aforementioned topics that emerged from the symposium, therefore, either appear at great length in this volume or are implicated in the discussions within. I use the term *discussion* in at least two senses: First, the thirteen chapters in this volume emerged from discussions in the 1993 symposium; from conversations among the various contributors in 1995 and 1997, who convened at the University of Washington through funding from The Ford Foundation, the National Endowment for the Humanities, and the University of Washington Hylan Lecture Fund for working sessions and a campus American Studies conference; and from presentations and discussions at the session, "Coalition or Collision: Territory, Difference, and the Institution," convened by the Minority Scholars Committee of the American Studies Association at the 1997 conference in Washington, D.C. Second, I use the term *discussion* because the book is written with the expectation of engaging a broad audience interested in the productive, generative, and highly valued discussions of the meaning of scholarship on and teaching about the U.S. American experiences of socially constructed, racialized ethnic minorities as they intersect with those of the socially constructed nonracialized Americans.

Color-Line to Borderlands is not intended to be a definitive work on Ethnic Studies. In fact, a number of omissions prevent it from providing a complete overview of the field. Because the contributors decided themselves how to approach their chapters, some essays focus primarily on the historical development of Ethnic Studies or of an ethnic-specific field; others provide analyses of the relationships in Ethnic Studies among ideology, related fields of study, scholarship, methodology, and pedagogy; still other chapters provide a combination of these two approaches. The volume does not include an essay on the development of Latino/a Studies or Puerto Rican Studies, as originally intended, because I was unable to find a readily available contributor. For similar reasons there is no specific discussion of gender, Black Women's Studies, or Chicana Studies. Rather than covering the all-salient components and issues of Ethnic Studies, which would have demanded at least a two-volume work, I have judiciously chosen (I hope readers agree) to cover what appeals to a wide audience—a readership not necessarily conversant with Ethnic Studies, many of whom have never seriously thought of Ethnic Studies as an entity integral to the liberal arts.

Resistance to the Institutionalization of Ethnic Studies

Most symposium attendees had experienced to varying degrees difficulties with higher administration—ranging from problems with administrative support of the intransigence of "mainstream" scholarship and positionality to destructive intradepartmental and intraprogrammatic tensions rooted in protective and fearful identity politics that the administration refused to tackle head-on. *Color-Line to Borderlands* narrates the issues surrounding the development of Ethnic Studies and the struggle to produce scholarship that reflects humanity's fullness in its complexities, conflicts, and complements. That narrative is fragmented, almost lost it seems, in the often simplistic interpretations of "diversity" and fear of the displacement and discomfort of living multiculturally.

Reviews of Ronald Takaki's book, *A Different Mirror: A History of Multicultural America*, provide insight into the difficulty of the institution-alization of Ethnic Studies in U.S. higher education. This work, whatever the criticisms, is the first comprehensive attempt to tell the story of the United States in a way that reflects the interconnectedness of events, actions, expe-riences, and perspectives, addressing raced, classed, and gendered realities. In relating the beautiful and the ugly, as Langston Hughes urged his read-ers, Takaki incorporates the contemporaneous emotional responses to events, something that might be read as a postmodern act of re-memory with the Ethnic Studies goal of connection. As a professor of Ethnic Studies and a leading scholar in the field, Takaki's work over the years reflects the spirit of Louis Chu, Vine Deloria, Frederick Douglass, Maxine Hong Kingston, Joyce Ladner, Amerigo Paredes, and other historians, creative writ-ers, literary scholars, and social scientists who have sought to illuminate ways of understanding the particularity of the experiences of racialized ethnic groups in the context of the larger U.S. experience. Takaki's book is a quin-tessential and masterful beginning to the inclusive historiography since that signaled by the works of African Americanists such as Mary Berry, St. Clair Drake, Vincent Harding, Joy James, Manning Marable, and other lesser known teachers and scholars.

Yet in major reviews only Harding has expressed Takaki's triumph, observing that "at his best, Takaki writes a history that touches us . . . [draw-ing] us into the multicultural rehearsal for the nation's wholeness, remind-ing us that the ashes we possess are for both mourning and building."[9] Many reviewers denied that one can select, even after much research and study, sev-eral groups that reflect the dynamics of the nation's history; while others did not discuss the historiography at all. Rather, for example, Andrew Hacker, professor and frequent review essayist for the *New York Review of Books*, imposed an essentialist view on Takaki's book, seeing it as a "clean account of the basic assumptions and intentions of the advocates of diversity . . . a manifesto for the future . . . that desires Americans to sustain their ancestral identities."[10] Reviewer George Fredrickson praised Takaki's attempt "to view all of American history from a multicultural perspective," adding that the work represents a "laudable effort—humane, well-informed, accessible and often incisive." He faults Takaki's approach, however, which he claims has its "own kind of one-sidedness and partiality." He cites omissions that he considers to demonstrate that minorities have had some White support throughout U.S. history, arguing that such omissions create the impression that White support is only exceptional. Interestingly, Fredrickson offers the metaphor of "a slowly simmering stew" to describe the formation of the national identity, rather than that of the often cited "mosaic" or "melting pot."[11] These reviews and others reflect the responses of faculty and administration to Ethnic Studies scholarship and teaching that the emerging field has encountered over the past thirty years. At worst, these comments are scathingly dismissive and even fearful; at best, they are ambivalent, as Fredrickson's "slowly simmering stew" undoubtedly reveals. Minority faculty are not immune from expressing similar or analogous views.[12]

The Problem of Naming and Definition

Naming in a nation that has not resolved the problem of its racialist and ethnocentric heritage is always problematic. For example, the Irish were viewed as a "race" in the mid-nineteenth century and well into the twentieth century. Historian Karen Brodkin has reminded readers that "the U.S. 'discovery' that Europe was divided into inferior and superior races began with the racialization of the Irish in the mid-nineteenth century and flowered in response to the great waves of immigration from southern and eastern Europe that began in the late nineteenth century. Before that time, European immigrants—including Jews—had been largely assimilated into the White population."[13] But Whiteness eventually "solved" the resulting problems of the racialization of European immigrants to the United States, as they developed an Americanized ethnicity that quickly translated as White. African Americans, however—the diametrical opposite of this Whiteness—have struggled over the years with such imposed labeling as "colored," "negro," "nigra," and "nigger." To signal the cultural and human content of their racialized identity, they devised such solutions as Afro-Saxon, Negro, Afro-American, Black, and African American, always with the problem about capitalization. The term *African American* evolved from the attempts of Black Americans to convey a cultural-ethnic content to the naming of their reality and experiences. Black, originally intended to signal diasporic connections, fell prey to the insistence of the mainstream use of "Black" having racial or skin-color connotations only.

Similarly, Chicano/a and Latino/a Studies reflects the insistence on recognition by Chicana and Latina feminists. When used together, Chicano/a and Latino/a Studies implies the insistence of Chicanos/as that theirs is the largest group of Spanish-speaking Americans and that they have a claim to an indigenous heritage. Asian American is argued to be a political term, reflecting a conscious coalition (as one argument goes) and an imposed identity (as goes another). The terms American Indian Studies and Native American Studies, although often used interchangeably, sometimes signify to some the acceptance of the colonial designation for the former and the recognition of the indigenous positionality of the latter. Both terms are problematic, however, as they do not reflect the individual nations of Native peoples and imply to many outsiders American ethnic political and cultural groups.

Questions remain about how to reckon with the East Indian American, the Haitian American, and the Southeast Asian American. Where do these lives, literary expressions, and U.S. political experiences relate to what is called Ethnic Studies? And what about the term *Ethnic Studies* itself? What about the Euro-American, the European immigrant and the relationship between assimilation and racism? Although these questions linger, as the following chapters demonstrate, Ethnic Studies in academia today reflects a necessarily complicated response. The term itself, as discussed at length in the following essays, is problematic in that it focuses on the racialized ethnic groups in the United States and not on White, European ethnic groups that once constituted "immigrant studies." Some programs and departments include comparative texts as well as historical and policy analogies of Jewish American, Irish American, and other Euro-American ethnicities in courses to further explore the context and expand the understanding of U.S. cultural and political dynamics. In most cases, however, "Ethnic Studies" refers to U.S. racialized ethnic groups.

Recent studies of Whiteness suggest a broader understanding of racialization and hold significance for Ethnic Studies and American Studies, as Whites are viewed as racialized and of a cultural entity. Both fields are in considerable flux due to this development. However, as constituted in most colleges and universities today, Ethnic Studies is the interdisciplinary and comparative study of the social, cultural, political, and economic expression and experience of U.S. racialized ethnic groups and of U.S. racialization and its effects. It refers to the racial groups in the United States that have historically and continually been excluded from citizenship or full participation on the grounds that they have been:

- Perceived, imaged, and treated as either inhuman or as noble savages and treated legally as colonized peoples with limited legal rights (American Indians).
- Perceived, imaged, and treated legally as being inhuman, having no culture, ethnicity, or legal rights (African Americans).

- Perceived, imaged, and treated ambivalently as having an inferior culture or ethnicity, stemming from their mixed racial and cultural heritage and treated ambivalently legally (Chicanos/as and Latinos/as).
- Perceived, imaged, and treated as savages with no culture or ethnicity or treated ambivalently as exotic, model cultural groups; and treated legally as a people to exclude or include physically and culturally, depending on the perceived relationship to racialization at a given time (Asian Americans).
- Perceived, imaged, and treated as any of the above based on phenotypes and stereotypes that resonate with U.S. racialization (East Indian Americans, Haitian Americans, Central Americans).

Rather than being "victim studies," as some critics have referred to the field, Ethnic Studies seeks to identify, assert, and study the cultural realities of these groups, their relation to the body politic, and their unassimilated status because of racism and ethnocentrism intertwined with sexism, heterosexism, and classism, as well as religious, age, and physical ability discrimination. Ethnic Studies seeks to illuminate the possibility of a vibrant, multiracial, and multiethnic national culture and a just society.

Institutional Ambivalences toward Ethnic Studies and Attitudes toward Interdisciplinary Studies and Structures

What might be called institutional ambivalences toward Ethnic Studies stem from the refusal of most faculty and administrators to embrace the challenges that Ethnic Studies, either in its comparative or ethnic-specific forms, presents to scholarship, methodology, pedagogy, syllabi, institutional structure, and composition of faculty and student body. A few signs of administrative and faculty ambivalences are:

- Viewing and treating Ethnic Studies simultaneously as simply an academic endeavor and as a "minority department" that must be endured as long as there is community pressure of some kind.
- Hiring faculty in Ethnic Studies who have only discipline-based interests, with little interest in or understanding of interdisciplinary studies.
- Supporting departmental hires of faculty on the basis of racial-ethnic parity, of skin color, or of racial-ethnic heritage rather than on the basis of academic scholarship and demonstrated teaching ability in Ethnic Studies.
- Failing to intervene on justified academic grounds for fear of being called racist by the offending parties when difficulties arise in Ethnic Studies departments.
- Taking a position with a faction in an Ethnic Studies department because of pres-

sure from faculty of color outside the department who have various ideas of what Ethnic Studies should and should not be and various reasons (few, if any, academic) for wanting to be associated with the department.

- Supporting intra-racial and interracial conflicts within the department by viewing the department as a minority preserve rather than an academic department, thereby encouraging racial-ethnic essentialism rather than the serious study of key, excluded groups.

Judith Thompson Klein, Professor of Humanities at Wayne State University, and William H. Newell, Professor of Interdisciplinary Studies at Miami University, have reminded scholars that "approaches vary and disputes over terminology continue" regarding interdisciplinary studies.[14] They broadly define interdisciplinary studies (IDS) as: "A process of answering a question, solving a problem, or addressing a topic that is too broad or complex to be dealt with adequately by a single discipline or profession. Whether the context is an integrated approach to general education, a Women's Studies program, or a science, technology, and society program, IDS draws on disciplinary perspectives and integrates their insights through construction of a more comprehensive perspective. In this manner, interdisciplinary study is not a simple supplement but is complementary to and corrective of disciplines."[15] Varying approaches and disputes over terminology for interdisciplinary studies often places Ethnic Studies in a state of limbo, subjected to the whims of prevailing custom on a given campus and within its own department. To distinguish interdisciplinary studies that provide an "integrated approach" and a "more comprehensive perspective" suggests a type of methodology, one that studies a topic through the integration of various methodologies as well as through the lens of various disciplines. For example, often a simplistic lining up of courses from different disciplinary departments serves as an Ethnic Studies, African American Studies, or Asian American Studies, Chicano/a, Latino/a, or Native American program.

In such instances, with few or no courses connecting content, group experiences, and methodologies, Ethnic Studies is viewed simply as a programmatic entity that has little cohesion except the demands of people of color and some White faculty that it be taught. When campuses refuse to establish procedures that require discipline-based departments to coordinate and conduct hires in areas that overlap with interdisciplinary departments, duplication then occurs in hiring and the long-established, familiar discipline-based departmental program is favored to teach courses on or reflective of "race." In addition, faculty development projects in interdisciplinary Ethnic Studies, both comparative and ethnic-specific, are often merely tolerated by higher administration, used as a basis for securing other unrelated funding, or not continued with institutional funding. The content of Ethnic Studies thus remains marginal. Faculty in Ethnic Studies programs and departments too frequently assume that Ethnic Studies is a place to house cultural studies, interdisciplinary-based work that is unwelcome in "traditional" departments. Often they develop programs and departments with no resonance to the field of study over time, ignorant or dismissive of the intellectual narrative of Ethnic Studies.

"Other" Studies and Ethnic Studies: A Necessary Dialectic

T. V. Reed, in the final chapter of this book, discusses the problematic of the various "studies" that examine difference in the United States. The current tension on campuses between the well-established American Studies programs and departments and the ambivalently accepted African American, Asian American, Native American, Chicano/a, Latino/a, and Ethnic Studies programs and departments exemplifies the crucial, long-simmering conflict that multiculturalism has brought to a near boil. As I discuss in my chapter "Ethnic Studies as a Matrix for the Humanities, the Social Sciences, and the Common Good," that tension is exacerbated by the development of a seemingly all-encompassing cultural studies in the United States largely in isolation from Ethnic Studies. Are we willing in academic institutions and as a nation to provide the space to study seriously and learn respectfully, in as complete a way as possible, U.S. history so that we can simultaneously build toward a just and equitable future? Now, at the turn of the century, Ethnic Studies is needed in its various forms as an academic, scholarly entity that serves simultaneously as a corrective and reconstructive enterprise for scholarship and teaching. American Studies is needed as an academic, scholarly entity that works with so-called traditional disciplines and Ethnic Studies departments, programs, scholars, and students to discover its limitations and to redefine its textual bases and assumptions. Both fields are routes for higher education to connect with its communities, the citizenry of this nation. Together, these fields provide the necessary dialectic to investigate the distortions, reinstate the omissions, and embrace the fullness of our conflicted, limited, joyous, and painful human experience, so we can retell the national story with an honesty that allows us to understand the present and build on honesty and justice.

Color-Line to Borderlands is a work of generative scholarship, a result of what preceded it. This work is to be advanced by further scholarship, future institutional structures, and incoming faculty and students. The goal of that advancement is not the reduction of re-memory, re-vision, transformation, and the change that inclusion can bring through a reification of the narratives of domination and victimhood. Rather, the generative goal of Ethnic Studies actively seeks the realization of an educated citizenry in an equitable and just democracy, a citizenry that enjoys an education that meaningfully connects to everyday lives, to public policy, and to institutional structure.

Notes

1. W. E. B. Du Bois, *The Souls of Black Folk* (1903; reprint, New York: Alfred A. Knopf, Everyman's Library, 1993), 16, 37, and 9.

2. Ibid., 149.

3. Ibid., 88.

4. Ibid., 88–89.

5. Contemporary readings of W. E. B. Du Bois frequently fail to acknowledge the dialectics that are replete throughout his life and work even when they purport to do so. Most often, they fail to view Du Bois's thinking as a continuum and often reflect the critics' own ambivalences and prejudices about Africa and African American life and culture, rather than reflecting Du Bois's constant attempts to engage the complexities and the best of the old and the new. For example, see Arnold Rampersad's introduction to the 1993 Everyman's Library edition of *The Souls of Black Folk;* Henry Louis Gates, "African American Studies in the Twenty-First Century," *The Black Scholar* 22 (3): 20–29; and Henry Louis Gates and Cornel West, *The Future of the Race* (New York: Alfred A. Knopf, 1998). See my refutation of the reading of Du Bois's concept of double consciousness that is characteristic of African American Studies in Butler, "African American Studies and the 'Warring Ideals': The Color Line Meets the Borderlands," in Manning Marable, ed., *Dispatches from the Ebony Tower: Intellectuals Confront the African American Experience* (New York: Columbia University Press, 2000); and Joy James's comprehensive analysis of contemporary African American intellectual leadership in James, *Transcending the Talented Tenth: Black Leaders and American Intellectuals* (New York: Routledge, 1997).

6. The following scholars participated in the Ethnic Studies Symposium,

April 23–24, 1993, hosted by the Department of American Ethnic Studies at the University of Washington-Seattle: convener Johnnella E. Butler, chair, Department of American Ethnic Studies, University of Washington; Marilyn Bentz, senior lecturer, American Indian Studies Center, University of Washington; Pedro Cabán, chair, Puerto Rican and Hispanic Caribbean Studies, Rutgers University; Larry Estrada, vice provost and director, American Cultural Studies Program, Western Washington University; Evelyn Hu-De Hart, director, Center for the Study of Race and Ethnicity, University of Colorado-Boulder; Rhett S. Jones, director, Center for the Study of Race and Ethnicity, Brown University; Ron La France, director, American Indian Program, Cornell University; Franklin Odo, director, Ethnic Studies, University of Hawaii; Robert Perry, chair, Department of Ethnic Studies, Bowling Green State University; Refugio Rochin, professor, Department of Agricultural Economics/Chicano Studies Program, University of California-Davis; Marcia Sawyer, visiting assistant professor, Department of American Ethnic Studies, University of Washington; Ines Talamantez, associate professor of religion, University of California-Santa Barbara; L. Ling-Chi Wang, chair and associate professor, Department of Ethnic Studies, University of California-Berkeley; Brackett Williams, director, African American Studies Program, University of Arizona-Tucson; and William Williard, chair, Department of Comparative American Cultures, Washington State University.

Additional participants included the following members of the Department of American Ethnic Studies, University of Washington: Albert Black, senior lecturer, Afro-American Studies; Guadalupe Friaz, assistant professor, Chicano Studies; Erasmo Gamboa, associate professor, Chicano Studies; Tetsuden Kashima, associate professor, Asian American Studies; Linda Revilla, assistant professor, Asian American Studies; Elizabeth Salas, assistant professor, Chicano Studies; Joseph W. Scott, professor, Afro-American Studies; Liang Tien, assistant professor, Asian American Studies; John C. Walter, professor, Afro-American Studies; and Shawn Wong, associate professor, Asian American Studies.

7. Pedro Cabán, "Connecting Our Differences," *Common Purposes,* October 1992.

8. Franklin S. Odo, "Cultural Preservation Policy: Is There a Future for Our Past?" in Bill Ong Hing and Ronald Lee, eds., *The State of Asian Pacific America: A Public Policy Report, Policy Issues to the Year 2020* (Los Angeles: LEAP Asian Pacific American Public Policy Institute and UCLA Asian American Studies Center, 1996), 113–25.

9. Vincent Harding, "Healing at the Razor's Edge: Reflections on a History of Multicultural America," *Journal of American History* 81 (2): 571–84.

10. Andrew Hacker, *New York Review of Books,* October 7, 1993.

11. George Fredrickson, *New York Times Book Review,* August 22, 1993, p. 17.

12. Reminiscent of the late 1960s, the student hunger strikes at UCLA and the University of California-Berkeley during spring 1999, when Ethnic Studies was threatened by the anti-affirmative action initiatives and an overall climate negative to the field's development in California and Washington state, indicate another dimension of Ethnic Studies: its role in addressing for students the need for an inclusive education, one that engages the complexities of U.S. life and culture. As Professor L. Ling-Chi Wang, chair of Ethnic Studies at Berkeley, stated on May 4, 1999: "I am both sad and angry that the legitimate issues affecting the future of the Department of Ethnic Studies had to result in the mass arrest and detention of the best and the brightest of the future leaders of California and the nation early this morning. . . .Years of neglect and indifference toward Ethnic Studies precipitated the current crisis. When students experience dwindling faculty and thinning curricula and when they see overworked faculty and canceled classes, they know the department is dying of a slow death. They did what they felt was necessary to call the Chancellor's attention to these problems. I have nothing but respect and admiration for their commitment and courage. Being new to the Berkeley campus, I know Chancellor [Robert M.] Berdahl is not personally responsible for the problems now facing Ethnic Studies. I also know he wants to reverse the trend and restore the preeminence of Ethnic Studies among the universities across the nation." E-mail forwarded to me that May from aaascommunity@lists.u.oregon.edu.

13. Karen Brodkin, *How Jews Became White Folks and What That Says about Race in America* (New Brunswick, N.J.: Rutgers University Press, 1998), 27.

14. Julie Thompson Klein and William H. Newell, "Advancing Interdisciplinary Studies," in William H. Newell, ed., *Interdisciplinarity: Essays from the Literature* (New York: College Entrance Examination Board, 1998), 3.

15. Ibid.

ETHNIC STUDIES AS A MATRIX: MOVING FROM COLOR-LINE TO BORDERLANDS

Multiculturalism: Battleground or Meeting Ground?

RONALD TAKAKI

It is very natural that the history written by the victim does not altogether chime with the story of the victor.

—*Jose Fernandez of California, 1874*

IN 1979, I EXPERIENCED THE TRUTH OF THIS STATEMENT when I found myself attacked by C. Vann Woodward in the *New York Review of Books*. I had recently published a broad and comparative study of Blacks, Chinese, Indians, Irish, and Mexicans, from the American Revolution to the U.S. war against Spain. But, for Woodward, my *Iron Cages: Race and Culture in Nineteenth-Century America* was too narrow in focus. My analysis, he stridently complained, should have compared ethnic conflicts in the United States to those in Brazil, South Africa, Germany, and Russia. Such an encompassing view would have shown that America was not so "bad" after all.

The author of scholarship that focused exclusively on the American South, Woodward was arguing that mine should have been cross-national in order to be "balanced." But how, I wondered, was balance to be measured? Surely, any examination of the "worse instances" of racial oppression in other countries should not diminish the importance of what happened here. Balance should also insist that we steer away from denial or a tendency to be dismissive. Woodward's contrast of the "millions of corpses" and the "horrors of genocide" in Nazi Germany to racial violence in the United States seemed both heartless and beside the point. Enslaved Africans in the American South would have felt little comfort to have been told that conditions for their counterparts in Latin America were "worse." They would have responded that it

3

mattered little that the Black population in Brazil was "17.5 million" rather than "127.6 million" by 1850, or whether slavery beyond what Woodward called the "three-mile limit" was more terrible and deadly.

What had provoked such a scolding from this dean of American history? One might have expected a more supportive reading from the author of *The Strange Career of Jim Crow*, a book that helped stir our society's moral conscience during the civil rights era. My colleague Michael Rogin tried to explain Woodward's curious reaction by saying that the elderly historian perceived me as a bad son. History had traditionally been written by members of the majority population; now some younger scholars of color like me had received our Ph.D.s and were trying to "re-vision" America's past. But our critical scholarship did not chime with the traditional version of history. Noting my non-Whiteness, Woodward charged that I was guilty of reverse discrimination: my characterization of Whites in terms of rapacity, greed, and brutality constituted a "practice" that could be described as "racism." Like a father, Woodward chastised me for catering to the "current mood of self-denigration and self-flagellation." If and when the mood passes," he lamented, "one would hope a more balanced perspective on American history will prevail."[1]

Looking back at Woodward's review today, we can see that it constituted one of the opening skirmishes of what has come to be called the "culture war." Some of the battles of this conflict have erupted in the political arena. Speaking before the 1992 Republican National Convention, Patrick Buchanan urged his fellow conservatives to take back their cities, their culture, and their country, block by block. This last phrase was a reference to the National Guard's show of force during the 1992 Los Angeles riot. On the other hand, in his first speech as president-elect, Bill Clinton recognized our ethnic and cultural diversity as a source of America's strength.

But many of the fiercest battles over how we define America are being waged within the academy. There minority students and scholars are struggling to diversify the curriculum, while conservative pundits like Charles J. Sykes and Dinesh D'Souza are fighting to recapture the campus.[2] The stakes in this conflict are high, for we are being asked to define education and determine what an educated person should know about the world in general and America in particular. This is the issue Allan Bloom raises in his polemic, *The Closing of the American Mind*. A leader of the intellectual backlash against cultural diversity, he articulates a conservative view of the university curriculum. According to Bloom, entering students are "uncivilized," and faculty have the responsibility to "civilize" them. As a teacher, he claims to know what their "hungers" are and "what they can digest." Eating is one of his favorite metaphors. Noting the "large Black presence" at major universities, he regrets the "'one failure' in race relations—Black students have proven to be 'indigestible.'" They do not "melt as have *all* other groups." The problem, he contends, is that "Blacks have become Blacks": they have become "ethnic." This separatism has been reinforced by an academic permissiveness that has befouled the curriculum with "Black Studies" along with "Learn Another Culture." The only solution, Bloom insists, is "the good old Great Books approach."[3] Behind Bloom's approach is a political agenda. He asks, What does it mean to be an American? The "old view" was that "by recognizing and accepting man's natural rights," people in this society found a fundamental basis of unity. The immigrant came here and became assimilated. But the "recent education of openness," with its celebration of diversity, is threatening the social contract that had defined the members of American society as individuals. During the civil rights movement of the 1960s, Black Power militants had aggressively affirmed a group identity. Invading college campuses, they demanded "respect for Blacks as Blacks, not as human beings simply" and began to "propagandize acceptance of different ways." This emphasis on ethnicity separated Americans from each other, shrouding their "essential humankindness." The Black conception of a group identity provided the theoretical basis for a new policy, affirmative action, which opened the doors to the admission of unqualified students. Once on campus, many Black students agitated for the establishment of Black Studies programs, which in turn contributed to academic incoherence, lack of synopsis, and the "decomposition of the university."[4]

Bloom's is a closed mind, unwilling to allow the curriculum to become more inclusive. Fortunately, many other educators have been acknowledging the need to teach students about the cultural diversity of American society. "Every student needs to know," former University of Wisconsin chancellor Donna Shalala has explained, "much more about the origins and history of the particular cultures which, as Americans, we will encounter during our lives."[5] This need for cross-cultural understanding has been grimly highlighted by racial tensions and conflicts such as the Black boycott of Korean stores, Jewish-Black antagonism in Crown Heights, and especially the 1992 Los Angeles racial explosion. During the days of rage Rodney King pleaded for calm: "Please, we can get along here. We all can get along. I mean, we're all stuck here for a while. Let's try to work it out." But how should "we" be defined?[6]

Earlier, the Watts riot had reflected a conflict between Whites and Blacks, but the fire this time in 1992 Los Angeles highlighted the multiracial reality of American society. Race includes Hispanics and Asian Americans. The old binary language of race relations between Whites and Blacks, *Newsweek* observed, is no longer descriptive of who we are as Americans. Our future will increasingly be multiethnic in the twenty-first century; the western edge of the continent called California constitutes the thin end of an entering new wedge, a brave new multicultural world of Calibans of many different races and ethnicities.[7] If "we" must be more inclusive, how do we "work it out"? One crucial way would be for us to learn more about each other—not only Whites about peoples of color, but also Blacks about Koreans and Hispanics about Blacks. Our very diversity offers an intellectual invitation to teachers and scholars to reach for a more comprehensive understanding of American society. Here the debate over multiculturalism has gone beyond whether or not to be inclusive. The question has become, "How do we develop and teach a more culturally diverse curriculum?"

What has emerged are two perspectives, what Diane Ravitch has usefully described as "particularism" versus "pluralism." But, by regarding each as exclusive, even antagonistic, Ravitch fails to appreciate the validity of both viewpoints and the ways they complement each other.[8] Actually, we need not be forced into an either-or situation. Currently, many universities offer courses that study a particular group, such as African Americans or Asian Americans. This focus enables students of a specific minority to learn about their history and community. These students are not necessarily seeking what has been slandered as self-esteem courses. Rather, they simply believe that they are entitled to learn how their communities fit into American history and society. My grandparents were Japanese immigrant laborers, and even after I finished college with a major in American history and completed a Ph.D. in this field, I had learned virtually nothing about why they had come to America and what had happened to them as well as other Japanese immigrants in this country. This history should have been available to me.

The particularistic perspective led me to write *Strangers from a Different Shore: A History of Asian Americans*. This focus on a specific group can also be found in Irving Howe's *World of Our Fathers: The Journey of the East European Jews to America*, Mario Garcia's *Desert Immigrants: The Mexicans of El Paso, 1880–1920*, Lawrence Levine's *Black Culture and Black Consciousness*, and Kerby Miller's *Emigrants and Exiles: Ireland and the Irish Exodus to North America*.[9] Increasingly, educators and scholars are recognizing the need for us to step back from particularistic portraits in order to discern the rich and complex mosaic of our national pluralism. While group-specific courses have been in the curriculum for many years, courses offering a comparative and integrative approach have been introduced recently. In fact, the University of California-Berkeley has instituted an American cultures requirement for graduation. The purpose of this course is to give students an understanding of American society in terms of African Americans, Asian Americans, Latinos, Native Americans, and European Americans, especially the immigrant groups from places like Ireland, Italy, Greece, and Russia.

What such curricular innovations promise is not only the introduction of intellectually dynamic courses that study the criss-crossed paths of America's different groups but also the fostering of comparative multicultural scholarship. This pluralistic approach is illustrated by works like my *Different Mirror: A History of Multicultural America* as well as Gary Nash's *Red, White, and Black: The Peoples of Early America*, Ivan Light's *Ethnic Enterprise in America: Business and Welfare among Chinese, Japanese, and Blacks*, Reginald Horsman's *Race and Manifest Destiny: The Origins of American Racial Anglo-Saxonism,* and Benjamin Ringer's *"We the People" and Others: Duality and America's Treatment of Its Racial Minorities.*[10]

Even here, however, a battle is being fought over how America's diversity should be conceptualized. For example, Ravitch avidly supports the pluralistic perspective, but she fears national division. Stressing the importance of national unity, Ravitch promotes the development of multiculturalism based on a strategy of adding on: to keep mainstream Anglo-American history and expand it by simply including information on racism as well as minority contributions to America's music, art, literature, food, clothing, sports, and holidays. The purpose behind this pluralism, for Ravitch, is to encourage students of "all racial and ethnic groups to believe that they are part of this society and that they should develop their talents and minds to the fullest." By "fullest" she means for students to be inspired by learning about "men and women from diverse backgrounds who overcame poverty, discrimination, physical handicaps, and other obstacles to achieve success in a variety of fields." Ravitch is driven by a desire for universalism: she wants to affirm our common humanity by discouraging our specific group identities, especially those based on racial experiences. Ironically, Ravitch, a self-avowed proponent of pluralism, actually wants us to abandon our group ties and become individuals.[11]

This privileging of the "unum" over the "pluribus" has been advanced more aggressively by Arthur Schlesinger Jr. in *The Disuniting of America*. In this jeremiad, Schlesinger denounces what he calls "the cult of ethnicity"—the shift from assimilation to group identity, from integration to separatism. The issue at stake, he argues, is the teaching of "*bad* history under whatever ethnic banner." After acknowledging that American history has long been written in the "interests of white Anglo-Saxon Protestant males," he describes the enslavement of Africans, the seizure of Indian lands, and the exploitation of Chinese railroad workers. But his discussion on racial oppression is perfunctory and parsimonious, and he devotes most of his attention to a defense of traditional history. "Anglocentric domination of schoolbooks is based in part on unassailable facts," Schlesinger declares. "For better or worse, American history has been shaped more than anything else by British tradition and culture." Like Bloom, Schlesinger utilizes the metaphor of eating. "To deny the essentially European origins of American culture is to falsify history," he explains. "Belief in one's own culture does not require disdain for other cultures. But one step at a time: no culture can hope to ingest other cultures all at once, certainly not before it ingests its own." Defensively claiming to be an inclusionist historian, Schlesinger presents his own credentials: "As for me, I was for a time a member of the executive council of the *Journal of Negro History*. . . . I have been a lifelong advocate of civil rights."[12]

But what happens when minority peoples try to define their civil rights in terms of cultural pluralism and group identities? They become targets of Schlesinger's scorn. This "exaggeration" of ethnic differences, he warns, only "drives ever deeper the awful wedges between races," leading to an "endgame" of self-pity and self-ghettoization. The culprits responsible for this divisiveness are the "multicultural zealots," especially the Afrocentrists. Schlesinger castigates them as campus bullies, distorting history and creating myths about the contributions of Africans.[13]

What Schlesinger refuses to admit or is unable to see clearly is how he himself is culpable of historical distortion: his own omissions in *The Age of Jackson* have erased what James Madison had described then as "the black race within our bosom" and "the red on our borders." Both groups have been entirely left out of Schlesinger's study: they do not even have entries in the index. Moreover, there is not even a mention of two marker events, the Nat Turner insurrection and Indian removal, which Andrew Jackson himself would have been surprised to find omitted from a history of his era. Unfortunately, Schlesinger fails to meet even his own standards of scholarship: "The historian's goals are accuracy, analysis, and objectivity in the reconstruction of the past."[14]

Behind Schlesinger's cant against multiculturalism is fear. He worries what will happen to our national ideal of "e pluribus unum." Will the center hold, or will the melting pot yield to the Tower of Babel? For answers he looks abroad. "Today," he observes, "the nationalist fever encircles the globe." Angry and violent "tribalism" is exploding in India, the former Soviet Union, Indonesia, Guyana, and other countries around the world. "The ethnic upsurge in America, far from being unique, partakes of the global fever." Like Bloom and Ravitch, Schlesinger prescribes individualism as the cure. "Most Americans," he argues, "continue to see themselves primarily as individuals and only secondarily and trivially as adherents of a group. The dividing of society into "fixed ethnicities nourishes a culture of victimization and a contagion of inflammable sensitivities." This danger threatens the "brittle bonds of national identity that hold this diverse and fractious society together." The Balkan present, Schlesinger warns, may be America's prologue.[15]

Are we limited to a choice between a "disuniting" multiculturalism and a common American culture, or can we transform the "culture war" into a meeting ground? The intellectual combats of this conflict, Gerald Graff suggests, have the potential to enrich American education. As universities become contested terrains of different points of view, gray and monotonous cloisters of Eurocentric knowledge can become brave new worlds, dynamic and multicultural. On these academic battlegrounds scholars and students can engage each other in dialogue and debate, informed by the heat and light generated by the examination of opposing texts such as Joseph Conrad's *Heart of Darkness* and Chinua Achebe's *Things Fall Apart*. "Teaching the conflicts has nothing to do with relativism or denying the existence of truth," Graff contends. "The best way to make relativists of students is to expose them to an endless series of different positions which are *not* debated before their eyes." Graff turns the guns of the great books against Bloom. By viewing culture as a debate and by entering a process of intellectual clashes, students can search for truth, as did Socrates "when he taught the conflicts two millennia ago."[16]

Like Graff, I welcome such debates in my teaching. One of my courses, "Racial Inequality in America: A Comparative Historical Perspective," studies the character of American society in relationship to our racial and ethnic diversity. My approach is captured in the phrase "from different shores." By "shores" I intend a double meaning. One is the shores from which the migrants departed, places such as Europe, Africa, and Asia. The second is the various and often conflicting perspectives of shores from which scholars have viewed the experiences of racial and ethnic groups. By critically examining these different shores, students address complex comparative questions. How have the experiences of racial minorities such as African Americans been similar to and different from those of ethnic groups such as Irish Americans? Is race the same as ethnicity? For example, is the African American experience qualitatively or quantitatively different from the Jewish American experience? How have race relations been shaped by economic developments as well as by culture—moral values about how people think and behave as well as beliefs about human nature and society? To wrestle with these questions, students read Nathan Glazer's analysis of assimilationist patterns as well as Robert Blauner's theory of internal colonialism, Charles Murray on Black welfare dependency as well as William Julius Wilson on the economic structures creating the Black underclass, and Thomas Sowell's explanation of Asian American success as well as my critique of the "myth of the Asian-American model minority."[17]

The need to open American minds to greater cultural diversity will not go away. Faculty can resist this imperative by ignoring the changing racial composition of student bodies and the larger society, or they can embrace this timely and exciting intellectual opportunity to revitalize the social sciences and humanities. "The study of the humanities," Henry Louis Gates Jr. observes, "is the study of the possibilities of human life in culture. It thrives on diversity. . . . The new [Ethnic Studies] scholarship had invigorated the traditional disciplines."[18] What distinguishes the university from other battlegrounds, such as the media and politics, is that the university has a special commitment to the search for knowledge, one based on a process of intellectual openness and inquiry. Multiculturalism can stoke this critical spirit by transforming the university into a crucial meeting ground for different viewpoints. In the process perhaps we will be able to discover what makes us an American people.

Whether the university can realize this intellectual pursuit for collective self-knowledge is uncertain, especially during difficult economic times. As institutions of higher learning face budget cuts, calls for an expansion of the curriculum often encounter hostility from faculty in traditional departments determined to protect dwindling resources. Furthermore, the economic crisis has been fanning the fires of racism in society: Asian Americans have been bashed for the seeming invasion of Japanese cars, Hispanics accused of taking jobs away from Americans, and Blacks stereotyped as enjoying a dependency on welfare and special privileges of affirmative action. This context of rising racial tensions has conditioned the culture war. Both the advocates and the critics of multiculturalism know that the conflict is not wholly academic; the debate over how America should be defined is related to power and privilege. Both sides agree that history is power. Society's collective memory determines the future. The battle is over what should be remembered and who should do the remembering.

Traditionally excluded from the curriculum, minorities are insisting that America does not belong to one group and neither does America's history. They are making their claim to the knowledge offered by the university, reminding us that Americans originated from many lands and that everyone here is entitled to dignity. "I hope this survey do a lot of good for Chinese people," an immigrant told an interviewer from Stanford in the 1920s. "Make American people realize that Chinese people are humans. I think very few American people really know anything about Chinese." As different groups find their voices, they tell and retell stories that liberate. By writing about the people on Mango Street, Sandra Cisneros explained, "the ghost does not ache so much." The place no longer holds her with "both arms. She sets [Cisneros] free." Indeed, stories may not be as innocent or simple as they might seem. They "aren't just entertainment," observed Native American novelist Leslie Marmon Silko.[19]

On the other side the interests seeking to maintain the status quo also recognize that the contested terrain of ideas is related to social reality. No wonder conservative foundations like Coors and Olin have financed projects to promote their own political agenda on campuses across the country, and the National Association of Scholars has attacked multiculturalism by smearing it with a brush called "political correctness." Conservative critics like Bloom are the real campus bullies; they are the ones unwilling to open the debate and introduce students to different viewpoints. Under the banner of intellectual freedom and excellence, these naysayers have imposed their own intellectual orthodoxy by denouncing those who disagree with them as "the new barbarians," saluting Lynne Cheney, the former head of the National Endowment for the Humanities, for defending traditional American culture, and employing McCarthyite tactics to brand Ethnic Studies as "un-American."[20]

How can the university become a meeting ground when the encounter of oppositional ideas is disparaged? What Susan Faludi has observed about the academic backlash against women's liberation can also be applied to the reaction to multiculturalism. "The donnish robes of many of these backlash thinkers cloaked impulses that were less than scholarly," she wrote. "Some of them were academics who believed that feminists had cost them in advancement, tenure, and honors; they found the creation of Women's Studies not just professionally but personally disturbing and invasive, a trespasser trampling across *their* campus." Her observation applies to multiculturalism; all we need to do is to substitute "minority scholars" for "feminists" and "Ethnic Studies" for "Women's Studies." The intellectual backlashers are defending "their" campuses against the "other."[21]

The campaign against multiculturalism reflects a larger social nervousness, a perplexity over the changing racial composition of American society. Faludi's insights may again be transferable. The war against women, she notes, manifests an identity crisis for men: what does it mean to be a man? One response has been to reclaim masculinity through violence, to "kick ass," the expression George Bush used to describe his combat with Geraldine Ferraro in the 1984 vice-presidential debate. Eight years later, during the Persian Gulf war against Saddam Hussein, Bush as president demonstrated masculine power in Desert Storm. In a parallel way, it can be argued, the expanding multicultural reality of America is creating a racial identity crisis: what does it mean to be White?[22]

Demographic studies project that Whites will become a minority of the total U.S. population some time during the twenty-first century. Already in major cities across the country, Whites no longer predominate numerically. This expanding multicultural reality is challenging the traditional notion of America as White. What will it mean for American society to have a non-White majority? The significance of this future, *Time* observed, is related to our identity—our sense of individual self and nationhood, or what it means to be American. This demographic transformation has prompted E. D. Hirsch Jr. to worry that America is becoming a "Tower of Babel," and that this multiplicity of cultures is threatening to tear the country's social fabric. Nostalgic for a more cohesive culture and a more homogeneous America, he contends, "If we *had* to make a choice between the *one* and the *many*, most Americans would choose the principle of unity, since we cannot function as a nation without it." The way to correct this fragmentation, Hirsch argues, is to promote the teaching of "shared symbols." In *Cultural Literacy: What Every American Needs to Know,* Hirsch offers an appendix of terms designed to create a sense of national identity and unity—a list that leaves out much of the histories and cultures of minorities.[23]

The escalating war against multiculturalism is fueled by a fear of loss. "Backlash politics may be defined as the reaction by groups which are declining in a felt sense of importance, influence, and power," observed Seymour Martin Lipset and Earl Raab. Similarly, historian Richard Hofstadter described the impulses of progressive politics in the early twentieth century in terms of a "status revolution"—a widely shared frustration among middle-class professionals who had been displaced by a new class of elite businessmen. Hofstadter also detected a "paranoid style in American politics" practiced by certain groups such as nativists who suffered from lost prestige and felt besieged by complex new realities. Grieving for an America that had been taken away from them, they desperately fought to repossess their country and "prevent the final destructive act of subversion."[24]

A similar anxiety is growing in America today. One of the factors behind the backlash against multiculturalism is race, what Lawrence Auster calls "the forbidden topic." In an essay published in the *National Review*, he advocates the restriction of immigration for non-Whites. Auster condemns the White liberals for wanting to have it both ways—to have a common culture and also to promote racial diversity. They naively refuse to recognize the danger: when a "critical number" of people in this country are no longer from the West, then we will no longer be able to employ traditional reference points such as "our Western heritage" or speak of "our Founding Fathers." American culture as it has been known, Auster warns, is disappearing as "more and more minorities complain that they can't identify with American history because they 'don't see people who look like themselves' in that history." To preserve America as a Western society, Auster argues, America must continue to be composed mostly of people of European ancestry.[25] What Auster presents is an extreme but logical extension of a view shared by both conservatives like Bloom and liberals like Schlesinger: they have bifurcated American society into "us" versus "them." This division locates Whites at the center and minorities at the margins of our national identity. "American," observed Toni Morrison, has been defined as "White." Such a dichotomization denies our wholeness as one people. "Everybody remembers," she explained, "the first time they were taught that part of the human race was Other. That's a trauma. It's as though I told you that your left hand is not part of your body."[26]

In their war against the denied parts of American society, the backlashers are our modern Captain Ahabs. In their pursuit of their version of the white whale, they are in command; like Ahab directing his chase from the deck of the *Pequod*, they steer the course of the university curriculum. Their exclusive definition of knowledge has rendered invisible and silent the swirling and rich diversity below deck. The workers of the *Pequod* represent a multicultural society—Whites like Ishmael, Pacific Islanders like Queequeg, Africans like Daggoo, Asians like Fedallah, and American Indians like Tashtego. In Melville's powerful story, Ishmael and Queequeg find themselves strangers to each other at first. As they labor together, they are united by their need of mutual survival and cooperation. This connectedness is graphically illustrated by the monkey-rope. Lowered into the shark-infested water to secure the blubber hook into the dead whale, Queequeg is held by a rope tied to Ishmael. The process is perilous for both men. "We two, for the time," Ishmael tells us, "were wedded; and should poor Queequeg sink to rise not more, then both usage and honor demanded that, instead of cutting the cord, it should drag me down in his wake." Though originally from different shores, the members of the crew share a noble class unity. Ahab, however, is able to charm them, his charisma drawing them into the delirium of his hunt. Driven by a monomanic mission, Ahab charts a course that ends in the destruction of everyone except Ishmael.[27]

On college campuses today, the voices of many students and faculty from below deck are challenging such hierarchical power. In their search for cross-cultural understandings, they are trying to re-vision America. But will we as Americans continue to perceive our past and peer into our future as through a glass darkly? In the telling and retelling of our particular stories, will we create communities of separate memories, or will we be able to connect our diverse selves to a larger national narrative? As we enter the twenty-first century dominated by ethnic and racial conflicts at home and throughout the world, we realize that the answers to such questions will depend largely on whether the university will be able to become both a battleground and a meeting ground of varied viewpoints.

Notes

This chapter is a reprint of the article that appeared in *Annals of the American Academy of Political and Social Science* (November 1993): 109–21, reprinted with permission of the author. Despite the years since publication, the issues Professor Ronald Takaki so cogently discusses remain salient today, with the context being arguably strikingly similar, anti-affirmative action movements notwithstanding. The source for the epigraph quotation is David J. Weber, ed., *Foreigners in Their Native Land: Historical Roots of the Mexican Americans* (Albuquerque: University of New Mexico Press, 1973), vi.

1. C. Vann Woodward, "America the Bad?" *New York Review of Books,*

November 22, 1979; Ronald Takaki, *Iron Cages: Race and Culture in Nineteenth-Century America* (New York: Knopf, 1979).

2. Charles J. Sykes, *The Hollow Men: Politics and Corruption in Higher Education* (Washington, D.C., and New York: Regnery Gateway, 1990); Dinesh D'Souza, *Illiberal Education: The Politics of Race and Sex on Campus* (New York: Free Press, 1991).

3. Allan Bloom, *The Closing of the American Mind: How Higher Education Has Failed Democracy and Impoverished the Souls of Today's Students* (New York: Simon & Schuster, 1987), 19, 91–93, 340–41, 344.

4. Ibid., 27, 29, 33, 35, 89, 90, 347.

5. Donna Shalala, *University of Wisconsin-Madison: The Madison Plan* (Madison: University of Wisconsin, 1988).

6. For Rodney King's statement to the press, see *New York Times*, May 2, 1992, p. 6.

7. "Beyond Black and White," *Newsweek*, May 18, 1992, p. 28.

8. Diane Ravitch, "Multiculturalism: E Pluribus Plures," *American Scholar* 59 (3): 337–54.

9. Ronald Takaki, *Strangers from a Different Shore: A History of Asian Americans* (Boston: Little, Brown, 1989); Irving Howe, *World of Our Fathers: The Journey of the East European Jews to America and the Life They Found and Made* (New York: Simon & Schuster, 1976); Lawrence W. Levine, *Black Culture and Black Consciousness: Afro-American Folk Thought from Slavery to Freedom* (New York: Oxford University Press, 1977); Mario T. Garcia, *Desert Immigrants: The Mexicans of El Paso, 1880–1920* (New Haven, Conn.: Yale University Press, 1981); Kerby A. Miller, *Emigrants and Exiles: Ireland and the Irish Exodus to North America* (New York: Oxford University Press, 1985).

10. Ronald Takaki, *A Different Mirror: A History of Multicultural America* (New York: Little, Brown, 1993); Gary Nash, *Red, White, and Black: The Peoples of Early America* (Englewood Cliffs, N.J.: Prentice-Hall, 1974); Ivan Light, *Ethnic Enterprise in America: Business and Welfare among Chinese, Japanese, and Blacks* (Berkeley: University of California Press, 1972); Reginald Horsman, *Race and Manifest Destiny: The Origins of American Racial Anglo-Saxonism* (Cambridge: Harvard University Press, 1981); Benjamin Ringer, *"We the People" and Others: Duality and America's Treatment of Its Racial Minorities* (New York: Tavistock, 1983).

11. Ravitch, "Multiculturalism," 341, 354.

12. Arthur M. Schlesinger Jr., *The Disuniting of America: Reflections on a Multicultural Society* (Knoxville, Tenn.: Whittle Communications, 1991), 2, 14, 24, 81–82.

13. Ibid., 58, 66.

14. James Madison, quoted in Takaki, *Iron Cages*, 80; Arthur M. Schlesinger Jr., *The Age of Jackson* (Boston: Little, Brown, 1945); Schlesinger, *Disuniting of America*, 20.

15. Schlesinger, *Disuniting of America*, 2, 21, 64.

16. Gerald Graff, *Beyond the Culture Wars: How Teaching the Conflicts Can Revitalize American Education* (New York: W. W. Norton, 1992), 15.

17. Nathan Glazer, *Affirmative Discrimination: Ethnic Inequality and Public Policy* (New York: Basic Books, 1975); Robert Blauner, *Racial Oppression in America* (New York: Harper & Row, 1972); Charles Murray, *Losing Ground: American Social Policy, 1950–1980* (New York: Basic Books, 1984); William Julius Wilson, *The Truly Disadvantaged: The Inner City, the Underclass, and Public Policy* (Chicago: University of Chicago Press, 1987); Thomas Sowell, *Ethnic America: A History* (New York: Basic Books, 1981); Takaki, *Strangers from a Different Shore*. For an example of the debate format, see Ronald Takaki, *From Different Shores: Perspectives on Race and Ethnicity in America* (New York: Oxford University Press, 1987).

18. Henry Louis Gates Jr., *Loose Canons: Notes on the Culture Wars* (New York: Oxford University Press, 1992), 114.

19. Pany Lowe, interview, 1924. Survey of Race Relations, Hoover Institution Archives, Stanford, Calif.; Sandra Cisneros, *The House on Mango Street* (New York: Vintage, 1991), 109–10; Leslie Marmon Silko, *Ceremony* (New York: New American Library, 1978), 2.

20. Dinesh D'Souza, "The Visigoths in Tweed," in Patricia Aufderheide, ed., *Beyond PC: Towards a Politics of Understanding* (St. Paul, Minn.: Graywolf Press, 1992), 11; George Will, "Literary Politics," *Newsweek*, April 22, 1991, p. 72; Arthur Schlesinger Jr., "When Ethnic Studies are Un-American," *Wall Street Journal*, April 23, 1990.

21. Susan Faludi, *Backlash: The Undeclared War against American Women* (New York: Doubleday, 1992), 282.

22. Ibid., 65.

23. William A. Henry III, "Beyond the Melting Pot," *Time*, April 9, 1990, pp. 28–31; E. D. Hirsch Jr., *Cultural Literacy: What Every American Needs to Know* (Boston: Houghton, Mifflin, 1987), xiii, xvii, 2, 18, 96, 152–215.

24. Seymour Martin Lipset and Earl Raab quoted in Faludi, *Backlash*, 231; Richard Hofstadter, *The Age of Reform: From Bryan to F.D.R.* (New York: Random House, 1955), 131–73.

25. Lawrence Auster, "The Forbidden Topic," *National Review*, April 27, 1992, pp. 42–44.

26. Toni Morrison, *Playing in the Dark: Whiteness in the Literary Imagination*

(Cambridge: Harvard University Press, 1992), 47; Bonnie Angelo, "The Pain of Being Black," *Time*, May 22, 1989, p. 121, reprinted by permission of Time, Inc., copyright 1989.

27. Herman Melville, *Moby Dick* (Boston: Houghton Mifflin, 1956), 182, 253, 322–23.

Ethnic Studies as a Matrix for the Humanities, the Social Sciences, and the Common Good

JOHNNELLA E. BUTLER

I am because we are; we are, because I am. (I am we.)

—*West African proverb*

IN THE EARLY 1960S, WHEN I WAS THIRTEEN OR FOURTEEN, my father invited Mr. Mikali, a South African, to dinner. Mr. Mikali told our family something that I have always remembered, something that in my life as a teacher-scholar I have grown to understand all too well. He said that people of African ancestry in the United States and South Africa would win their respective struggles for civil rights and against apartheid, but only then will the real battle become apparent: the battle for minds. He referred to the struggle for the right to know one's heritage, to name oneself, and to have one's values, aesthetics, and ways of seeing become a functioning part of America or South Africa. I remember thinking then that that was what the Civil Rights movement was about: the struggle for the United States to change to accept who Negroes are and have been.

Rather than reducing the goal of democracy and higher education to a melting pot of forced and synthetic binaries, fighting the battle for minds means seeking to build on the humanity of individuals and expanding the possibility of individuals and groups to know, respect, and grow from an understanding of their heritages and the interconnection of their heritages with others. It means situating the lives of individuals and the experiences of groups as informed by conflictual and complementary heritages, all directed toward the common good, while embracing either synthesis or the generative engagement of binaries that respects and works with difference, discovering in the process similarities and connections on which to build. This battle for minds also calls for educational, legal, and social institutions as well as public policy that constantly adjusts for equity and justice, identifying and addressing the harsh legacies of racism and other discriminations.

Moving from Substance to Significance

At the beginning of the twenty-first century, diminished access to higher education, the increasing diversity of the nation's population, the rollback of affirmative action and civil rights gains, computer technology that offers more information as well as the possibilities of new pedagogies and challenges to traditional student-teacher and student-student interaction all augur for a prolonged state of change in higher education. In association with the humanities and social sciences, Ethnic Studies, if supported, can serve as a matrix for producing courses of study, scholarship, methodology, and pedagogy that will assist in reinforcing the educational values necessary for higher education institutions and students to respond to the realities and needs of the changing population and cultural realities. As an interdisciplinary field of study, Ethnic Studies encompasses the content of the humanities and social sciences while paradoxically being excluded from these fields. But as a matrix, Ethnic Studies provides the situation within which (and through association with) the humanities and social sciences may realize the potential of their educational missions.

Manifestations of the paradigmatic shift inexorably occurring in the academy include the development of Ethnic Studies, diversity projects, multiculturalism, feminism, Queer Studies, the new multicultural American Studies, Afrocentrism, curriculum transformation, and critical race theory. Signaled by the recognition in the early part of the twentieth century that the United States could not be defined in only male, European aesthetic, social, and political terms, this shift was continued in the 1960s with the push for voting rights and the desegregation of higher education by racialized ethnic groups, more precisely by African Americans who had been segregated institutionally and culturally from White America. Hostilities, joys, and confusions resulted from the crossing of the color-line with scholarly and pedagogical attempts to clarify the significances of class and ethnicity, the exposure of heterosexism, as well as gender, age, and physical ability discriminations and attempts at equity. Many in the academy work to give all students the *substance*, that is, the content and the perspectives to help them understand the complexity of the United States, its values, its conflicts, and its potential, so that students can move to the *significance* of their education. In so doing, students will inevitably encounter the nation's diversity and the need to maintain equity and social justice as active goals.

Literary scholar Paul Lauter has pointed out that over the years very little thought has been given to the evolution of the liberal arts in the United States. In his book *Canon and Contexts* he examines issues of literary study and the canon in societal and academic institutional contexts, recognizing that "the literary canon is, in short, a means by which culture validates social power."[1] Elizabeth Karmarck Minnich's *Transforming Knowledge* discusses ways to rethink the assumptions of the liberal arts as they evolve to encompass and reflect more than a small segment of humanity.[2] Johnnella E. Butler and John C. Walter's *Transforming the Curriculum: Ethnic Studies and Women's Studies* demonstrates the role of Ethnic Studies and Women's Studies in the transformation and evolution of the humanities and the social sciences as scholars incorporate the categories of race, ethnicity, gender, and class in their teaching and writing into scholarship, content, and pedagogy.[3] What these three works have in common with one another and with Ethnic Studies scholarship is a view of the humanities and social sciences as evolving to meet the fundamental human and social needs of students and the larger society; and the search for a pluralistic paradigm that strives for equity and justice in a participatory democracy. The inclusion of the excluded in the curriculum is, then, a climactic point in the evolving understanding of the liberal arts.

If the substance is inclusive and engaging of the complexities, its significance will lead to an understanding of diversity and a positing of our actions based on fundamental realities of our shared society. Traveling from substance to significance is the ideal journey of the teacher-scholar and the student-scholar. Education's goal is the leading of the student out of himself or herself—from the Latin root *educare* (*ex + ducere*)—to guide the student's sensibilities so that their familiar experiences, sensibilities, and ideas encounter other experiences, sensibilities, and ideas. It may seem old-fashioned to think of education in this way, but this conceptualization is among the best of our liberal arts traditions. It is not very distant from the late Brazilian educator Paulo Freire's concepts of education aimed at liberating the human spirit to be able to name, encounter, and engage the world. Such journeys from substance to significance constitute education.

Ethnic Studies, the Humanities
and Social Sciences, and the Matrix Potential

Given the racialized history of the United States and its extended and related legacies, Ethnic Studies—the interdisciplinary and comparative study of the social, cultural, political, and economic expression and experience of U.S. racialized ethnic groups and of U.S. racialization—together with the humanities and the social sciences potentially provides a matrix yielding clarification, accuracy, and connection among human difference. Despite its difficulties in institutionalization, its sometimes shortsighted approaches to giving voice to those historically excluded from and distorted by the academy, and its struggle to define, practice, and distinguish between interdisciplinary and multidisciplinary methodology, Ethnic Studies has hewn the road from substance to significance. In so doing, Ethnic Studies offers a next stage in the development of the humanities and the social sciences toward the realization of their potential through a dialogue with Ethnic Studies.

In *One America Indivisible* scholar Sheldon Hackney, the recent director of the National Endowment for the Humanities, offers an elegant and poignant definition of the humanities, which "broadly understood" are "the natural intellectual prism through which to explore our pluralism."[4] The humanities, history, philosophy, literary, and religious studies form "that body of thought that tells us what we think about ourselves, what we see as admirable behavior, what we believe it means to be human, what we recognize as the human condition, what we learn from human experience as a just society, what we decide we owe to each other, what we understand as the way the world works. . . . They are our self-conscious investigations into our past—our joint and singular narratives, our self-imaginings and self-representations, the ways in which we picture ourselves."[5] The social sciences—sociology, psychology, anthropology, economics, and political science—identify patterns of human behavior and examine individual and group relationships to society and societal structures. Studied and practiced without the humanities' function of offering and revealing meaning, the social sciences quickly become abstract and distant from the very lives they describe. Studied and practiced without the social science function, the humanities thus become solipsistic. Without interaction with distinct Ethnic Studies scholarship, the humanities and the social sciences are therefore incomplete and inaccurate.

Being the interdisciplinary, comparative study of the cultures of U.S. racialized ethnic groups as they interact with each other and with the larger American culture, Ethnic Studies content and methodology is located in the humanities and the social sciences as well as in the convergence of the two fields. Ethnic Studies therefore functions as a matrix for the academic struggle to define and make sense of interdisciplinary methodology and structures within the academy. As faculty seek to develop interdisciplinary and comparative scholarship that examines national, regional, diasporic, and transnational realities—while remaining accountable to the dominant discipline structure of higher education—questions arise about the criteria for scholarship, pedagogy, and even the parameters of disciplines, as established fields and disciplines recognize and interact with the coherence and content of Ethnic Studies. The resulting struggles can prove instructive for the academic organization of the humanities and the social sciences. Such encounters demand, on the one hand, dialogics among the disciplines in the humanities and the social sciences, including Ethnic Studies as a separate interdisciplinary discipline, and on the other hand, dialogics among self-reflection, "old" and "new" scholarship, methodology, pedagogy, cultural and societal significance, cultural expression, and societal structures.

Racialization, Assimilation, and Whiteness in the Institutionalization of Ethnic Studies

The spiraling trajectory of the development of Ethnic Studies in higher education during the twentieth century demands recognition in the face of the constant threat of erasure.[6] Ethnic Studies grapples with the repetitive forces of assimilationist imperatives that choke not some essentialized sense of ethnic identity, but rather individual and group selfhood and agency. During its early years, from the late 1960s through the early 1970s, the field was encouraged by the Black Arts movement and academic assertions of the selfhood and agency of Blackness and of the Black experience.[7] What came to be known in the United States as Ethnic Studies challenged the assimilationist imperatives that masked the White supremacy in such accepted histories as those written by Ulrich B. Phillips and Henry Steele Commager.[8]

These imperatives became entrenched in mainstream scholarship on "race relations," scholarship that defined the image and the interpretation of African American lives and expressions, scholarship that ultimately defined government policy toward African Americans. Not surprisingly,

African American literature and theater led the challenge, with an energetic voice that spoke to Black communities and beyond. From African American anthologies of folk literature, fiction, and poetry, to Puerto Rican and African American street poets, to the 1975 Asian American anthology *Aiiieeeee!*, which sought to shatter the stereotyped cry of the "Asian" caricature, Ethnic Studies grew from contributions-focused courses that proclaimed "We are here!" to courses that began simultaneously to recover the obscured and distorted past and to critique the racialized ethnic's reality.[9] Scholarship in Black Studies probed beyond Janheinz Jahn's pioneering works on West African culture, synchronized with extraordinary studies of African history and civilization by Basil Davidson, Cheikh Anta Diop, and St. Clair Drake, and produced works examining the African transformations in "new world" culture.[10]

Ethnic Studies seeks connection without a dehumanizing form of assimilation, is simultaneously distinct from and a part of Whiteness, and works to change "the battle for the minds" to a cooperative human quest for knowledge, understanding, and a better life. Reading in tandem Stow Persons's *Ethnic Studies at Chicago, 1905–45* and Jack Bass's *Widening the Mainstream of American Culture: A Ford Foundation Report on Ethnic Studies* clarifies the challenges to and the challenges offered early on by Black Studies and other racialized Ethnic Studies in this quest.[11] Persons tells the story of Robert E. Park's Chicago school of Ethnic Studies and its most influential sociological scholarship as it developed from the cultural imperative of the Anglo-American norm of assimilation, a norm that had its expressed beginnings with Benjamin Franklin and William Smith's fear that the Germans migrating to the colony of Pennsylvania in the 1750s would "Germanize" that colony:

The reaction of the Anglo-Americans led by Benjamin Franklin and William Smith proved to be *typical of their response to ethnic challenges for the next two centuries.* Franklin and Smith declared Anglo-American culture to be in jeopardy, doubting its ability to "Americanize" the mounting number of Germans who were swarming into the colony. They proposed a range of measures designed to assure the ultimate assimilation of the newcomers. Chief among these were to be free English-language schools for German children; disqualification for any position of trust, honor, or profit of those who could not speak English; restriction of further German immigration; and the finding of some means to disperse the Germans as widely as possible among the English-speaking population.

Franklin candidly admitted his color prejudices, not only deploring the "darkening" of the white American color through miscegenation but also expressing his distaste for the "swarthy" complexioned Europeans. Only the English and the Saxons were white; and Franklin hoped that America might be reserved for their increase.[12]

It is clear that Franklin, Smith, and their progeny viewed ethnicity as a social construct, one that could be altered with the appropriate push toward assimilation. During the forming of the U.S. Constitution, however, race was viewed as an essential fact, with racism as the vehicle to deliver the fruits of what Persons has called "the Anglo-American burden," the transformed English and Saxon heritage that became Anglo-American cultural imperatives (very ironic, given the Germanic origins of the Saxons!). As time passed, rather quickly those who were not considered "swarthy" assimilated to these Anglo-American cultural imperatives. Just as quickly, that Anglo-American cultural imperative transmogrified into White supremacist ideology, veiled by democratic aspirations and reinforced by the racist essentialism.

The Chicago school of Ethnic Studies and its most celebrated Black student, E. Franklin Frazier, identified race with nationality. As Persons explains:

A racial culture thus became the basis of a distinct nationality. Wherever immigration and race mixing occurred the inherited racial temperament would be broken up. Although this had clearly happened in America, Park said nothing to indicate an awareness of its implications for American nationality. His purpose rather was to consider the problems of blacks and Orientals in the same terms with which European immigrants would be discussed. He admitted that Americans had proved themselves capable of assimilating every kind of difference except color differences, but he did not avail himself of the distinction made by later commentators between ethnicity and race. Rather, he sought to minimize the importance of color by pointing out that it had significance for secondary-group relations, but not for primary relationships.[13]

For Park, as for Frazier, prejudice evolved from "economic conflicts between racial groups with different standards of living . . . Race prejudice and the elaboration of caste systems were the response of the dominant race to the threat to its livelihood." He dismissed "the idea that race prejudice reflected ignorance and misunderstanding to be dispelled by knowledge."[14] Thus, in American sociology (the academic site for the study of race relations) race was rather clumsily associated with ethnicity, and African Americans were seen, as in Frazier's work, as having no cultural-national heritage except that of White America.[15] Equating the migration from plantation to ghetto with European immigration, Frazier "appl[ied] the full range of Chicago ethnic theories to black problems."[16]

By 1970, according to The Ford Foundation report *Widening the Mainstream of American Culture,* the Foundation had funded fifty-nine grants in Ethnic Studies. These grants encompassed the development of undergraduate and graduate curricula in Ethnic Studies within traditional disciplines; the creation of discrete Afro-American Studies programs at colleges and universities; the development of faculty curriculum and research seminars on race and minority problems, on the Black student experience, and on Black history and culture; the development of library, museum, and historical documentation support of Black history; the creation of seminars for teacher preparation of Chicanos and Chicanas, social studies research on Mexican Americans, graduate program support in Mexican American Studies, and the establishment of the *Chicano Chronicle,* a newspaper of Mexican American history; the foundation of a research study of the Puerto Rican migration experience and the establishment of the Center for Puerto Rican Studies at the City University of New York; the development of a graduate program in American Indian Studies, the documentation of Native American history and educational materials, and the development of a mobile library, and the creation of sixteen Ph.D. fellowships for study on American Indians and 338 fellowships in Ethnic Studies from 1970 to 1973.[17]

The report's narrative belies the very tension that Ethnic Studies has attempted to address that plagues it from within and without: the battle against scholarship and teaching that reinforces through its theory and epistemology the racist assimilationist imperatives through the development of scholarship and teaching that both critiques those imperatives and collects, analyzes, and uses the significance of the multiple stories that should inform the scholarship about the United States.[18] For example, the report's opening paragraph lists, with no differentiation, scholars with disparate perspectives and conclusions as "black and white scholars like E. Franklin Frazier, Melville Herskovits, W. E .B. Du Bois, Charles S. Johnson, Robert Park, John Hope Franklin, Gunnar Myrdal, and Carter G. Woodson [as doing] important research during the first half of the twentieth century."[19] By doing so, Bass expresses implicitly the contradictions that students in the report expressed in "confusing and sometimes separatist" demands and that professors' comments and program funding reflected.[20] For example, he cites the noted historian John Blassingame as writing that "black studies is too serious . . . has too many exciting possibilities of liberating the racially shackled American mind, for intellectuals to shirk their responsibility to organize academically respectable programs. This possibility of curricular innovation must . . . take advantage of the opportunity to enrich the educational experiences of all students and teach them to think and to understand more clearly the problems of their age."[21]

Ford funding of Chicano and Chicana activists and scholars in tackling "a particular problem affecting the Mexican American community—a severe shortage of public school teachers trained as bilingual/bicultural specialists"[22]—challenged the ingrained racist imperative that Benjamin Franklin had leveled against the Germans in the Pennsylvania colony. The Center for Puerto Rican Studies at CUNY was founded on the principle that "departments of Puerto Rican Studies on the various CUNY campuses are 'organic extensions of the community and not remote outposts in an alien space that only a few are privileged to penetrate'" and were to provide "an intellectual and educational resource to which policy-makers may turn for information and advice in addressing the myriad problems facing the Puerto Rican community in New York."[23] As Mack Jones, the chair of the Department of Political Science at Atlanta University, put it: "Teaching from a black perspective . . . does not mean that students would know any less about the world. It means that the assumptions that determine which facts are deserving of attention and emphasis . . . will grow out of the experiences of black people. To argue against the validity of such a perspective is to suggest that only the Anglo-Saxon experience is of sufficient quality for serious intellectual inquiry."[24]

Such principles and objectives challenged the ingrained concept of universities as the carriers of Anglo-American values and as the domain of the elite. The ensuing contradictions present themselves in both ethnic-specific and comparative programs and departments as a methodological conflict: whether Ethnic Studies should be situated in the humanities or the social sciences; whether programs and departments should engage in interdisciplinary methodology and pedagogy in either the humanities or the social sciences or within both areas; and whether sociology should provide the methodological and assumptive bases for Ethnic Studies.[25] The methodological conflict is shaped and exacerbated by institutional demands, problems of disciplinary turf, and ethnocentrism.

It seems that the questions raised by younger scholars who see themselves using the methodology of cultural studies, the perspectives of transnational and diasporic positionalites, and the conscious articulation of the study of Whiteness and critical race theory in American Studies have the strength to push Ethnic Studies to embrace without contradiction interdisciplinary and cross-disciplinary study. The problem is, however, that Ethnic Studies and other various interdisciplinary studies and methodologies engage in little if any dialogue. The spring 1990 international conference "Cultural Studies Now and in the Future," held at the University of Illinois at Urbana-Champaign, serves as a relevant example. Although attended by about nine hundred invitees, in attendance were "more people of African descent from London . . . than from the United States."[26] About the reception of cultural studies in the United States, scholar Cornel West observed that race has to be given "a tremendous weight and gravity if we're going to understand the internal dynamics of U.S. culture[?] There's no escape . . . Yes, race is there in Britain, as we all know, but with very different histories, different developments. And similarly so in terms of gender. . . . How are we to understand the moment of the intervention of Afro-American studies in the academy? Let's read that history next to the intervention of cultural studies in Britain."[27] In a discussion session, West spoke briefly about "the silencing of Afro-American intellectuals in this country":

There is an intellectual and social chasm between large numbers of persons in Afro-American Studies programs and persons in interdisciplinary studies, or cultural studies. Now why does this chasm exist, that's a much longer story that has to do with what particular schools of thinking have shaped significant numbers of Afro-American scholars who are in Afro-American studies programs vis-à-vis the kinds of developments that have been going on in literary criticism and cultural studies and so forth. There is this *de facto* segregation, when we actually look at what some of the dynamics have been in a variety of different institutions, between black scholars and left intellectuals. . . . It has to do with the very deep racist legacy in which black persons, black intellectuals are guilty before being proven innocent, in terms of perceiving them capable of intellectual partnership, capable of being part of a serious conversation.[28]

The problem expands to the question of how do scholars within and outside Ethnic Studies engage Afrocentricity, Black feminism, Chicana Studies, Asian American transnational scholarship, diasporic studies, and so on? As West puts it, "We have yet actually to create contexts in which Black intellectuals, brown intellectuals, red intellectuals, White intellectuals, feminist intellectuals, genuinely struggle with each other."[29] Ethnic Studies in its programmatic and professional organization struggles to provide that context, despite the particular divisiveness of racism, classism, sexism and heterosexism, and despite methodological conflict arising from its history and from the nature of higher education and of the United States.

The Palimpsest of the Black-White Binary

A major, largely unrecognized dilemma for Ethnic Studies today is presented by the need to provide a foreground for the analysis of Whiteness. Whiteness has been implicitly a part of the field from its inception. The question is, how do Ethnic Studies scholars explicitly study Whiteness? That is, how do we appropriately expose and foreground racialized Whiteness without displacing the focus on the dynamics that heretofore unstated racialized Whiteness produces for U.S. racialized minorities? Pioneering Black Studies scholar and sociologist Herman Blake, as quoted by Jack Bass in *Widening the Mainstream of American Culture*, observed: "From the perspective of the liberal arts [Blake says] it is my responsibility *not* to say what [only] is pleasing but to keep [minority students] disturbed, troubled, and shaken up so that they are asking critical questions about what it is that pleases them."[30] Bass continues: "Although he [Blake] believes minority students must be secure and positive in their ethnic identity, [he] is concerned that some students may fail to go beyond that point. Minority students are not fully free, he says, until liberated from the need to be 'anything but human.' At the same time, he notes, 'we must not ignore their need to understand how they can apply what they're learning to the communities from which they came.'"[31]

Black Studies and other Ethnic Studies came so hard won, and the need to reach minority students remains so urgent, that it is difficult for many to accept, even if they see the need, the added complexities of foregrounding the implicit engagement of Whiteness. Furthermore, as more White students take Ethnic Studies seriously and as more traditional departments claim inclusive curricula, the scholarly and the societal value of Ethnic Studies— although it does not diminish—is frequently dismissed by administrators who consolidate programs ostensibly for budgetary reasons and the like.

Ironically, as pointed out in various chapters in this volume, Ethnic Studies in the academy refers to racialized U.S. ethnic groups. This is in partial response to the denial of African American ethnicity (culture) and the degradation of the ethnicities of other racialized American ethnic groups. The legal and cultural mores, as well as the history of U.S. society, demonstrate *the defining character* of the Black-White racial binary and all its manifestations to the Asian American, the Chicano/a, the Latino/a, and the American Indian. As we peel away the layer of the Black-White binary, its imprint remains on the social, cultural, legal, political—even economic in some instances—realities of other U.S. racialized ethnics. As legal scholar Derrick A. Bell has persuasively argued, the Anglo-American burden evolved quickly into Whiteness as property, such that "even those whites who lack wealth and power are sustained in their sense of racial superiority and are thus rendered more willing to accept their lesser share, by an unspoken but no less certain property right in their 'Whiteness.'"[32] With corroboration from the historians Edmund Morgan and David Brion Davis, Bell points out:

Working class whites did not oppose slavery when it took root in the mid-1660s. They identified on the basis of race with wealthy planters . . . even though they were and would remain economically subordinate to those able to afford slaves. But the creation of a black subclass enabled poor whites to identify with and support the policies of the upper-class. And large landowners, with the safe economic advantage provided by their slaves, were willing to grant poor whites a larger role in the political process. Thus, paradoxically, slavery for blacks led to greater freedom for poor whites, at least when compared with the denial of freedom to African slaves. Slavery also provided mainly propertyless whites with a property in their whiteness.[33]

Bell details the role Blacks continue to play as buffers between the most advantaged Whites and the least advantaged Whites and as signaling property in their Whiteness to maintain an economic and social status quo. His description reflects what the late African American literary critic George Kent identified as the "list of cultural drives on which America as a Western exaggeration has attempted to place a pre-empting signature." In his essay "Faulkner and the Heritage of White Racial Consciousness: Notes on White Nationalism in Literature," Kent lists eight unconscious White imperatives:

1. Endorsement of intense individualism and extreme self-consciousness, often leading to alienation.

2. Drive to mastery over nature—often creating uneasiness regarding relationship to nature.

3. Pre-emption of the doctrine of evolution and progress for evidence of Western status as a natural outcome.

4. The drive for massive and intricate organization.

5. Possession of Christianity as a statute-endowing religion and a validation of the role of Western white men (negative ordering of the flesh—*Light in August*).

6. Versions of rationality and common sense as efficient tools for dealing with reality.

7. Possession of a problem-solving optimism.

8. Economic self-interest and concentrated exploitation.[34]

When confronting Blackness, these imperatives, continues Kent, "create a mythicization of the designated stranger and Blackness, a proliferation of racial myth and ritual, and a use of the designated stranger and Blackness for the validation of Whiteness. Our evidence is the frequency and intensity with which certain images of Blackness are hungrily insisted upon, which notify us that we are being offered grains of reality upon a ground of myth."[35] Therefore, the "otherness" of Blackness, and by extension with variation, the "otherness" of other U.S. people of color, not only defines Whiteness, but also defines and gives material value to Whiteness. Thus, I propose that the question studies of Whiteness raises for Ethnic Studies is not what lies *beyond* the Black-White binary, but what is built on it, palimpsestically.

As historian David R. Roediger has observed in a cover blurb for Ethnic Studies scholar George Lipsitz's book *The Possessive Investment in Whiteness,* Lipsitz "break[s] decisively with the tendency of studies of whiteness to reduce race to a black-white binary."[36] However, more to my point, Lipsitz analyzes how the Black-White racial binary defines in some instances, and shapes in others, the racialization of and racism experienced by Asian Americans and Latinos/Latinas in the United States as well as the nation's interactions with people of color beyond its shores. He demonstrates how Ethnic Studies illuminates the way active agency on the part of, for example, African Americans reveals the effects of and actions based on Whiteness as property, as he calls it, "the possessive investment in Whiteness":

People of color have never been merely passive victims of white supremacist power. The active agency of aggrieved communities has always served as an important counterweight to white power. In the process of defending themselves and advancing their own immediate interests, individuals and communities struggling against white supremacy have often created ways of knowing, forms of struggle, and visions of the future important to all people. Even seemingly insignificant cultural expressions often prove to be important reservoirs of collective memory and cultural critique about the possessive investment in Whiteness. Scholarly studies of racism in the United States suffer when they fail to recognize the knowledge about social relations contained in music, literature, and folklore, but those scholars who develop respect and understanding for popular ways of knowing can create highly enlightening and important works.[37]

Black Studies brought race to the foreground in the academy, just as Black access to higher education in the 1960s brought racism in the academy to the foreground. As Asian American Studies, Chicano/a Studies,

Puerto Rican Studies and other Latino/a Studies, and American Indian Studies forged their places in the academy, they foregrounded the racialization of immigrants and of colonized peoples within the United States. These places in the academy grew, in an academic sense, from the challenges scholars in different fields brought to the Chicago school of Ethnic Studies. As the politics of race and racism met the optimism engendered by the legal victories of the 1950s and 1960s, it continued the work of pioneers from Carter G. Woodson, to Américo Paredes, to Ella Cara Deloria, to John Okada in order to have the United States examine generatively the many stories that make up the one. In challenging the "ground of myth" by explicating, analyzing, and expanding the "grains of reality," the matrix of Ethnic Studies examines the many stories that constitute the single story, moving toward the full realization of humanity. The dilemmas raised by the resistance to engaging difference through Ethnic Studies reflect the national dilemma that the convergence of race, racism, and the Anglo-American burden poses.

In the epilogue to his book *One America Indivisible,* Hackney states the dilemma from the national perspective:

My own belief is that there is an overarching national identity that we can share in a way that brings us together so that we can more easily solve our common problems, but a national identity that also honors our differences. Based in democracy, this identity guards individual rights but recognizes the need for a sense of duty to the community. I worry that rights-based individualism on the Left, and market-driven libertarianism on the Right, will leave insufficient room for a common vision of the common good. Surely even the most committed ideologue recognizes that no individual can thrive if the community is failing. The question absent from our national catechism is, "What do I owe my fellow citizens?"[38]

Ethnic Studies' first response to Hackney's query is that he and all of us of whatever racial designation, owe to our fellow citizens the rejection of any participation or investment in Whiteness as property. That is a huge task that implies pedagogical, scholarly, community, and national work on all our parts. In one way or another—whether financially, morally, stereotypically, or fancifully—all of us reflect in obvious or discrete ways in our lives and in our work the legacy of the Anglo-American burden, the legacy of Whiteness. Academically, for Ethnic Studies specifically, this means actively engaging the study of Whiteness as well as womanist and feminist scholarship and perspectives. As early scholarship by U.S. women of color reminds us to invoke a reference to Gloria T. Hull, Patricia Bell Scott, and Barbara Smith's title of their pioneering work, scholars and all of us still proceed as if all the women are White, all the people of color are men, and White men are an exclusive patriarchy.[39] Maulana Karenga's second edition to his *Introduction to Black Studies* is a major step in the appropriate analytical inclusion of women in Black Studies, which indicates recognition of the need for continuing and improving the transformation of Ethnic Studies to include expanded race analysis as well as gender and sexual identity analysis.[40]

The second response of Ethnic Studies to Hackney's query is its demand for a national identity that does more than "also honor[ing] our differences." To recognize and embrace a shared national identity, the past that Ethnic Studies has insisted on recovering demands, like the blues, a fingering of the jagged grain of its pain and triumphs, an owning of its ugliness and an engaging of the possibilities Ethnic Studies offers to the present. This means engaging differences as well as analyzing and picking apart binaries to reveal the difficult generative possibilities. Bell achieves this so masterfully throughout his work that, to paraphrase Vincent Harding, no illusions are allowed.[41]

The move from the color-line to the borderlands means living in the generatively tense spaces of race, ethnicity, gender, sexual identity, and class, and their interactions with other markers that also have social and thus life significance (such as age and physical ability). For Ethnic Studies, this move increases the field's importance as an academic space for teaching and producing scholarship that seeks the closest approximation of accuracy while it continues to develop as a field to be engaged by the established fields of study that are considered "traditional." This move challenges Ethnic Studies to wrestle with its own demons of the racist assimilationist scholarly perspectives that accompanied its formulation; the interethnic and intra-ethnic rivalry exacerbated by the assimilation of the individualistic, abstract objectification of self and others that is now called postmodern; and its gender and sexual identity biases and omissions. The move from color-line to borderlands also, however, challenges the humanities and the social sciences to work with Ethnic Studies to correct their exclusionary universalistic theories and scholarly expressions of a national self-understanding birthed in slavery, racism, and colonialism. Only then can the community that Hackney seeks become transformed, embracing and generatively using its differences. Only then will the similarities or samenesses—the unity—be able to emerge and be recognized and built on.

Transformation and a Cooperative, Relational Pluralism

Transformation of the humanities and social sciences to reveal their useful-
ness to humanity in this world that is drastically different from the world that
first envisioned these studies is inextricably related to the development of
Ethnic Studies. Such transformation must involve the philosophic transformation of revealing the unity among human beings and the world as well as
revealing important differences within the context of that unity. It implies
acknowledging and benefiting from interaction among sameness and diversity, among groups and individuals, among disciplines, among disciplines and
interdisciplinary fields of study. Resting on the maxim "I am we," it allows
for constant dialogical movement from thesis and antithesis to synthesis, the-
sis, and antithesis; to coexisting thesis and antithesis; to an ultimate, possible, but not a necessary or imposed synthesis. This, simply, is a form of
reasoning that goes beyond the oppositional dialectical to an inclusive dialogical that is reflective of the matrix-like ideal of a cooperative, relational
pluralism.

In *The Opening of the American Mind*, historian Lawrence Levine reminds
readers that "pluralist ideas [such as those expressed early in this century by
Horace Kallen, Randolph Bourne, and W. E. B. Du Bois] were overwhelmed
by the certainty that ethnic distinctions were in the process of inevitable distinction." Furthermore, "as late as 1966 the influential sociologist Talcott
Parsons wrote that 'emancipation' from such 'particularist solidarities' as ethnicity, religion, regionalism, and class was accelerating as society adopted 'universalistic norms.'"[42] While some continue to share Parson's view, today many
others seek a pluralism that can serve as a matrix for democracy to be realized. Although at various stages of development, perspectives within Ethnic
Studies relied on identity politics and a strategic and sometimes desperate
separatism in response to the intransigence of racism, it is reasonable to view
the development of Ethnic Studies as an effort to provide the academic and
societal basis for the recognition of the agency of racialized ethnic minorities. An enabling form of pluralism is implicit in most Ethnic Studies scholarship and programs, despite the structural distance from traditionally
accepted departments. That pluralism may be termed a cooperative, relational
pluralism, characterized by dialectical and dialogical interaction with the
unstated (and perhaps even unanticipated) goal of merging to create something new—a concept of American that is multiple-centered, varied, and
reflective of overlapping, merging, and simultaneously similar and distinctly

different heritages. Moreover, the implicit pluralism suggests individual and group agency reinforced by the evolution of distinct identities to fluid multi-layered and multicentered identities.

In 1973 scholars Madelon D. Stent, William R. Hazard, and Harry N. Rivlin offered the following definition of cultural pluralism: "A state of equal co-existence and cooperation in a mutually supportive relationship with the boundaries or framework of one nation of people and diverse cultures with significantly different patterns of belief, behavior, color, and in many cases with different languages. To achieve cultural pluralism, each person must be aware of and secure in his own identity, and be willing to extend to others the same respect and rights that he expects to enjoy."[43] My reworked definition (additions are shown in italic) expresses the type of pluralism inherent in Ethnic Studies:

A state of equal co-existence and cooperation in a mutually supportive relationship with the boundaries or framework of one nation of people of *differing ethnicities* and diverse cultures with significantly different patterns of belief, behavior, color, and in many cases with different languages. To achieve cultural pluralism, *the nation, the communities, the individuals must constantly seek to identify and work within the context of identifying the unity that is in diversity, and work generatively with the tensions between the individual and the group. Within this context of a generative, cooperative pluralism,* each person must be aware of and secure in *his/her* own identity, and be willing to extend to others the same respect and rights that *he/she* expects to enjoy, *and the "one," the "unum," of the nation is contextualized by the "pluribus," the recognition of and engagement of multiple perspectives, multiple centers of being, beliefs, and behavior. Boundaries and limits of behavior are established, reconsidered and re-established through mutual consideration, mutual resources, and mutual sharing of resources.*[44]

This definition places the interaction between individual and community, between self and other, between difference and similarity as key to nation building and seeks the mutual restriction of power and dominance. It is based on the acknowledgment of a secure but generative sense of self and respect for the rights of self and others.

The Ethnic Studies Major as Catalyst

The University of California-Berkeley, Bowling Green State University, the University of Washington, the University of California-San Diego, and the University of Colorado-Boulder have undergraduate majors in Ethnic Studies that are interdisciplinary and comparative. Many colleges and universities offer Ethnic Studies through American Studies, American cultures and American civilization programs, and through Centers for the Study of Race and Ethnicity. Other colleges and universities offer majors in Africana Studies, African American Studies, Asian American Studies, Chicano/a Studies, Latino/a Studies, Puerto Rican Studies, and American Indian Studies. Examples of majors, regularly updated and with course descriptions, may be found on the Web sites of the various universities. The institutionalization of majors through departmental or program structure depends on the history of each campus and the structures available for interdisciplinary studies. However, it is useful to identify certain characteristics of the Ethnic Studies major that allow for its matrix-like possibility.

Some of these key characteristics of the Ethnic Studies major are interdisciplinary and comparative connections to and among disciplines in the humanities and the social sciences; a paradoxical existence, marked by institutional, scholarly, and societal realities that simultaneously endanger and sustain innovation; content that simultaneously challenges and enhances traditional scholarship; attention to race as a meaningful and oppressive social construction; interdisciplinary departments and programs that function and challenge the rigid disciplinary academic structures that house them; joint appointments and cross-listed courses across departmental boundaries; undergraduate and graduate studies that cross disciplines, modify chronologies, and expand reading lists; attempts at collegial cooperation across methodological and departmental turf borders and across lines of raced and ethnocentric power.

In addition, Ethnic Studies has its problems, mostly in its historically ambivalent relationship to gender and sexual identity. Born reflecting White, male, Euro-centered scholarly and pedagogical methodology while simultaneously challenging that methodology, Ethnic Studies has much too slowly in its courses reflected the race, gender, and class analyses in the works of such scholars as Patricia Hill Collins, Beverly Guy-Sheftall, Darlene Clark Hine, Robin D. G. Kelley, George Lipsitz, Audre Lorde, Lisa Lowe, Manning Marable, Tey Diana Rebellodo, Barbara Smith, and others. These problems, however, are shared with the humanities and the social sciences and are connected to the general tendency to describe rather than to examine the significances of domestic colonial, colonial, postcolonial, post-civil rights, regional, national, global, diasporic, and transnational experiences and identities.

The elusive color-line in the borderlands threatens the realization of an equitable participatory democracy, even if we solve all of the problems related to the human alienation encouraged by a potentially beneficial technology that if misused can distance us from one another and from ourselves; even if we solve the economic problems related to the distribution of wealth, the expansion of a permanent underclass and of a diminished middle class, the color-line ultimately threatens the dialogic reconciliation of the binary of individual/community, dooming us to repeat divisive hostilities and aborted expressions of democracy because of racism. The creative and enabling characteristics of the Ethnic Studies matrix offers higher education the ability to assure that our scholarship, methodology, and pedagogy counters the hegemony of the color-line and the ethnocentrism, classism, and gender and sexual discrimination that accompanies it.

The task is so fundamental and of such a magnitude that it demands a rethinking of the ways knowledge and information are organized, engaged, and taught. And here lies the rub, because our academic, pedagogical, and now technological narratives and discourses influence the conceptualization of individual and community, as well as our personal, political, and policy-driven attitudes and actions toward one another. Ethnic Studies, which began our national concern with what are now many types of multiculturalism (as the essays in this book attest), has attempted to engage in the academy the contextualized, fallible, and generative objectivity that literary theorist Satya Mohanty has described in his post positivist realist analysis of postmodern literary theory.[45] Viewing "multiculturalism as an aspect of a theory of social justice," Mohanty's work illuminates the conflictive academic context in which Ethnic Studies has persisted, a context that parenthetically reveals the depth of the misconception that teachers and students in colleges and universities exist in ivory towers.[46]

Because Ethnic Studies assumes the significance of cultural identities to individual agency as well as to oppressive constructs, it has from its beginning been a touchstone. It is hoped that Ethnic Studies has been a wellspring for those who see understanding how, why, and to what effect cultural identities, often read as racial identities, exist in relation to the group and national narrative. As Mohanty sees it, "Cultural identities are good everyday instances of our deepest social biases; even when they are openly espoused, they are often based on submerged feelings and values, reflecting areas of both sensibility and judgment. They are neither to be dismissed as mere social constructions, and hence spurious, nor celebrated as our real unchanging essences in a heartless and changing world. We have the capacity to examine our social identities, considering them in light of our best understanding of other social facts and our other social relationships. Indeed this is what we do whenever we seek to transform ourselves in times of social and cultural change."[47] Understood as such, then, cultural identities are pivotal in this time of social and cultural change in order to understand and intervene in the national consciousness in ways that reconnect with both the beautiful and ugly of the ancestral and more immediate pasts. Examining the multiple binaries of our cultural identities is the work of the generatively merged double consciousness of Du Bois or of Gloria Anzaldúa's mestiza consciousness, work that helps us to understand and engage productively the complexities of the self and others and of the present as well as legacies of the past.[48]

To paraphrase Floyd W. Hayes in his introduction to *A Turbulent Voyage: Readings in African American Studies*, the quest of Ethnic Studies in U.S. higher education is to challenge America to refashion its self-understanding.[49] To do so as a nation, a necessary and fundamental step is to provide a place in U.S. colleges and universities where scholar-teachers and students can identify the excluded narratives; analyze the results of their inclusion with traditionally taught narratives that they reflect, contradict, conflict, and agree with; and reconsider and re-narrate the various expressions of the national self-understanding in accord with these analyses. The matrix of Ethnic Studies—composed of the study of race and racialization, of the experience of racialized U.S. ethnic groups, of the study of Whiteness, and of the study of the expressive culture that reflects the fullness of the human experience in the United States—is that place of salvation for the humanities and the social sciences. Moreover, it is a most generative space for the continued aspiration for higher education to engender an equitable and just democracy that exists for the common good.

Notes

1. Paul Lauter, *Canons and Contexts* (New York: Oxford University Press, 991), 23.

2. Elizabeth Karmarck Minnich, *Transforming Knowledge* (Philadelphia: Temple University Press, 1990).

3. Johnnella E. Butler and John C. Walter, *Transforming the Curriculum: Ethnic Studies and Women's Studies* (New York: SUNY Press, 1991).

4. Sheldon Hackney, *One America Indivisible: A National Conversation on*

American Pluralism and Identity (Washington, D.C.: National Endowment for the Humanities, 1997), 5.

5. Ibid., 5.

6. There is no other field of study in academia that at least once a year on most campuses is the subject of a student article or editorial questioning its validity; that has to offset the effects of faculty and others outside the department or program advising against courses or the major; or that politicians outside the area of study and outside the academy in general feel they can question not only its validity but also the field's very right to existence. This is what I mean by the constant threat of erasure.

7. Works such as Addison Gayles, *The Black Aesthetic* (Garden City, N.Y.: Doubleday, 1971); Stephen Henderson, *Understanding the New Black Poetry: Black Speech and Black Music as Poetic References* (New York: Morrow, 1975); and Toni Cade (Bambara), ed., *The Black Woman* (New York: New American Library, 1970) lay the foundation for reconceptualizing the African American experience in terms of its cultural expression and social reality in relation to both itself and the larger U.S. American culture.

8. Ulrich B. Phillips, *American Negro Slavery: A Survey of the Supply, Employment, and Control of Negro Labor as Determined by the Plantation Regime* (New York and London: D. Appleton, 1918); Henry Steele Commager, *The First Book of American History* (New York: F. Watts, 1957).

9. Frank Chin et al., eds., *Aiiieeeee! An Anthology of Asian-American Writers* (New York: Anchor Press/Doubleday, 1975).

10. There is an extraordinary amount of scholarship on African civilization and African transformations in the "new world," extending from the 1960s through the 1980s, that is rarely recognized or used today in literary, historical, or cultural studies. Relevant texts are by Jahn, Davidson, Diop, and Drake. One might begin with Jahnheinz Jahn, *Muntu: The New African Culture* (New York: Grove Press, 1961); Basil Davidson, *The Black Man's Burden: Africa and the Curse of the Nation-State* (New York: Times Books, 1992); Basil Davidson, *The African Slave Trade* (Boston: Little, Brown, 1980); Cheikh Anta Diop, *The Cultural Unity of Negro Africa: The Domains of Patriarchy and of Matriarchy in Classical Antiquity* (Paris: Présence Africaine, 1962); and St. Clair Drake, *Black Folk Here and There: An Essay in History and Anthropology* (Los Angeles: CAAS Publications, 1987).

11. Stow Persons, *Ethnic Studies at Chicago, 1905–45* (Urbana: University of Illinois Press, 1987); Jack Bass, *Widening the Mainstream of American Culture: A Ford Foundation Report on Ethnic Studies* (New York: Ford Foundation, 1970).

12. Persons, *Ethnic Studies at Chicago*, 2; italics added.

13. Ibid., 82.

14. Ibid., 83.

15. E. Franklin Frazier, *Black Bourgeoisie: The Rise of a New Middle Class in the United States* (New York: Collier Books, 1962).

16. Persons, *Ethnic Studies at Chicago,* 131.

17. See Bass, *Widening the Mainstream of American Culture, a Ford Foundation Report.*

18. Assimilation is not inherently racist or undesirable. However, as experienced in the United States, the process is racialized and assumes racist norms.

19. Bass, *Widening the Mainstream of American Culture,* 1.

20. Ibid., 3.

21. Ibid.

22. Ibid., 10.

23. Ibid., 19.

24. Ibid., 18.

25. During the discussions of the Ethnic Studies Symposium at the University of Washington, which form the basis of this book, this issue surfaced. One participant contentiously equated Ethnic Studies with sociology and the traditional mainstream study of race relations (see symposium transcript, April 24, 1993).

26. Of the thirty-nine papers published in *Cultural Studies,* the 1992 volume of that conference, it appears that only two are by Ethnic Studies scholars: Chicano/a Studies and African American Studies, to be exact. See Grossberg et al., eds., *Cultural Studies* (New York: Routledge, 1992), 699.

27. Ibid., 694.

28. Ibid., 699.

29. Ibid., 696.

30. Herman Blake, quoted in Bass, *Widening the Mainstream of American Culture,* 14.

31. Ibid.

32. Derrick A. Bell, "White Superiority in America: Its Legal Legacy, Its Economic Costs," in *Black or White: Black Writers on What It Means to Be White* (New York: Schocken Books, 1998), 145.

33. Ibid., 143–44.

34. George Kent, "Faulkner and the Heritage of White Racial Consciousness: Notes on White Nationalism in Literature," in Kent, *Blackness and the Adventure of Western Culture* (Chicago: Third World Press, 1972), 166.

35. Ibid., 166. Kent's observations are similar to those of James Baldwin and Toni Morrison. See in particular Baldwin, "Faulkner and Desegregation" in Morrison, ed., *Baldwin, Collected Essays* (New York: Library of America, 1998), 209–14; and Morrison, *Playing in the Dark: Whiteness and the Literary Imagination* (Cambridge: Harvard University Press, 1992).

36. George Lipsitz, *The Possessive Investment in Whiteness: How White People Profit from Identity Politics* (Philadelphia: Temple University Press, 1998).

37. Ibid., 158.

38. Hackney, *One America Indivisible,* 128.

39. Feminist works of the late 1970s and 1980s established the groundwork for Black Women's Studies, Chicana Studies, and works on Asian American feminism. Key texts are Cade (Bambara), *Black Woman;* Rosanne P. Bell et al., eds., *Sturdy Black Bridges* (Garden City, N.Y.: Anchor, 1979); Angela Davis, *Women, Race, and Class* (New York: Random House, 1981); Gloria T. Hull, Patricia Bell Scott, Barbara Smith, *All the Women Are White, All the Blacks Are Men, but Some of Us Are Brave* (Old Westbury, N.Y.: Feminist Press, 1982); Barbara Smith, ed., *Home Girls: A Black Feminist Anthology* (New York: Kitchen Table Press, 1983); Cherríe Moraga and Gloria Anzaldúa, *This Bridge Called My Back: Writings by Radical Women of Color* (Watertown, Mass.: Persephone Press, 1983); Asian Women United of California, eds., *Making Waves: An Anthology of Writings by and about Asian American Women* (Boston: Beacon Press, 1989); and Shirley Geok-lin Lim, Mayumi Tsutakawa, and Margarita Donnelly, eds., *The Forbidden Stitch: An Asian American Women's Anthology* (Corvallis, Ore.: Calyx Books, 1989).

40. Maulana Karenga, *Introduction to Black Studies,* 2d ed. (Los Angeles: University of Sankore Press, 1993). As evidence of the continuing efforts of Ethnic Studies to include gender and sexuality identity analysis, the spring 2000 conference of the National Council for Black Studies held a preconference on gender in conjunction with its twenty-fourth annual meeting.

41. This is from a typed manuscript by Vincent Harding that is in my possession. I cannot locate the publication citation. The contemporary writer that most closely represents the sentiment of African American history allowing for no illusions is, in my opinion, Derrick A. Bell, particularly in his trilogy of works, *And We Are Not Saved: The Elusive Quest for Racial Justice* (New York: Basic Books, 1987), *Faces at the Bottom of the Well: The Permanence of Racism* (New York: Basic Books, 1992), and *Gospel Choirs: Psalms of Survival for an Alien Land Called Home* (New York: Basic Books, 1996).

42. Lawrence Levine, *The Opening of the American Mind: Canons, Culture, and History* (Boston: Beacon Press, 1996), 114–18.

43. Madelon D. Stent, William R. Hazard, and Harry N. Rivlin, eds., *Cultural Pluralism in Education: A Mandate for Change* (New York: Appleton-Century-Crofts, 1973), 14.

44. The quotation, with my additions shown in italic, is based on the definition of cultural pluralism as offered by Stent, Hazard, and Rivlin, eds., *Cultural Pluralism in Education,* 14. My thinking here is most influenced by conversations

and joint writing with the American Commitments National Panel of the American Association of Colleges and Universities, funded by the Ford Foundation, 1993–96. See in particular a result of this panel, *The Drama of Diversity and Democracy: Higher Education and American Commitments* (Washington, D.C.: American Association of Colleges and Universities, 1995).

45. Satya Mohanty, *Literary Theory and the Claims of History: Postmodernism, Objectivity, Multicultural Politics* (Ithaca, N.Y.: Cornell University Press, 1997). See also Martha Nussbaum, "The Hip Defeatism of Judith Butler: The Professor of Parody," *New Republic,* February 22, 1999, on Judith Butler and postmodernism's logical end of abstraction and therefore no action.

46. Mohanty, *Literary Theory and the Claims of History,* 198.

47. Ibid., 201.

48. See Johnnella E. Butler, "Reflections on Borderlands and the Color-Line," in Shirley Geok-lin Lim and María Herrera-Sobek, eds., *Power, Race, and Gender: Strangers in the Tower?* (New York: Modern Language Association, 2000), in which I discuss the parallels between W. E. B. Du Bois's delineation of African American double consciousness in 1903 and Gloria Anzaldúa's concept of Chicana mestiza consciousness. See Du Bois, "Of Our Spiritual Strivings" in *The Souls of Black Folk* (1903; reprint, New York: Everyman's Library, Alfred A. Knopf, 1993), 7–15; and Anzaldúa's *Borderlands/La Frontera* (San Francisco: Spinters/Aunt Lute, 1987), 77–91.

49. Floyd W. Hayes III, ed., *A Turbulent Voyage: Readings in African American Studies* (San Diego, Calif.: Collegiate Press, 1992), xi-xlvii.

The Problematics of Ethnic Studies

MANNING MARABLE

ANY DISCUSSION ABOUT RACE AND ETHNICITY AS SOCIAL forces within the contemporary American experience must begin from the vantage point of history. In the development of U.S. society, there were three great social divisions that, from the very beginning, fostered social hierarchies of power and privilege and sets of dependent relations. The first was the division between Europeans versus non-Europeans (particularly African slaves and American Indians); the second was the division between capital and labor, the conflict between those privileged elites who controlled the land and productive resources versus those who lived by their labor power; and third, the gender stratification between men and women, the superiority granted to males by the patriarchal weight of law, property ownership, political enfranchisement, and physical violence and control. Each of these great divisions contributed to the historical construction of a national identity of America that was largely defined by "Whiteness": a racial category of privilege that rationalized and justified the domination and exploitation of "Others" who are non-European, poor, and/or female.

These three very different yet overlapping hierarchies of domination shaped the foundations for what Michael Omi and Howard Winnant have termed a "racial formation."[1] What emerged was a racial system of meanings, discourses, and hierarchies of power that was inherently unstable and constantly changing, as new immigrants entered the racial formation and created fresh interactions between groups. Nevertheless, as cultural anthropologist Faye V. Harrison reminds us, the instability of racialized institutions was "constrained by poles of difference that have remained relatively constant: White supremacy and the Black subordination that demarcates the social bottom. Although Whiteness and Blackness have not had fixed meanings and boundaries, the opposition between them has provided the stabilizing backbone for the United States' racialized social body."[2]

Theoretical Questions on Race and Ethnicity

In practice what this has meant historically is that "Whiteness" evolved as a racial category of privilege, which was accessible only to immigrants of European origin, with some exceptions. Whiteness was the entry point or passage through which Euro-Americans competed against each other for power and status. The White community was deeply stratified by class and gender inequalities, but all individuals who claimed the status of Whiteness stood above the abyss of inferiority and subordination, to which people of African descent and Native Americans had been plummeted. Phenotype and physical features were used in this system as a rough symbolic indicator to determine the individual's access to resources, property, and power. But as powerful as the code of color was, class divisions still prefigured the range of possibilities for the dynamics of racialized ethnicity and gender. In short, every racial formation exists within a political economy and a class structure that does not dictate but does prefiguratively set the possible alternatives that develop in all social relations. As modes of production develop and change, as the organization of labor and the economy move forward, the social configuration and social manifestations of race also mutate into new forms. Thus race and racism in 1895, when Booker T. Washington articulated his separate-but-equal compromise address in Atlanta, Georgia, was not the identical racial formation that was the context for Louis Farrakhan's Million Man March in Washington, D.C., a century later.

 White racial consciousness became a central ideological theme in the political construction of what would become the United States. But from the beginning, Whiteness itself was vacuous and sterile as a cultural entity. As historian David Roediger explains, "It is not merely that whiteness is oppressive and false; it is that whiteness is *nothing but* oppressive and false. . . . It is the empty and terrifying attempt to build an identity based on what one isn't and on whom one can hold back."[3] By the late seventeenth and early eighteenth centuries, immigrants from mostly western European countries who came to the American continent had assimilated and constructed for themselves a new racial identity called "White." After the establishment of the United States, Whiteness was literally codified as part of the Constitution, particularly in Article I, section 2, which defined Black slaves for the purposes of taxation and representation as the equivalent of three-fifths of a human being.

"Race" is therefore a dynamic social construct that has its roots in the transatlantic slave trade, the establishment of plantation economies based on slave labor, and in the ideological justification for the vast extermination of millions of indigenous Americans. White Americans have thought of themselves in terms of racial categories for several centuries. By contrast, "ethnicity" is a relatively recent concept. There are no references to "ethnicity" per se in the social science literature of the nineteenth and early twentieth centuries. Rather, it surfaced as an important social science category of analysis in the writings of sociologists during the Great Depression, as a means to describe the diverse immigrant populations largely from southern and eastern Europe. Later, ethnicity was utilized to describe the development of modern European nationalism and conflicts developing between various communities defined by their cultural and social traditions. Manning Nash defines ethnicity as a set of "cultural markers" that give a collective identity to a group, such as kinship, rituals, communality, or language.[4] Anthropologist Leith Mullings has also provided a good working definition of ethnicity: "group identification, by self or others, on the basis of phenotype, language, religion, or national origin."[5]

Because of the hegemony of race and racism in the social development of the United States, European immigrants who arrived here quickly learned that the key to their advancement and power was to claim the status of being White. In other words, during the nineteenth century "race" was much more powerful than what we might today call "ethnicity" in determining the life chances of most new immigrants. The Irish, who for centuries had been an oppressed nation, experienced severe discrimination upon their arrival. But within several generations in the United States they had become "White." They had assimilated the values of privilege and the discourses and behaviors of domination, which permitted them to claim status within the social hierarchy.

Conversely, immigrants from Latin America and Asia were frequently "racialized" by both legislative means and by de facto segregation. For example, Chinese immigrants were subjected to legal restrictions as early as 1870. In 1875 the U.S. Congress essentially prohibited Chinese women from entering the country. The Chinese Exclusion Act of 1882 banned "idiots," "lunatics," and "Chinese laborers." Legislation severely restricting Japanese immigration was passed by Congress in 1907 and again in 1924. Asian Indians were limited from coming into the United States in 1917; Filipino immigration was curtailed in 1934. In 1942, after the outbreak of World War II, 110,000 Japanese American civilians were forcibly removed from their homes to detention camps. It was only with the passage of the 1952 McCarran-Walter Act that Asians born outside the country were allowed to become U.S. citizens.[6] An even more complicated racial coding process developed with Mexican Americans. After the U.S.-Mexican war of 1846–48, the United States incorporated roughly one-half of Mexico's entire territory into its own legal boundaries. Slavery, which had previously been abolished by the Mexican government, was reestablished. Only Mexicans who were defined as Spanish or White could claim U.S. citizenship. Indians, peasants, and mestizos were treated as inferior groups.[7]

Currently there are major academic disagreements over the meanings and materiality of race and ethnicity. For example, should race be subsumed under ethnicity as a subcategory? Or is race an exceptional social category in its own right, because of its peculiar historical development, discourses, relations with culture, and so on, which sets it apart from ethnicity? To what extent, if at all, should race be measured by biological, genetic, or cultural differences between groups? Can racialized ethnic minorities such as African Americans be "racists" themselves? And what of the complex relationships between racialized ethnicities—Asian Americans, American Indians, Latinos, and Black Americans?

Many different theoretical approaches have been proposed to address these questions. At one end of the ideological spectrum are the racial-ethnic theorists, or the multiculturalists. One prominent example of such work is that by historian Ronald Takaki. In several influential studies Takaki basically states that racialized minorities are fundamentally different from other ethnic groups because of their common history of oppression. African Americans came to this country involuntarily, in chains. Only American Indians were subjected to a deliberate policy of genocidal extermination. A common history of residential segregation, economic subordination, and political disfranchisement have created the basis for a comprehensive approach to the study of these ethnic minority groups.[8] Closely paralleling Takaki is the work of Ethnic Studies scholar Johnnella E. Butler, who defines "people of color" as a social category that includes "those who have not and do not assimilate." Despite the many differences between these groups, Butler notes, "there are enough similarities in the American experiences of all these peoples to provide an imperfect yet workable construct of social organization—individual and group behavior—created by the peoples themselves and reflected in the academy." Butler defines this as a "matrix construct . . . a flexible diverse construct with multiple connections and interactions."[9]

A political economy approach to issues of race has been used by social scientists such as Robert Allen and Robert Blauner. Both argue that racialized minorities not only share uniquely different social histories from Whites, but that their existence is strikingly similar to that of a colonized nation. In *Black Awakening in Capitalist America*, Allen suggests that Black America is an oppressed internal colony inside the United States. The capitalist economic system thus uses racism as a means to exploit Black and brown labor power and to divide and confuse White workers from recognizing their true interests. Blauner's *Racial Oppression in America* argues that White ethnic groups may have experienced intolerance and exploitation, but that they were never "colonized." The structure of racial power confines African Americans and other racialized minorities to a subordinate status. The process of racial and class underdevelopment was therefore not accidental but absolutely essential in the consolidation of White power.[10]

At the opposite end of the spectrum are the cultural universalists, who for very divergent reasons attack or dismiss Ethnic Studies. The most influential "old school" universalists on issues of race and ethnicity are Nathan Glazer and Daniel Patrick Moynihan, authors of *Beyond the Melting Pot* and other works. These scholars have argued that ethnicity is not biologically based, but rather a product of social forces and voluntary choices people made about expressing their identities. As for Black Americans, Glazer and Moynihan essentially proposed a universalist model with Whites as the standard, wherein Blacks should strive to acquire the lifestyles, family patterns, and work habits of Whites to diminish racial tensions. This theoretical orientation logically led Moynihan to his infamous 1965 "Black Matriarchy Thesis," attacking the matrifocal family structure of the Black community as the principal cause of poverty and juvenile delinquency. Similarly, Glazer's subsequent hostility toward affirmative action programs, minority economic set-asides, and Ethnic Studies programs reflects his universalist convictions that "color-blindness" should be society's ultimate goal. Therefore, any policy compensating for the special handicaps or barriers that still affect Blacks and other people of color, such as affirmative action, unjustly discriminates against innocent Whites.[11]

Then there are the "new school" universalists, who imply that any recognition of a unique status for racialized ethnic groups veers dangerously toward racial essentialism and separatism. Two leading intellectuals in this school of thought are Werner Sollors, a professor in Harvard's African American Studies program, and Sean Wilentz, director of American Studies at Princeton University. In a series of provocative works, Sollors vilifies those who emphasize the discontinuities and conflicts among various racial and ethnic groups. For Sollors, "ethnicity" as a social construct is an "invention," nothing more. In this view all Americans, regardless of their respective racial or ethnic identities, share far more in common within each other, culturally, socially, and politically.[12] In a 1996 article in the *Chronicle of Higher Education*, Wilentz accuses many Ethnic Studies scholars of depicting "the United States chiefly in terms of ethnic (or racial) identities and antagonisms and, in some cases, to proclaim that ethnic groups should defend their cultures from assimilation into a hegemonic mainstream 'American' civilization." Princeton's American Studies program, however, has taken a different approach by emphasizing fundamental cultural commonalities rather than differences. Wilentz states: "We fear, as the historian Arthur M. Schlesinger, Jr., has observed, that a fixation on ethnic differences presents a distorted picture of the United States as a country that is all 'pluribus' and no 'unum.' We are equally convinced, however, that an ethnic or racial approach, narrowly conceived, does not do justice to the numerous ethnic and racial components of American culture. . . . To paraphrase the writer Ralph Ellison, Americans are all 'cultural mulattos.'"[13] Wilentz's color-blind formulation defies common sense and denies the crucial difference race still makes in daily American life.

Finally, there are also social theorists of race and ethnicity who frankly do put forward essentialist and identity-bound models of cultural difference. The most influential school of thought presently expressed in most Black Studies programs is "Afrocentrism," a concept initially developed by Molefi Asante, former chair of Black Studies at Temple University. The rationalization for Afrocentrism is constructed around its oppositional stance toward Eurocentrism, the cultural ideology and supremacist practices of the White West. Several Afrocentrists even claim that racism is not socially constructed but rather a product of genetic or physical deficiencies among Euro-Americans. It is therefore not surprising that the national conversation around Ethnic Studies continues to be so politically charged and confrontational. People from universities and public schools alike talk past each other precisely because there is no consensus, in abstract theory or in the real world, about what is meant by race and ethnicity.

Ethnic Studies: Intellectual Contours and Structures

Ethnic Studies as a field of scholarship is the intellectual product of vast historical and social changes within U.S. society. It has evolved from different types of academic institutions, both public and private, and in some quarters it still speaks the passionate language of the various social protest movements that gave the field life a generation ago. Ethnic Studies as an intellectual project is still evolving, but its essential character was forged in the demographic, political, and cultural transformations within twentieth-century American society that have occurred around the issue of difference. At the dawn of the twentieth century racial discourse was rigidly framed on a bipolar model, Black versus White. Ninety percent of all African Americans lived in the South, and roughly 80 percent were farmers or sharecroppers. Jim Crow segregation had been institutionalized throughout the South and was informally extended to govern race relations in the Northeast and Midwest. White insurgent movements seeking social change—such as the women suffragists, trade unionists, and middle-class Progressives—largely excluded Negroes. The few Asian Americans who had been permitted to remain in the United States were marginalized and controlled by the same powerful forces that perpetuated Black inferiority and subordination. Diversity in major U.S. cities was reflected largely through the complex patterns of European languages, religions, nationalities, and cultural traditions that had come to dominate urban life.

American universities rarely focused on racialized ethnic groups, except to explore these communities as "problems" (e.g., "The Negro Problem"). Black higher education was confined to about a hundred public and private academic institutions that had been constructed in the decades after the Civil War. What today is called Black Studies, or more accurately the Black intellectual tradition of scholarship in the humanities, social sciences, and physical sciences, was nurtured first at these unfunded but proud colleges. The research of African American scholars such as W. E. B. Du Bois, Charles S. Johnson, and E. Franklin Frazier formed the foundation for a critical and serious understanding of African American life and history. Interest in African affairs in the aftermath of World War II fostered the establishment of African Studies programs and centers at predominately White institutions, such as Northwestern University in 1948. Nevertheless, such programs were relatively isolated and few in number, reflecting the marginality of racialized minorities in the larger scope of American academe and civil society. The barrier of race structured the boundaries of knowledge and legitimate intellectual inquiry for most White Americans.

Several events and factors were responsible for transforming the study of race and ethnicity in American higher education. As northern industrial and manufacturing jobs became available to Blacks before and during World War I, millions trekked out of the South in the Great Migration. Hundreds of thousands of immigrants from the Caribbean came to the East Coast. In the 1940s and 1950s several million Mexicans who had frequently crossed the border to obtain work began to resettle the U.S. Southwest. By the 1960s there were substantial racialized ethnic populations in almost every major U.S. city. These demographic changes inevitably influenced American popular culture. Everything from professional sports and popular music to films, and the media began to be profoundly shaped and interpreted through the prism of minority group cultures. The Civil Rights movement represented a "Second Reconstruction" for Black America, with the dismantling of legal segregation. The civil rights campaigns of the 1950s and 1960s helped give shape and impetus to other new protest movements, reflecting the demands and agendas of Chicanos, Puerto Ricans, feminists, lesbians, and gays, American Indians, and many other groups. These profound movements for social reform, in turn, pressured predominantly White colleges and universities to open their doors to racialized ethnic minorities for the first time. For example, between 1976 and 1993 the number of Asian Americans enrolled in colleges soared from 198,000 to 724,000. By 1993 college enrollment for Latinos reached one million.

The newly arrived racialized ethnic groups on White campuses quickly demanded changes in the curriculum that reflected their own historical experiences, cultures, and respective intellectual traditions. The first institutionalized expression of these demands was in the field of African American Studies. By the late 1960s African American Studies programs were established at more than a hundred colleges; within ten years the number of Black Studies programs exceeded 350. In the U.S. Southwest more than fifty Chicano Studies programs were formed within a decade. In the eastern states Puerto Rican Studies centers and programs were established. Most of these earlier programs

were conceptually defined by the social reality of a specifically racialized experience and the cultural parameters of the heritages and traditions of specific
non-White populations. For example, African American Studies generally
focused on the cultural connections among Africa, the Caribbean, and Black
America, the construction of Black culture and society inside the United States,
and the patterns of resistance against racial discrimination.

The development of Native American Studies was in several critical
respects different from Black, Latino, and Asian American Studies programs.
The study of American Indian cultures and societies as a field of scholarship
was for years dominated by White anthropologists, who frequently viewed
their subjects through ethnocentric and even racist perspectives. Indians usually thought of themselves in terms of their tribal identities. All of this began
to change in the 1950s, when the federal government initiated a policy called
"termination," which in effect expelled more than one hundred tribes off lands
that had been promised to them by historical treaty obligations. This policy
crisis pushed tribal groups toward a pan-Indian cultural identity. New organizations such as the National Congress of American Indians and the United
Native Americans were formed. In the late 1960s the radical American Indian
Movement (AIM) fostered a new wave of militancy among Indians throughout the United States. But it was not until 1980 that a group of Indian scholars met to establish the Native American Studies Association.

As a result of its development, the field has two very different types of
academic institutional structures: many traditional programs initiated and
led by White scholars at predominantly White universities, which focus on
anthropological, linguistic, historical, and folkloric themes; and the more radical Indian Studies programs, frequently connected with the network of tribal
colleges. This second group of Indian scholars often define their research outside the boundaries of Ethnic Studies, for the simple reason that Indians are
the only "indigenous" people in the United States. Indians are not an ethnic
group because they did not immigrate to this country. This is why much of
the best new scholarship in the field, such as the outstanding work of Vine
Deloria, is concerned with the issues of law, such as treaty obligations and
territorial rights.

As the new academic programs were established, two distinct curricular and research models emerged nationally. The vast majority were interdisciplinary undergraduate programs, which characteristically had a director
and a list of affiliated faculty who were located in disciplinary-based departments. The director usually advised majors, taught the core required courses,

and supervised a modest program of lectures and campus-based activities. These programs almost always linked their central courses to their college's general education requirements or its core curriculum. The departments of Black Studies, Chicano Studies, and Ethnic Studies were almost always located at large public institutions. At Ohio State University and Temple University, for instance, Black Studies had more than sixteen full-time faculty and graduate degree programs. In 1996 there were approximately forty-five Black Studies full departments, seventeen Chicano and Puerto Rican Studies departments, and eight Asian American Studies departments.

Both programmatic models of racialized Ethnic Studies had their own sets of problems, however. The departments often tended to suffer "ghettoization." For example, traditional departments sometimes would not cross-list Black and Latino Studies courses. The criteria for appointment, promotion, and tenure in the new departments were considered lacking sufficient academic rigor and intellectual viability. Faculty in these departments were often marginalized from the academic life of the campus community, in effect, preaching to their own racial constituency. Conversely, the interdisciplinary programs often lacked any academic coherence or intellectual integrity. The curricula were often eclectically organized, relying on faculty who had little academic relationship with each other. One recurrent problem was that departments typically recruit, promote, and tenure their faculty on their own set of criteria, which might have little relationship with the interdisciplinary scholarship, publications, and research of African American, Latino, or Ethnic Studies.

Princeton and Harvard Universities represent two of the most influential models of African American Studies. In the 1980s Princeton recruited a cohort of outstanding scholars and writers, including the novelist Toni Morrison, the historian Nell Painter, and the social philosopher-theologian Cornel West. Each was given the resources to establish an interdisciplinary set of courses, visiting professorships, and to sponsor major events, such as the April 1994 "Race Matters" conference. Harvard had been pressured by student protesters in the late 1960s to establish an African American Studies department. For more than a decade the institution treated the department as a pariah, however, with limited influence and few resources. A research institute named for W. E. B. Du Bois was also established to promote the development of Black Studies on the campus. In 1989, Harvard recruited literary scholar Henry Louis Gates Jr. as director of African American Studies and almost overnight committed massive financial resources and assistance in program development. Gates successfully recruited major intellectuals, such as Cornel West from Princeton and sociologist William Julius Wilson from Chicago, and in the process attempted to redefine the field's entire scope and direction. Gates was able to control seven full-faculty appointments and was given the resources through the institute to sponsor a major journal, *Transition*, as well as a series of academic conferences and publications projects.

The evolution of Ethnic Studies programs was largely preceded by the creation of these other racial-ethnic programs. The first of the major Ethnic Studies departments to develop were, not surprisingly, in ethnically diverse California. The Department of Ethnic Studies at the University of California-Berkeley was founded in 1969, at the height of the antiwar and Black Power movements. It was originally conceived as an umbrella-like structure, with four interdependent programs operating within one department. Four separate majors and curricula were established in Native American Studies, Chicano Studies, Asian American Studies, and Afro-American Studies. Within a few years, however, several serious problems had developed in the program. Because each major focused on a single racial ethnicity, students and faculty tended to function only in their narrow area of scholarly interest. There were relatively few faculty at the time who were involved in comparative research in the field of Ethnic Studies. Compounding all of these issues was the internal competition for resources. The department's administration received its budgetary allocation and made the determination for how much each program would receive for the academic year. Cooperation among the various programs suffered and sometimes broke down completely. By 1973, Afro-American Studies made the decision to leave Ethnic Studies and demanded the right to become a department. Several years later Native American Studies also broke from Ethnic Studies. Although the department has for years continued to be the home of several outstanding scholars, such as Ronald Takaki and Michael Omi, it has never received the full institutional support that it merits. Despite these problems, by the early 1990s the Ethnic Studies department had more than 150 undergraduate majors and a small but successful doctoral program.[14]

For nearly twenty years Berkeley's Ethnic Studies department was the most influential model for new program development. Dozens of Ethnic Studies academic units were initiated during these years. In 1979, for example, Bowling Green University established a Department of Ethnic Studies, which included an undergraduate degree in three areas: Latino Studies, Black Studies, and general Ethnic Studies. In 1983, Washington State University created a Department of Comparative American Cultures, which within several years had ten faculty and offered curricula with concentrations in Native American, Asian American, Chicano, and African American Studies.[15] Most of these Ethnic Studies units were interdisciplinary programs rather than departments and frequently were unable to exercise authority in faculty recruitment and tenure or with their own curricula. At a number of smaller colleges Ethnic Studies was offered as a minor concentration through traditional departments, such as sociology and anthropology.

By the mid-1980s the distinctive racial-ethnic composition of California's university campuses was no longer confined to the West Coast. Significant numbers of Asian American students were enrolling in elite universities throughout the country. In 1983, for example, 5.5 percent of Harvard's entering first-year class was Asian American; in 1990 Asian Americans constituted 19.7 percent of the new first-year class. Asian American organizations initiated legal challenges against several institutions that were charged with carrying out discriminatory policies or quotas to restrict Asian American admissions. In 1988 the U.S. Department of Education investigated both Harvard and UCLA to determine whether they had "established illegal quotas limiting the number of Asian-American students they admit."[16] Just as the explosion of the African American student population at predominantly White institutions created the pressure to launch hundreds of Black Studies programs, the hundreds of thousands of new Asian American students made similar demands for diversity within their curricula. Their presence on campuses helped to promote a new approach to teaching Ethnic Studies with a broader comparative and global focus.

The Department of Ethnic Studies at the University of California-San Diego was representative of the new directions in the field. Courses previously taught under separate academic menus of Asian American, Chicano, American Indian, and Afro-American Studies were fully integrated, with emphasis on a rigorous, comparative core curriculum. By 1996 the department had nine core faculty who were all tenured or tenure-track within Ethnic Studies. More than twenty additional faculty in other departments taught regularly in Ethnic Studies. Instead of an umbrella model, where scholars focused solely on their own racial-ethnic topical fields, faculty were recruited largely on their academic interest in comparative ethnic research. The department has also begun the process to initiate master's and Ph.D. programs. The department currently has about ninety majors, with more than five hundred students enrolled in upper-level courses each academic year.

A similar transition occurred at the University of Colorado-Boulder. In 1987 an interdepartmental committee recommended the establishment of CSERA, the Center for Studies in Ethnicity and Race in America. The CSERA was given the authority to recruit a series of senior scholars who in most cases would be jointly appointed with traditional departments. The selection of historian Evelyn Hu-DeHart as CSERA's director symbolized the new focus on comparative ethnicity. Born in China, Hu-DeHart's scholarship ranges from studies of Native Americans in the Latino Southwest, to patterns of slavery and indentured servitude of Chinese immigrants in the Caribbean. The CSERA's early years were marked by some tensions, as several faculty who had originally been hired to teach in only one racial-ethnic area resisted the new comparative emphasis. By 1995, however, the CSERA had received departmental status and had consolidated itself as a successful program.

Other institutions created similar programs. In 1985, for example, the University of Washington-Seattle established the Department of American Ethnic Studies, which developed from an Afro-American Studies program created fifteen years earlier. Curricula in Asian American and Chicano Studies were enriched, and the three studies expanded into a single degree program with ethnic-specific concentrations and comparative and capstone courses.[17] In 1988, Brown University established the Center for the Study of Race and Ethnicity in America to support courses and research on racialized ethnic groups; Brown has also developed a Department of American Civilization with nine faculty positions. In 1996, Stanford University created the Institute for Comparative Studies in Race and Ethnicity (CSRE), which integrates undergraduate majors in Asian American, Native American, Chicano, and comparative studies through introductory-level and senior-level courses. The institute also develops close curricular connections with African and Afro-American Studies and Jewish Studies. The proposal for the establishment of the CSRE stated that a "comparative focus on the subjects of race and ethnicity, in the U.S. and abroad, is fundamental to all majors. . . . No individual ethnic-specific major has the capacity to provide the comparative dimension by itself." The proposal also emphasized the importance of the CSRE's "global dimension. . . . CSRE goes beyond the American experience to incorporate the study of international issues and experiences."[18]

As of 1996 there were nearly one hundred Ethnic Studies programs throughout the United States, of which approximately thirty are full departments. The programs within this field that have been most successful have had several common characteristics. First, is the issue of the undergraduate core curriculum or general distribution requirements. A number of the program's courses must be offered as an integral part of the college-wide core curriculum. Other courses should be cross-listed with traditional departments when possible. Second, successful departments avoid "racialization" and ghettoization. The study of race and ethnicity should not be confined solely to Latino, Asian American, American Indian, and Black American students and scholars. Programs must be seen as being central to the intellectual life and academic culture of the whole community. Ideally, Ethnic Studies should assume a significant role in the strategic planning of a university.

Successful programs nearly always have the authority to initiate appointments and to recruit and retain their own faculty. Absolute tenure control is not necessary for a department to be successful, and in many cases it has been a severe handicap. At several large Black and Latino Studies departments and research centers, for example, a number of faculty who had been hired in the initial wave of institutionalization lacked scholarly credentials or were never actively engaged in research. By the mid- to late 1980s many of this veteran group had been tenured, but they had ceased to function as intellectuals beyond their normal responsibilities as classroom instructors. Sometimes a siege mentality would set in, as junior faculty were admonished never to work in collaboration with traditional departments or other interdisciplinary programs like Women's Studies. Tenure and promotion reviews have sometimes degenerated into contests over petty administrative power.

Such problems have always been part of the academic politics of American universities and are hardly unique to Ethnic Studies. What perhaps is most desirable is the recruitment of faculty who are both well-grounded in a traditional academic discipline and who define their primary scholarship as being broadly interdisciplinary and comparative. W. E. B. Du Bois, for example, was the chief architect for modern Black Studies, and he was simultaneously an outstanding historian and sociologist. The detailed, multidisciplinary and interdisciplinary research in Ethnic Studies has and will continue to generate new knowledge and innovative ways of thinking about traditional ideas. Much of the most innovative and creative scholarship is produced at the borders, the intellectual spaces between old disciplines. The life of the mind in a university should never be "fixed." What Ethnic Studies at its best can accomplish is an expansion of scholarly discourse and knowledge, new modes of examination and inquiry.

Inequality and the New Color-Line

The central recurring dilemmas of Ethnic Studies scholarship are the twin problems of cultural amalgamation and racial essentialism. I say "twin problems" because these two different tendencies nevertheless have a subterranean unity. Many advocates of diversity and the study of racialized ethnicities tend to homogenize groups into the broad political construct known as "people of color." The concept "people of color" has tremendous utility in bringing people toward a comparative, historical awareness about the commonalities of oppression and resistance that racialized ethnic groups have experienced. Our voices and visions cannot properly be understood or interpreted in isolation from one another. But to argue that all people of color are therefore equally oppressed, and share the objective basis for a common politics, is dubious at best. The opposite tendency, toward racial-ethnic "identitarianism," to recall literary critic Gayatri Spivak's term, encapsulates our respective racialized groups within the narrow terrain of our own experiences. In our own separate languages, from the vantage point of our respective grievances, we trust only in ourselves, cursing the possibility that others unlike ourselves share a common destiny.

Most Ethnic Studies scholars do not fall into either trap. Rather, we recognize both the profound divergence and parallels in the social construction of ethnicity. Different ethnic groups retain their own unique stories, insights and reflections, triumphs and tragedies from their sojourns through American life. None of this can take away from the deep structural similarities, especially in the processes of racial oppression, the struggles for survival and resistance, and the efforts to maintain cultural and social integrity and identity, which create the dynamic social framework that brings us together. But let us take seriously the dynamic, dialectical characteristics of social change that define the framework of American race and ethnicity. Most scholars agree that racialization is a social and historical process; that "races" are not fixed categories. Rather, they are permeated by the changing contours of class, gender, nationality, and sexual orientation. If this is true, we must also recognize that an "oppressed race" in one historical epoch, such as the Irish and the Ashkenazi Jews, can later be incorporated into the privilege strata of Whiteness. Racial designations of identical cultural groups may differ from country to country and from diverse places and times.

Moreover, the state always has a vested interest in the management of diversity. The U.S. government's decision in 1971 to create a new "ethnic, but

not racial" category of "Hispanic" is the best recent example of state manip-
ulation of the politics of difference. The designation *Hispanic* was imposed
on more than fifteen million citizens and resident aliens who had very
different nationalities, racial-ethnic identities, cultures, social organizations,
and political histories. But the government's attempt to regulate "difference"
as a matter of public policy inevitably affects how most people perceive themselves in daily life. Are Chicanos also Hispanics, or are they Latinos, or
Mexicans who now live in territories that once belonged to them? The
Hispanic category encompasses extraordinarily different groups: upper-
middle-class immigrants from Argentina, Uruguay, and Chile, who are phe-
notypically White and culturally European; Black working-class Panamanians
and Dominicans; the anti-Castro Cuban exiles of 1959–61 who now form much
of Florida's Dade County ruling political elite and professional class; and
Chicano farmworkers in California's agricultural districts. Which of these distinct nationalities and cultural groups will largely set the standards for what
.the Hispanic legal and social construct may become? As in every social construct, each group's collective identity is a product of political and social con-
testations, ideological conflicts, class and gender stratifications. It seems
probable that in the near future some of these racialized ethnics will increasingly be incorporated into the White social category of privilege, through a
combination of upward class mobility, racial-ethnic intermarriage, residential segregation, and their assimilation of White conservative political behavior and voting patterns.

The general tendency of most people in the United States is to think about
race and racism parochially, solely within a North American context and
within the current moment in history. A much richer perspective about race
as a social construct, however, can be obtained from a comparative approach
to the study of other racial formations. In South Africa, for example, a very
different racialized society developed, with a colored group forming something of a buffer stratum between Blacks and Whites. Under the former regime
of apartheid, certain Asian nationalities, such as Japanese, could be classified
as "White," while others like the Chinese were relegated to the lower status
of "coloreds." In colonial Brazil the importation of more than four million
African slaves was the foundation for the construction of a distinctive racialized society. Color and phenotype were important criteria for placing an individual within the racial hierarchy. But social class status, education, family
background, and other elements were also extremely important in interpreting
racial distinctions. For more than a century the Brazilians have used the expres-

sion "Money lightens the skin." For a minority of Brazilian Blacks it has been possible to scale the hierarchy of Whiteness through the acquisition of material wealth and cultural capital. Until recently, that was rarely the case in the United States. But new developments have been introduced that have fundamentally altered the old racial reality.

The central driving force today behind the configuration of the U.S. racial formation is immigration. In the 1980s there were 8.6 million immigrants who legally entered the United States, more than in any decade since 1900–10. In 1989 alone about 1.1 million immigrants were admitted for permanent residence, the highest number since 1914. By 1996 there were five million illegal immigrants in the United States, with more than 60 percent of them from Central America and Mexico. Illegal immigration has become a multibillion-dollar enterprise. Nationwide, about one-third of the total growth rate of the U.S. labor force comes from legal and illegal immigration. In New York City, for example, in 1990 there were forty-five hundred businesses that employed fifty thousand illegal immigrants in sweatshop conditions. Asian American Studies scholar Peter Kwong has observed that much of the international traffic of immigrants is essentially indentured servitude: "Smugglers are now charging $28,000 to bring in Indians and Pakistanis, and $8,000 to bring Poles through Native American reservations on the New York-Canada border. The cost to Southeast Asian women is years of indentured service as 'white slaves' in the prostitution industry."[19]

According to an Urban Institute study, more than 90 percent of this new immigrant population settles in urban areas where there are high concentrations of Black Americans. The conditions have been created where native-born Black workers increasingly find themselves in sharp competition with foreign-born non-Whites.[20] In his research on urban employment patterns, the sociologist William Julius Wilson found that employers usually prefer to hire immigrant Mexicans over Blacks, because they perceive Mexicans to be more reliable. In some cities Blacks complain that they have been fired or have lost low-wage jobs because they were not fluent in Spanish. Increasingly, some Latino and Asian American groups have used the antidiscrimination laws achieved by the Civil Rights movement to attack what many African Americans feel are hard-won gains. For instance, in late 1994 Tirso del Junco, the only Latino on the U.S. Postal Service Board of Governors, charged that African Americans were "overrepresented" within the postal service workforce. Using Los Angeles as a prime example, del Junco observed that in 1993 Blacks comprised only 10 percent of the area's workforce but made up 62 percent of all regional postal employees, while Latinos constituted 35 percent in the region but held only 15 percent of postal jobs.[21]

In the area of education, the gains achieved by African Americans in terms of access and opportunities during the 1960s and 1970s began to be reversed. The percentage of graduating Black seniors who went on to college leveled off and started to descend in the 1980s. By contrast, 51 percent of all 1980 Asian American high school seniors had enrolled in four-year colleges by February 1982, compared with 37 percent of all White seniors, 33 percent of African Americans, and 20 percent of Hispanics. In terms of business development, the U.S. Census Bureau's 1987 Survey of Minority-Owned Business Enterprises indicated that Asian American businesses increased from 187,691 to 335,331 between 1982 and 1987, a 79 percent growth rate. The census also estimated the same year that about 6 percent of all Asian Americans owned businesses, compared with 6.5 percent of all Whites, 2 percent of Hispanics, 1.5 percent of African Americans, and 1 percent of Native Americans.[22]

By 1992, Koreans owned 38 percent of all retail outlets in Los Angeles County. Korean American businesses in Los Angeles had grown by 27 percent in the two years just before the city's massive unrest.[23] In the area of home mortgages, banks and lending institutions continued their discriminatory practices toward the great majority of racialized ethnics, but they treated Asian Americans very differently. According to a 1997 study by the Federal Financial Institutions Examination Council, banks, credit unions, and mortgage companies turned down 48.8 percent of all applications for home-purchase loans from Black Americans. The denial rates were 50.2 percent for American Indians, 34.4 percent for Hispanics, 24.1 percent for Whites, and only 13.8 percent for Asian Americans.[24] These and other striking differences in opportunities and upward mobility of racialized ethnics set the context for increasing social and legal conflicts. For example, much of the Black and Latino violence in the 1992 Los Angeles rebellion was aimed squarely against Korean establishments. According to Peter Kwong, 1,867 Korean American businesses were looted and burned during the civil unrest, "representing one-half of the total lost from the riots." Most of the destroyed businesses had been located in Koreatown, an urban neighborhood that was 26.5 percent Asian American and more than 50 percent Latino. Almost one-half of all people arrested by the police during the disturbance were Latinos.[25]

Two years later, when Californians debated Proposition 187, which denied undocumented immigrants educational access and health-care services, the explosive politics of racialized ethnicity once again surfaced. Most local Black elected officials and community leaders voiced their opposition but did relatively little to defeat the proposition. On election day Proposition 187 easily passed. Asian Americans had voted overwhelmingly for the initiative. Most Black voters rejected the measure but by a narrow margin: 53 percent opposed and 47 percent in favor. Black voter turnout was also unusually low, which also contributed to the Proposition 187 victory. With the initiative's passing, Black and Latino conflict intensified in poor urban communities such as Compton, where underfunded schools, public health facilities, and social services had already reached a breaking point.[26]

Any discussion concerning these and other conflicts between America's racialized ethnics should take into account that there are significant differences—based on social class, nationality, language, and religion—that subdivide each grouping. Significantly less than half of all Asian Americans are of Japanese and Chinese origin or descent. The Asian American category includes Japanese Americans, who have higher median family incomes than Whites, and the Hmong of Southeast Asia, who are one of the poorest U.S. population groups. There is also significant class stratification and polarization within the Chinese community, with a growing professional and corporate elite as well as tens of thousands of working-poor people. The construction of a pan-ethnic "Asian American" identity and cultural-political consciousness is historically a very recent phenomenon and remains extremely contested. Much of the focus surrounding Asian American Studies, for example, has concentrated largely on the research pertaining to the historical and recent experiences of Japanese and Chinese immigrants. But as Arabs, Cambodians, Indians, Indonesians, Pakistanis, Vietnamese, and others increasingly enter the discussion regarding the definition of what the "Asian American" category should mean, this process becomes even more complicated.[27]

Another factor that may come into consideration is the continuing attempt to differentiate some "model minorities" from other minorities, in what can be termed "geopolitical-cultural capital." In this era of globalization corporate capital requires a multicultural, multinational management and labor force. Racialized ethnic consumer markets in the United States represent hundreds of billions of dollars; Black Americans alone spend more than $350 billion annually. To better exploit these vast consumer markets, capital has developed "corporate multiculturalism," the manipulation of cultural diversity for private profit maximization.

In terms of the governmental, financial, and corporate interests, certain ethnic minorities are viewed as being connected with powerful geopolitical countries such as China and Japan. The prestige or power of a nation-state's economy in the global marketplace inevitably is symbolically transplanted into public policies, which in turn affect the representation and treatment of its former citizens or their cultural descendants. Another way of looking at this is from the disadvantaged position of the Third World. Sub-Saharan Africa, with some notable exceptions such as South Africa, is an economic basket case. East Asia's "four tigers"— Hong Kong, Singapore, South Korea, and Taiwan—recorded 9.4 percent annual growth in per capita gross domestic product in the 1980s, compared with Sub-Saharan Africa's annual growth rate of negative 0.9 percent. As of 1997, South Korea has a per capita income of $10,000 a year; the Congo, recently freed from thirty years of authoritarian rule by a U.S.-supported dictator, has an annual per capita income of $150.[28] Japan alone has invested billions of dollars in U.S. property, corporations, and financial markets. Power is often understood and interpreted through the prism of cultural hierarchy. Ideologically and culturally, the so-called backward peoples who are ethnically identified with Africa, the Caribbean, and much of Latin America and southern Asia are at a distinct disadvantage in racist Western societies. This does not, by any means, minimize the significance of class stratification or the social dynamics of economic exploitation and conflicts generated by ethnic intolerance within Third World societies.

A new racial formation is evolving rapidly in the United States, a new configuration of racialized ethnicity, class, and gender stratification and divisions. The phenotypical color-based categories of difference, which only a generation ago appeared extremely rigid and fixed, are increasingly being restructured and reconfigured against the background of globalized capitalism and neoliberal governmental policies worldwide. In a curious way William Julius Wilson was both right and wrong about "the declining significance of race" prediction nearly two decades ago.[29] Traditional White racism, as configured by class and state forces over several centuries, is certainly declining. Its place is being taken by a qualitatively new color-line of spiraling class inequality and extreme income stratifications, mediated or filtered through old discourses and cultural patterns more closely coded by physical appearance, legal racial classification, and language. What the critical study of racialized ethnicities can bring into focus is how and why these domestic and global processes are currently unfolding and what can be done to challenge them.

Notes

Much of the background information from various Ethnic Studies programs throughout the country mentioned in this chapter was compiled during my participation in a Columbia University advisory committee on Ethnic Studies. This committee had been created following campus unrest and student takeovers of several college buildings in the spring semester of 1996. Data from two unpublished documents was extremely helpful: the final report, "Guidelines and Recommendations," drafted by the advisory committee in January 1997; and Jorge Coronado and Maggie Garb, "Report to the Special Faculty Committee on Ethnic Studies," September 1996. Also many key ideas in this chapter were conceived together with my intellectual partner Leith Mullings. This essay also appears in Manning Marable, ed., *Dispatches from the Ebony Tower: African American Intellectuals Confront the African American Experience* (New York: Columbia University Press, 2000); it was written in 1997 for *Color-Line to Borderlands*.

1. See Michael Omi and Howard Winnant, *Racial Formation in the United States: From the 1960s to the 1990s*, 2d ed. (New York: Routledge, 1994).

2. Faye V. Harrison, "The Persistent Power of 'Race' in the Cultural and Political Economy of Racism," *Annual Reviews in Anthropology* 24 (1995): 47–74, 58–59.

3. David Roediger, *The Wages of Whiteness: Race and the Making of the American Working Class* (New York: Verso, 1991), 13.

4. See Manning Nash, *The Cauldron of Ethnicity in the Modern World* (Chicago: University of Chicago Press, 1989).

5. Leith Mullings, *On Our Own Terms: Race, Class, and Gender in the Lives of African American Women* (New York: Routledge, 1997), 160.

6. Richard L. Worsnop, "Asian Americans," *Congressional Quarterly Researcher*, December 13, 1991, p. 955.

7. M. Menchacha, "Chicano Indianism: A Historical Account of Racial Repression in the United States," *American Ethnologist* 20 (3): 583–603; and John J. Miller, "Paragons or Pariahs? Arguing with Asian-American Success," *Reason* 25 (7): 48–50.

8. See Ronald Takaki, *Iron Cages: Race and Culture in Nineteenth-Century America*, 2d ed. (New York: Oxford University Press, 1990); and Takaki, ed., *From Different Shores: Perspectives on Race and Ethnicity in America* (New York: Oxford University Press, 1987).

9. Johnnella E. Butler, "Ethnic Studies: A Matrix Model for the Major," *Liberal Education* 77 (2): 26–32, 26. Also see Johnnella E. Butler and John C. Walter,

eds., *Transforming the Curriculum: Ethnic Studies and Women's Studies* (Albany: SUNY Press, 1991).

10. See Robert Allen, *Black Awakening in Capitalist America* (Garden City, N.Y.: Anchor, 1969); and Robert Blauner, *Racial Oppression in America* (New York: Harper and Row, 1972).

11. See Nathan Glazer and Daniel Patrick Moynihan, *Beyond the Melting Pot: The Negroes, Puerto Ricans, Jews, Italians and Irish of New York City,* 2d ed. (Cambridge: MIT Press, 1970); and Glazer, *Affirmative Discrimination: Ethnic Inequity and Public Policy* (New York: Basic Books, 1975).

12. See Werner Sollors, ed., *The Invention of Ethnicity* (New York: Oxford University Press, 1989); and Sollors, *Beyond Ethnicity: Consent and Descent in American Culture* (New York: Oxford University Press, 1986).

13. Sean Wilentz, "Integrating Ethnicity into American Studies," *Chronicle of Higher Education,* November 29, 1996.

14. Butler, "Ethnic Studies," 32.

15. Ibid.

16. Worsnop, "Asian Americans," 950.

17. Butler, "Ethnic Studies," 32.

18. Report on "The Purpose and Rationale of the Program in Comparative Studies in Race and Ethnicity," Stanford University, School of Humanities and Sciences, October 2, 1996.

19. Jack Miles, "Blacks vs. Browns," *Atlantic Monthly,* October 1992, pp. 41–68; and Peter Kwong, *Forbidden Workers: Illegal Chinese Immigrants and American Labor* (New York: New Press, 1997), 172–73, 235.

20. Salim Muwakkil, "Color Bind," *In These Times,* March 6, 1996, pp. 15–17.

21. Peter Skerry, "The Black Alienation," *New Republic,* January 30, 1995, pp. 19–20.

22. Worsnop, "Asian Americans," 950–53.

23. Peter Kwong, "The First Multicultural Riots," *Village Voice,* June 9, 1992, pp. 29–32, 31.

24. "Rejections for Mortgages Stay Higher for Blacks," *New York Times,* August 5, 1997. The Federal Financial Institutions Examination Council is a coordinating body for five federal agencies. The 1997 survey covered 14.8 million home-loan applications from ninety-eight hundred lending institutions.

25. Kwong, "First Multicultural Riots," 31.

26. Larry Aubry, "Proposition 187 and African Americans: Harmful Short-sightedness," *Los Angeles Sentinel,* November 10, 1994; Jim Cleaver, "Passage of Prop. 187: Maybe Now the Lesson Will Hit Home," *Los Angeles Sentinel,* November

17, 1994; Charles S. Lee and Lester Sloan, "It's Our Turn Now," *Newsweek*, November 21, 1994, p. 57; Mike Davis, "The Social Origins of the Referendum, " *NACLA Report on the Americas* 29 (November/December 1995): 24–28; Katheryn Flewellen, "Whose America Is This?" *Essence*, February 1996, p. 154; and Joe Domanick, "The Browning of Black L.A.," *Los Angeles Magazine*, May 1996, pp. 74–79.

27. See William Wei, *The Asian American Movement: A Social History* (Philadelphia: Temple University Press, 1993).

28. Nicholas D. Kristof, "Why Africa Can Thrive Like Asia," *New York Times*, May 25, 1997.

29. See William Julius Wilson, *The Declining Significance of Race: Blacks and Changing American Institutions*, 2d ed. (Chicago: University of Chicago Press, 1980); and Wilson, *The Truly Disadvantaged: The Inner City, the Underclass, and Public Policy* (Chicago: University of Chicago Press, 1987).

The Influence of African American History on U.S. History Survey Textbooks since the 1970s

JOHN C. WALTER

THE PAST THREE DECADES HAVE GENERATED A WEALTH OF historical scholarship about the African American experience. Historians August Meier and Elliott Rudwick wrote in their 1986 book, *Black History and the Historical Profession, 1915–1980*: "The score of years beginning in 1960 witnessed an enormous scholarly output in the history of race relations and the Afro-American experience. There was a quickening of publication in the early 1960s, and by the end of the decade Afro-American history had become fashionable, a 'hot' subject finally legitimated as a scholarly specialty. At bottom, this development was the fruit of the social consciousness that came with the zenith of Black activism and changes in American race relations. At the same time the intellectual origins and trajectories of these historians making contributions to the field became more varied."[1] Meier and Rudwick have both been eminently fair in all of their writings. They describe in great detail this "quickening of publication in the early 1960s" in African American history, discussing how and why it became such a hot topic by the end of the decade. But the authors do not deal with professors in the classroom, where statements are made that do not appear in print, statements that in many cases are lifted from or corroborated by publications including survey texts.[2]

African Americans understand that without the Civil Rights movement of the 1950s and 1960s, the state of African American history today would, in all likelihood, approximate that of the 1940s. By the mid-1960s it became clear to White academicians that a profound civil rights movement engineered by Black people would soon change race relations in America, and that this change would qualify ultimately as an important historical development. Many White academicians, mostly in history departments but also in other fields, realizing that a career could be made by writing about a people and a history Whites had once denigrated and disdained, rushed to republish articles and books, which in their original presentations were not so much about Black people as they were about race relations, usually unsympathetic to Black people's efforts to achieve equal opportunity in American life.

Soon a host of historians who had done work on slavery could now pass off their books and articles as "Black history," important enough to attract graduate students, even though too many of these authors remained prejudiced. Many White graduate students, sensing the employment and commercial possibilities of the movement, began to major in African American history, and before long the academic community witnessed a massive increase of young White scholars looking for jobs in the field. The speed with which any number of professors jumped into the field of African American history was directly correlated to the extremely uneven quality of their work. The result was squadrons of young, newly minted assistant professors of questionable knowledge, doing immeasurable damage to undergraduate and graduate students with their "Sambo thesis," which was later widely criticized for arguing that within the Southern slave population an infantile "Sambo" Black population developed.[3] The thesis suggested that slavery was not so bad after all.[4]

Possibly one of the best critiques of this phenomenon is historian Thomas Holt's critique of the writings on Reconstruction in his essay "Reconstruction in United States History Textbooks," in which Holt notes that "the traditional narrative of the Reconstruction era tends toward intellectual incoherence. That incoherence leads historians ultimately to invoke either inappropriate psychological analyses (of individuals or groups) or literary flourishes about tragic flaws in the American character—all in lieu of probing the historical forces at work. In its abbreviated form, as found in many United States history surveys, that narrative conveys the sense that there were several parallel sequences of events and developments, which were largely unrelated and disconnected."[5] For most Black people the burgeoning interest in what was called in the 1960s and later "The African American Experience" was uplifting, despite survey texts dealing with Reconstruction that, as Holt noted, "fail[ed] adequately to account for the collapse of Reconstruction, especially the betrayal of the political and economic aspirations of the freed people."[6]

Similarly most of the newly minted (and most of the old) American historians failed and continue to fail to adequately account for the collapse of the "Second Reconstruction" and the legacy of that collapse. The result is that at the end of the twentieth century the African American population's condition relative to the White population eerily resembles that at the end of the nineteenth century, yielding such extremely flawed analyses as that of the historians Stephan and Abigail Thernstrom.[7] Yet Black people expected this variegated analytical phase and hoped that in time it would be reversed. Black graduate students of the 1960s, such as myself, were delighted to find elegant and reliable survey texts such as John Hope Franklin's *From Slavery to Freedom*, first published in 1947 and revised in 1967.[8] Available also was Meier and Rudwick's *From Plantation to Ghetto* (1966, reprinted 1970), and Benjamin Quarles's *The Negro in the Making of America* (1969) and *The Negro in the American Revolution* (1961).[9] Then, of course, there was the *Journal of Southern History*, which despite its name, we graduate students called "The Journal of Black and White Southern History." Meier and Rudwick noted that in the 1960s this journal looked very much like the *Journal of Negro History* in content.[10]

From the mid-1960s to 1980, at meetings of the Association for the Study of Afro-American Life and History, there was always a significant number of White professors. It was generally thought that soon a dialogue would ensue that would ultimately eliminate racism in historical scholarship and in other academic disciplines, thereby making academic life a model for the rest of America. By the mid-1980s, however, White attendance declined from its high of approximately 30 percent in the 1970s to less than 1 percent today. There was also a concomitant decline in book publishers' displays at the meetings.

By the 1980s, with the demise of the Civil Rights movement, partisan racism resurged with the re-election of Richard Nixon in 1972, finding full fruition in the 1980 election of Ronald Reagan. In the same period a significant segment of White faculty members, who had never been comfortable with what they considered to be irritating questions from students of color, began withdrawing into neutral and even hostile territory. For these scholars the African American Studies movement was no longer profitable, and their latent racism eventually emerged in their lectures and writings.[11] It was an easy transition for such people because Black students, now without the support of the expired Civil Rights movement, were increasingly loathe to challenge racist statements in class, and professors of color were so few that alternative courses were in extremely short supply. The inevitable backlash in academia came swiftly, inexorably propelled with the parallel rise of the so-called moral majority, appeals by conservative politicians for "law and order," and the subsequent frenzy against affirmative action—all expressions of the desire to return America to the comfortably racist ethos of the 1940s and the 1950s, if not the period between the "First Reconstruction" and World War II.

So intimidatingly pervasive was the return to racialist conservatism on campuses that many young Black Studies departments and programs were downgraded while others were eliminated, with impunity. A few fortunate Black professors were transferred to "traditional" departments such as history, where perhaps their courses might count toward a major in American history. The unlucky ones, if not fired, found themselves teaching courses for elective purposes only. Concomitantly, White professors with little training in African American Studies became heads of Black Studies departments and programs. This development inevitably affected students, as many African American graduate students avoided majoring in African American history, knowing what might await them upon graduation. Over the years many African American students have informed me that they shunned a major in Black history "to avoid the stigma."

Meier and Rudwick have shown that there was excellent scholarship in African American history between the 1960s and today. But, as they demonstrate, the incorporation of that scholarship into mainstream scholarship on slavery, for example, was highly dependent upon individual historians responding to "the social and intellectual climate of his generation" and upon the "autonomous nature of the way in which most of the involved scholars came to their conclusions, and given the variety of intellectual underpinnings for what appears to be a consensus about slave culture and community, we think that it would be inaccurate to consider this seeming unity of perspective as a genuine paradigm."[12] Given this conclusion from their analyses of African American history and the historical profession, it is hardly surprising that American history textbooks have been slow to incorporate much of Black history. These omissions are usually justified on the grounds that textbooks have to cover the entire American experience and therefore only so much space can be devoted to African Americans. That is understandable, of course, but why so little space and why so many distortions and negative, if not racist, exaggerations, descriptions, and ascriptions?

Methodology

This chapter reviews three major U.S. history survey textbooks, using in each case a 1970s edition and a 1990s edition to assess the progress made in the incorporation, manner of presentation, and analysis of the history of African Americans within the larger context of U.S. history. This approach, which examines significant although smaller subjects—rather than defining subjects such as slavery and its causes, the Civil War and its causes, the Reconstructions, their intentions and failures—sheds considerable light on the long-standing conflicts in writing about and teaching the history of these subjects and events. These textbooks were selected on two criteria: they had to be in print since the 1970s and to be currently available in revised editions. As modern revised editions, it is reasonable to expect progress in all areas, certainly with reference to African Americans. The texts examined were written by distinguished historians, and it was assumed that because of these scholars' standings in academia, their judgments would be impartial, unprejudiced, and consonant with the best in historical development. The textbooks used in this study are as follows:

1. Richard Current, T. Harry Williams, and Frank Freidel, *American History: A Survey*, 4th ed. (New York: Alfred A. Knopf, 1975). Alan Brinkley, *American History: A Survey*, 9th ed. (New York: McGraw-Hill, 1995). Hereafter this text is referred to as *American History* (1975) and *American History* (1995).

2. John Blum, Bruce Catton, Edmond Morgan, Arthur Schlesinger Jr., Kenneth Stampp, and C. Vann Woodward, *The National Experience: A History of the United States*, 3d ed. (Fort Worth, Tex.: Harcourt, Brace & World, 1973). John Blum, William S. McFeely, Edmund Morgan, Arthur M. Schlesinger Jr., Kenneth Stampp, and C. Vann Woodward, *The National Experience: A History of the United States*, 8th ed. (Fort Worth, Tex.: Harcourt Brace & World, 1993). Hereafter this text is referred to as *National Experience* (1973) and *National Experience* (1993).

3. Charles Sellers and Henry May, *A Synopsis of American History*, 1st ed. (Rand McNally & Co., 1974). Charles Sellers, Henry May, and Neil R. McMillen, *A Synopsis of American History*, 7th ed. (Chicago: Ivan R. Dee Publishers, 1992). Hereafter this text is referred to as *Synopsis* (1974) and *Synopsis* (1992).

Historical Periods

This review deals with two periods of American history: the Progressive Era, which is rarely thought of as a significant period in African American history, and the Civil Rights era. The periodization for the Progressive Era is generally understood as lasting from 1900 through World War I, but the Civil Rights era is not as well delineated. For the purposes of this review, the period spans 1954 through 1972. I chose 1954 as the beginning year because that year's U.S. Supreme Court decision *Brown v. Board of Education* catalyzed the slow march that eventually rendered "separate but equal" legally indefensible.

I originally thought that for the Progressive Era at least eleven events would serve as assessment criteria. Certainly included would be the founding of the National Urban League and the National Association for the Advancement of Colored People (NAACP), the continued lynching and attempts to outlaw it through legislative action. Upon reflection, however, I concluded that such expectations were too high. Rather, it would be fairer to reduce the number to just six items of such importance that they, by any criteria, could not be left out of any useful survey text. These items, taken together, are the Niagara Movement, the Springfield Riots of 1908, and the founding of the NAACP in 1909; the founding of the Urban League; the Brownsville Riot of 1906 and the Houston Riot of 1917; the role of African Americans in World War I; the Great Migration; and the Garvey movement.

Similarly, for the Civil Rights era, I originally considered thirteen items, as more events should be considered in this period because these African American activities dominated the news for nearly two decades. Certainly, because this era is generally accepted to have started with the *Brown* decision, followed by the Montgomery Bus Boycott the next year, these two events should be included. Eleven other items, including the desegregation of Southern universities, the role of rock 'n' roll, and the important Supreme Court cases such as *United States v. Jefferson County Board of Education* and *Swann v. Charlotte-Mecklenburg Board of Education,* which ushered in the era of busing, should be included. Upon reflection, however, I reduced this group of thirteen to seven. The "must include" list covered the Montgomery Bus Boycott of 1955–56; the Civil Rights marches on Washington in 1957, 1960, and 1963; the student movement in Greensboro, North Carolina, and the formation of the Student Non-Violent Coordinating Committee (SNCC); the Freedom Summer of 1963; the Black Panthers; the three Supreme Court cases of *Cooper v. Aaron* (1958), *Loving v. Virginia* (1967), and *Swann v. Charlotte-Mecklenburg* (1971); and so-called Black music, or rock 'n' roll.

The Importance of Selected Events: The Progressive Era

The Niagara Movement, the Springfield Riot, and the Founding of the NAACP. Taken together, these events are important because the Niagara Movement, begun in 1905 by Dr. W. E. B. Du Bois, brought together a number of Black intellectual leaders to develop a movement for liberal education, which would set the political and social agendas for a Black population not long out of slavery. This movement attracted a great deal of attention because it came ten years before the death of Booker T. Washington and was seen as a counterbalance to the vocational education program promulgated by Washington and the so-called Tuskegee Machine. The movement declined within four years because there was not yet the critical mass of interested, educated, and wealthy Black women and men necessary for the movement's survival. Lacking funds and mobility, the movement soon died. The connection between the Niagara Movement and the founding of the NAACP was Du Bois. At the NAACP's founding, he exerted considerable influence on the NAACP's program and eventually ended up as its director of research and publisher of the NAACP's newspaper, *The Crisis*. Du Bois was not the association's founder, however, as is so often stated. Those who had supported the Niagara Movement supported the NAACP because their goals were similar. With the incorporation of wealthy White patrons, the NAACP attained the success and longevity that had escaped the Niagara Movement. It was the coming together of White liberals, deeply upset by the barbarity of the 1908 riot in Springfield, Illinois, the home town of Lincoln, that stimulated the founding of the NAACP. This is considered a significant development in African American history, surely significant enough for inclusion in any U.S. history survey text.

The Urban League. Founded one year after the NAACP, the Urban League, unlike the NAACP (which emphasized liberal education, political action, and eventually litigation to achieve racial equality), was geared toward social welfare and improving job possibilities for African Americans. The fact that the league has lasted successfully through today, like the NAACP, is testimony that it was a significant development in an area that had previously been ignored.

Brownsville Riot of 1906 and the Houston Riot of 1917. These two "racial confrontations" are of great importance in African American history, because in both cases Black people, when physically attacked by White persons, substantially returned the favor. It is also significant that in both cases the Black persons involved were soldiers. Although the Black participants were dealt with harshly by the courts and by the country, these two confrontations marked the beginnings of what many African American historians consider the gradual development of a militant posture by African Americans against long-standing abuses by the White population. In the case of the Houston riot, the soldiers involved were part of the so-called Buffalo Soldiers. As part of their punishment, the unit was disbanded and never served together again.

African Americans in World War I. A significant number of Black men served in World War I. Although in segregated units, they served with distinction far beyond the expectations of the White population to such an extent that most chronicles of the war remark on the exceptional bravery these Black soldiers exhibited. News of their exemplary performance created great pride at home, and African American scholars credit these men with contributing significantly to the post-World War I concept of the "New Negro."

The Great Migration. This massive migration of Blacks from the South to the North between the world wars had its antecedents in earlier migrations to the Southwest and West. This was due in large part to the attraction to cheap land opportunities to establish independent all-Black communities as well as to escape persecution and poor economic opportunities at home in the South. The beginning of World War I marked a shift in northern migration, and by the war's end the Black population in Northern cities rose significantly, causing conflict with older White residents who resented this massive Black influx. These conflicts resulted in serious race riots in such cities as Houston, Chicago, and East St. Louis in 1917, where forty Black people were killed. Yet these resettlements soon created economic and political opportunities for assertive Black individuals and a renewed sense of community, resulting in increased political and economic power in Northern cities. This great migration radically changed the condition of cities north and south. Its occurrence cannot be relegated to a minor event in American history.

Marcus Garvey. Founder of the Universal Negro Improvement Association (UNIA), often labeled the "Back to Africa Movement," during World War I, Garvey is remembered today in the African American population and throughout the African Diaspora, not only because of his still little-understood movement, but also for his forceful contention that Black people were as good as White people and that Black is beautiful. Although his movement failed, Garvey remains in the consciousness of Black people and is seen by many as the father of the concept of the African Diaspora. This concept provided the stimulus for renewed interest in pan-Africanism as well as a revision of the view of Africa as a backward "dark continent."

The Importance of Selected Events: The Civil Rights Era

Montgomery Bus Boycott. Although it generated a federal court decision, *Browder v. Gayle* (1956), which ended racial segregation on buses in Montgomery, Alabama, the boycott set the stage for the eventual successful desegregation of public transportation throughout the South. Significantly, it occurred shortly after the landmark Supreme Court decision in *Brown v. Board of Education,* which outlawed segregation in public schools. The combination of the Court's decision, coupled with the boycott's success, provided a powerful stimulus for the eventual ending of segregation in the South as well as in the North. The boycott also launched the career of Dr. Martin Luther King Jr., one of the best-known names of the twentieth century. Therefore, no U.S. survey text can be considered complete without a discussion of the Montgomery Bus Boycott.

Civil Rights Marches on Washington in 1957, 1960, and 1963. It is well documented in African American history texts that the 1963 March on Washington had antecedents and that there was a linear relationship between the marches of 1957, 1960, and 1963. The 1957 march forced the U.S. government to establish in the U.S. Justice Department an Office of Civil Rights. This was the first such entity that concerned itself with the civil rights of Black people, and for African Americans it was an important first step forward. A similar march in 1960 caused the U.S. government to expand the Office of Civil Rights and to issue regulations protecting the voting rights of Blacks in the South. The 1963 March on Washington is well known, most likely because of King's famous "I Have A Dream" speech. Nevertheless, historians credit this march to have placed enough pressure on President John F. Kennedy and ultimately the U.S. Congress to write and soon after pass the Civil Rights Act of 1964. Taken as a group, these three marches are important, and any discussion of the 1963 march without reference to the preceding marches ignores its precedents.

The Student Movement in Greensboro, North Carolina, and the Formation of the Student Non-Violent Coordinating Committee (SNCC). The student movement is undoubtedly important because it marked the first time that young Black men and women became involved in a large-scale national civil rights movement of any kind, providing that youthful energy and a different orientation from the older civil rights organizations. SNCC represented a new approach to civil rights protests, moving beyond boycotts to nonviolent physical confrontation, along with a revitalized Congress of Racial Equality (CORE). Significantly, both SNCC and CORE were highly interracial groups, clearly demonstrating the possibilities of Black and White cooperation.

Freedom Summer of 1963. This is an important development in U.S. history because it marked the first time large numbers of young people, Black and White, risked and in many cases lost their lives in the South, particularly in Mississippi, in an attempt to educate Black people to exercise their right to vote, to read and write, and to understand their rights as American citizens. There is no doubt that Freedom Summer and subsequent summers of similar activity directly contributed to Black political progress in the South. This summer's remarkable contributions still stand, as the South has more elected and appointed Black officials today than any other region in the country.

The Black Panthers. Formed in Oakland, California, in 1966, the Black Panther Party displayed a unique approach to achieving civil rights for Black people. They were not averse to meeting White physical violence with retaliatory violence in self-defense. In a show of determination the Black Panthers invaded the California legislature in 1967 with guns at the ready. This militant posture branded them as pariahs to police departments and the FBI, which successfully infiltrated the Black Panthers and, with the Chicago police, murdered Panther leader Fred Hampton in 1969. The party declined soon after, and many former members are now successful mainstream politicians, including Democratic U.S. Representative Bobby Rush from Chicago.

U.S. Supreme Court Cases. Three Court cases representative of the Civil Rights period—*Cooper v. Aaron* (1958), *Loving v. Virginia* (1967), and *Swann v. Charlotte-Mecklenburg* (1971)— indicate the progress Black people made in the United States during the 1960s in reclaiming their civil rights through aggressive litigation. Without the Court's decision in *Cooper*, the integration of Little Rock Central High School in Arkansas and other high schools elsewhere might have taken longer and involved serious injuries if not deaths. In *Loving* the Court ruled that a state ban on interracial marriage was unconstitutional. This decision is of major importance, because in addition to approving interracial marriage, it also removed the fear of prosecution and persecution in southern states with laws against "miscegenation." This was a very important development in African American and American life because many states had had such laws on the books for more than a century. The Court ruling in *Swann* marked the Court's resolve to achieve immediate integration in the South sixteen years after the second *Brown* decision (known as "Brown II"), which ruled how *Brown v. Board* should be implemented. Busing students across traditional racial lines was approved, ushering in a period of protests and protracted litigation.

So-called Black Music, or Rock 'n' Roll. Listening to the radio today, one is struck by the number of songs from the 1950s and 1960s that are used successfully in commercials. The number of radio stations that play only songs of that period is also astonishing. Songs from this era mark a relationship between music and social change that had not characterized America until then, except perhaps during the Civil War. Rock 'n' roll, as differentiated from the later hard rock, acid rock, and the like, was the product of Black Americans, and its incidence marked the first time that Black people in large part were able to write, produce, and sell their own songs, not as supplicants to White producers and corporations. This development marked a significant change in the material and structural relations between Blacks and Whites.

A Note on Prefaces in the Textbooks

Although students are usually under the impression that history texts are written by scholars with total objectivity (after all, these are just the facts!), textbooks contain prefaces that state the authors' intent. Because race and racism has always been a challenge (or a bother) to most historians, those segments of the prefaces that best represent the authors' intents and views are included here.

A Synopsis of American History

In *Synopsis* (1974) the authors describe the text as a "brief summary" of American history, designed to be read by "adults who are beginning the study of the subject." The authors state that the work should be read in conjunction with other selections from the *Berkeley Readings in American History* series. They intended to say "little directly about social and intellectual history" and expressed the belief that "political history affords the clearest organization of American history."[13] This statement is dismaying because, apart from the dubious proposition of the superior merits of political history, such an approach would automatically omit many of the activities of African Americans to regain their civil rights, lost by statutes and court decisions after Reconstruction to the present. Yet given the minimal criteria used for this review, I expected that *Synopsis* would claim a passing grade. In the preface for *Synopsis* (1992) the authors restate the emphasis on political history but add that they also analyze "the social, cultural, economic, and intellectual currents of American life."[14] This was encouraging, because I could now expect that the most important events in African American history would be included.

The National Experience: A History of the United States

In *National Experience* (1973) the authors state that the textbook "examines both the aspirations (often contradictory among themselves) and the achievements (often less grand than the best hopes) of the American people . . . the ideas, the institutions, and the processes that fed hope and affected achievement . . . [and] emphasizes public policy." They believe that this emphasis on public policy "reveals the fabric and experiences of the past more completely than does any other kind of history." They contend that because of the "increasing complexity of public issues in the recent past," they devote "half of this volume to the period since Reconstruction, indeed more than a third to the twentieth century."[15] In *National Experience* (1993) the same preface appears and introduces a new author, William S. McFeely, who has rewritten the pre-Civil War, Civil War, and Reconstruction chapters.[16]

American History: A Survey

The preface is interesting in this text, because in the first edition (1963) (which is not reviewed here), the authors stress the complexities of history, the difficulties in representing a consensus, and note that in deciding on the inclusion of material and the handling of controversial issues, "we have tried wherever possible to reflect the consensus of contemporary historical scholarship."[17] They use not only the research of the textbook's authors but that of "hundreds" of historical scholars. In American History (1975) the preface is rewritten and refers to the "new history," *"which pays attention to the role of minorities and women."¹⁸*

Professor Alan Brinkley of Columbia University has taken sole responsibility for *American History* (1995). He states that instead of just adding or changing language here and there, he made substantial rewrites. This "rewriting" seems to be what Thomas Holt has called for when he described the need for "revised calculus" rather than "simple addition."¹⁹ The text's focus, Brinkley states, is on "new history," previously uncovered history, with less emphasis on great men and great events. He considers the book's greatest strengths to be its connection of "new history" to the more traditional stories of politics, diplomacy, and great events in U.S. history.

Review of Texts: The Progressive Era

The Niagara Movement, the Springfield Riot, and the Founding of the NAACP

Synopsis. Nothing appears in *Synopsis* (1974) about the Niagara Movement or the 1908 riot in Springfield, Illinois, but in dealing with the progressive impulse at the turn of the century, the authors state that a few progressives, including Oswald Garrison Villard and Clarence Darrow, "agitated openly for Negro rights and even joined the Black militant, W. E. B. Du Bois, in organizing the National Association for the Advancement of Colored People in 1909."²⁰ This statement has been bandied about in many history textbooks, but the authors are in error. Jane Addams, Darrow, Mary White Ovington, Villard, and Lillian Wald, among others, were outraged by the 1908 riot that ensued after a Black man was lynched, most likely because he was married to a White woman. Happening in Springfield, the birthplace of Abraham Lincoln, made the incident even more repugnant to Ovington and Villard. They were the founders of the NAACP who had invited Du Bois to join them. Ovington, writing about the formation of the NAACP, has documented that fact. Du Bois was well known for his earlier failed attempts to establish a similar organization, the Niagara Movement. These progressives, being in tune with Du Bois's idea of full civil equality for Black people, invited him to join their movement. It was not the other way around. *Synopsis* (1992) is not improved: the earlier statement remains.²¹

National Experience. The 1973 edition mentions the Niagara Movement and the NAACP, but its language suggests that the NAACP was a direct outgrowth of the Niagara Movement. "Abandoning the program of Booker T. Washington, Du Bois and his associates demanded immediate action to achieve political and economic equality for Blacks. With some support from informed Whites, the Niagara movement was transformed in 1909 into the National Association for the Advancement of Colored People."[22] Again, the statement that the Niagara Movement was "transformed" into the NAACP is erroneous, and the suggestion therefore that the principal mover in its founding was Du Bois is wrong. Quite the opposite is the truth. In *National Experience* (1993) the language is similar except in this instance: "white supporters" are now transformed into "white sympathizers."[23]

American History. In the 1975 edition the Niagara Movement is also mentioned as a forerunner of the NAACP. This text states that "at first Du Bois and a group of like-minded reformers, Black and White, met from time to time in a fellowship known as the Niagara Movement. Then, on Lincoln's Birthday in 1909, they organized the National Association for the Advancement of Colored People. White men were named to most of the offices of the NAACP, but Du Bois as its director of publicity and research remained the guiding spirit."[24] This statement is deeply in error because no history of the Niagara Movement mentions the presence of White people, and as the historian Benjamin Quarles has pointed out, even after the Niagara Movement had established a number of branches throughout the country, "a white member was a rarity, and the movement received almost no support from the Negro masses."[25] Furthermore, the statement that "they" (that is, members of the Niagara Movement) organized the NAACP, is also in error. As previously stated, the principal moving spirits in the formation of the NAACP were Villard and Ovington, and the suggestion that the Niagara Movement directly metamorphosed into the NAACP is without foundation.

American History (1995) shows some improvement, however. It states that "Du Bois and a group of his supporters met at Niagara Falls to launch the Niagara Movement." No mention is made here of White people being there. Yet the text remains almost the same as it continues, "Four years later, after a race riot in Springfield, Illinois, they joined with white progressives sympathetic to their cause to form the National Association for the Advancement of Colored People (NAACP)."[26] This statement is unsupported by the facts, because by 1910 the Niagara Movement had declined to such an extent that virtually only Du Bois remained its symbol. The suggestion that "they joined" I suspect means that the Niagara group formally joined with progressives. None of this is factual, however.

The Urban League

Synopsis. The National Urban League is not mentioned either in the 1974 or 1992 edition.

The National Experience. The National Urban League is mentioned in the 1973 text but only in regard to its work in the 1960s. Nothing is said of its founding or its importance thereafter. Far more interesting is that in the 1993 edition, mention of the Urban League is omitted totally.

American History. In neither the 1975 or 1995 edition is the Urban League mentioned.

The Brownsville Riot of 1906 and the Houston Riot of 1917

Synopsis. In the 1974 edition nothing is said of the Houston riot, but the Brownsville riot is mentioned regarding President Theodore Roosevelt's rash action when "he discharged without honor three divisions of highly decorated Black soldiers on unfounded charges of rioting at Brownsville, Texas."[27] Furthermore, nothing is said of why the riot occurred or of the effect on or the response of the Black community to Roosevelt's egregious behavior. Interestingly, in the 1992 edition neither Brownsville nor Houston is mentioned at all.

The National Experience. The 1973 text includes a paragraph on the Brownsville riot under the heading of "Roosevelt and World Power: National Power and Responsibility." The authors describe the incident thus: "His [Roosevelt's] zeal for discipline and morale, however, led him to discharge without honor the Black troops who refused to reveal the names of a few soldiers who had allegedly shot up the anti-Negro town of Brownsville, Texas in 1906."[28] Stated this way, with the phrase "shot up," the description suggests that the Black soldiers had gone on a rampage. This is not true, and even if they had gone on some sort of retaliatory excursion, it was not without severe provocation, and this should be made clear. The Houston riot is not mentioned at all.

In *National Experience* (1993) the language regarding the Brownsville riot is changed. In a section dealing with Roosevelt, the authors write: "Much worse, in 1906 the president revealed a cruel prejudice by discharging without honor Black troops who refused to reveal the names of a few of their fellows who had allegedly shot up the racially prejudiced town of Brownsville, Texas."[29] There is improvement here because "allegedly" has been added to qualify "shot up," and Roosevelt is finally revealed as exhibiting "cruel prejudice."[30] Nevertheless, even "allegedly shot up the racially prejudiced town of Brownsville" leaves out what had previously transpired that caused the Black soldiers to take the "alleged" action. Again, the Houston riot is not mentioned at all.

American History. This text has nothing to say about Brownsville, either in its 1975 or 1995 edition, and the Houston riot is absent from the 1975 edition. The 1995 edition, however, has one sentence on Houston listed under "Significant Events": "1917, Racial tensions lead to violence among soldiers based in Houston."[31] This statement is utterly false. The violence was not among the soldiers but between Black soldiers and the racist Houston population.

African Americans in World War I

Synopsis. Neither the 1974 nor the 1992 edition has anything to say about African Americans in World War I, despite the fact that in the war the 369th Regiment so distinguished itself that the entire regiment was decorated by the French for exceptional bravery. Many scholars argue that the exploits of this regiment and others like it contributed greatly to the renewed militance of Black people, particularly in northern cities after the war.

National Experience. Black participation in the war is not mentioned in the 1973 edition. However, in the section entitled "Race Hatred" in the chapter marked "War and Its Sequel," the authors state that "more and more Blacks, for their part, educated by the experience of military service, by the war's avowedly democratic aims, and by the inequities they met in the North, began to demand rights long denied them, particularly higher wages, equal protection of the law, and the chance to vote and hold political office."[32] In *National Experience* (1993) this sentence is restated, except that "Blacks" are now "Black citizens."[33] This statement says nothing of the military conduct of Black soldiers and makes no reference to the fact that these men, though highly regarded by the French, were reviled by Americans on their return. Indeed, many were shot to death simply because White people feared them for their military experience. The statement about "inequities met in the North" also makes very little sense. "Inequities" were far more prevalent in the South, and Black resistance in the South beginning in the World War I era led directly to the Civil Rights movement of the 1950s and 1960s.

American History. There is some improvement here over the previous texts. In the 1975 edition the authors state: "Some 400,000 blacks served in the army, half of them in Europe, where the local people usually drew no color line. Black veterans returned with a new-found sense of respect and dignity and with a determination to improve their status at home. They had fought in a war to 'make the world safe for democracy,' and some of them now applied the slogan to the United States. Speaking for the returning blacks, the NAACP magazine, *The Crisis* proclaimed in 1919: 'Make way for Democracy! We saved it in France, and by the Great Jehovah, we'll save it in the USA, or know the reason why.' They were soon disillusioned."[34]

Although nothing is said of the heroism of these Black soldiers, what is stated here is passable for a survey text.

The 1995 edition is greatly improved, however. It gives the topic almost an entire half-page. Dealing with the returning Black veterans, Brinkley makes the point that Black soldiers were an inspiration to thousands of urban African Americans. He states that "in fact, that black soldiers had fought in the war had almost no impact at all on White attitudes. But it did have a profound affect on black attitudes: it accentuated African-American bitterness—and increased black determination to fight for their rights. . . . Just as black soldiers expected their military service to enhance their social status, so black factory workers regarded their move north as an escape from racial prejudice and an opportunity for economic gain."[35] This treatment can hardly be faulted. It represents a model approach. One could quibble about the word *urban*, because the soldiers' experience affected rural Blacks as well.

The Great Migration

Synopsis. The migration of Blacks from the South to the North before and during World War I is absent from the 1974 edition. In *Synopsis* (1992), however, under the topic "America at War," the authors declare that "the labor shortage, exacerbated by male military enlistments and declining immigration, created unprecedented opportunities for minorities and women. Blacks, welcome only in the most menial industrial jobs up to this time, found their labor in high demand. Between 1916 and 1918, nearly 500,000 Afro-Americans left the South for wartime jobs in northern cities."[36] Treating the Great Migration in this way, the impression is that Black migration was little different from other migrations. Better economic opportunities up North were not the only major cause. Just as important was the South's sustained high rate of lynching and casual violence, including murders, rapes, and beatings. Furthermore, nothing is said here about the migration's effects on the northern communities to which they migrated. Also important are the responses Blacks encountered in the North as well as the Southern White population's reactions to Blacks leaving in such numbers.

National Experience. In the 1973 edition the migration is characterized thus: "In response to wartime labor shortages, several hundred thousand blacks had moved from the South to Northern industrial centers."[37] In the 1993 edition the same language occurs but with this addition: "Those migrants brought their poverty with them."[38] A brief discussion of how job competition created hatred on the part of the Whites with whom the Black migrants were competing follows, but the faults here are the same as in the previous texts.

American History. The 1975 edition provides the best account on this topic so far. Under the heading "Xenophobia and Negrophobia" the authors wrote: "No other group suffered so much from the postwar wave of intolerance as did the Negroes. For many of them the war had seemed to offer an opportunity to break out of the narrow oppressive caste system of the South. Hundreds of thousands moved to the industrial centers of the North to get employment in the booming war industries and, they hoped, to find a less discriminatory society."[39] The authors also note that these migrants faced animosity from unskilled White workers with whom they competed for low wage jobs and that they had to live in slums.

American History (1995) is greatly improved. Almost an entire page is dedicated to the Great Migration under the heading "1915 Great Migration of Blacks to the North Begins."[40] The migration is described as having both a "push" and a "pull" catalyst. For the author "the push was the poverty, indebtedness, racism, and violence most blacks experienced in the South. The pull was the prospect of factory jobs in the urban North and the opportunity to live in communities where blacks could enjoy more freedom and autonomy."[41] The text also notes that agents had been dispatched down South to recruit African American workers, that Black newspapers advertised prospects for employment in the North, and that "most important, those who migrated first sent word back to friends and families of the opportunities they encountered—one reason for the heavy concentration of migrants from a single area of the South in certain cities in the North."[42] As a result some of the older Black residents of these cities were "unsettled by these new arrivals, with their country ways and their revivalistic religion; the existing African-American communities considered the newcomers coarse and feared that their presence would increase their own vulnerability to white racism."[43] The author also noted that new churches sprang up as a consequence of this migration, that there was inadequate housing and crowding, which created health hazards, and that the notorious riot in East St. Louis, Illinois, on July 2, 1917, was a consequence of this migration. Given the acknowledged scarcity of space, this sketch is as good as can be expected.

Marcus Garvey

Synopsis. In the 1974 edition, in a discussion of the New Negro movement, the authors wrote: "In a parallel development, the inarticulate black denizens of the nation's industrial slums found a symbol of race pride in the exotic figure of Marcus Garvey and his Universal Negro Improvement Association. Unlike either Booker T. Washington or W. E. B. Du Bois, Garvey stirred the imagination of the impoverished black masses. His back-to-Africa movement, like his dream of an African Empire, died in embryo. But his immense popularity (estimates of his following range from one to four million) exposed as perhaps never before the depths of the Afro-American despair."[44]

In *Synopsis* (1992) there is no improvement on this careless and unsympathetic portrayal. It retains the same language and therefore the same problems as the 1974 edition.[45] In the above quote one is immediately struck by the phrase "black denizens." *Webster's Ninth New Collegiate Dictionary* defines *denizen* as an inhabitant and also as an alien; but in ordinary parlance a denizen is typically understood to be a negative word, a person who is not part of ordinary or mainstream society. The phrase "black denizens" gives the false impression that Garvey's followers were mostly deviant slumdwellers. Highly respected works on Garvey show that the leadership of the UNIA was solidly middle-class African American, and the membership was dispersed over all social strata, in the United States and elsewhere. In *Black Moses: The Story of Marcus Garvey and the Universal Negro Improvement Association*, historian E. David Cronon has noted that although the precise number of UNIA members is unknown, estimates ran the gamut from twenty thousand to six million. Even the U.S. government estimated that "between 30,000 and 40,000 Negroes" invested in Garvey's shipping line.[46] This figure would not include others who had not invested. It is not likely that all of these people were "inarticulate black denizens of the nation's industrial slums." In my own book, *The Harlem Fox,* former UNIA member J. Raymond Jones remembers that the New York membership was a mix of all social strata.[47] A significant segment of the UNIA was in fact Anglophone West Indian immigrants, a group that was never inarticulate, most of whom were solidly middle class.

Furthermore, the statement that "unlike either Booker T. Washington or W. E. B. Du Bois, Garvey stirred the imagination of the impoverished black masses" is also without basis.[48] Although this can be argued, not everyone Garvey inspired was impoverished. And the conclusion that "his immense popularity . . . exposed as perhaps never before the depths of Afro-American despair" is based on ignorance of African American history.[49] Rather than indicating "despair" or utter hopelessness, Garvey's movement demonstrated quite the opposite. Garvey and the UNIA membership certainly showed none of that. Scholars have shown that people joined the UNIA because it suggested an alternative to the pervasive racism and containment that was characteristic of African American life at that time. The Garvey movement said in effect: "We are as good as anyone else despite what racist white people say." In that respect it had much in common with the later Civil Rights and Black Arts movements, which were telling White people to "get off our backs" and that Black, indeed, was beautiful.

National Experience. The 1973 edition refers to Garvey thus: "By 1923 about a half a million blacks had joined the Universal Negro Improvement Association of Marcus Garvey, a Jamaican black nationalist who proposed to create a new empire in Africa with himself on the throne. That wild scheme collapsed, but its transient appeal to American blacks rested on the need they felt for self-identity, racial pride, and an escape from a society that denied them dignity, opportunity and even personal safety."[50] In the 1993 edition the language of the earlier edition remains unchanged except for this: "Garvey had a fundamental appeal to Black Americans. Touching their traditional sensibilities, he used religious symbols and rituals in his organizational meetings. His attacks on the oppression of his race were based on Christian ethical standards. Though Garvey's financially flimsy scheme for an empire collapsed, his movement met a powerful need of Black Americans for self-identity, racial pride, and an escape from a society that denied them dignity, opportunity, and even personal safety."[51]

In the twenty years since the 1973 edition, the editors clearly have made little progress. Garvey is still a Jamaican nationalist with "wild schemes," but now he is nearly a "man of the cloth" because his appeals are based on "Christian ethical standards." Although this is a moderate improvement, the statement "Garvey had a fundamental appeal to Black Americans" is extremely misleading. It is a common fault of historians to lump all African Americans together, and this remark is highly representative of that practice. Garvey's movement did not meet the powerful need of all Black Americans for self-identity because, if so, Garveyism would most likely be alive and well today. In fact, a segment of Black Americans led the charge to undermine his movement in collaboration with the federal government, which saw Garvey as a threat to a racist status quo, and to send him to jail and eventual deportation.

American History. In the 1975 edition, after describing the "terrors" of lynching and urban riots, the authors wrote: "These terrors led millions of Negroes to follow a persuasive charlatan, Marcus Garvey, founder of the Universal Negro Improvement Association. In return for their contributions he promised to take them home to an African empire. In 1923 Garvey was convicted of swindling and sentenced to federal prison, but Negro nationalism nevertheless persisted."[52] The use of the word *charlatan* suggests that all along Garvey intended to cheat his followers out of their money, that he knew his movement could not possibly be successful. When this prejudiced description is followed up by the statement that in 1923 Garvey was convicted of "swindling," the conviction makes it seem as if the authors' characterization of the man is justifiable. No serious scholar of Garvey's movement concludes that he was a "charlatan." In fact, today among African Americans, and in the Caribbean and elsewhere, Garvey is viewed as a true nationalist, a man who dared to take on a racist society with a counter-proposal that Black was beautiful in his cry, "Up ye mighty race."

Interestingly, in *American History* (1995), Garvey was no longer a charlatan but a Black nationalist, with almost a half-page (rather than three sentences) devoted to him. He now "encouraged African Americans to take pride in their own achievements" (and here the phrase "African Americans" is used instead of "Negroes") and to "develop an awareness of their African heritage—to reject assimilation into White society and to develop pride in their own race and culture (which was, he claimed, superior to that of White society)."[53] Garvey and his UNIA are credited in the 1995 edition with launching a chain of Black-owned grocery stores and other businesses, and no longer is it claimed that he intended to take African Americans home to an African empire; rather, Garvey is now merely urging his supporters to leave America and return to Africa, where they could create a new society of "their own."[54] There is further improvement, as Brinkley states that "the allure of black nationalism, which he helped to make visible to millions of African Americans, survived in black culture long after Garvey himself was gone."[55] This is more to the point and emphasizes the fact that Black nationalism existed before Garvey. More than anything else, what Garvey reignited in America was the flame of Black nationalism, which had burned low by World War I.

Review of Texts: The Civil Rights Era

As in the review of the Progressive Era material, the methodology remains the same; that is, the same three texts, each of two editions (one from the 1970s, the other from the 1990s), is assessed. Six topics are reviewed: the Montgomery Bus Boycott (1955–56); the Civil Rights marches on Washington in 1957, 1960 and 1963; the student movement in Greensboro, North Carolina, and the formation of SNCC; the Freedom Summer of 1963; the Black Panthers; three U.S. Supreme Court decisions: *Cooper v. Aaron* (1958), *Loving v. Virginia* (1967), and *Swann* (1971); and so-called Black music, or rock 'n' roll.

Montgomery Bus Boycott

Synopsis. In the 1974 edition the Montgomery Bus Boycott is mentioned, with six sentences devoted to it. Among other things the authors wrote: "More important than any government action was the new determination of Southern Negroes to achieve equality for themselves. . . . Similar efforts, carried on with remarkable discipline in the spirit of passive resistance, made further gains in desegregating transportation, restaurants, and housing. More progress was made by the Southern Negro than in any decade since Reconstruction."[56] Despite the space limitations, this description is misleadingly incomplete. Mere boycotting of the Montgomery bus system was not enough. It took a Supreme Court decision to give the boycott legal standing, and that is not mentioned here. In *Browder v. Gayle* (1956) the Court affirmed a lower court ruling that segregation on buses violated "the due process and equal protection of the law clauses of the 14th Amendment of the Constitution of the United States."[57] This decision prevented further attempts at resegregation. Boycotts alone do not ensure continued success. Astonishingly, in the 1992 edition there is only one sentence devoted to the Montgomery Bus Boycott: "In 1955–56 blacks in Montgomery, Alabama, led by young Martin Luther King, Jr., launched a successful boycott to end segregation in that city's buses."[58] Why the curtailed space and decline in importance? Perhaps times have changed and there is less pressure to give adequate space to African American contributions to American social and moral progress.

National Experience. The 1973 edition treats the Montgomery Bus Boycott in very much the same manner as *Synopsis* (1974), although the authors explained that King, strongly influenced by Thoreau and Gandhi, counseled his followers to avoid provocation and to confront "physical force with an even stronger force, namely, soul force."[59] Further, the authors noted that suits in federal courts "achieved the desegregation of the bus system in a year."[60] By 1993, however, *National Experience* devoted similar space to the boycott, but it placed greater stress on the role of law in the desegregation of the buses. The authors write, "Lawyers like Thurgood Marshall of the NAACP argued the constitutional cases," and they tell the story as in the 1973 edition, emphasizing the importance of the Supreme Court decision.[61]

American History. In the 1975 edition the Montgomery Bus Boycott is entirely omitted. Happily, in the 1995 edition the most lengthy treatment of the boycott is found. Perhaps this felicitous change is due to Brinkley's role as the lone author. He starts appropriately by mentioning the Court's 1954 *Brown* decision as a catalyst for the attitude change of Montgomery Negroes, such as Rosa Parks. Brinkley also emphasizes that without the *Brown* decision "still the boycott might well have failed had it not been for a Supreme Court decision late in 1956, inspired in part by the protest, that declared segregation in public transportation to be illegal. The buses in Montgomery abandoned their discriminatory seating policies, and the boycott came to a close."[62] Furthermore, he shows that the victory in Montgomery established a new form of racial protest. Brinkley accurately notes that this boycott gave King national prominence as well as his later authority as the major leader of the Civil Rights movement.

Marches on Washington in 1957, 1960, and 1963

Synopsis. The 1974 edition omits both the 1957 and 1960 marches. As for the 1963 march, the text states that "in August, the nation seemed profoundly impressed by a peaceful march of a quarter of a million people in Washington, under the leadership of Martin Luther King."[63] There is no mention of its provenance, no mention of its effects, and no mention of its legacy. In *Synopsis* (1992) the 1957 and 1960 marches are still omitted, and the entry for the 1963 march remains unchanged from the 1974 edition.[64] There is error in both editions because King did not lead the 1963 march. Rather, that march was the creation of the venerable A. Philip Randolph, aided greatly by Bayard Rustin. This is the same Randolph whose threatened March on Washington in 1941 had forced Roosevelt to issue Executive Order 8802, which prohibited racial discrimination in employment in U.S. defense industries and established the oversight Fair Employment Practices Committee (FEPC).

National Experience. National Experience shows no improvement over *Synopsis* on this subject. The authors describe the 1963 march as a "great march" and mention the "I Have A Dream" speech, quoting King's speech at length, but they say nothing of the march's antecedents or its consequences.[65] The 1993 edition particularly regresses on this topic. There is no mention of the earlier marches, and space allotted to the 1963 march is smaller than in the 1973 edition.[66] As evident elsewhere, with some topics this shrinking coverage seems to be a trend.

American History. In the 1975 edition the 1957 and 1960 marches are absent and the 1963 march consists of two short, useless sentences.[67] *American History* (1995), however, while also omitting the 1957 and 1960 marches, describes the 1963 march as: "The greatest civil rights demonstration in the nation's history. President Kennedy, who at first opposed the idea of the march, in the end gave it his open support after receiving pledges from organizers that speakers would not criticize the administration. Martin Luther King, Jr., in one of the greatest speeches of his distinguished oratorical career, roused the crowd with a litany of images prefaced again and again by the phrase 'I have a dream.' The march was the high-water mark of the peaceful, interracial civil rights movement—and one of the last moments of real harmony within it."[68]

The 1963 march deserves a better description than these flimsy comments on interracial strife and the decline in harmony. To the student unfamiliar with African American history, the impression could easily be that the march marked the decline of a previously glorious movement. In fact, quite the opposite happened. Interracial strife within the Civil Rights movement did not reach injurious magnitude until after the summer of 1964. Today, African Americans believe and distinguished historians of African American history argue persuasively that the 1963 march had profound consequences. Historian William H. Chafe regards the march as "a political triumph."[69] Meier and Rudwick state unreservedly that "the Civil Rights Act of 1964 would not have been passed were it not for a series of developments that converged at the March on Washington in August 1963."[70]

The Student Movement in Greensboro, North Carolina, and the Formation of SNCC

Synopsis. Although SNCC became as powerful during the 1960s as the Congress of Racial Equality (CORE) and the NAACP, and was the guiding force in coordinating young people's activities in what came to be called the "student movement," SNCC is not mentioned in *Synopsis* (1974). In the 1992 edition, however, the following appears: "In 1966, both the Student Non-Violent Coordinating Committee (SNCC) and the Congress of Racial Equality (CORE) officially abandoned their philosophical traditions of biracialism and non-violence."[71] This careless language suggests conditions and developments quite different from the truth, implying that SNCC had become racist and violent, particularly because this immediately follows a paragraph describing the rise of the Black Power movement and quotations of "Off the Pigs" and "Kill Whitey." The situation is not helped either when immediately after the sentence on SNCC and CORE, the text mentions the "paramilitary Black Panther party and the Nationalist Republic of New Africa" and ends the paragraph thus: "The themes of black chauvinism and retaliatory violence, once preached primarily by the Nation of Islam (Black Muslims), seemed increasingly attractive to young innercity blacks."[72] Juxtaposed in this fashion, SNCC is lumped with pariah groups, misplaced in negative territory with no mention of the group's wonderful nascence, the many sufferings its members endured, and the positive things it accomplished before a change in leadership.

National Experience. National Experience has nothing to say of SNCC in its 1973 and 1993 editions. In both, however, under the heading "The Student Movement," the authors state that "passive resistance was widely used in the winter of 1959–60 to challenge the refusal to serve Blacks at Southern lunch counters. The rapid spread of 'sit-in' demonstrations through the South and the support they evoked in the North and among moderate Southern whites testified to the rising moral force of the protest against segregation."[73] What seems to have escaped these authors is that SNCC started the student movement, members of which not only "sat-in" but gave their lives and suffered broken bodies at the hands of racist Whites. For SNCC to be disregarded in this manner is a prime example of the authors' lack of concern for important elements in American history concerning African Americans.

American History. Until review of SNCC coverage, *American History* has consistently treated African American history topics in a slightly more comprehensive and sensitive manner than the other textbooks under review.

Nevertheless, in its 1975 edition, although one sentence is given to the student movement, SNCC is not mentioned at all.[74] Fortunately, in the 1995 edition, under the heading of "Expanding Protests," SNCC is properly placed within the enlarging Civil Rights movement and given credit for its grassroots work in urban and rural communities. Although space is limited, John Lewis (now a respected congressman from Georgia) should have been mentioned, for his is an epic story from SNCC's fiery chair during the 1960s to a respected U.S. representative.

Black Panthers

Given their high visibility during the 1960s and the dramatic ways in which that movement rose and declined, it is expected that the Black Panthers would have secured at least a long sentence in any U.S. history survey textbook.

Synopsis. In the 1974 edition the Black Panthers are nowhere to be found, but in the 1992 edition the following appears: "Such Marxist-oriented revolutionary movements as the paramilitary Black Panther party and the nationalist Republic of New Africa advocated the territorial separation of Black from White. The themes of Black chauvinism and retaliatory violence, once preached primarily by the nation of Islam (Black Muslims), seemed increasingly attractive to young innercity blacks."[75] The Black Panthers seem to be easy prey to prejudiced historians. Like Black America in general, the Panthers are often labeled as somehow deviant as they responded in kind to the savagery and violence inflicted on them.

For example, the conclusion of the previous quotation—"the themes of black chauvinism and retaliatory violence . . . increasingly attractive to young innercity blacks"—leaves the impression that the Panthers, even though they previously had not preached violence, were predisposed toward violence.[76] This view, espoused by the FBI and various police departments, resulted in an estimated twenty-eight Panthers murdered by the police in 1969 alone.[77] *Chauvinism* is a prejudiced word here too, because the literal meaning of this word is "excessive or blind patriotism or undue partiality or attachment to a group or place to which one belongs or has belonged."[78] Applied to the Black Panthers, the word is thus inappropriate, because their patriotism was by no means excessive or blind. Rather, theirs was very much in the American tradition—that is, to believe that Black people are as good as White people and that assertion was a direct response to centuries of White chauvinism. To call the Black Panthers chauvinists and label them as given to retaliatory violence is to woefully mischaracterize them. In fact, the use of such descriptors expresses prejudice against them.

National Experience. More space is given to the Panthers in *National Experience, in which (*unlike the prejudiced statements in *Synopsis)* the leaders are actually named. Eldridge Cleaver's 1967 book *Soul on Ice* is credited with being "a strong statement of the Black Panther ethos."[79] Yet these authors call Cleaver's book "a disturbing fusion of sensitivity and savagery." The word *savagery* has been used in the White vernacular to describe Black people since the seventeenth century; some White historians have also frequented the term when referring to Blacks. Although Cleaver's work might have been "disturbing," there is no need to describe it as "savage." The authors are also egregiously misleading when they write: "The unprovoked murder by Chicago police of two Panthers in 1969 increased black resentment (though the theory of a national police campaign to kill Panthers turned out, on investigation, to be groundless").[80] This statement, frankly, is slick and disingenuous. Most likely, no documentary evidence will ever be found of a national police conspiracy, for there was no need. But because police killed an estimated twenty-eight Black Panthers throughout the country, and only two are reported in the text, clearly the authors are less than fair in their presentation.

Remarkably, in the 1993 edition the paragraph dealing with the Panthers disappears, replaced with a picture of Huey Newton (perhaps the easiest Panther to discredit by implication because of his contradictory keen intellectualism, desperate rhetoric, and sad demise) in an inset reprinted from the July 3, 1967, issue of *The Black Panther,* headed "In Defense of Self Defense." This inset is titled "The Case for Violence," and on the facing page is another inset labeled "The Case against Violence," with a quote from King. What is to be made of this bizarre juxtaposition? Apparently the authors meant to show that a conflict on the use of violence existed in the African American community, but presented in this form there is no inclusion of the new scholarship on the police and FBI war against the Panthers, Co-Intel Pro (the FBI's infiltration of the Panthers, where its agents spread lies about the Panthers' criminal activities, eventually setting up Chicago's Black Panther Party leader Fred Hampton for murder by Chicago police in 1969), and sabotage (including misinformation within the Panther Party by FBI agents). The absence of any commentary, as there was in the 1974 edition, is perhaps evidence of the authors' decision to avoid uncomfortable subject matter.

American History. It is especially dismaying that in the 1975 edition, thus far typically a bit better than the other texts under review, the Black Panthers were not mentioned. In the 1995 edition, however, author Brinkley saves the day, noting that although the Panthers existed "outside the mainstream of the civil rights movement" and were "particularly alarming to many whites . . . they were, in fact, more the victims of violence from the police than they were practitioners of violence themselves."[81] And though Brinkley mentions Huey Newton's phrase of the willingness to fight for justice "through the barrel of a gun," nowhere in the 1995 edition is there any mention of Black chauvinism and savagery as there was in *Synopsis*. There is also no insinuation of unprovoked violence as suggested in *National Experience*. Though brief, in this treatment of the Panthers, as with most other African American topics, *American History* (1995) tries diligently in most instances to present African American history with fairness and sensitivity.

The U.S. Supreme Court Cases

The three important Court cases of the period are *Cooper v. Aaron* (1958), *Loving v. Virginia* (1967), and *Swann* (1971).

Synopsis. In the 1974 and 1992 editions these cases are not mentioned. This is very poor history. At the least *Loving v. Virginia* should have been mentioned, because this case ended the practice of Southern states prosecuting individuals who married interracially, while *Swann* is generally accepted as one of the two Court cases that launched the era of busing.

National Experience. In the 1973 edition only *Swann* is cited. The authors note that a unanimous Court ruled that reasonable busing could be used to integrate schools, but they immediately add: "Nonetheless, in extreme cases busing raised real problems, especially when children were bused from good and safe school districts to inferior and hazardous schools."[82] Phrased this way, it appears as if Black litigants wanted children bused from good and safe school districts to inferior ones. Quite the opposite was the objective of Black people, however. What they expected was the integration of schools because the schools for Black children were indeed inferior because of meager funding and the absence of good teachers, which resulted in inferior education.

In the 1993 edition the trend continues: whereas the years go by, topics previously treated at some length now become either extinct or treated in shorter versions. *Swann* is an excellent case in point. In the 1993 edition in a reference to the Supreme Court the authors write: "It sustained the cause of school desegregation, approving mandatory busing in *Swann v. Charlotte-*

Mecklenburg (1971)."[83] This, perhaps, could be seen as an improvement over the earlier edition.

American History. None of these cases appear in the 1975 edition, although *Swann* is cited in the 1995 edition. The authors remark that "the new Court, however, fell short of what the President and many conservatives had expected. Rather than retreating from its commitment to social reform, the Court in many areas actually moved further. In *Swann* (1971), it ruled in favor of the use of forced busing to achieve racial balance in schools. Not even the intense and occasionally violent opposition of local communities such as Boston and Louisville, Kentucky, was able to weaken the judicial commitment to integration."[84]

This treatment of *Swann* is passable, but it is strange that *Swann* appears while other Court decisions just as important do not. For example, in *Cooper v. Aaron* the Court ruled that Black children's constitutional rights "are not to be sacrificed or yielded to the violence and disorder which have followed upon the actions of the Governor and Legislature. Thus, law and order are not here to be preserved by depriving the Negro of their constitutional rights."[85] The Court unanimously rejected the Board of Education's argument, knowing without doubt from vivid television pictures that the savage violence destructive to normal educational activities was the work of White persons, showing the school board's argument as a repugnant lie.[86] There was also a progressive ancillary result from this case: when Louisiana attempted to avoid integration of its schools through interposition statutes, lower federal courts relying on the language of *Cooper* ruled them unconstitutional. It is astonishing that this case is missing in all texts.

Similarly disconcerting is the absence of *Loving v. Virginia.* Simply stated, the Court ruled that a White man could marry a Black woman and vice versa without government interference.[87] This case was extremely important, putting an end to the concept of "miscegenation" as a legal entity and depriving the word of its power to encourage lynch mobs.[88] Perhaps the absence of cases in these works reflects a strong tradition in textbook production to avoid court cases except in extreme circumstances. Legal history seems not to meld well with political, economic, and social history. This is unfortunate because by now historians should understand that most Black Americans—historically lacking financial and political power in the United States—have had little recourse but to object to injustice through public protests and to demand that the courts live up to the principles of the Bill of Rights and the Constitution.

So-Called Black Music, or Rock 'n' Roll

Synopsis. There is no mention of rock 'n' roll music in either edition.

National Experience. Interestingly, the entry on rock 'n' roll is the same in both editions: "Music played a vital role in the formation of the counter-culture. English groups, especially the Beatles and later the Rolling Stones, registered the trajectory of the young—from the communal 'We All Live in a Yellow Submarine,' through their psychedelic 'Lucy in the Sky with Diamonds,' to Mick Jagger's sinister 'Sympathy for the Devil.' Bob Dylan was the generation's American bard, singing his poignant and evocative songs—first social conscience and then folk rock—and offering open and honest talk about drugs, race, sex, life and memory."[89] Nowhere in this quote is there any reference to Black people's role in the development of rock 'n' roll. After all, they created this brand of music. Indeed, what the authors deem rock 'n' roll, such as the Beatles's "We All Live in a Yellow Submarine," was in fact not rock 'n' roll at all. The Rolling Stones came closest to perpetuating the rock 'n' roll tradition, but by the end of the 1950s rock 'n' roll had declined in popularity, supplanted by White folk rock, hard rock and the like, and thereafter rock 'n' roll was heard mostly in Black clubs. Informed texts and Black people call the music Blacks created rock 'n' roll. The spelling is important, for the music came from Blacks "down South" and that is how they pronounced it.

American History. Although nothing is said of rock 'n' roll in the 1975 edition, Brinkley writes in the 1995 edition:

And perhaps the most pervasive element of the new youth society was one that even the least radical members of the generation embraced: rock music. Rock 'n' roll first achieved wide popularity in the 1950s, on the strength of such early performers as Buddy Holly and, above all, Elvis Presley. Early in the 1960s, its influence began to spread, a result in large part of the phenomenal popularity of the Beatles, the English group whose first visit to the United States in 1964 created a remarkable sensation, "Beatlemania." For a time, most rock musicians—like most popular musicians before them, concentrated largely on uncontroversial romantic themes. One of the first great hits of the Beatles was a song with the innocuous title, "I Want to Hold Your Hand." By the late 1960s, however, rock had begun to reflect many of the new iconoclastic values of its time. The Beatles, for example, abandoned their once simple and seemingly innocent style for a new, experimental, even mystical approach that reflected the growing popular fascination with drugs and Eastern religions. Other groups, such as the Rolling Stones, turned even more openly to themes of anger, frustration, and rebelliousness. Many popular musicians used their music to express explicit political radicalism as well—especially the leading folk singers of the era, such as Bob Dylan and Joan Baez. Rock's driving rhythms, its undisguised sensuality, its often harsh and angry tone—all made it an appropriate vehicle for expressing the themes of the social and political unrest of the 1960s.[90]

Although *American History* gives greater space to rock 'n' roll as an important development in the Civil Rights era, like *National Experience* the textbook sees music as part of the "counterculture" of the 1960s. The author treats the music of the 1950s and 1960s entirely as White music, starting with Buddy Holly and Elvis Presley to the Beatles and ending with the Rolling Stones, Bob Dylan, and Joan Baez.

There is no attempt to deal with the origins of rock 'n' roll; no mention of the father of rock 'n' roll, Chuck Berry, to whom Elvis Presley and the Beatles paid homage.[91] What about other Black rock 'n' rollers such as Little Richard, Fats Domino, Big Joe Turner, Bo Diddley, Big Mamma Thornton, Ivory Joe Hunter, and Aretha Franklin—all of whom bridged the 1950s and 1960s and who were the progenitors and transformers of rock 'n' roll? Today and in recent decades documentaries and programs populate television dealing with the vast influence of the Motown Sound produced by Smokey Robinson, the Commodores, and Diana Ross and the Supremes, to name but a few who changed the American musical scene. There are also a host of radio stations that play mostly Black rock 'n' roll, and television is awash with commercials using rock 'n' roll backgrounds. There is currently a rock 'n' roll revival in night clubs and musical festivals, and "the beat goes on . . ."

Conclusion

Three popular surveys of U.S. history, published in the 1970s and revised in the 1990s, were reviewed in this chapter for content and content changes, accuracy, and sensitivity of language in covering African American history in the Progressive and Civil Rights eras. The presumption was that in the 1970s, given the significant increase in the volume of historical works on the African American experience, survey texts would reflect to some significant degree the new scholarship. Until the 1960s such texts had largely ignored the presence of Africans, except when discussing slavery, the Civil War, and Reconstruction. I presumed that the survey texts revised in the 1990s would be near ideal works.

The Progressive Era was chosen because survey texts produced as late as the 1960s seldom mentioned Black people's presence in that era, except sporadically in reference to race riots such as those in Brownsville or in East St. Louis. These were negative affairs that seemed to assume importance for White historians because of the large number of people who had died or were injured, or as in the case of Brownsville because of President Theodore Roosevelt's egregiously unfair behavior. But Black Americans strove hard and accomplished a great deal in this era, despite very limited opportunities, and ample coverage is certainly warranted. I expected that at least some of the new scholarship would have found its way into these survey texts. Similarly, I had hoped that the Civil Rights era would have generated a larger African American presence in the texts under review, because the scholarship on this era was even more voluminous and the events more immediate. This was not the case, however. All texts reviewed, with the one exception of Brinkley's *American History* (1995), showed evidence of omissions, distortions, and inaccuracies to the astonishing degree detailed in this chapter.

Yet there were also indications of various degrees of progress. Unfortunately, *Synopsis* (1974) was extremely lacking in content, sensitivity, and scholarly rigor with respect to African American topics. Even more disturbing, the 1992 edition, for the most part, remained unimproved. In some instances an important topic appears in the 1974 text only to disconcertingly disappear in the 1992 edition, as was the case of the 1906 Brownsville Riot. Less flawed by omissions and deletions than *Synopsis*, both editions of *National Experience* are plagued more so by error and careless writing. Most depressing was no evidence in the 1993 edition of any attempt to improve on the 1973 edition, except in the case of the Brownsville Riot. But what accounts for the fact that the 1963 March on Washington is given less space in the later edition than in the 1973 edition? In all of the 1970s editions the African American experience of the Civil Rights era is poor, almost as thin, inaccurate, and negatively slanted (if not prejudiced) as the treatment of Blacks in the Progressive Era.

A review of the treatments in the survey texts of the causes and legacy of slavery, the Civil War, and Reconstruction exceeds the space limitations of this chapter, but the approach I have undertaken here illuminates the exaggerations, prejudice, omissions, and biased interpretations that perhaps indicate the magnitude of the problem of treating larger, defining subjects such as slavery, the Civil War, and Reconstruction. It was therefore enormously heartening to review *American History* (1995), under the sole authorship of Professor Alan Brinkley of Columbia University, which omits only one topic, the National Urban League, from the list of twelve under review. Although

Brinkley neglects to give full credit to African Americans for the birth and development of rock 'n' roll, I expect the next edition will remedy this, given Brinkley's excellent work in transforming the 1975 edition into a near model of integrating African American history into a U.S. history survey text. It is hoped that other historians will follow his example.

Notes

1. August Meier and Elliott Rudwick, *Black History and the Historical Profession, 1915–1980* (Chicago: University of Illinois Press, 1986), 161.

2. For example, as a graduate student I remember quite clearly being told, while attending a historical conference, that the enslavement of Blacks after 1790 resulted from an increased need for labor. Further, many students still complain to me that their professors argue that Reconstruction failed because of Black people's lack of readiness for nineteenth-century industrial life.

3. See, for example, Stanley Elkins, *Slavery: A Problem in American Institution and Intellectual Life* (Chicago: University of Chicago Press, 1959).

4. See, for example, Robert William Fogel and Stanley L. Engerman, *Time on the Cross*, vol. 1, *The Economics of American Slavery*, and vol. 2, *Evidence and Methods—A Supplement* (Boston: Little, Brown, 1974); for a superb critique, see Paul A. David et al., *Reckoning with Slavery: A Critical Study in Quantitative History of American Negro Slavery* (New York: Oxford University Press, 1976).

5. Thomas Holt, "Reconstruction in United States History Textbooks," *Journal of American History* 81 (March 1995): 1641–51.

6. Ibid., 1641.

7. Stephan Thernstrom and Abigail Thernstrom, *America in Black and White: One Nation, Indivisible* (New York: Simon & Schuster, 1997).

8. John Hope Franklin, *From Slavery to Freedom: A History of Negro Americans*, 3d ed. (New York: Alfred A. Knopf, 1967).

9. August Meier and Elliott Rudwick, *From Plantation to Ghetto*, 2d ed. (New York: Hill & Wang, 1970); Benjamin Quarles, *The Negro in the Making of America*, 2d ed. (New York: Collier Books, 1969), and Quarles, *The Negro in the American Revolution* (Chapel Hill: University of North Carolina Press, 1961).

10. Meier and Rudwick, *Black History and the Historical Profession.*

11. A similar withdrawal of political supporters of the Negro occurred after the "First Reconstruction."

12. Meier and Rudwick, *Black History and the Historical Profession*, 276. Meier and Rudwick, writing about the historical profession from 1915–80, conclude that

Black history, after being a "hot field" during the 1970s, by the 1980s became a specialty among specialties. However, their concluding optimistic prediction that the ranks of full professors minted during the 1960s and 1970s will remain "sensitive to the importance of Afro-Amerian history" and become the "dominant group in the profession" has failed (308). See chapters 4 and 5.

13. Charles Sellers and Henry May, *A Synopsis of American History*, 1st ed. (Rand McNally, 1974), preface.

14. Charles Sellers, Henry May, and Neil R. McMillen, *A Synopsis of American History*, 7th ed. (Chicago: Ivan R. Dee Publishers, 1992), preface.

15. John Blum, Bruce Catton, Edmond Morgan, Arthur Schlesinger Jr., Kenneth Stampp, and C. Vann Woodward, *The National Experience: A History of the United States*, 3d ed. (New York: Harcourt, Brace & World, 1973), vii.

16. John Blum, William S. McFeely, Edmund Morgan, Arthur M. Schlesinger Jr., Kenneth Stampp, and C. Vann Woodward, *The National Experience: A History of the United States*, 8th ed. (Fort Worth, Tex.: Harcourt College Publishers, 1993), vii.

17. Preface in *American History: A Survey* (1963).

18. Preface in *American History* (1975), emphasis added.

19. Holt, "Reconstruction in United States History Textbooks," 1642.

20. *Synopsis* (1974), 289.

21. *Synopsis* (1992), 287.

22. *National Experience* (1973), 513.

23. *National Experience* (1993), 559.

24. Richard Current, T. Harry Williams, and Frank Freidel, *American History: A Survey*, 4th ed. (New York: Alfred A. Knopf, 1975), 580.

25. Benjamin Quarles, *The Negro in the Making of America* (1969; reprint, New York: Touchstone Books, 1987), 205.

26. Alan Brinkley, *American History: A Survey*, 9th ed. (New York: McGraw-Hill, 1995), 592.

27. *Synopsis* (1974), 291.

28. *National Experience* (1973), 526.

29. *National Experience* (1993), 572.

30. *National Experience* (1973), 526.

31. *American History* (1995), 647.

32. *National Experience* (1973), 576.

33. *National Experience* (1993), 632.

34. *American History* (1975), 636.

35. *American History* (1995), 644.

36. *Synopsis* (1993), 309.

37. *National Experience* (1973), 576.

38. *National Experience* (1993), 632.

39. *American History* (1975), 636.

40. *American History* (1995), 647.

41. Ibid., 635.

42. Ibid.

43. Ibid.

44. *Synopsis* (1974), 340.

45. *Synopsis* (1992), 327.

46. E. David Cronon, *Black Moses: The Story of Marcus Garvey and the Universal Negro Improvement Association* (Madison: University of Wisconsin Press, 1955), 206.

47. John C. Walter, *The Harlem Fox: J. Raymond Jones and Tammary, 1920–1970* (Albany: State University of New York Press, 1989), 37–43.

48. *Synopsis* (1974), 340.

49. Ibid.

50. *National Experience* (1973), 576.

51. *National Experience* (1993), 633.

52. *American History* (1975), 636.

53. *American History* (1995), 645, 646.

54. Ibid., 646.

55. Ibid.

56. *Synopsis* (1974), 418.

57. Richard Bardolph, ed., *The Civil Rights Record: Black Americans and the Law, 1849–1970* (New York: Thomas Y. Crowell Company, Inc., 1970), 519.

58. *Synopsis* (1992), 407.

59. *National Experience* (1973), 745.

60. Ibid.

61. *National Experience* (1993), 825.

62. *American History* (1995), 806.

63. *Synopsis* (1974), 433.

64. *Synopsis* (1992), 412.

65. *National Experience* (1973), 769.

66. *National Experience* (1993), 845.

67. *American History* (1975), 790.

68. *American History* (1995), 827.

69. William H. Chafe, *The Unfinished Journey: America since World War II* (New York: Oxford University Press, 1995), 311.

70. August Meier and Elliott Rudwick, *From Plantation to Ghetto*, 3d ed. (1970; reprint, New York: Hill & Wang, 1976), 289.

71. *Synopsis* (1992), 422.

72. Ibid.

73. *National Experience* (1973), 745.

74. *American History* (1975), 789.

75. *Synopsis* (1992), 422.

76. Ibid.

77. Chafe, *Unfinished Journey*, 413.

78. "Chauvinism" entry in *Webster's Ninth New Collegiate Dictionary* (Springfield, Mass.: Merriam-Webster, Inc., 1988), 229.

79. *National Experience* (1973), 783.

80. Ibid.

81. *American History* (1995), 830.

82. *National Experience* (1973), 816.

83. *National Experience* (1993), 883.

84. *American History* (1995), 871.

85. Quoted in Derrick Bell, *Race, Racism, and American Law*, 3d ed. (Boston: Little, Brown, 1992), 548.

86. Ibid. See also J. Harvie Wilkinson III, *From Brown to Bakke: The Supreme Court and School Integration, 1954–1978* (New York: Oxford University Press, 1978), 92–95.

87. There had been an earlier case concerning interracial marriage, *McLaughlin v. Florida* (1964), but *Loving* is considered the definitive case.

88. Several authorities consulted note that the word *miscegenation* did not enter the American language until approximately 1864, after which it was a serious crime to violate miscegenation laws in many Southern states. In Kentucky by 1889, for example, intermarriage between Blacks and Whites was punishable by three years in jail. Many lynchings throughout the South resulted from mob opposition to miscegenation. Although the legal term *miscegenation* appears to have been a nineteenth-century coinage, there were laws as early as 1664 in Maryland that made any White woman marrying a slave a slave herself as well as her children. Perhaps the best history of this concept is Joel Williamson, *New People: Miscegenation and Mulattoes in the United States* (New York: Oxford University Press, 1984).

89. *National Experience* (1973), 789, and *National Experience* (1993), 859.

90. *American History* (1995), 852.

91. Charlie Gillett, *The Sound of the City: The Rise of Rock and Roll* (New York: Pantheon Books, 1983), introduction and chapter 1.

II INSTITUTIONAL STRUCTURE AND KNOWLEDGE PRODUCTION

Ethnic Studies in U.S. Higher Education:
The State of the Discipline

EVELYN HU-DeHART

SINCE ITS FOUNDING MORE THAN THIRTY YEARS AGO, ETH-
nic Studies is increasingly being institutionalized on U.S. college and university
campuses, even as it continues to struggle for recognition, legitimacy, and
credibility. How the practitioners of Ethnic Studies define the field and go
about doing their work is the primary focus of this chapter. But before that
discussion, a bit of history and background is in order.

A Brief History of Ethnic Studies

Inspired by the Civil Rights movement and buoyed by the energy of the antiwar movement, a generation of American college students invaded administrative offices in the late sixties and through the seventies, demanding
fundamental changes in higher education. The occupation of campus buildings by students of color (then called Third World students) and their White
supporters startled and no doubt terrified a few university presidents, deans,
and professors. At this time school administrators were almost exclusively
White and predominantly male, and the student body was predominantly
White and male. The curriculum had been fairly static since the early
decades of the twentieth century, and the term *multiculturalism* had not yet
been invented. Exactly what the students and their community supporters

wanted was clear, however: access to higher education, changes in the curriculum, the recruitment of more professors of color, and the creation of Ethnic Studies.

Working on the implicit assumption of buying "fire insurance," colleges and universities—beginning in 1968 on such California campuses as San Francisco State, UC Berkeley, and UC Santa Barbara—acquiesced to the founding of Black Studies, Chicano/a Studies, Native American Studies, and Asian American Studies, the origins and core of what later became known collectively as Ethnic Studies. Over the ensuing thirty-plus years, Black Studies programs have led the way to an Ethnic Studies proliferation. At the end of the twentieth century, more than seven hundred Ethnic Studies programs of some kind have been identified on campuses across the country.

The creation of Ethnic Studies in the late sixties and seventies also mirrored the changing perspectives and values among U.S. minorities or "Third World peoples"—from the desire for assimilation into the Euro-American mainstream of the postwar era to the push for cultural autonomy and national self-determination, values that simultaneously reflected the Third World's own struggle for decolonization, national liberation, and sovereignty. In the process efforts by U.S. minorities to erase race toward a "color blind" society gave way to a new kind of race and color consciousness, this time named by those previously oppressed and excluded by the color-line. Thus the color pride movements of Black Power as well as brown, red, and yellow power also undergirded the founding of Ethnic Studies.

Perhaps no symbol captured this yearning for self-determination better than "Aztlán," defined by Chicano/a Studies as the original homeland (practically a nation-state) of the Chicano/a people and the fountainhead of Chicano/a identity and culture. For identity reasons, but also serving as an intellectual organization principle, Black Studies began to elaborate the idea of the African diaspora, whereby peoples of African descent in the Western hemisphere are bound to each other and to mother Africa by the unique, defining core experience of New World slavery. The diaspora approach globalized Black Studies and provided a natural means toward comparative Black Studies, which in time would influence the course of all Ethnic Studies. For example, within Asian American Studies today the Asian diasporas (Chinese, Japanese, Filipino, and so on) are quickly gaining currency among students and scholars alike.

The globalization of American Ethnic Studies has been aided by another significant development in U.S. society. As those sectors of American society represented by peoples of non-White or non-European heritage—those generally defined socially as "minorities"—greatly expanded and came of college age in the late 1980s and 1990s, Ethnic Studies received renewed impetus after being institutionally weakened during the relatively quiescent mid-1970s to the mid-1980s. The revitalized communities of color, particularly those defined as Latino/a or Asian-Pacific American, are overwhelmingly of immigrant backgrounds. Furthermore, the recent arrivals have significantly diversified each of these broadly defined communities, so that Latinos/as are no longer only from Mexico and Puerto Rico but also from countries in Central America, the Spanish Caribbean, and South America. They are of African descent, of indigenous or mestizo heritage, and even "White" (as in the case of some upper-class South Americans) or "Asian" (as in the case of the Cuban Chinese). Even more internally diverse is the Asian-Pacific American category, which includes more than twenty distinct ethnicities, with as many languages and almost as many religions. Latinos/as and Asian-Pacific Americans also constitute the fastest-growing communities, which together are projected to become more than one-third of the nation's population within the twenty-first century.

The upshot of these demographic changes for Ethnic Studies is manifold. They have expanded the boundaries of Chicano/a Studies to include Puerto Rican (or Boricua) Studies, Cuban Studies, Dominican Studies, or a broad-based Latino/a Studies. They have compelled Asian American Studies to move beyond the traditional concerns of Chinese and Japanese Americans to include other Asian American communities, notably Filipinos, South Asians, Koreans, Vietnamese, and to incorporate the diasporic experiences of some of these groups. Together with the reawakening of interest in Native American Studies, brought about largely by the Columbus quincentenary, Ethnic Studies has become "bigger and better." The field is here to stay for good. Finally, and most important, the expansion of ethnic-specific focuses within Ethnic Studies has encouraged a movement toward reconceptualizing Ethnic Studies along comparative lines. This multiplicity of variegated programs has been represented since the late 1970s by several active professional associations, among them the National Council of Black Studies, the National Association of Chicana/o Studies, the Asian American Studies Association, the National Association of Ethnic Studies. The newest may be the Puerto Rican Studies Association, founded in 1992.

Ethnic Studies Defined

A common mistake is to confuse or conflate Ethnic Studies with global or international studies, on the basis that they are both "non-Western" and are usually organized as nondepartmental interdisciplinary programs. Various area studies arose out of the context of U.S. imperialism in the Third World and bear such names as African Studies, Asian Studies, and Latin American and Caribbean Studies. The original, founding purpose of these area studies was to focus on United States-Third World relations and to train specialists to uphold U.S. hegemony in these regions of the world in which the United States had heavy economic and political investments. Rather than truly interdisciplinary, these programs can better be described as multidisciplinary. American Studies scholar Shirley Hune discusses the relationship between area studies and Ethnic Studies in her chapter in Part 3 of this volume.

Having grown out of student and grass-roots community challenges to the prevailing academic power structure and Eurocentric curriculum of U.S. colleges and universities, Ethnic Studies were insurgent programs with a subversive agenda from the outset. Hence, they were considered suspect and illegitimate even as they were grudgingly allowed into the academy. The founders of Ethnic Studies—students, faculty, and community supporters alike—did not mask their objective of systematically examining and dismantling institutional racism. Within the academy Ethnic Studies scholars today work to define a distinct epistemology; they struggle consciously to break or transcend the bounds of traditional disciplines in their search for new methodologies; and they wrestle more deliberately to articulate a genuine interdisciplinary approach to the discovery of new knowledge. Ethnic Studies scholars argue for a holistic or organic approach to the understanding of minority experiences in America and for an emic or insider approach. In American Indian Studies, for example, the faculty speak of an "indigenous model."[1]

Program definitions vary from campus to campus and change over time. The curriculum or course offerings are not uniform and do not conform to a prescribed pattern, although they generally fall within the broad categories of historical, sociological, and cultural. What they have in common is a specific or comparative focus on groups socially constructed as "minorities" in U.S. society for their shared history of having been racially constructed as distinct from the European immigrants and their descendants. The latter have dominated the United States and defined its identity as White, Western, and therefore superior, who see differences among themselves as strictly "cultural" or ethnic. The racially defined, non-European-descended groups in the United States have a "social trajectory and outcome quite diverse from that of people categorized only by cultural standards, that is, Irish Americans, Jewish Americans, Italian Americans, and Polish Americans."[2] By recognizing this distinction between *race* and *ethnicity*, Ethnic Studies scholars confront the irony that the very name of their intellectual and political project is problematic. "The term Ethnic Studies is a misleading one," Black studies scholar Rhett S. Jones of Brown University has noted, "confusing our students, and lending itself to much mischievous hostility by those academics who would rather not have studies of people of color in the university at all." Jones has concluded that the field should be renamed "race studies."[3]

Sociologist John Liu, in presenting his case for the consideration of Ethnic Studies as a separate and distinct discipline, begins with this crucial difference: "Race and ethnicity represented divergent experiences, with never the twain to meet because of instructionalized racism."[4] He argues that race, ethnicity, and institutionalized racism form the central core disciplinary concepts of Ethnic Studies.[5] This assertion is sharply at odds with the views of such influential social scientists as Nathan Glazer and Daniel P. Moynihan, Alejandro Portes and Robert Bach, and Thomas Sowell, all of whom maintain that race is merely one type of ethnicity and that in due time all groups plunge into the "melting pot" and become Americans.[6]

In advancing its own coherent methodological orientation, the Ethnic Studies approach to knowledge, described as interdisciplinary, must be more than "simply separate applications of discipline-based methodology."[7] Unlike traditional disciplines, which are long divorced from any community base or origins, Ethnic Studies scholars must ask the question, Why do research and for whom? After all, its *raison d'etre* is to correct the omissions and distortions in mainstream academia. Ethnic Studies must "give voice to the excluded" and to "involve racial groups in the articulation of their own existences through various means."[8] Therefore, oral history and participatory research are important tools in Ethnic Studies research. Furthermore, "the enunciation of a people's voice has led many ethnic scholars to organize their research around communities."[9]

Ethnic Studies scholars should also dispute the assertion that good scholarship is necessarily "objective" and nonpolitical, again in contrast to values in traditional disciplines. On the contrary, they openly acknowledge a moral and political purpose in their work, because they are simultaneously committed to scholarship and social change, to a "more equitable social order," and to "creating new social realities."[10] A good definition of comparative race and Ethnic Studies can be found in the founding document of the Ethnic Studies Department at the University of California-San Diego. The stated purpose is to focus "on immigration, slavery, and confinement, those three processes that combined to create in the United States a nation of nations. Ethnic Studies intensively examines the histories, languages, and cultures of America's racial and ethnic groups in and of themselves, their relationships to each other, and particularly, in structural contexts of power."[11] The attention here is on the recovery of knowledge denied or submerged and the construction of new knowledge from the perspectives of historically marginalized and powerless groups.

To many in Ethnic Studies, the field's purpose also has to include a fundamental and explicit challenge to the dominant paradigms of academic practices. Although he was specifically addressing the goals of Puerto Rican Studies, Frank Bonilla, founder and director of Hunter College's Centro de Estudios Puertorriqueños, expressed guiding principles applicable to all Ethnic Studies: "We have set out to contest effectively those visions of the world that assume or take for granted the inevitability and indefinite duration of the class and colonial oppression that has marked Puerto Rico's history. All the disciplines that we are most directly drawing upon—history, economics, sociology, anthropology, literature, psychology, pedagogy—as they are practiced in the United States are deeply implicated in the construction of that vision of Puerto Ricans as an inferior, submissive people, trapped on the underside of relations from which there is no foreseeable exit."[12] In the words of another scholar, Jesse Vasquez, Ethnic Studies is a "liberating educational process"[13] that challenges the triumph of Western Civilization on U.S. soil—Eurocentrism—and its claims to objectivity and universalism." In Ethnic Studies peoples of color are constructed not as mere objects to study but rather as "creators of events" and agents of change. Ethnic Studies scholars recognize the importance of perspective, and that "perspectives ... are always partial and situated in relationship to power."[14] More concretely, "it is both practically and theoretically incorrect to use the experiences of white ethnics as a guide to comprehend those of nonwhite, or so-called 'racial' minorities."[15]

Another expression of the distinctive nature of Ethnic Studies scholarship is the "matrix model," that is, "looking at the matrix of race, class, ethnicity, and gender ... within the contexts of cultural, political, social, and economic expression."[16] The purpose of this new academic field is to recover and reconstruct the lived historical experiences and memories of those Americans whom history has neglected, to identify and credit the contributions of those Americans to the making of U.S. society and culture, to chronicle protest and resistance, and to establish alternative values, visions, institutions and cultures.

Ethnic Studies and Liberal Education

Not surprisingly, renewed interest in and the proliferation of Ethnic Studies programs have called new attention to this academic enterprise. Ongoing controversies regarding diversity and multiculturalism in higher education have unavoidably placed Ethnic Studies in the eye of the storm; this is particularly true of Black or African American Studies. Critics have singled out Afrocentric scholars and curricula for especially harsh scrutiny and sometimes ridicule, deliberately lumping all African-centered scholarship under one rubric. In 1998 regent Ward Connerly of the University of California system suggested it is important to find out "whether the classes are truly academic or just a lot of warm, feel-good stuff that we created years ago just to be politically correct."[17]

With these and similar broadsides directed against curricular reforms designed for greater gender and racial-ethnic diversity and inclusion, one might conclude that higher education is in an unprecedented period of crisis— at least, that is the impression created by the authors of such books bearing the ominous titles of *Closing of the American Mind* (Alan Bloom), *Illiberal Education: The Politics of Race and Sex on Campus* (Dinesh D'Souza), and *The Disuniting of America* (Arthur M. Schlesinger Jr.).[18] Bloom, D'Souza, Schlesinger, and others who decry the intrusion of multiculturalism into higher education express particular outrage at the inclusion of multiple voices, values, and perspectives in the core or general education requirements of a liberal education, one that, they strenuously assert, has been correctly anchored by the values and principles of Western civilization. Women and minorities, these critics argue, are either wrong or wrongheaded when they attempt to challenge the primacy of Western civilization in the formation of the United States or in the articulation of its culture.

Although there is no question that Ethnic Studies represents a sharp departure from the traditional course of study offered in U.S. colleges and universities, the criticisms of Ethnic Studies and their practitioners are built on two fallacious arguments: that Ethnic Studies and the move toward a more multicultural curriculum are unprecedented curricular discussions in the history of U.S. higher education, and that some of the underlying motivation for establishing Ethnic Studies has no basis at all in U.S. academic tradition. In fact, Ethnic Studies enjoys some fine company and is central to the reconceptualization of liberal studies for the twenty-first century. Contrary to the critics' alarming warning, the so-called crisis in American higher education is nothing new; higher education has constantly been contested over the years in one way or another. Moreover, at every institution of higher learning the curriculum undergoes periodic reform or re-examination. Education historian W. B. Carnochan has argued that far from being of transhistorical value, liberal education should exemplify what universities do best, which is to study "currents and crosscurrents of change over time."[19]

Carnochan also reminds readers that in this heated debate over curriculum, most often forgotten or ignored by critics of curricular change is the rationale that Harvard University president Charles William Eliot employed in the late nineteenth century to replace a fixed curriculum with a free elective system as the underpinning of a modern, liberal education. Eliot wanted to ensure a flexible curriculum that could incorporate new subjects and thereby expand the existing body of knowledge to "enlarge the circle of the liberal arts." Just as he believed that within the liberal arts, different subjects should be held in equal regard, so too he believed that the many cultures immigrants brought to America should be equally respected. At the time Eliot expressed these ideas, the United States was experiencing its highest volume of immigration, unprecedented in both numbers and diversity. According to Carnochan, Eliot was inspired by the egalitarianism of this still relatively new nation, which he described in powerful terms as "a volatile combination of meritocracy and democracy, an adaptive response to the heterogeneity of an immigrant society."[20]

One hundred years after Eliot and his curricular reforms at Harvard, American society has become even more heterogeneous. This is the result not only of another period of large-scale immigration, this time overwhelmingly from non-European countries, but also because for the first time in U.S. history the country has officially renounced White supremacy and has recognized the multicultural heritages and contemporary makeup of the American people. Based since its inception on an expanding curriculum that prepares students "to reflect on the habits of thought and familiar frameworks in the light of new subjects, critiques, and alternatives," liberal education becomes ever more crucial in the pluralistic democracy multicultural America strives to honor.[21] Ethnic Studies, the critical part of multicultural curricular reform in U.S. colleges and universities, occupies a place of central importance in conceptualizing and designing liberal education for the twenty-first century.

Notes

This chapter has been constructed from the author's previously published articles on Ethnic Studies: "Ethnic Studies in U.S. Higher Education: History, Development, and Goals," in James A. Banks and Cherry A. McGee Banks, eds., *Handbook of Research on Multicultural Education* (New York: Macmillan, 1995); "Reconceptualizing Liberal Education: The Importance of Ethnic Studies," *Educational Record: The Magazine of Higher Education* (spring/summer 1995): 23–31.

1. M. Annette Jaimes, "American Indian Studies: Toward an Indigenous Model," *American Indian Culture and Research* 11 (3): 1–16.

2. John Liu, "Asian American Studies and the Disciplining of Ethnic Studies," in G. Nomura, Russell Endo, Stephen H. Sumida, and Russell Long, eds., *Frontiers of Asian American Studies* (Pullman: Washington State University Press, 1989), 273–83, 275.

3. Rhett S. Jones, "Ethnic Studies: Beyond Myths and into Some Realities: A Working Paper," Center for the Study of Race and Ethnicity in America, Brown University, 1993.

4. Liu, "Asian American Studies," 276.

5. Ibid., 274.

6. Liu is referring to Nathan Glazer and Daniel P. Moynihan, eds., *Ethnicity: Theory and Experience* (Cambridge: Harvard University Press, 1975); Alejandro Partes and Robert Bach, *Latin Journal: Cuban and Mexican Immigrants in the United States* (Berkeley: University of California Press, 1985). However, in a reversal of his earlier position, Glazer, in *We Are All Multiculturalists Now* (Cambridge: Harvard University Press, 1997), recognizes that at least one group has not been assimilated within the national body in the way he and Moynihan projected. He concludes that "we never found a way to properly include African Americans in the great project that called for and fostered assimilation" (20). Thomas Sowell, ed., *Essays and Data on American Ethnic Groups* (Washington, D.C.: Urban Institute, 1978).

7. Johnnella E. Butler, "Ethnic Studies: A Matrix Model for the Major," *Liberal Education* 77 (2): 26–36, 26.

8. Liu, "Asian American Studies," 279.

9. Ibid., 280.

10. Ibid., 281–82.

11. University of California-San Diego, "Proposal for the Creation of a Department of Ethnic Studies at the University of California, San Diego," University of California-San Diego, Department of Ethnic Studies, January 25, 1990, p. 2.

12. Frank Bonilla quoted in Jesse M. Vasquez, "The Co-opting of Ethnic Studies in the American University: A Critical View," *Explorations in Ethnic Studies* 11 (1): 23–34, 25.

13. Vasquez, "Co-opting of Ethnic Studies," 26.

14. University of California-San Diego, "Proposal for the Creation of a Department of Ethnic Studies," 5–6.

15. E. Annette Charfauros, "New Ethnic Studies in Two American Universities: A Preliminary Discussion," Program on Non-Profit Organizations, Yale University, 1991, p. 25.

16. Butler, "Ethnic Studies," 29.

17. John H. Bunzel, "Validity of College Ethnic Studies Programs Challenged" in *Las Vegas Review-Journal*, November 18, 1998.

18. Alan Bloom, *Closing of the American Mind* (New York: Simon & Schuster, 1987); Dinesh D'Souza, *Illiberal Education: The Politics of Race and Sex on Campus* (New York: Free Press, 1991); and Arthur M. Schlesinger Jr., *The Disuniting of America: Reflections on a Multicultural Society* (New York: Norton, 1992).

19. W. B. Carnochan, *The Battleground of the Curriculum: Liberal Education and the American Experience* (Stanford, Calif.: Stanford University Press, 1993), 6.

20. Ibid.

21. Elizabeth Kamarck Minnich, "The New Academy: Reconfiguring Common Grounds for Liberal Learning and Democracy," unpublished manuscript, 1995.

From Ideology to Institution:

The Evolution of Africana Studies

RHETT S. JONES

THIS CHAPTER BEGINS WITH AN EXAMINATION OF FIVE pamphlets that provide a useful introduction to Black Studies. Pamphlets or booklets occupy a different place in scholarship than do books or articles in academic journals. Despite recent advances in technology, it still takes time to publish a book, and it takes time for a paper to make its way from an author to an editor, through reviewers, back to the editor and the author, and finally into print. Pamphlets are different, however. Whether supported by influential and wealthy institutions such as The Ford Foundation, by progressive organizations such as the A. Philip Randolph Fund, by student groups, or by individuals willing to pay to see their own words in print, pamphlets have an immediacy about them. Because they can be quickly published, pamphlets often reflect the concerns of the moment in a way unlike other publications. The five booklets selected here have an emotional immediacy that embodies the urgency many scholars felt about Africana studies as it emerged as a distinct discipline in the late 1960s.

Before turning to these pamphlets, however, a word on terminology is necessary. Throughout the chapter I use the terms Africana studies, African American Studies, Afro-American Studies, and Black Studies interchangeably, although some scholars insist that one term is more appropriate than the others. Some reject Black Studies because, they argue, it masks the com-

113

plex relations between Africans and persons of African descent elsewhere in the world. Others oppose Afro-American Studies because, despite the grammatical rules that create the prefix "Afro," there is no such person as an "Afro." The term Africana Studies was created to emphasize the importance of Africa, while not limiting the field to the study of Africa. Still other scholars have argued that the field ought to be called Africanology to emphasize its unity. At the University of Louisville and at Sacramento State University the discipline has long been called Pan-African Studies, thereby anticipating the field's recent diasporic orientation. On the one hand, there has been a general shift away from using the term Black Studies, so that Black Studies at the University of Rhode Island became African and African American Studies, while Black Studies at Vassar and Wellesley Colleges became Africana Studies. On the other hand, the newly established program at Providence College is called Black Studies, and the academic units at Brown, Harvard, and Smith retain the title Afro-American Studies, so named when the programs were established in the late 1960s. As these examples suggest, the field's title has great meaning to some scholars, and one need not be a linguist to understand the link between a name and a political philosophy. But the interchangeable terms used throughout this chapter carry no political meaning; I merely use them as a way of making for less fatiguing reading, as using these many alternatives has made for less fatiguing writing.

Reacting to a New Field: Early Responses to Africana Studies

Published by the A. Philip Randolph Educational Fund in 1969, just as many Black Studies programs were getting off the ground, the pamphlet *Black Studies: Myths and Realities* included contributions by some of the nation's best-known scholars and activists, nearly all of whom had serious reservations about the emerging discipline.[1] Contributors include Andrew Brimmer, Kenneth Clark, Norman Hill, Martin Kilson, Roy Wilkins, and C. Vann Woodward. Wilkins referred to "black Jim Crow studies," while Clark's letter of resignation from the Antioch College board of directors protested the college's proposal to establish "an all-Negro Black Studies institute." Brimmer's essay, which appears near the end of the booklet, embodies the concerns of the other contributors:

I am greatly disturbed by the proliferation of programs variously described as "Black Studies" or "Afro-American Studies" and by the growing tendency of numerous Negro students to concentrate in such areas or to substitute such courses for more traditional subjects in undergraduate programs (especially the social sciences and humanities). . . . [Black students] should have no illusions about the extent to which they are likely to acquire in "Black Studies" programs the mental discipline, technical skills, and rigorous training in problem-solving that they will so desperately need in their future careers.[2]

In his introduction editor Bayard Rustin was more temperate than most of the contributors, writing that "there is no reason why the passionate hopes and strivings of young black people must be satisfied *at the expense* of intellectual objectivity and academic standards."[3] He thereby suggests that passion and objectivity were not mutually exclusive categories.

In their 1979 pamphlet *Unfair Harvard: Racism and the University*, students in the Harvard/Radcliffe Racial Issues Study Group questioned the intellectual objectivity of American higher education: "The traditional exclusion of the study of Black people from American scholarship is an important example of institutional racism. In the United States Blacks were enslaved for two hundred and forty-four years, segregated for nearly one hundred more, and forcibly relegated to the lower rungs of society where we remain today. With this kind of history, it is not hard to imagine why racism would affect America's educational institutions."[4] These students were not alone in their opinion. Ten years after the initial battles over Africana Studies many students, and not a few faculty and administrators, argued that U.S. higher education was not an objective enterprise. Rather, it was systematically biased against persons of African descent.

Yosef ben-Jochannan took this argument further, arguing in his early 1980s pamphlet *Cultural Genocide in the Black and African Studies Curriculum* that "the BLACK EDUCATOR must be free to criticize and question ANYONE, ANYTHING, ANYTIME. He or she [the Black educator] is the only person capable of achieving the 'TRUE KNOWLEDGE' about what it is to be BLACK or AFRICAN-AMERICAN. For there is not a single WHITE man, woman, or child, living or dead, who knows what it is to be 'BLACK.' Thus, THE FINAL AUTHORITY ON BLACKNESS can only come from the BLACK EDUCATOR."[5] He continues, noting that the mere fact of being Black does not qualify a person to teach Black Studies any more than the fact of being White can make any White person an "AUTHORITY ON WHITE STUDIES." Ben-Jochannan insisted that only Black people could interpret the Black experience and construct a valid Black Studies curriculum.

In his 1985 *Afro-American Studies: A Report to The Ford Foundation*, historian Nathan Huggins took a different approach from that of ben-Jochannan, the contributors to the Rustin pamphlet, and the Harvard and Radcliffe students. He suggested that the Afro-American Studies movement could best be understood by viewing it as the confluence of two separate social forces: first, "change taking place at American colleges and universities and, second, the struggle of blacks for social justice."[6] Huggins attempted, but only with partial success, to place Black Studies in a larger context, thereby bridging the gap between social and intellectual history. Whereas the contributors to the Rustin collection, the Harvard and Radcliffe students, and ben-Jochannan were each passionately involved in discussions around the emergence of African-American Studies—not afraid to admit their emotions were engaged—Huggins took some distance from the discipline, treating it in the detached manner of the historian. Many scholars in Afro-American Studies criticized Huggins and The Ford Foundation: Huggins for not seeming to understand that the discipline was more than simply another academic discipline, but part of the continuing Black American struggle, and the Foundation for selecting Huggins in the first place to write about the field. Although few questioned Huggins's scholarly credentials, many wondered why the Foundation had not selected one of the many distinguished scholars involved in and committed to Africana Studies to write the pamphlet. Huggins was regarded as an outsider, one who had been careful to distance himself from the battles over Black Studies.

In 1989, The Ford Foundation published *Black Studies in the United States: Three Essays*, with contributions by Robert L. Harris Jr., Darlene Clark Hine, and Nellie McKay. McKay held an appointment in Afro-American literature at the University of Wisconsin, while Hine's work in Black history had earned her a chair at Michigan State University. By this time Afro-American Studies had already been criticized for its sexism, as many argued that the field had systematically excluded women and failed to take into consideration Black women's special perspectives. By including essays by Hine and McKay, the foundation implicitly acknowledged the validity of this criticism. It also tacitly agreed that the earlier choice of Huggins may not have been wise by including in the later work the viewpoints of scholars who were clearly knowledgeable of Africana Studies and of the changing intellectual, academic, and social framework within which the discipline now operated.

In choosing Harris to contribute an essay, the Foundation had selected a scholar who was not only knowledgeable of Black American organizations, having written extensively on them; he was also an insider in the Black Studies movement. Together with sociologist James Turner and psychologist William Cross, Harris had been instrumental in the development of the Africana Studies and Research Center at Cornell University. Harris had replaced Turner, considered by many to be one of the founding fathers of Africana Studies, as the center's director. Harris's essay, "The Intellectual and Institutional Development of Africana Studies," demonstrated both the passionate commitment to the field of ben-Jochannan and the scholarly detachment of Huggins.

Harris traced the evolution of African American Studies "as an area of scholarly inquiry" through four stages. The first phase began in the 1890s and lasted until World War II, a period in which a number of organizations studied, documented, recorded, and analyzed Black culture. The second stage emerged in the context of racist assumptions about Blacks in the social sciences. The third period stemmed from the Civil Rights revolution, the Black Power movement, and the Black Consciousness movement, ranging from about the mid-1960s to the mid-1980s, "a period of legitimization and institutionalization" for the discipline. Of the fourth stage Harris, writing as an insider, suggested that "in general, the field is in fairly good condition, but there are some problems, or perhaps opportunities to improve it." He suggested that Black Studies needed to broaden and deepen the field of inquiry. This prospect, he wrote, becomes

somewhat difficult for those departments and programs with limited numbers of faculty. Small faculties are stretched thin, when they attempt to offer a major and cover Africa, Afro-America, and the Caribbean. Offering a comprehensive program in Africana Studies has meant that some departments and programs play primary service roles in providing distribution requirements for graduation. These efforts have little opportunity to supply depth in the field of study. Faculty become very much occupied with servicing large introductory courses and have little time for research and writing in an area of specialization. There is a tendency for faculty to become generalists familiar with a broad range of knowledge rather than specialists who advance the frontiers of specific areas of knowledge.[8]

Harris's essay demonstrated how far Afro-American Studies had come from the early period in which the field was denounced by such scholars as Andrew Brimmer and Kenneth Clark, each of whom eventually changed his position. In later years Brimmer and Clark participated in programs sponsored by Brown University's program in Afro-American Studies. As Harris clearly illustrated, the field had developed to a point at which it was able to criticize itself, look at where it had been, and outline an agenda for the future. His work demonstrates a mature confidence in Black Studies.

Finding the Roots: The Social Foundations of Africana Studies

Taken together, these five pamphlets provide a useful overview of the many important issues in the growth of African American Studies. But just as their strength is their immediacy, an aggressive determination to address the issues of the moment, their weakness is their failure to take the long view and to see that the beginnings of Black Studies are located not in the twentieth century but in the eighteenth century, where the roots of American ideas about race are found. In the 1700s African Americans, who then had no U.S. ethnic identity, were seen as Blacks, while Europeans who came to America, fleeing ethnic identity, saw themselves as White. Although Whites were the more powerful determinants, together Whites and Blacks agreed to ignore the complex reality of Native American nations and to create a simple figure called the Indian. Using their political and economic power, Whites created a reality in which persons studied and discussed only Black-White relations or Indian-White relations, but seldom examined the complexities of relations among Whites, Native Americans, and Blacks. This bipolar model not only shaped and dominated literature and scholarship on White-Black relations, but also that on White-Indian relations and on White-European immigrant relations. Whites were considered the hub of the wheel, while all other groups—Blacks, Indians, European immigrants, and later Asians, Asian Americans, and Latinos—were studied in terms of their relations with Whites. Comparatively few studies explored the relationship between Asians and Latinos or between Native Americans and immigrants.

Inheriting this White-oriented, bipolar model, Ethnic Studies scholars attempted to work beyond it and present America as it is and always has been— a multireligious, multicultural, multiethnic, and multiracial society. But to get to that point, Ethnic Studies has had to get by Black Studies. Viewed in one way, Ethnic Studies is the result of an evolutionary process that began with Black Studies; but seen from another perspective, Black Studies and Ethnic Studies have been in conflict, with gains in Ethnic Studies in higher education often coming at the expense of Black Studies. Black Studies clearly came first, propelled by Black students' demands in the late 1960s that White colleges study African American history and culture. Black students at some of the nation's most prestigious colleges and universities—Brown, Berkeley, Cornell, Harvard, Michigan, Smith, Vassar, Wisconsin, and Yale, for example—demanded that more Black students be admitted, that more Black faculty be hired, and that Black Studies departments be established. These Black students were supported at these and other universities by White faculty, administrators, staff, and students.

Why did Black students begin the struggle? Why not Native American, Asian American, or Latino/a students? The answer is to be found not in the twentieth century, but in the long relationship between Blacks and Whites in the United States. Although Africa clearly had an impact on African American culture, for the most part Blacks accepted much, though not all, of European American culture early on. Although they retained many African words and some aspects of a West African worldview, many accepted English as their language, Christianity as their religion, and most of European American culture as their own. But if African Americans accepted America, America certainly did not accept them. Blacks were therefore placed in the position of being *in* America but not *of* America.

As ideas about who was and was not considered an "American" began to crystallize, most Whites agreed that the American was White, therefore excluding Indians and Blacks. Blacks did not stand on the sidelines, however, waiting for Whites to decide whether or not Blacks were Americans. Even before the new nation became independent, Blacks insisted that they were Americans and thus fully entitled to liberty, equality, and justice. As legal scholar and federal judge A. Leon Higginbotham Jr. has pointed out in his book *In the Matter of Color: Race and the American Legal Process: The Colonial Period*, the founding fathers made, from their perspective and from that of their racist descendants, a mistake in declaring that "all men" were created equal.[9] Of course, as Higginbotham goes on to demonstrate, they did not really believe that Blacks were the equal of Whites or that Whites from the lower classes were equal to the ruling elite for that matter. And they certainly did not believe that women were the equals of men. But the founding fathers were pragmatic propagandists, and in casting about for a rationalization for the break with Great Britain, they shrewdly calculated that high-sounding phrases couched in terms of the universal rights of mankind would justify rebellion. Every bit as pragmatic as their fellow Whites, Blacks quickly seized on the rhetoric of the Revolution, asking why, if all men were created equal, Blacks were being held as slaves. Slavery and revolutionary rhetoric seemed incompatible to almost all Blacks and to a number of Whites as well. Before, during, and after the Revolution, Blacks filed court suits, petitioned the government, and otherwise demanded the end of slavery.

The continuation of slavery, along with the hypocritical refusal to use the term *slave* in the Constitution, and the fact that many of the states denied Blacks the vote, gave Black Americans a unique perspective on America. Black Americans grew up contrasting the difference between what the United States claimed it offered all of its citizens and the reality of the nation's treatment of Americans of African descent. In his 1829 "Appeal to the Coloured Citizens of the World, but in Particular, and Very Expressly, to Those in the United States of America," the Boston-based free Black David Walker wrote: "Now, Americans! I ask you candidly, was your sufferings under Great Britain, one hundredth as cruel and tyrannical as you have rendered ours under you?"[10] With the institution of slavery as their target, free African Americans entered early, eagerly, and aggressively into the civic life of the first new nation. They challenged slavery, the racist assumptions on which it was based, and the moral hypocrisy on which it rested. Because in most states, North and South, African Americans were not permitted to participate fully in the political process, they became shrewd and watchful observers. Much like sports fans watching from the sidelines, African Americans were often more knowledgeable of the game than the players themselves, as the players are in the ebb and flow of the game itself.

African Americans early on took a different perspective from most European Americans. They realized that the growing strength of racism rendered meaningless for Blacks the American ideal of individualistic achievement. The rights to vote, own property, obtain bank loans, and receive police protection were denied Blacks not because of an individual character defect but simply because they were Black. Moreover, the one-drop rule meant that the children of African Americans, and in turn all of their descendants, would forever be excluded from the American dream. With little opportunity to rise as individuals, Black Americans therefore understood that they had to fight against slavery and racism if they were to become full participants in U.S. society. Yet many still loved America, warts and all. One of the differences between Blacks and Whites was that White Americans loved a romantic image of America—a nation free, open to all, resting on the principles of fair play. Blacks knew America was none of these things, yet they loved it anyway. This love did not prevent them from becoming the nation's first and strongest critics, however. Forced to be outsiders, yet lacking an alternative

ethnic political base, Black Americans provided a unique critical perspective
on the United States.

No other race or ethnic group was able to offer such a perspective, as no
other group was simultaneously within and outside of American society.
Native Americans were aggressively critical of White America, but as members of independent nations, they were outsiders and not very interested in
the many failures of the United States to live up to its own ideals. Rather,
they were concerned with how these internal failures affected their nations.
To be sure, there were Indians who broke with tradition and became, or sought
to become, U.S. citizens, but decisions to renounce Indian nationality and
voluntarily become citizens of a country that regarded Native Americans as
second-class persons blunted the impact of their criticism. Moreover, by entering the political, philosophical, and social debates characteristic of the early
years of the new republic, these Indians sometimes cut themselves off from
their own people. In short, Native American critics of the United States were
doubly damned: to participate in the debates over who was an American was
to abandon their tribal traditions for which American discussions had little
relevancy, damning them in the eyes of their own people; and to join in these
discussions also invited the damnation of Whites, as most regarded Native
Americans as inferior.

The nation's ethnic groups were often critical of ethnic, religious, and
cultural discrimination, but Irish, French, German Americans, and others who
set themselves apart and were set apart by "genuine" or White Americans settled on a strategy that blunted their criticism of U.S. institutions. These groups
accepted, endorsed, and eagerly participated in America's political and economic institutions. For the most part these systems had their origins in English
law and economic assumptions. Few White Americans challenged these
assumptions, and when they did the criticisms were not from an ethnic base.
For example, although some Irish Americans rejected Anglo-American economic and political institutions, they did not do so as Irish Americans; in
fact, most Irish Americans accepted these institutions. Most ethnic groups
tactically chose to create and maintain control over separate religious, educational, fraternal, and other cultural organizations, while benefiting from
participation in the country's governmental and financial systems. These
groups therefore offered few criticisms of the basic workings of American
society, which—as they in effect "became White"—they saw as benefiting
themselves and their children.

parallel institutions — but not "outside"

Because they viewed U.S. society as flawed, African Americans criticized the nation's institutions in a fundamentally different way than did Euro-American ethnics. When Latinos and Asian Americans arrived or were forcibly incorporated into the United States in the nineteenth century, they vigorously attacked the nation's racist assumptions. By the time they joined their voices with those of Blacks, African Americans had already been at such criticism for nearly two centuries. Because Blacks were the nation's first and strongest critics, it is not surprising that Black Studies should have preceded Ethnic Studies. The African American political and scholarly perspective on Black people in U.S. society is therefore far older than the Black Studies movement of the 1960s. This perspective originated in the separate experience of Black Americans and in the segregation that produced separate Black institutions. Because Blacks were Americans, these institutions—whether school, church, newspaper, fraternal organization, burial society, or college, to list but the most obvious—tended, at least in formal structure and stated purpose, to resemble their White counterparts. This modeling sometimes embodied a desire for assimilation, but at other times it reflected the reality that a Black population forced into the Euro-American world had no other models. For example, when Black men established college fraternities in the early years of the twentieth century, they gave Greek letter names to their organizations, like White fraternities.

This did not mean that Black organizations were identical to White ones, however. They differed in three respects. First, although their charters often claimed otherwise, many Black organizations were created because the White counterparts were either closed to Blacks, or if they accepted Blacks, the groups denied them any real power or influence. African American churches grew and flourished because when admitted to White church membership, Blacks were forced to sit apart from Whites and were seldom allowed to participate in church governance. Second, Black institutions were influenced by African culture, with the interaction among members determined more by African ideas about how persons ought to treat one another than by formal European rules. Third, as compared with their White counterparts, Black institutions were always underfinanced. Because Black people were typically poorer than White people, Black organizations were poorer than White ones. Few African American organizations were endowed. Operating institutions that on paper were identical to White institutions—but without the financial resources Whites took for granted—forced Blacks to embrace a number of innovative strategies. For example, unlike their White counterparts, Black sororities could seldom afford sorority houses and had therefore to develop other ways to foster close ties among their members.

Despite these differences, Black organizations not only survived but many flourished. Within them, Blacks learned to support one another as an oppressed, despised people, while never losing sight of the reality that their organizations pursued goals identical to White organizations. This organizational experience paid off when in the late 1940s and 1950s Blacks began an all-out assault on Jim Crow and an attack to gain for themselves full U.S. citizenship. Although Black churches have traditionally (and deservedly) received most attention as institutions within the vanguard of the Civil Rights movement, Black unions, fraternal and professional organizations, and a host of other Black institutions were involved. Their members had learned how to achieve goals without money by the means of discipline, hard work, support of one another, and determination.

The movement's success, crowned by the passage of Civil Rights Acts of 1964 and 1965, was intoxicating. Black Americans could now do things White Americans had long taken for granted. When hungry, they could stop and buy a meal without wondering whether or not the restaurant "served Negroes," and they could send their children to the nearest school instead of having them bused to a distant Black institution. Although some Blacks understood that support by other Americans made possible this racial transformation of the landscape, other Blacks viewed this change as brought about solely by Blacks themselves. Nonetheless, Black Americans clearly formed the leadership and vanguard of the struggle and suffered greatly from physical and economic attacks. In the wake of the movement's success, Black pride and self-confidence grew. The nation, indeed the world, had gained a new respect for African Americans. Black riots in the cities transformed the dominant European American image of African Americans as a docile folk into that of a dangerous group. Over the course of the 1960s and 1970s Black organizations flourished, in part supported by newly confident Blacks, in part by a newly fearful White establishment. Blacks opened theaters, founded Black museums, and established Black publications. Such older African American organizations as churches, sororities, banks, and colleges took on a new life. The Black Studies movement was part of this assertive confidence among Black Americans.

As the previous brief review of the five pamphlets demonstrates, the conventional interpretation of the beginning of Black Studies locates it in Black college students' demands that more Black students be enrolled, that they be supported with scholarships, and that more Black faculty be hired. The origin of Black Studies is far more complex, however, for at the same time students wrote their manifestos, Black intellectuals established think tanks, Black communities attempted to gain control over their schools, and Black publications appeared. But the essence of Black Studies—reflections on the state of Black communities linked to moral criticism of White America—was an older enterprise, dating back to the eighteenth century. This moral criticism and its antiracist ideology involved Black churches, schools, colleges, and other institutions in what later generations would call Black Studies. "Lift Every Voice and Sing," by J. Rosamond Johnson and James Weldon Johnson, known by many as the Negro national anthem and sung wherever Black Americans gathered for public ceremonies, reflected the study of Blacks and the condemnation of racism that were at the very heart of the Africana Studies movement.

Mirroring Ideological Divisions: Africana Studies Textbooks

This movement, never a united one, soon splintered. Despite a shared culture, the Black community had never been politically unified. In his autobiography, Roy Wilkins, longtime head of the NAACP, said he tired of persons always coming up to him and asking why African Americans did not stick together, "as though blackness was some kind of glue."[11] Blacks were separated by the same educational, regional, religious, class, and generational differences that divided Whites, to which they added strong, often bitter, debates over the significance of Africa and the meaning of color. These divisions soon found their way into Africana Studies in the most public and rancorous ways. Because the field was not new, it inherited the existing divisions among African American intellectuals, broadly divided among nationalist, integrationist, and Marxist lines.

other divisions

The development of nationalist and integrationist ideologies dated back to the beginnings of African American culture and reflected the conflicting impulses of Black Americans on the one hand to fully join in American society, and on the other hand, to create a separate society, community, or nation of their own. Some nationalists urged a return to Africa, a movement to Haiti, the creation of separate Black settlements on the frontier, or the development of all-Black towns. Others favored Black control of Black neighborhoods, Black support for Black business, and the development of Black educational institutions. Still other nationalists urged separatism as a temporary strategy, a way in which Blacks could consolidate their strengths and escape racism within the safe confines of Black-controlled environments. To some, separatism seemed a desirable end itself, a way of permanently separating Blacks from Whites for the good of Black people. These separatist viewpoints sometimes carried overtones of Black supremacy.

Integrationists, as the term suggests, generally pressed for full integration of African Americans into American life. Insisting that Blacks were as American as any other group of Americans, integrationists sought to gain for Blacks the rights of U.S. citizens. Integrationism was both a means and an end, as its Black practitioners whenever possible sought to establish biracial organizations to end racism. Although chronologically the Marxists were the last to offer an interpretation of Black life in America, they quickly won the attention of the African American community in general and African American intellectuals in particular with their vigorous, outspoken, and courageous attacks on the society that made racism possible. On the eve of the appearance of the Black Studies movement, nearly every Marxist party in the United States, and there were a number of them, had both a line on the "Negro problem" and usually a small number of committed Black intellectuals as members.

Those who founded Black Studies were usually oriented toward one of these intellectual traditions, so that although the Marxists continued their attacks on non-Marxists, for example, they also managed to find sufficient energies to attack one another (in the best American Marxist tradition). The nationalists were divided into those committed to the economic development of African America and those who believed Blacks needed first to understand, address, and resolve cultural issues. Integrationists attacked Marxists and nationalists for prejudging issues and using biased methods to study Blacks. Nationalists and Marxists attacked integrationists for pretending to be neutral while using paradigms created by racists. The late 1960s and early 1970s were exciting times in sloganeering, with economic nationalists described as "pork chop" nationalists and integrationists denounced as "running lackeydogs of capitalism/imperialism."

These divisions are reflected in the three best-known texts in the field. Written by the nationalist Maulana Karenga in 1982, *Introduction to Black Studies* situated the emergence of the discipline in the long worldwide struggle of persons of African descent against slavery, racism, and the systematic distortion of their culture by White intellectuals.[12] Although Karenga was widely attacked as a "reverse racist" by opponents of Black Studies and of

Black people, he acknowledged in the early pages of his book the important role of people of color and of Whites, especially students of color and White students, in the battle for Africana Studies. Not surprisingly, the Marxist-oriented editorial collective known as People's College authored the 1977 *Introduction to Afro-American Studies*, which placed the emergence of Black Studies in the worldwide struggle of oppressed peoples. The book noted that "the real test of new ideas is not just in how well they help us to understand the world; the real test comes in applying these new ideas to building a new and better world for the masses of people."[13] Karenga and the Marxist-oriented collective shared the idea that Black Studies was not a neutral discipline, one isolated in an ivory tower, but a subject to be mastered and then used to better the position of Black people in the United States and in the world at large.

By emphasizing that their 1982 book *Long Memory: The Black Experience in America* was a work of history and that although historians learn from others they also "learn from other historians," authors Mary Frances Berry and John W. Blassingame excused themselves from the responsibility of addressing whether the knowledge gained from their book needs to be applied.[14] *Long Memory*, which significantly does not use the term Black Studies in its title, concludes with an essay that argues that Black nationalists have shifted their emphasis to the struggle in Africa from that in the United States. Lacking a crystal ball, however, neither author foresaw the rise of Afrocentrism. Beyond the pages of their book, the commitment of Blassingame and Berry to equality and justice for Blacks are well known. Within the work's pages they make clear they side with Blacks, not with their oppressors. It is therefore perhaps unfair that *Long Memory* has been viewed by many scholars as the "safe" integrationist alternative to the nationalist *Introduction to Black Studies* or the Marxist-oriented *Introduction to Afro-American Studies* when it comes to selecting a text.

Black Studies has from its beginnings been concerned with Black culture, with the divisions among scholars reflected in these three texts, divisions that stemmed in part from differing ideas on the origin of Black culture. In general, nationalists tend to emphasize the links between Africa and African American culture, Marxists tend to situate African American culture in the culture of the working class, and integrationists tend to emphasize that Black Americans are above all part of U.S. culture. In 1984 scholar Amuzie Chimezie sought to demonstrate the independence of Afro-American culture in his *Black Culture: Theory and Practice*, aligning himself with those "who affirm the validity of black culture," rather than with those who deny its existence or view it as a pathological variant of middle-class Euro-American culture.[15] In the introduction to his 1988 anthology, *Introductory Readings in African American Culture*, Gerdes Fleurent, musicologist and former chair of Black Studies at Salem State College in Massachusetts, also emphasized the importance of Black culture, choosing to include contributions by those thinkers who expressed a clear belief in the autonomy of Black culture.[16] In the 1987 *Slave Culture: Nationalist Theory and the Foundations of Black America* historian Sterling Stuckey found a strong continuing link between African and African American culture.[17]

Some of the more recent textbooks in Africana Studies reflect a continuing concern with culture as well as some of the political and intellectual divisions of the earlier texts. With the 1995 publication of *Exploring the African-American Experience*, Lincoln University became the first historically Black college to offer a text on the Black experience in the New World. Former university president Niara Sudarkasa, one of the volume's editors, makes it clear that students continue to play a role in the evolution of Black Studies: "The eagerness of today's African American students to better understand their history, and the readiness of some of them to continue the painstaking work to set it right, is nowhere more evident than at Lincoln University. It was the students who suggested that Lincoln should have an African American Studies course that would be required of them all. By instituting this requirement, we have sought to engage our students in some of the seminal discussions and debates surrounding the history of Africa's descendants in America, on the continent and elsewhere."[18] The book grew out of the Black Studies course and, with a few exceptions, all of the contributors are part of the Lincoln University faculty. As Sudarkasa suggests, Lincoln defines African American Studies in such a way as to include Africa and the African diaspora outside U.S. borders. Although there is no claim that Blacks are better qualified than others to interpret the African American experience, all the contributors to *Exploring the African-American Experience* are in fact Black.

Longtime editor of the *Western Journal of Black Studies*, Talmadge Anderson takes a somewhat different approach in his 1993 work, *Introduction to African American Studies*, writing:

The purpose of this book is to provide students and other readers historical, theoretical and philosophical concepts of the African American experience from a black perspective. Thus, much of the theories, concepts and perspectives discussed are those of African American scholars and writers who by their apparent philosophy and professional work have demonstrated a proclivity towards social and psychological blackness. Yet, a work of this nature could not have been possible without including the studies and perspectives of respected non-Black or White scholars who, because of their racial fairness and academic integrity, have also contributed much towards demystifying the African American past and present.[19]

Later Anderson makes his position more clear: "Others may contribute their perspectives [on Black Studies], but the initiative and final definition must be from an African ethos or worldview."[20] His position is important because he founded and served for many years as the editor of the *Western Journal of Black Studies*, one of the leading journals in the field. The journal has published writers of all colors, but Anderson continues to believe that Blacks have a special insight, a scholarly edge in understanding Afro-American life and culture.

Similarly, Floyd W. Hayes III, the editor of *A Turbulent Voyage: Readings in African American Studies* (1993), has a long history as a committed African American Studies insider, having taught the field at both San Diego State and Purdue Universities.[21] If Anderson's book reflects the continuing intense and often emotional engagement of Black Studies scholars with their discipline and American racism, Hayes's anthology reflects an attempt at a more distant, yet engaged interpretation of the African American experience. Hayes does not address the place of Afro-Americans within the African diaspora; instead, he focuses on the United States. He is also wary of orthodoxies, writing: "In fact, one must ask whether there should be conformity to a model curriculum and a single theoretical or ideological orientation in African American Studies. Most fields of study do not display this kind of uniformity. Perhaps an alternative is to allow a more flexible and innovative atmosphere in which African American Studies can continue to grow and develop."[22] Hayes carries this perspective into *A Turbulent Voyage*, including selections from persons from a variety of ideological positions, although almost all of the contributors are Black.

In 1997's *Leading Issues in African-American Studies* editor Nikongo BaNikongo of Howard University attempts to provide a variety of conflicting interpretations of Black American life and culture.[23] He begins by noting that "the definition which the student gets of Afro-American Studies is almost totally dependent on where the definition is given, from whom and the objective the giver has in mind."[24] BaNikongo seems comfortable engaging a range of different perspectives, including the Black conservatives who generally find little place (save as scapegoats, straw men, and alleged apologists for racism) in most Africana Studies publications. And instead of settling for cultural explorations of the African diaspora, his contributors address how the diaspora's political manifestation of Pan-Africanism is working itself out in international political and economic confrontations. Not all of the contributors to *Leading Issues* are Black.

These recent books in Afro-American Studies demonstrate that some of the issues raised in the early years of the field remain unresolved. What is African American culture? The answer to this question influences, but does not determine, whether African American Studies should be seen as a distinct discipline and whether Black Americans are seen as best qualified to undertake the study of Black people. Because racism remains a powerful force in American life, and the position of the majority of African Americans appears to be getting worse not better, scholars continue to debate these issues.

Institutionalizing the Field: Africana Studies Organizations

Beneath their differences, however, a new discipline is growing. Between 1966 and 1972, Africana Studies programs grew rapidly, with nearly five hundred established. In 1975 at the invitation of Bertha Maxwell, chair of Afro-American Studies at the University of North Carolina-Charlotte, a number of Black Studies scholars met to consider some of the problems resulting from this rapid growth. Later that year a follow-up meeting was held at the Educational Testing Service in Princeton, New Jersey. The National Council for Black Studies (NCBS) grew out of these two meetings. Appropriately, Maxwell was elected as the council's first president, serving from 1976–78, followed by William King (1978–80), William "Nick" Nelson (1980–82), Carlene Young (1982–84), Delores Aldridge (1985–88), Selase Wayne Williams (1988–92), and William Little (1992–98). James B. Stewart is president at this writing. Headquartered first at Indiana University, with Joseph Russell as executive director, the NCBS was a grass-roots movement built from the ground up by chairs of Afro-American Studies departments, their faculty, and supportive students, staff, and administrators. The national office remained at Indiana until 1991, when it was moved to Ohio State University. While there, the NCBS appointed Jacqueline Wade as executive director. From Ohio State the office was shifted to California State University-Dominguez Hills, where Josiah A. M. Cobbah was appointed executive director in 1996.

Early development of the Council grew from the recognition that its initial strength would come from regional and state associations, groups that would link the council to the local, grass-roots efforts that were the heart of Black Studies. Among the strongest of these were the New England Regional Conference of the NCBS and the Illinois Council for Black Studies. John C. Walter, first of Bowdoin College and later at Smith College, was central in organizing the New England Regional Conference, while Gerald McWorter of the University of Illinois built up the Illinois council. Each organization hosted the annual NCBS meeting, Illinois in 1982 and the New England Regional in 1986. Working with People's College, the Illinois council issued a number of publications, among them the aforementioned *Introduction to Afro-American Studies*. The New England Regional, first in association with the Five College Consortium on Black Studies and later independently, published the *New England Journal of Black Studies*. The Regional also published *Green into Black: Outside Funding for Afro-American Studies*, a guide to grant writing and obtaining outside funding for Black Studies programs.[25] The Regional recognized early that obtaining funds from outside the university gave Africana Studies programs the autonomy many considered desirable. The Regional encouraged New England Black Studies programs to engage in writing grants, just as it supported workshops on administration, research, curriculum, and teaching. Brown University's Afro-American Studies Program obtained more than $700,000 in outside funding in a little more than a decade. In 1979, African American and Ethnic Studies professor Johnnella E. Butler, then of Smith College, collaborated with Margo Culley, a Women's Studies colleague from the University of Massachusetts, and was awarded the first major curriculum transformation grant of its kind, encouraging the overdue partnership of Black Studies and Women's Studies faculty and scholarship. The result was a $125,000 FIPSE grant for a two-year faculty seminar and a disseminating conference to bring analyses of sexism and gender to Black Studies and analyses of racism and race to Women's Studies.

The NCBS provides guidance for African American Studies departments and programs, helps colleges to recruit Black scholars, devises and implements educational programs in elementary, secondary, and postsecondary schools, promotes African-centered research on the Black experience, makes information on Black life available to the public, serves as a consultant to policy makers, and encourages national and international links among scholars interested in the study of persons of African descent. With support from a major grant from The Ford Foundation, the NCBS hosts Summer Institutes organized for the purpose of introducing the field to faculty trained in one of the traditional disciplines and provides ongoing support for Institute graduates. Administrative Institutes supported by the NCBS train new Africana Studies chairs. The NCBS also holds occasional mini-conferences such as the one held at Temple University in 1995 on curriculum development. Jointly with the University of Ghana, the Council offers an African Language Institute. With support from The Ford Foundation, the NCBS has engaged in curriculum development and trained Afro-American Studies faculty. The Council evaluates and reviews Black Studies programs for colleges and universities. It also facilitates the international development of the discipline—important, given the field's increasing focus on the African diaspora—by holding meetings outside of the United States. Over the years conferences have been held in Guyana, Ghana, and South Africa. The NCBS meets annually; its governing board convenes as needed. Regional and state affiliates may meet more often.

The Council's quarterly newsletter, *The Voice of Black Studies*, publishes short articles on the field, information on its history, brief essays from persons well-known in African American Studies, news from the national office, reviews, and job listings. In the early 1990s an agreement with Sage Publications briefly provided the *Journal of Black Studies* to all NCBS members as part of the benefits of membership. In 1993 the council began publication of its own refereed journal, *The Afrocentric Scholar*. But Afrocentricity, the African-centered approach to scholarship most fully developed by Molefe Kente Asante in *Afrocentricity* and *The Afrocentric Idea*, has always been controversial in the NCBS.[26] Not all members of the council subscribed to Afrocentricity, though in the late 1980s and early 1990s the majority of those on NCBS's governing board and elected officers were Afrocentrists. They used their influence in choosing a name for the new journal.

During this period many of those committed to Africana Studies—including a number of the discipline's founders—who did not consider themselves Afrocentrists, left the NCBS. Others continued as members but, believing their perspectives on teaching, research, and service were ignored at the national level, focused on issues at their individual colleges. The elaborate web of relations among individual colleges, regional or state organizations, and the National Council, so carefully constructed and nurtured by the founders of Black Studies, was broken. It shattered on the belief of many that a commitment to Afrocentrism had become a litmus test for membership in the NCBS. Then council president William Little, an Afrocentrist, swiftly

moved to make it clear that being an Afrocentrist was not a requirement for
NCBS membership, and all those interested in Black Studies, regardless of theoretical orientation or political position, were welcome. In this spirit the NCBS
journal was renamed the *International Journal of Africana Studies*. In 1995 the
council established its own publishing house and named Diedre Badejo, then
of the University of Louisville, as journal editor.

The NCBS was not the only Africana Studies organization. The National
Association of African American Studies (NAAAS), established in 1993, works
at bridging the gap between community and academy by opening membership to all those interested in the Black experience and by maintaining
archives for this purpose. Under the leadership of executive director Lemuel
Berry Jr. of Virginia State University, the Association has recently met with
the National Association of Hispanic and Latino Studies. These meetings suggest a willingness on the part of many involved in Black Studies to reach out
to other Ethnic Studies organizations and to explore ways in which they might
work with them. The NAAAS is committed to activism. Article 3 of the NAAAS
Constitution reads: "Any person who has performed notable service for the
cause of African Americans may be elected to honorary life membership in
the Association without payment of membership dues."[27]

In the 1982 program of the NCBS's annual meeting a small notice
appeared, inviting persons to join the Southern Conference on Afro-American
Studies Incorporated (SCAASI). Organized by faculty at historically Black colleges, and growing out of a meeting held at Texas Southern University in
February 1979, SCAASI is interested in Blacks "especially in the deep south
and southwestern states of the United States," and it "is neither in competition with or trying to subvert any already existing group."[28] The conference
now meets annually, publishes a newsletter and a journal, *The Griot*. According
to a recent issue of *The Griot*, SCAASI was formed because "even though the
southern states contained, perhaps, a majority of Afro-Americans, most of
the intellectual activities geared at interpreting and preserving Afro-American
history and culture were centered elsewhere."[29] The conference intends to
meet in "each former Confederate and border state" and when possible at
the historically Black colleges. Although SCAASI has continued to meet in
the South, articles in *The Griot* have not been concerned exclusively with the
South. The journal's editorial home has in recent years been located at Berea
College in Kentucky.

SCAASI has achieved its early goals. Meetings have been held in nine southern states and at such historically Black colleges as Alabama State University, Clark-Atlanta University, Dillard University, Florida A&M University, Jackson State University, LeMoyne-Owen University, Morehouse College, North Carolina A & T State University, Paul Quinn College, Southern University, Texas Southern University, Tougaloo College, and Virginia State University. But SCAASI's early history illustrates the complex relations between Africana Studies and historically Black colleges. Many Black colleges took the position that they did not need Afro-American Studies departments because of their long interest in Black history and the fact that the majority of their students were Black. Although an African American Studies department was established at Howard University, considered to be one of the nation's leading Black colleges, few others followed suit. Some historically Black universities and colleges resisted the idea of even offering a Black Studies minor. SCAASI's long-time secretary-treasurer Howard Jones, then of Texas Southern University, regarded by many as the conference's founding father, was rebuked in 1979 by a university administrator for his efforts on behalf of Africana Studies. At the time the field remained controversial, and many administrators at historically Black colleges thought it prudent to distance themselves from it. Jones had made it clear that SCAASI "would always go to the black community rather than away from it as the other [Black Studies] groups are doing."[30] Many administrators at Black colleges were leery of emergent links between such organizations as SCAASI and what they perceived as radical elements in the Black community. They also believed that scholarship should be detached from activism.

Student Leadership and Black Studies

Like SCAASI, the Student Organization for Black Unity (SOBU) had its origin in a southern Black college and had a strong community orientation. SOBU grew out of a meeting held at North Carolina A & T State University in 1969. Students there had agreed that "anything short of an independent political body could not adequately meet the needs of students of African descent."[31] Aggressively led and committed to Black control of Black schools, the struggle for South African liberation, and the problems of Black students in predominantly White colleges, SOBU soon moved North, involving Black students at Harvard and Brown, among other colleges and universities. Independent of SOBU, Black student organizations sprang up around the nation; Black student unions were common, both influencing and being influenced by Black Studies. Black student unions were often at the forefront of the demands to create Black Studies departments, and at some colleges they had considerable influence on the way in which these departments were organized.

At Brown University, for example, the Afro-American Studies Planning Committee, established in 1968, consisted of faculty, administrators, undergraduate students, and a graduate student. As Brown's Black Studies program had been created in response to Black student demands, it was thought appropriate that students should serve on the committee to develop Afro-American Studies and that they should play an advisory role in the evolution of the program. Students also served on the search committees for the director of Black Studies at Brown. But times changed. As Afro-American Studies departments matured, they tended to limit the role of students. At Harvard, for example, the place of students in Black Studies became controversial when music historian Eileen Southern replaced Professor Ewart Guinier in 1976. Guinier had been a popular chair, aggressively insisting that Harvard should live up to its early commitments to Africana Studies and involve itself in resolving the many problems of Black people. As the students saw it: "With the transfer of leadership in the Department, Afro-American Studies at Harvard changed drastically. As chairperson of the AASD, Eileen Southern ended student input in running the Department by abolishing the managing (executive) committee in 1976. This act, which was in direct contradiction to Faculty legislation, lessened the 'threat' of student involvement in University decision-making. Her style of operation, backed up by her position as the only senior [tenured] faculty member in AASD, has resulted in her domination of the Department."[32]

Similar developments took place throughout the country as Africana Studies faculty, growing in numbers and in confidence, reduced the contributing role of students. Even where faculty sought to retain student participation, many undergraduates newly arrived on campuses were no longer interested. By the early 1980s most students viewed the battle for Black Studies as fought and won. They were content to focus on their studies, a role many argued ought to be their central concern. At Brown the program's faculty made provisions for representatives of both the undergraduate Black student organization and the graduate minority student organization to regularly attend faculty meetings, but few students came. The close working relationship between Black students and faculty so characteristic of Brown in the early 1970s did not exist a decade later.

Moving off Campus: Independent Africana Studies Institutions

The Black Studies movement was not confined to campuses. The Institute of the Black World, initially based in Atlanta under the aegis of the Martin Luther King Memorial Center, described itself as "a community of black scholars, artists, teachers, and organizers who are coming together—to commit their talents and skills to the future liberation and independence of African peoples."[33] As this word choice indicates, the Institute did not view itself as just another academic think tank, but instead saw itself as community oriented and involved in the struggle against racism. It anticipated the future orientation of African American Studies toward the African diaspora by committing itself to African liberation. The Institute, which later separated from the King Center, published in 1970 seminal pamphlets by two of the leading intellectuals in the Black Studies movement: Lerone Bennett Jr.'s *The Challenge of Blackness* and Vincent Harding's *Beyond Chaos: Black History and the Search for the New Land*.[34] Bennett brought Black history to the masses by regularly writing in the pages of the popular magazine *Ebony*. In a sense his writings helped those who read the magazine, and those who read his many other publications to bridge the gap between the Marxist and the nationalist perspectives. Although he agreed with Marxists that the origins of racism were found in the self-centered greed of America's ruling elite, Bennett refused to see Blacks as mere victims of capitalist exploitation. Instead, he emphasized the power of the culture the slaves had created, which their descendants had maintained.

Harding brought together those who approached Afro-American Studies solely as an academic discipline and those who embraced the field as part of a moral struggle. By taking the risky position of linking Africana Studies to Christianity, along with theology scholars Gayraud Wilmore and James Cone, Harding emphasized the liberation qualities and potential of slave religion and its organizational progeny. Black scholars, and for that matter Black people, have always been ambivalent about Christianity. For many it has been the opiate of the masses, foisted on African Americans by slaveholders with the aim of encouraging them to focus on the next world and to ignore their exploitation in this one. Part of Malcolm X's appeal to Blacks was that he denounced Christianity, arguing that Afro-Americans could free themselves by breaking with the faith of the slaveowner. Harding linked the Black struggle to Black Christianity, reminding his readers that in many ways Whites were as morally maimed by practicing racism as were Blacks who suffered from it.

Bl. Catholics

Other Black Christians were also influenced by Africana Studies. Black Catholics, for example, a doubly marginalized group, constituted a tiny minority of American Catholics and a small percentage of African American Christians. Unlike Catholics of African descent elsewhere in the hemisphere, who had created such African-based faiths as Santeria, Voudon, and Candomble within the framework of Catholicism, Black American Catholics operated almost exclusively within organizations controlled by Whites. But Black Catholics were not immune to the Afro-American Studies movement. In 1978 the National Black Catholic Clergy Caucus sponsored the Black Catholic Theological Symposium (BCTS) and two years later established the Institute for Black Catholic Studies at Xavier University. In 1991 symposium participants decided it should be an "interdisciplinary theological society which would meet annually."[35] BCTS members now meet to discuss their scholarly and pastoral work. The symposium, like the Institute for the Black World and other organizations that had their beginnings in the 1970s, sees itself as linking scholarship and activism. Although knowledge is viewed as important in itself, Black Catholic scholars are expected to apply their knowledge to meet the many problems confronting persons of African descent throughout the world.

Full membership in the BCTS is open to Roman Catholics of African descent who hold a doctoral degree or its equivalent within a theological or theologically related discipline. These disciplines include but are not limited to anthropology, history, literature, philosophy, psychology, and sociology. According to a BCTS brochure, however, the symposium also offers a "limited number of Affiliate memberships . . . to selected scholars and persons, both black and non-black whose research, writing and ecclesiastical appointments focus on black Catholics."[36] The organization defines itself as primarily but not exclusively Black. By offering affiliate membership to Whites, the BCTS seeks to avoid the charge, so often made in the 1980s, that all-Black organizations were guilty of reverse racism. Many other Black institutions have adopted a similar strategy by making it clear that membership is primarily Black but that they are open to all people.

The Institute of the Black World, the BCTS, and similar organizations were part of a movement that reached beyond campuses, and as such they affect nearly every aspect of scholarship in the United States. American museums, long the intellectual stronghold of Eurocentrism and, many argue, racism, did not escape. Black museums were established in many of the nation's larger cities and soon began to explore ways of working together. In the late 1960s

museums

Margaret Burroughs, founder of Chicago's DuSable Museum of African American History, and Charles Wright, founder of the Afro-American Museum of Detroit, hosted a series of conferences for Black museums. In 1969, Wright invited representatives of a number of Black museums to Detroit to discuss the formation of a national association. Early in the 1970s Tom Lloyd, director of the Storefront Museum in New York City, established the National Association of Museums and Cultural Organizations, the first formal Black museums association. The association failed for lack of funding, however. Most Afro-American museums were small and poor. They lacked both the personnel and financial resources to support a national organization. Moreover, many of them operated in isolation, so that no network existed on which to build a national organization.

But Black museum professionals continued to push for a formal organization for the movement. Beginning in 1975, Burroughs sponsored a series of meetings of museum professionals and scholars known as the Black Seminar Group. This time money made the difference. In early 1978 a consortium of Black museums, with funding under the National Museum Act and supported by the Smithsonian Institution, organized a series of conferences at Black museums. Responding to a consensus for the need for a national Black museums association, Edmund Barry Gaither of Boston's Museum of the National Center of Afro-American Artists served as chair of a group that formulated bylaws for the African American Museums Association (AAMA). These rules were approved in a meeting held in Detroit in February 1978, and lacking a home of its own, the AAMA was headquartered for two years at the National Center. With support from Betty Thomas, then the director of the Mary McLeod Bethune Museum and Archives, the AAMA established headquarters in Washington, D.C., in 1980. In the same year the association hired its first full-time executive director, Joy Ford Austin.

Throughout the 1980s the AAMA became an aggressive, race-conscious, and vigorous force among U.S. museums, helping curators in planning exhibits, administrators in recruiting staff, scholars in conducting research, collectors in making donations, trustees in meeting responsibilities, and artists wishing to exhibit. Rowena Stewart, founder of the Rhode Island Black Heritage Society and later director of Philadelphia's African American Historical and Cultural Museum, served as president of the AAMA from 1981 to 1984. Stewart played a central role in encouraging Black museums to seek funding that had traditionally gone to White institutions. Together with Austin, Stewart established a process for reviewing and accrediting

Afro-American museums. Black Studies scholars, among them Spencer Crewe, later to head the National Museum of American History of the Smithsonian Institution (1994–present), were drawn into the review process. In 1984 Stewart and Austin participated in the NCBS's annual meeting held at Cornell University, urging more Black scholars to involve themselves in the Afro-American museum movement. The AAMA also worked closely with the American Association of Museums, the American Association for State and Local History, the National Endowment for the Arts, the National Endowment for the Humanities, and a number of other scholarly and cultural organizations.

Despite its many achievements, the AAMA found itself in difficulty at the end of the 1980s. The association became a victim of its own successes, as White museums—with far greater resources than Black ones and under increasing pressure to reflect the nation's cultural diversity in their exhibits—began to compete with Black museums for funds to support programs on Black Americans. Many White museums engaged in the most crass forms of tokenism, conducting business as usual, with perhaps a single Black exhibit a year. But because of their clout and connections, they took funding away from Black museums. The racist backlash to Black achievements in the 1980s, combined with the organizational and financial problems of the always underfunded AAMA, created additional problems for the organization. In 1991 the association closed its Washington office and formed an Interim Governing Committee, headed by Stewart. The National Afro-American Museum and Cultural Center, located in Wilberforce, Ohio, provided support for the national office, which reopened in 1992.

The Afro-American Studies movement also had an impact on traditional disciplines. Black scholars in anthropology, literature, political science, and sociology organized separate groups within their disciplines. Black scholars sometimes remained as a caucus within a larger organization, while at other times they created an independent organization or evolved within the context of a larger professional association. The history of the Association of Black Anthropologists (ABA) is one example of the nature of this evolution and of the impact Africana Studies had on an established discipline. In 1970 the American Anthropological Association (AAA), concerned with the small number of people of color who were anthropologists, established a Committee on Minority Participation in Anthropology. The Caucus of Black Anthropologists emerged out of the committee's regular meetings, and by the early 1970s the caucus, composed for the most part of junior faculty members and graduate students in anthropology, agreed on the need to move from an informal group to a formal association. The caucus was reorganized into the Association of Black Anthropologists at the AAA's annual meeting in 1975.

In 1973 the caucus initiated publication of *Notes from the Natives*, originally a four-page newsletter written by Black anthropologists who viewed themselves simultaneously as both the natives so often studied by anthropologists and as members of the anthropological establishment who studied them. In 1978 then University of Chicago graduate student Sheila Walker originated the newsletter and oversaw the creation of a larger version, renamed *Notes from the ABA*. The publication carried news of the profession, political commentaries, book reviews, abstracts of papers delivered by Black anthropologists, job listings, and scholarly notes. With support from the AAA the newsletter gradually evolved into a full-fledged, refereed journal, once again renamed, *Transforming Anthropology*. This incarnation of the journal was committed to research on "race, ethnicity, class, gender, and other invidious distinctions; and the development of research that involves both the peoples studied and local scholars in all stages of investigation and dissemination of findings."[37] As was the case with Africana Studies departments and with independent Black research organizations, the ABA sought to meet the needs of scholarship and the needs of the Black community.

Publishing the Word: Africana Studies Periodicals

As the history of the journal *Transforming Anthropology* demonstrates, the growth of African American Studies was reflected in the appearance of such periodicals as *Afro-Americans in New York Life and History*, *Black Academy Review*, *The Black Scholar*, *Black World*, and the *Western Journal of Black Studies*. *Black Academy Review* shifted publication from the United States to Nigeria. The journal *Black Images*, published in Canada, espoused a strong concern early on with the African diaspora. Not all of these first-generation Africana Studies journals survived, however. No longer published are *Contributions in Black Studies*, the *New England Journal of Black Studies*, *Review of Afro-American Issues and Culture*, *Studia Africana*, *Studies in Black Literature*, and *Umjoa*. Also no longer published is a series of working papers, the University of Illinois Afro-Scholars Working Paper Series, as well as the journal once supported by the Association of Black Sociologists.

But many other periodicals continue to flourish. Among them are *African American Review* (although the journal has undergone a number of name changes), *Afro-Americans in New York Life and History*, *The Black Scholar*, the *Journal of Black Psychology*, the *Journal of Black Studies*, and the *Western Journal of Black Studies*. Such long-established journals as the *Journal of Negro Education* and the *Journal of Negro History* received new life as a result of the Black Studies movement and also remain in publication. Newer journals are also thriving. Among them are *Callaloo*, *The Griot*, the *Langston Hughes Review*, *Trotter Institute Review*, and more recently the *Afrocentric Scholar* (the name of which has been changed to the *International Journal of Africana Studies*), the *Journal of African American Men*, the *Journal of African American Male Studies*, and *Race and Reason*. The appearance of other periodicals, such as the *Afro-American Journal of Philosophy*, the *Journal of Pan-African Studies*, *Wazo Weusi: A Journal of Black Thought*, and *Word: A Black Culture Journal*, have had shorter careers.

The history of *Black World*, edited by the iconoclastic Hoyt Fuller, exemplifies how the issues over which Blacks differed affected the success (or demise) of Black journals. Published by the Black-owned Johnson Publications Company, the publisher of such popular Black publications as *Ebony* and *Jet*, the nationalist-oriented *Black World* served as the voice for many of the early participants in Black Studies. The cover of *Black World* usually included Black faces or a striking picture portraying issues important to Black people. The cover also carried the names of well-known Black scholars, activists, and intellectuals. It was sold on newsstands and sought to attract both those African Americans who would recognize the names and those who would be drawn by the cover picture. More interesting than the front covers were the back ones. For example, one back cover pictured a young Black man, wearing an African-like garment and carrying an automatic weapon. Next to the picture appeared the caption, "Would He Look Better in a Sweater and Chinos with a Science Book under His Arm?" Another back cover carried a photograph of a Black man, next to the statement, "When Is a Black Man Not an African?"[38] These and other back covers of *Black World* attacked White racism, colonialism, and imperialism, but they reserved their most scathing statements for African Americans in flight from Blackness. The cover image of the armed Black youngster read: "The black 'moderates,' that ever diminishing breed of success-oriented, middle-class straining-blacks, will follow the White liberals' lead, as they always do, routinely moaning about rampant racism while religiously adjusting to it. The black 'moderates,' to be sure, loathe the black 'militants' more even than the other groups. The militants threaten their unsteady perch upon the pedestal of security and stability."[39]

In fact, the growth of the Black Studies movement, the success of the Civil Rights movement, and the threat of the Black Power movement—of which *Black World* was a part—had increased, not diminished, the Afro-American middle class. This educated, striving group was buying *Black World*, but it was increasingly uncomfortable with the magazine's contents. The other back cover previously highlighted found that: "In most areas of the Americas, Africans have at times been characterized by pathetic attempts to reject their heritage, and millions have served the ends of self-degredation [*sic*] and White domination by gauging their own humanity by the yardstick of European morals, manners, and men. To these Africans in the Americas, it was easier to identify with even the faces and symbols of Asia than with the image of Africa. Many of the fashion-conscious among them recently hung Nehru suits and Mao jackets in their closets, for example, but have never owned a dashiki."[40] Middle-class, educated Black Americans were in the vanguard of the Africana Studies movement, but they now found themselves attacked by a publication that their sacrifices and struggles had created.

This partnership between a successful, capitalist Black publishing house and Fuller, who spent a good deal of time attacking Black capitalists, was an uneasy one from the beginning. Yet African American intellectuals were shocked when the Johnson Publications Company announced its suspension of support for *Black World* for the most businesslike of reasons: there were not enough subscriptions. The journal *First World*, a new publication edited by Fuller and published independently, also failed despite support from Black intellectuals and Black Studies departments. The back page carried a list of those departments and individuals who supported *First World* with contributions. Although it read like a *Who's Who* of those involved in Africana Studies, many names were conspicuous by their absence.

This history of *Black World* suggests the complex evolution of Black Studies, a discipline that sought to be both academic and community oriented, to work with established academic disciplines and create a new discipline of its own, to center research in the scholarship of Blacks yet remain open to Whites, and to include the many African American intellectual traditions. Paralleling this development of Black Studies journals has been the publication by Black Studies departments of newsletters that provide a window on Africana Studies research. Because most department newsletters are inexpensively printed, there is not a long delay between the formulation of an exciting research idea, the completion of research, and the publication of the research in the newsletter. These newsletters provide opportunities to learn of work in progress. Although most newsletters naturally are concerned with their sponsoring departments, and so in a sense are public relations vehicles, few limit themselves to narrow, local concerns. Most provide summaries of lectures given by visiting faculty and publish book reviews and overviews of recent doctoral dissertations. Other newsletters occasionally devote an entire issue to a single theme, such as Afro-Latinos or the plight of the Black male. Still others publish interviews with Black scholars, artists, businesspersons, union officials, and clergy. Because nearly all Afro-American Studies units are interdisciplinary, articles, commentaries, review essays, and interviews typically cover work in the arts, the humanities, and the social sciences and explore relationships among the various fields.

Reflecting the struggles of African American Studies departments, these newsletters are often irregularly published. I have identified twenty-five such newsletters, including those with such ordinary names as the *Africana Studies and Research Center Newsletter* (Cornell University), the *Afro-American Studies Newsletter* (University of Mississippi), the *Black Studies Newsletter* (University of Missouri), and simply *News* (University of Pennsylvania). Other titles are more venturesome, including the *Afroamericanist* (University of Illinois), *Atumpan* (Indiana University), *Burning Torch* (Temple University), *Crossroads* (University of Wisconsin), *The Diaspora* (University of California-Berkeley), *Du Bois Lines* (University of Massachusetts), *Elimu* (University of California-Santa Barbara), *Nommo* (Purdue University), *Nommo-South* (University of Georgia), and *Race and Reason* (Brown University).

The Africana Studies movement also spawned specialized newsletters in such disciplines as archaeology, folklore, museum studies, music, religious studies, and theater. The newsletter of the aforementioned National Council for Black Studies, *The Voice of Black Studies*, as well as that of the Southern Conference on Afro-American Studies, *Grapevine*, taken together with departmental newsletters and such regional newsletters as *Hantu* of the New England Regional Conference of NCBS, provide insight into the everyday workings of Black Studies from its beginnings to the present.

Continuing the Struggle: Ethnic Studies and Africana Studies

Black Studies departments, scholarship and books, student organizations, journals, newsletters, conferences and symposia, as well as the commentary on the role of Blacks in academe in such publications as *Black Issues in Higher Education* and the *Journal of Blacks in Higher Education* demonstrate the existence of a discipline. Ironically, this discipline has hampered the development of Ethnic Studies by institutionalizing the bipolar race model. There are some exceptions, however, as occasional articles and even special issues have appeared on Asian Americans, Latinos, and Native Americans in *Callaloo*, *The Trotter Review*, and the *Western Journal of Black Studies*. But these instances merely underline the fact that most African American Studies journals remain concerned with Blacks and with relations between Blacks and Whites. Ethnic Studies scholars have found themselves in the difficult position of having on the one hand to build on the work of Black Studies, while on the other having to persuade Black Studies scholars that they are not out to replace Black Studies with Ethnic Studies.

Relations between Black Studies and Ethnic Studies ought to be good, as most involved in Ethnic Studies frankly acknowledge that Black Studies was the first to appear as a distinct discipline. Such fields as Asian American, Chicano/a, Latino/a, and Native American Studies, to say nothing of Ethnic Studies itself, were modeled on Afro-American Studies. These race-specific studies clearly owe more to Africana Studies than to such established disciplines as anthropology, literature, and sociology. And clearly, each area of study has profited from the mistakes made as well as the successes and failures enjoyed by African American Studies. For example, Black Studies wrestled early on with the fact that many involved in the new discipline were themselves African American, leading to a set of questions about whether Blacks were best qualified to study Black people. To their credit, most—but not all—Black Studies scholars soon put this issue behind them, persuasively arguing that any scholar could examine the Black experience, provided he or she was willing to make the effort to take into consideration the unique history of African Americans. In turn, this led to discussions of methodological issues with some Afro-American Studies scholars—many of whom were not Black—arguing that models, paradigms, and theories developed to study White people could not be simply applied, unchanged, to the study of Black people. There were also debates over whether the best way to study Blacks was in separate Black Studies departments or by incorporating Black Studies into existing departments. Ethnic Studies has learned from these and other debates over Black Studies.

Yet the relationship between Ethnic Studies and Africana Studies has not always been cordial, with those in Ethnic Studies often arguing they are viewed with hostility by colleagues in Black Studies, and Black Studies scholars insisting that they are threatened by Ethnic Studies. There is, unhappily, a kernel of truth in each of these attitudes. At one university, for example, those attempting to organize a Chicano/a Studies program initially approached those in Black Studies, only to be told that although Black Studies would be supportive of such an effort, they would not do so at the expense of Black Studies. This not uncommon attitude was further complicated by administrators who thought it best to consolidate existing Afro-American Studies units with the emerging demands for the study of other racial groups. At a time when support for higher education was shrinking, some administrators preferred to set up a pool of faculty slots from which all appointments in Ethnic Studies would be made. Established departments were allowed to continue business as usual, while Asian American Studies, for example, was to grow at the expense of African American Studies.

At some universities Afro-American Studies departments were forcibly incorporated into new Ethnic Studies units despite their strong objections. Once inside they were told that because the number of Black Studies appointments already exceeded the number of appointments in Asian American, Latino and Latina, and Native American Studies, there would be no additional appointments in Black Studies. Furthermore, when Black Studies positions became vacant, they would be replaced by faculty interested in the study of another racial group. At some colleges such appointments made sense if the new Ethnic Studies programs were to be balanced, but at others administrators used appointments as a way of undercutting Ethnic Studies departments they did not want by dividing the field's supporters. Knowledge of the forced incorporation of Afro-American Studies into Ethnic Studies spread rapidly along Black Studies networks, with the result that Ethnic Studies came to be regarded with suspicious hostility by many involved in Black Studies.

Afrocentrism further complicated relations between Black Studies and Ethnic Studies scholars. Afrocentrism is a sensible scholarly perspective resting on two assumptions. First, much of the existing scholarship on Blacks is derived from disciplines that came into existence in the late nineteenth and early twentieth centuries, when racism was at its apogee. The failure of most of the "traditional" disciplines—anthropology is a notable exception—to acknowledge their racist roots and confront racism among their past and present members means that racism remains alive and well in most U.S. fields of study. Afrocentrists therefore argue that an alternative to the traditional approaches to the study of Blacks is needed. Second, if it makes sense to study White people from the perspective of disciplines created by Whites, it makes sense to study Black people from the perspective of disciplines created by Blacks. Afrocentric scholars argue that it does not make sense to accept uncritically the application of White Studies disciplines to the study of Blacks. Sensible as these assumptions may seem, however, they have not been accepted by all African American Studies scholars and are widely and rightfully debated. These debates have also affected relations between Black Studies and Ethnic Studies scholars, especially because many Afrocentrists view Ethnic Studies as an attempt to avoid discussions of racism by focusing on multiculturalism.

Under all of these debates runs a cynicism that yields a bitter twist. Black Studies had its beginnings in a time of euphoric expectations. Jim Crow was dead, and Blacks long barred from the nation's best universities and research institutions were now able to use these institutional resources to study race relations. As Blacks rented apartments, dined, used the toilet, and attended school wherever they wished—ordinary acts of everyday life that Whites long took for granted—it seemed as though the end of racism was just around the corner and the nation was about to turn it. But Blacks, other peoples of color, and their White allies learned over the course of the 1970s and 1980s that racism was so deeply woven into the fabric of America that it could not be easily ripped out. They had not anticipated the many justifications for racism that racists would find, all while denying they were racists. Many White Americans found excuses for behaving in racist ways without acknowledging they were in fact racists. The bitter reactions to this continuing racism spilled over into debates among those involved in Ethnic Studies and Black Studies, so that these fields sometimes turned on one another and instead of coming together, pulled apart. Ethnic Studies is a vibrant and lively discipline, engaging students, faculty, and Americans of all colors as they acknowledge the United States is and always has been a multiracial nation. Discussions of how ethnicity and race differ from one another, and of the relationship between Ethnic Studies and Black Studies, continue as we continue to seek to remove racism and ethnocentrism from the fabric of the nation.

Selected Bibliography

Adams, Russell. "Intellectual Questions and Imperative in the Development of Afro-American Studies." *Journal of Negro Education* 53, no. 3 (1984): 201–25.

Allen, Robert. "Politics of the Attack on Black Studies." *Black Scholar* 6 (September 1974): 1–7.

Anderson, Talmadge. *Black Studies: Theory, Method, and Cultural Perspective.* Pullman: Washington State University Press, 1990.

Azibo, Daudi Ajani ya. "Articulating the Distinction between Black Studies and the Study of Blacks: The Fundamental Role of Culture in the African-Centered Worldview." *Afrocentric Scholar* 1 (May 1991): 64–97.

Bailey, Ron. "Why Black Studies?" *Education Digest* 35, no. 9 (1970): 46–48.

Cruse, Harold. "Black and White: Outlines of the Next Stage." *Black World* 20 (January 1971): 19–41, 66–71.

Daniels, Philip T. K. "Black Studies: Discipline or Field Studies?" *Western Journal of Black Studies* (fall 1980): 195–99.

Davis, Charles. *Afro-American Studies, 1979–1980, Yale University.* New Haven, Conn.: Yale University Press, 1980.

Faculty of Arts and Sciences. *The First Three Years of the Afro-American Studies Department.* Cambridge: Faculty of Arts and Sciences, Harvard University, 1972.

Ford, Nick Aaron. *Black Studies: Threat or Challenge?* Port Washington, N.Y.: Kennikat Press, 1973.

Hall, Perry A. "Beyond Afrocentrism: Alternatives for Afro-American Studies," *Western Journal of Black Studies* 15 (winter 1992): 207–12.

Hare, Nathan. "The Battle for Black Studies." *Black Scholar* 3 (May 1972): 32–37.

Hutchinson, Janis Faye, ed., *Cultural Portrayals of African Americans.* Westport, Conn.: Bergin and Garvey, 1997.

Jones, Rhett S. "The Discipline of Black History since 1960." *New England Journal of Black Studies* 3 (fall 1981): 1–18.

———. "Pseudo Power and the Creation of African American Culture." *International Journal of Africana Studies* 4 (December 1996): 22–28.

Karenga, Maulana. "Black Studies and the Problematic of Paradigm: The Philosophic Dimension." *Journal of Black Studies* 18 (June 1988): 395–414.

Little, William A., Carolyn M. Leonard, and Edward Crosby. "The National Council for Black Studies: Black Studies/Africana Studies Holistic Curriculum Model." *Afrocentric Scholar* 2 (May 1993): 42–68.

Record, Wilson. "Can Black Studies and Sociology Find Common Ground?" *Journal of Negro Education* 154 (winter 1978): 63–81.

Robinson, Armstead L., et al., eds., *Black Studies in the University.* New Haven, Conn.: Yale University Press, 1969.

Steward, James B. "Reaching for Higher Ground: Toward an Understanding of Black/Africana Studies." *Afrocentric Scholar* 1 (May 1992): 1–63.

———. "Africana Studies: New Directions for the Twenty-First Century." *International Journal of African Studies* 4 (December 1995): 1–21.

Turner, James E. *The Next Decade: Theoretical and Research Interests in African Studies*. Ithaca, N.Y.: Cornell University Africana Studies and Research Center, 1985.

Williams, Selase W. "Black Studies: The Evolution of an Afrocentric Human Science." *Afrocentric Scholar* 2 (May 1993): 69–84.

Woodyard, Jeffrey L. "Evolution of a Discipline: Intellectual Antecedents of African American Studies." *Journal of Black Studies* 22 (December 1990): 239–51.

Notes

1. Bayard Rustin, ed., *Black Studies: Myths and Realities* (New York: A. Philip Randolph Education Fund, 1968).

2. Andrew Brimmer, "Education and Economic Opportunity," in Rustin, *Black Studies*, 40–42.

3. Rustin, "Introduction," in Rustin, *Black Studies*, 5. Emphasis in original.

4. Harvard/Radcliffe Racial Issues Study Group, *Unfair Harvard: Racism and the University* (Cambridge: Harvard/Radcliffe Racial Issues Study Group, 1979), 18.

5. Yosef ben-Jochannan, *Cultural Genocide in the Black and African Studies Curriculum* (New York: ABC Printers, n.d.), 57.

6. Nathan Huggins, *Afro-American Studies: A Report to The Ford Foundation* (New York: Ford Foundation, 1984), 5.

7. Robert L. Harris Jr., Darlene Clark Hine, and Nellie McKay, *Black Studies in the United States: Three Essays* (New York: Ford Foundation, 1989).

8. Robert Harris, "The Intellectual and Institutional Development of Africana Studies," in Harris, Hine, and McKay, *Black Studies in the United States*, 12, 13.

9. A. Leon Higginbotham Jr., *In the Matter of Color: Race and the American Legal Process: The Colonial Period* (New York: Oxford University Press, 1978), 372–73.

10. *David Walker's Appeal, in Four Articles; Together with a Preamble, to the Coloured Citizens of the World, but in Particular, and Very Expressly, to Those of the United States of America* (1829) (New York: Hill & Wang, 1965), 75.

11. Roy Wilkins with Tom Mathews, *Standing Fast: The Autobiography of Roy Wilkins* (New York: Viking Press, 1982), 215.

12. Maulana Karenga, *Introduction to Black Studies* (Los Angeles: University of Sankore Press, 1982).

13. People's College, *Introduction to Afro-American Studies* (Chicago: People's College Press, 1977), ii.

14. Mary Frances Berry and John W. Blassingame, *Long Memory: The Black Experience in America* (New York: Oxford University Press, 1982), xi.

15. Amuzie Chimezie, *Black Culture: Theory and Practice* (Shaker Heights, Ohio: Keeble Press, 1984).

16. Gerdes Fleurant, ed., *Introductory Readings in African American Culture* (Needham Heights, Mass.: Ginn Press, 1988),

17. Sterling Stuckey, *Slave Culture: Nationalist Theory and the Foundations of Black America* (New York: Oxford University Press, 1987).

18. Niara Sudarkasa *et al.*, eds., *Exploring the African-American Experience* (Lincoln, Pa.: Lincoln University Press, 1995), viii.

19. Talmadge Anderson, *Introduction to African Studies* (Dubuque, Iowa: Kendall/Hunt, 1993), ix.

20. Ibid., 4.

21. Floyd W. Hayes III, ed., *A Turbulent Voyage: Readings in African American Studies* (San Diego, Calif.: Collegiate Press, 1993).

22. Ibid., xxxix.

23. Nikongo BaNikongo, ed., *Leading Issues in African-American Studies* (Durham, N.C.: Carolina Academic Press, 1997).

24. Ibid., 5.

25. Rhett S. Jones, *Green into Black: Outside Funding for Afro-American Studies* (Providence, R.I.: Afro-American Studies Program, Brown University, 1977).

26. Molefi Kente Asante, *The Afrocentric Idea* (Philadelphia: Temple University Press, 1987); *Afrocentricity* (Trenton, N.J.: African World Press, 1988).

27. Article 3 of the National Association of African American Studies (NAAAS) Constitution.

28. NCBS Annual Meeting Program, 1982.

29. Southern Conference on Afro-American Studies, Inc. (SCAASI), statement on inside back cover of *The Griot* 13 (fall 1994).

30. Meeting newsletter, SCAASI, 1979.

31. "Work for African Liberation, with the Student Organization for Black Unity," pamphlet, n.d.

32. Harvard/Radcliffe Racial Issues Study Group, *Unfair Harvard: Racism and the University*, 20.

33. Lerone Bennett Jr., *The Challenge of Blackness* (Atlanta, Ga.: Institute of the Black World, 1970), inside back cover.

34. Ibid.; and Vincent Harding, *Beyond Chaos: Black History and the Search for the New Land* (Atlanta, Ga.: Institute of the Black World, 1970).

35. Black Catholic Theological Symposium brochure.

36. BCTS brochure.

37. *Transforming Anthropology* 1, no. 2, inside back cover.

38. "When Is a Black Man Not an African?" *Black World* 20 (April 1971), back cover; "Would He Look Better in a Sweater and Chinos with a Science Book under His Arm?" *Black World* 21 (April 1972), back cover.

39. "Would He Look Better," *Black World.*

40. "When Is a Black Man," *Black World.*

The Dialectics of Ethnicity in America:

A View from American Indian Studies

ELIZABETH COOK-LYNN & CRAIG HOWE

The problem with "ethnicity" for an Indians

THE DEVELOPMENT OF BLACK STUDIES, ASIAN AMERICAN
Studies, Puerto Rican, Chicano/a, and Latino/a Studies over the past thirty
years, and the move toward comparative study within what has come to be
called Ethnic Studies, has brought about the study of race and ethnicity within
a postcolonial, pan-American consciousness. The social structure of race in
many instances has become subsumed under ethnicity, and claims for understanding the uniqueness of individual groups are often dismissed and
ridiculed as "essentialist." This is especially true in the humanities and in the
social sciences, but is also evident in law and politics. This context and its ema-
nating themes—such as hybridity, ethnicity, border crossing, self-victimization,
assimilation, diversity, multiculturalism, and so on—cannot be discounted
when discussing the impetus for the development of American Indian Studies
as an academic discipline.

We can neither begin to define American Indian Studies nor measure
its progress until we understand the problem within the United States concerning ethnicity as prescribed in most Ethnic Studies curriculum development circles. The term *ethnic* refers to a social group within a broad cultural
system that is accorded special status on the basis of complex religious, linguistic, ancestral, or physical characteristics. This emphasis in curricular development is at the heart of the disagreement concerning treaty status of Indian

enclaves. In this context particularly rancorous and troublesome for many Ethnic Studies professionals is Native scholars' claim of First Nation status for Native enclaves within the United States. The nature of the study of ethnicity as social systems in the U.S. disputes trivializes, denies, and co-opts citizenship claims and treaty rights within nation-to-nation relationships.

Overview

The U.S. government, its educational systems, and America's earliest institutions have confused the issues of First Nation status in a number of ways. The Virginia colonial government, for example, promulgated its 1704 "race laws," which categorized Indians as participants on the "colored" side of the system. There was an attempt on the part of these early legislators to label Indians as "free persons of color," ignoring the indigenous, land-holding, First Nation, sovereign status of their origins. While these early designations of Indians as people "of color" have been repudiated and disavowed by Indians on the basis of indigenousness rather than color, confusion concerning indigenous populations in this country persists.

Most recently, in the educational systems across the country, American Indians have been labeled as "ethnic" divisions within American society. This deliberate obfuscation began as early as 1924, when the U.S. unilaterally conferred its citizenship on tribal peoples and then failed to take into account tribal nation objections.[1] Significantly, some groups, such as the Iroquois, did not "accept" U.S. citizenship; rather, they said they would ask for it if they so desired. The Tewa and others also resisted this political categorization into American society, but just as Christian missionaries had methods of carrying out surreptitious baptisms of unbelievers in Native enclaves, so too the U.S. federal government had methods of integrating unwilling Native citizens. In many cases U.S. citizenship was yet another federal policy forced on Indians.

The term ethnic pertains to a social group within a cultural and social system that claims or is accorded special status on the basis of complex often variable traits, including religious, linguistic, ancestral, or physical characteristics. Most Indians see ethnicity as an invention, a cultural construction structured within an Anglocentric, monocultural matrix. This is the construction used by sociologists, anthropologists, and some social scientists within the field of Ethnic Studies. Because this construct fails to account for the legal and indigenous treaty status of Native peoples, most Indians reject this mainstream perception of their status. Indians in America, as well as indigenous peoples everywhere who have experienced colonialism, face this conflict concerning status and identity, even though they might not have treaty relations with their colonizing powers. Native populations in the United States do not consider themselves just social groups within a cultural system called America. Rather, they define themselves as holding specific tribal legal status within the nation of the United States, and a "trust" status holds their reserved lands and resources within a protectorate. Unfortunately, the American Indian protectorate status has too frequently been defined as either ethnic or as a postcolonial dependency, and an entire body of law has been written, which seems to defend and deny variously the status of nations-within-a-nation.[2]

The reality is that Indian tribal peoples are the only groups in the United States that do not have a history of coming to this continent either through an immigrant system or through enslavement; they are the only groups to retain rightfully indigenous status and citizenship. Immigration is a fundamental organizing principle in Ethnic Studies and as such makes the integration of American Indian Studies into the episteme of Ethnic Studies problematic. Spiritual rootedness to the land through Native creation and genesis in North America is not just a belief system. It is a theory of origin from which the defense of tribalism emerges. In the methodological strategies of Native Studies, Indians are not studied as immigrants; instead, they are the only peoples indigenous to the continent who have signed binding nation-to-nation treaties with the U.S. federal government as evidence of their historical, spiritual, and indigenous presence. Indians also signed treaties with Canada, England, France, Holland, Spain, and other nations. Therefore, they cannot be designated "ethnic" populations. In addition to these historical and legal realities, Native enclaves continue to define themselves as peoples within specific age-old mythological and religious systems embedded in their own oral traditions and languages. Their separate and non-Christian origins are tribally specific (or nationalistic), although they often claim to be related obviously to one another through North American continental geography and experience.

These realities are historically prescribed in an inchoate, divisive, and controversial concept in American society called First Nation (Tribal) Sovereignty, which exempted American Indians from the U.S. Constitution (except as a commerce clause defines them) and can be thought of as a condition of self-determination developed throughout the treaty-signing period and later. The massive body of Indian law, which has developed in the past two hundred years, has largely upheld that concept, sometimes wholeheartedly, often reluctantly.[3] This essentially different perception of history and origin has always been at the heart of racial Indian-White conflict. It was one of the considerations in the initial rationale for the development of American Indian Studies as an academic discipline in the modern era. This difference is what makes the discipline of American Indian Studies reject as a postmodernist charade the study of Indians as "ethnics" or as U.S. "people of color." In the 1960s and 1970s, for example, militants, intellectuals, "bleeding hearts," anxious revisionists and nonrevisionists, and tribalists gathered on campuses throughout the country to argue about the forces that have shaped modern America. American Indians were on the list as those who represented remnants of a dark and troubled past, which meant that educational paradigms were wont either to ignore or distort the real and bloody past.

Nonetheless, a major topic of inquiry was, What does the future hold for American Indians? Were Indians going to oppose the United States and its perception of them as a disappearing minority, as ethnic, colonial, diverse "people of color," or as occupants of penal and poverty enclaves? Or were they going to fight for the right to nations-within-a-nation status? Was it possible for Indians to defend themselves, their status, their lands, in the face of a sophisticated American academic and political culture steeped in domination and imperialism? The answer to these questions are now self-evident. Cultural theory defined as "any developed comparative knowledge about the histories and forms of collective life" in the U.S. academy was about to undergo massive restructuring in the American Indian Studies canon.[4] Unfortunately, ideological difference and hostility would continue to plague this restructuring.

Toward an Intellectual Paradigm in American Indian Studies

When the paradigm of American Indian Studies as an academic discipline, commonly called Indian Studies, emerged in the late 1960s and early 1970s under the force of student militancy and the direction of a few credentialed Native scholars, it was envisioned as an intellectual paradigm directed toward the study of sovereignty and indigenousness—concepts largely unknown or neglected by mainstream scholars at the time. In 1980 historian and activist Roxanne Dunbar Ortiz organized a group of intellectuals who met as the first Native American Studies Association at San Diego State University. The group published this statement in their first newsletter: "The context of most Native American Studies components at present embodies imperialist and racist institutionalization. The built-in hindrances, which reflect the interests of the dominant society status quo, require that the stance of Native American Studies be one of challenge to that status quo."[5]

The first goal of the disciplinary thrust, then, was to develop intellectual strategies for political self-determination. That is, the aim was to find ways to defend the moral and legal rights of Indian peoples to determine fully their own political status and to pursue freely their economic, social, and cultural development, particularly on Native homelands but in urban enclaves as well. Indian scholars responded to the unilateral political "termination" and "relocation" policies of the U.S. government that had gained momentum in the 1950s, policies that amounted to the attempted dissolution of Indian tribes as distinctly separate political governments within special government-to-government (treaty) relationships with the United States.[6] Until that time there was little consideration of the concept of sovereignty as a function of culture and religion, or as endemic to indigenous societies as to cosmopolitan ones.

Scholarship in this area is often lacking in political theory, and there is even less written concerning the status of Native peoples throughout the world. An important collection of major pieces from *Center Magazine* since 1967 included an article by English sociologist Arnold Toynbee, which articulated a fear concerning the movement toward self-identity. The article suggested that the increasing political fragmentation of the human race could be described as the "worship of modern national states," and it was dangerous and progressive in its dangerousness.[7] Toynbee, a major intellectual on the matter of politics, wrote that the concept of national sovereignty originated only in the West and that it should be considered a flaw of human endeavors. This article also appeared in an influential journal published by the Center for the Study of Democratic Institutions, perhaps in response to the rise of nationalism worldwide.[8] This thinking affected the political apparatuses that influenced (and continue to influence) Native enclaves.

Despite such thinking by major intellectuals, U.S. federal Indian policy as it concerned sovereignty for First Nation status changed during the Nixon administration.[9] Political self-determination, according to the Nixon policy, could be thought of as a federally mandated legal right of Indian tribes to direct and control their own destinies while at the same time legally maintaining their trust relationships with the U.S. government. This mandate, no matter how it managed to assert itself during the Nixon political era, is challenged frequently by hostile state governments, and a plethora of court cases is typically on the agenda of many courts in the land.

Until the development of American Indian Studies curricula, the challenge to such political thinking and White-based ethnocentric or racist educational institutions across the United States had been an isolated problem area tended to mostly by tribal government entities and sympathetic church-related associations. Rather than referring to a secular authority useful for colonial empire building, "sovereignty" as it is described in Native Studies is a function of culture firmly embedded in the mythology and religion of indigenous groups that claim their origins in specific geographies. Outside of American Indian Studies, sovereignty has always seemed to be a function of tribal relationships to the U.S. federal government, not an innate and ✳ endemic source of power in indigenous theory.

American Indian Studies also sought to organize the bodies of tribal knowledge that form the conceptual and symbolic bases for social behavior, religion, and literature into a disciplinary model for higher education. In addition, the relationship between law and public opinion was a major evolving inquiry, deeply embedded in the impulse toward the development of the discipline of Native Studies. Native scholars articulated the notion that the rise and fall of civilizations in the course of history was largely a function of an organization of colonial codes of conduct and fundamental principles for decision making. Native scholars were determined that to study those phenomena would illuminate Indian-White race relations in the United States. It was envisioned that the model would start with such concepts as sovereignty and indigenousness and principles related to law and governance, continue to general knowledge courses, then to specialized and applied courses. In 1975, Congress passed the Indian Self-Determination and Educational Assistance Act, clarifying constituencies and goals.[10] Indian Studies centers and tribal enclaves had called for such legislation that would make official the responsibility of Indian Studies to develop professionals in the discipline who would seek employment with the tribes and the U.S. government, state schools systems, and legislatures to bring about an informed public. On campuses Indian Studies centers were to develop appropriate scholarly support for those persons in major academic disciplines and move toward the public arena to assist the country in beginning to understand itself, its histories, its responsibilities to Indian people, and its future as a culturally diverse, democratic nation.

Several scholarly journals began to emerge as early as 1959, when the *Journal of American Indian Education* was published at Arizona State

University by the School of Education. By 1990 the *American Indian Culture and Research Journal*, the *American Indian Quarterly*, the *Association for the Study of American Indian Literature*, and the *Wicazo Sa Review* had become well-established scholarly journals based at western universities and presses. World reports on the rights of indigenous peoples and ethnic minorities began to be published in academe through such journals as *Cultural Survival Quarterly*, which was founded in 1972 in Cambridge, Massachusetts.

Most Native scholars at the forefront of the movement to develop American Indian Studies recognized that termination and relocation, wars and genocide might not have been the persistent result of modern Indian-White relations if academic communities had not failed for a hundred years to place tribal nations-within-a-nation status in a rational light. At this point "deconstruction" thus became an important function of course development.[11] In addition, because Indians saw themselves as peoples who were not introduced to this continent like other peoples were, Native or indigenous intellectualism had to have as its essential function the examination of the question of what the legacy of indigenousness meant. Indigenousness and sovereignty, therefore, emerged as concepts vital to the discipline.

For the most part these concepts were either absent from the curriculum development in Ethnic Studies or else Native scholars did not view them as connected in any significant academic way to other American concepts such as slavery, racism, and immigration. The epistemology advocated by Native scholars who have followed the development of these concepts entails four aspects: spatial, social, spiritual, and experiential. The spatial aspect deals with the importance of land, of Indian land. It focuses on spatial instead of temporal concerns. The social aspect deals with tribes instead of individuals, with specific tribes. Tribal nationhood should be the focus of American Indian Studies, even if to do so might be detrimental to individual Indians. Instead of focusing on the rights of individuals, American Indian Studies should be more concerned with the rights of tribes. Whereas the spatial aspect opposes the dominance of Western abstract time, the social aspect opposes the dominance of individuals by Western thought and law. The focus is on American Indian lands and American Indian tribes.

The spiritual aspect reconceptualizes tribes as spiritual associations with eternal ties to specific landscapes of the Western hemisphere. No American Indian tribe claims to have immigrated to the Western hemisphere after emerging at some other place. As with the spatial aspect, the spiritual aspect also challenges the primacy of Western abstract time. Mythic events and sacred instructions are, by definition, beyond measured time, and the premises of spiritual associations are not temporally bound. Rather, they are eternal and everlasting. Similar to the social aspect of the epistemological focus, the spiritual aspect advocates the importance of traditions accepted and shared by members of a given tribe, not the unique beliefs held by individual citizens of a tribe. Finally, the experiential aspect has to do with the striving to develop American Indian Studies and its component parts in ways that support tribal sovereignty using indigenous models. It is intimately bound to living and interacting with American Indian peoples. It is inherently multisensory and interdisciplinary, and in the long run, political.

Dialectics of Opposition and Program Development

Hostile antagonists almost immediately challenged the goals and purposes articulated early on in American Indian Studies. In the implementation of curricula, Native Studies was often seen by mainstream professors and scholars even in cultural studies as an obstruction to the goals of assimilation and a democratic world in which comparativism was the preferred mode of analysis. The inevitable contrasts were avoided. Co-optation, tokenism, and discreditation was the result. One of the first charges was that American Indian Studies lacked a firm, wide intellectual base, a charge made largely by scholars who had either ignored or dismissed the oral traditions, believing them to be useless, traceless, and anti-intellectual. American democracy, this argument went, could trace its roots to Greek and Roman philosophers. Even Communism could trace its beginnings to Karl Marx and Frederick Engels. But who ever heard of American Indian intellectualism? There was only the famous but bogus speech by Chief Seattle or perhaps the 1868 Treaty of Fort Laramie, generally regarded as having been signed by thumbprint out there in the wilderness by savages who could not even speak English.[12] For some this put Indian Studies in the context of such bodies of thought and experience as fascism, magic, or Communism, or in any of the ideological, political, or philosophical movements that were perceived as a clear threat to established order.[13]

This perceived threat to the common good or the fear of what accurate Indian histories and the continued physical presence of tribal nations could mean to the vision America had of itself, it seems, continues to be as agonizing in modern American writing and thinking as it was during the Indian war period of the nineteenth century. Sovereignty, a major principle put forth in the curricular development of American Indian Studies, was thus set up by obstructionists to take the blame for much of society's ills, and the marketing of Indian pathology took over the social sciences. As just one example of the expression of this mainstream fear or threat, early in 1969, John Greenway, a well-established University of Colorado-Boulder anthropology professor, worried in an essay on Red Power, "will the Indians get Whitey?" His point was that "prevailing assumptions" or "shibboleths" long associated with American Indians (such as injustice, suffering, and victimization) had at that point reached such absurd proportions in the law and in education that this "deprived minority" could now accuse Whites of the crime of simply being Americans. Greenway described himself as a reasonable man and told his audience that this whole charade had gone on long enough.[14]

In today's often racist climate a White journalist named Fergus M. Bordewich found enthusiastic American audiences for his musings in *Killing the White Man's Indian*, as he worries about "the reinventing" of Native Americans in some false mode.[15] Bordewich argues that it is false to believe that the physical extermination of Native Americans was ever an official U.S. government policy. He continues, suggesting that Indians were wasteful (not environmentalists), that poor beleaguered scientists are now at the mercy of Indians, that the Indian Reorganization Act of 1934 formally ended repression, and that Indians are reinventing education and justice in inappropriate ways and exploiting the idea of sovereignty.[16] Bordewich says that America must very quickly amend the U.S. Constitution, telling Indian tribes once and for all that they are not sovereign, that they are merely "self-governing entities" that are "subject in every respect to the laws of the U.S." He further argues for a plan whereby American Indian tribes can be made into nonthreatening enclaves of capitalistic democracy.

For thirty years the struggle in American Indian Studies to articulate a future in which Native enclaves are defined as self-governing nations-within-a-nation has met with stiff resistance in the mainstream and academic communities. The concept of sovereignty for American Indian tribes is held suspect not only by scholars but by popular writers of history as well. According to some modern theorists, the study of ethnicity and its origins, as well as the place of such study in the intellectual and political life of America, has always had to do with fear and suspicion on the part of Whites and a sense of vulnerability on the part of Indians.[17] In the case of American Indians as an "other" in American society, tribal nation status has had as its major divisive feature the occupancy and ownership of land and resources.

Daniel Patrick Moynihan, the U.S. senator from New York, has perhaps articulated the general American attitude toward Indians as landholders when in a statement about American multiethnic society he observed: "Years ago, for example, [sociologist] Milton Gordon pointed out that in 1818 Irish charitable organizations in New York and Philadelphia had sought the aid of the federal government to provide land in the west on which to settle indigent Gaels. Not a chance, said Congress. Wisely. The United States in the main has been spared autonomous regions, bantustans, and enclaves. (Reservations, yes. Our worst mistake or worst dilemma, as you wish.) Such has to be the *policy* of a nation of immigrants."[18] This dismissal of five hundred years of the Native human history known to U.S. scholars is the only reference to American Indians in the entire volume dedicated to a discussion of U.S. and international politics from one of the major intellectuals of American political life.

In addition to criticism by Native scholars of the study of various aspects of Native life, analysis of the efforts to devise new approaches to the study of North American Indians was met with apprehension and doubt. As early as 1972, Native anthropologist Beatrice Medicine spoke for many concerned scholars when she wrote an analysis of "The American Indian and American Indian Studies Programs." The article illuminated not only the role of related disciplines but the consequences of specific focuses of activism and community structures.[19]

One of the first sites of serious departmental development of American Indian Studies was the University of Minnesota in 1968, after the frail beginnings at the University of Oklahoma- Norman and the University of Arizona-Tucson. Opposition to departmental status at Oklahoma had been so loud and long that departmental development was abandoned. Viola Fromer, the long-time friend of Salishan Indian scholar D'Arcy McNickle, put together an advisory and student services component at the University of Arizona, a model that was followed by many universities throughout the country. Such models were useful mainly for recruitment purposes, secondarily for Native student retention, and only incidentally for the development of American Indian Studies epistemology.

The plan for departmental status development at Minnesota seemed grand by comparison. Native scholars Dave Warren, Ed Dozier, and Roger Buffalohead, all well known in the inchoate American Indian Studies field, were hired. Dozier's early death, coupled with Warren's decision to stay at the Institute of American Indian Arts in Santa Fe, New Mexico, left Buffalohead in charge. Buffalohead ran the department for several years, struggling toward a meaningful curriculum. Next, Russell Thornton held the position for one year. Later, Gerald Vizenor headed the department, but his appointment to the tenure-track faculty position in American Indian Studies proved to be the last such position in that university's structure. Vizenor's tenure was fraught with the controversy and conflict that characterized the period, a reality that he has attributed to several factors, not the least of which was the rise of the American Indian Movement.[20] The university bought out Vizenor's contract in the late 1980s, and the tenure-track faculty position in American Indian Studies at the University of Minnesota was wiped from existence. Development at the university has been unstable ever since. At least part of the conflict and subsequent failure stemmed from the bureaucratic subordination inherent in the structures as well as the merging or co-opting by other disciplines.

Recommendations

Most Native scholars believe that placing the mechanisms of American Indian Studies within minority Studies programs such as Ethnic Studies at universities is a fatally flawed idea. Minority programs, these critics suggest, have become mechanisms that "confuse social issues and priorities" and are largely a "transparent devotion to posture and gloss at the expense of scholarly content."[21] William Willard, a professor of American Indian Studies and comparative cultures at Washington State University-Pullman and a founding editor of *Wicazo Sa Review,* and his co-author Mary Kay Downing have traced the progression of American Indian Studies in their 1991 article in *Wicazo Sa Review.* The informative article concerns the direction of what they call intercultural education. The authors conclude that American Indian Studies is "setting the stage for new strategies in interdisciplinary teaching about intercultural matters," but they have little to say about the future of the defensive, regulatory, and transformative functions of the American Indian Studies discipline as it regards the essential concepts of Native sovereignty in treaty and indigenous models.[22]

If those functions are to be achieved, several requirements must be met. First, an autonomous model with departmental status free from the constraints and interests imposed by related disciplines such as anthropology and history or even Ethnic Studies must be initiated as the component through which the discipline of American Indian Studies can be forged. This mechanism would oppose the marginality always accorded Native populations in classic disciplines and cultural studies areas as well as Ethnic Studies. Second, faculty positions and administrative positions must be filled by hiring persons with some of the following qualifications: They must be enrolled citizens of Indian Nations who hold academic credentials, and they must hold considerable tribally specific credentials (experience, language, politics, and other cultural ties to specific homelands, reservations). Further, they must have taken some American Indian Studies courses that provide them with an acquaintance of the bibliographies and models in Native Studies of the past twenty years. These requirements are admittedly idealistic and most practitioners in Native Studies today believe that although these requirements are ideal, substantial variation must be allowed.

Several objections to these requirements immediately arise. First, if only a few colleges have American Indian Studies courses, the question of whether it is wise to require faculty members to have taken them is problematic. Second, the requirement that faculty members be Indians is widely and loudly disputed as indefensible. Many believe that to require faculty persons to be of a particular political or legal or tribal category is essentialist, exclusionary, and racist. There is no doubt that some of these objections, as well as the requirements, need further analysis. There can be no doubt, however, that the success of American Indian Studies as an academic discipline goes hand in hand with the nurturing and development of intellectuals and scholars from within the target population. As a final requirement for disciplinary structure, an American Indian Studies model should include in its curriculum plan five parts: a Native language component, a political component, a legal component, an artistic component, and a research component. Some have suggested that a comparative religion background would be of greater value than the political component. Although, generally, this is a view of those who want to focus more fully on the discipline's cultural parameter than on the historical or legal factor, this is not an either-or matter. Perhaps the comparative religion requirement could be added in certain graduate programs or postgraduate or preparatory studies.

A long and complex route is required for dealing with an incredible number of communities to get a single course established, to say nothing of establishing an entire course of study. Yet, to be successful in the development of a new epistemology, course development and faculty and staff development must go hand in hand. As these matters now exist, a single American Indian Studies faculty person is hired by a university to begin or sustain a program.

He or she has little choice but to reach out to anthropology or history departments or humanities or social science entities for course development, using what many in American Indian Studies call an "old wine in new bottles" approach to curriculum development. Disorganization, conflict, and confusion often result. As American Indian Studies programs now exist at U.S. universities, they presume to serve five constituencies: students, faculty, staff, institutions, and communities, in that order. From their inception in 1969, these programs have offered either a certificate, a minor, or a major comprised of a collection of courses taught by faculty credentialed from a limited number of disciplines such as anthropology, history, literature, sociology, or politics. These courses would either have Native content added to pre-existing formats or have Native content framed and interpreted from status quo perspectives. Though largely taught by non-Native faculty, even Native faculty follow these patterns, in part because of training and indoctrination.

The power to change university systems and epistemologies resides in faculties. Because those in university systems know this to be true, and because there is a fear of deconstructing the mainstream cultural practices that amount to a reinscribing of White supremacy, one finds American Indians at work in universities in near isolation from one another. Understanding that this isolation is a function of racism and hegemony in university systems is critical to finding alternatives. Essential to the establishment of any new epistemology is a concentration of like-minded scholars in a place where intellectual and academic work can overlap, feed off one another, and provide the means to construct authority in a body of knowledge. Furthermore, many seasoned scholars in the discipline conceive of a department in which Native elders have status, where their unique knowledge and skills are used even though they do not have academic credentials. In the hierarchical world of academia, however, such scholars are rarely allowed, let alone nurtured.

If a university is unable or unwilling to meet these minimum standards and efforts in developing faculties, it should abandon its initiation of an American Indian Studies curriculum. Under no circumstances should a mere collection of courses be understood as a sufficient directive toward a disciplinary approach to indigenous knowledge bases. The idea that we must start with a collection of courses and then add to them, paying no attention to the development of a body of scholars to make up a tenured faculty system, is an idea that has already failed. It is time to realize that the postcolonial characteristics of American Indian Studies developments in U.S. universities will in no substantial way provide a case for nation-tribal identity, which is the discipline's main directive. It is time to realize that Native scholarship emerges not from subculture or class positions in American society but from traditions inherent in sovereign tribal nationhood.

As with all disciplines, a strategy is essential for evaluating and credentialing the faculty and the curricular development and the course of study. An association of American Indian Studies scholars is needed to serve as a certification board that would have information available to all university and professional components concerning standards. Legal scholar Vine Deloria Jr. has argued in a recent publication that the question of standards and "who is in charge?" are vital, especially in the light of more than twenty years of development and experience, some of it incredibly corrupt.[23] An invaluable tool for students, faculty, researchers, and intellectuals, such a board of examiners would articulate the function of scholarship as far as Native populations in this country are concerned. It could identify what is important concerning the "national" within Native Studies. Such a board might point the ways Native Studies as an academic discipline can be a tool for recovering from a damaging colonial past, both for Indians and others. It could also be helpful in devising strategies in assisting scholars in the ongoing bid for control of the definitions of national identity. Such a board might end the conflict between ethnicity and indigenousness, which is at the heart of American Indians' struggles to forge a new epistemology and move away from the confused directions the study of ethnicity in the United States is now taking.

American Indian intellectual traditions have been directly and negatively affected by cultural studies and components such as Ethnic Studies, which have a tendency to obliterate differences and assume commonalities across cultures. Many early textbooks in Ethnic Studies not only failed to include the concepts of "sovereignty," "nationalism," or "third world" that are essential to the Indian-White dialogue in America, they even rejected these concepts as a part of the U.S. reality, arguing instead that the more standard Ethnic Studies concepts—such as immigration, slavery, assimilation, multiculturalism, diversity, or postcolonial studies—could be used to describe the essential differences inherent in American Indian experiences. [*standard concepts*]

American Indian Studies pursues in its curriculum models an interrogation of the means by which a positive definition of tribal nationhood in contemporary American life might be articulated because Indian Nations, called First Nations in Canada, do exist in the modern U.S. social and political landscape. Their possession of land, language, and treaty rights cannot be subsumed, ignored, disguised, or deformed under the rubric of ethnicity, as they have been in scholarship and policy. To do so denies the historical fact that tribal peoples possessed this continent centuries before the United States existed and had a wide-ranging intellectual presence in this specific geography that deserves apprehension. The erasure of any such history might be called at the very least academic malfeasance; at worst, academic racism and colonialism.

Selected Bibliography

Annis, Robert, Beatrice Medicine, and Ken Coates. "American Indian Studies Programs in the United States: Growth and Development." In *Abstracts of Native Studies*, vol. 2. Brandon, Manitoba: Abstracts of Native Studies Press, 1985.

Ballinger, Franchot. *A Guide to Native American Studies Programs.* Association for the Study of American Indian Literatures, 1933.

Banks, James A. *Teaching Strategies for Ethnic Studies*, 3d ed. Needham Heights, Mass.: Allyn and Bacon, Inc., 1985.

Barnhardt, Ray. "Higher Education in the Fourth World: Indigenous People Take Control." *Canadian Journal of Native Education* 18 (2): 201–16.

Bataille, Gretchen, Miguel Carranza, and Laurie Lisa. *Ethnic Studies in the United States.* New York: Garland, 1996.

Bengelsdorf, Winnie. *Ethnic Studies in Higher Education.* New York: Arno Press, 1978.

Carter, Deborah J., and Reginald Wilson. *Minorities in Higher Education.* Washington, D.C.: American Council on Education, Office of Minorities in Higher Education, 1994.

Center for the Study of Democratic Institutions. *The Establishment and All That.* Santa Barbara, Calif.: Center for the Study of Democratic Institutions, 1970, p. 71.

Champagne, Duane. "American Indian Studies Is for Everyone." *American Indian Quarterly* 20 (1): 77–82.

Cook-Lynn, Elizabeth. "Who Stole Native American Studies?" *Wicazo Sa Review* 12 (1): 9–28.

———. "American Indian Intellectualism and the New Indian Story." *American Indian Quarterly* 20 (1): 57–76.

"Degrees Offered by College and Subject." In *The College Blue Book.* New York: Macmillan, 1994.

DeJong, David H. *Promises of the Past: A History of Indian Education.* Golden, Colo.: North American Press, 1993.

Deloria, Vine Jr. *Indian Education Confronts the Seventies.* 5 vols. Oglala, S.D.: American Indian Resource Associates, 1974.

Fuchs, Estelle, and Robert J. Havinghurst. *To Live on This Earth: American Indian Education.* Albuquerque: University of New Mexico Press, 1983.

Guyette, Susan, and Charlotte Heth. *Issues for the Future of American Indian Studies.* Los Angeles: American Indian Studies Center, University of California, 1985.

Hampton, Eber. "Toward a Redefinition of American Indian/Alaska Native Education." *Canadian Journal of Native Education* 20 (2): 261–310.

Jolola, Ted, ed. "Introduction" to special edition of *Wicazo Sa Review* 13(2): 5–17.

O'Brien, Eileen. "American Indians in Higher Education." *Research Briefs of the American Council on Higher Education* 3 (1993): 1–5.

Philp, Kenneth R. *Indian Self-Rule.* Salt Lake, Utah: Howe Brothers, 1986.

Reddy, Marlita, ed. *Statistical Record of Native North Americans.* Detroit, Mich.: Gale Research, 1993.

Reyhner, Jon, and Jeanne Eder. "A History of Indian Education." In Jon Reyhner, ed., *Teaching American Indian Students.* Norman: University of Oklahoma Press, 1992. Pp. 33–58.

Szasz, Margaret. *Education and the American Indian.* Albuquerque: University of New Mexico Press, 1974.

Notes

1. In 1924 Congress passed a statute conferring citizenship on all American Indians born within the United States. By reason of the Fourteenth Amendment, the grant of federal citizenship had the additional effect of making Indians citizens of the states where they resided. American Indians were not allowed to vote in Arizona until 1948 or in New Mexico until 1962, however.

2. Charles Wilkinson, *American Indians, Time, and the Law* (New Haven, Conn.: Yale University Press, 1987), provides a good overview of U.S. Supreme Court rulings relating to American Indian law from 1959 to the early 1980s.

3. For a thorough discussion of Indian law, see Felix Cohen, *Handbook of Federal Indian Law* (Washington, D.C.: U.S. Government Printing Office, 1942).

4. This definition is from Jose David Saldivar, *The Dialectics of Our America* (Durham, N.C.: Duke University Press, 1991), 149.

5. Newsletter distributed at the 1972 conference in San Diego.

6. In 1953 the U.S. Congress formally adopted House Concurrent Resolution 108, a policy of "termination," with the express aim to make American Indians within the United States subject to the same laws and entitled to the same privi-

leges and responsibilities as other U.S. citizens. In other words, the unique treaty relationship between Indian tribes and the federal government was to be unilaterally terminated. Tribal lands of the more than one hundred terminated tribes were thus to pass out of trust and be sold or mortgaged. Legislative and judicial responsibilities related to tribal affairs shifted from the federal government to various local state governments. Such federal services to tribes and tribal members as education, housing, emergency welfare, and health care were no longer available. Individual members of terminated tribes were no longer considered "Indians" for purposes of jurisdictional questions arising on Indian lands. Tribal governmental structures collapsed because most of their functions were terminated. Tribal and economic effects were tremendously negative, the ramifications of which are still felt today.

Public Law 280 was also passed in 1953, by which Congress empowered five states (Missouri, California, Nebraska, Oregon, Wisconsin) to take over civil and criminal jurisdiction of Indian reservations within their boundaries without consent of the tribes. So even if a tribe was not terminated, some of its functions were if its lands fell within the boundaries of those five states. At the same time as the termination policy took effect, the Bureau of Indian Affairs was encouraging Indians to leave the reservation under its "relocation" program. This program, which provided grants to American Indians to move to selected urban centers (Los Angeles, San Francisco, Oakland, Denver, Minneapolis, Dallas, Cleveland, Albuquerque), was supposedly developed in response to the high unemployment within reservations. A common result, however, was that Indian families joined the ranks of the existing urban poor in the relocation cities, plus the Indians experienced the trauma of dislocation from their tribal lands and communities.

7. In *The Establishment and All That: A Collection of Major Articles* for Center Magazine (Santa Barbara, Calif.: Center for the Study of Democratic Institutions, 1970).

8. Ibid.

9. In 1970 President Richard Nixon issued a statement on Indian affairs that declared termination to have been a failure, and he called on Congress to repudiate it as a policy. He stressed the continuing importance of the trust relationship between the federal government and the tribes, and he urged a program of legislation to permit tribes to manage their affairs with a maximum degree of autonomy. Spin-off effects of the administration's new policy included the Indian Financing Act of 1974, the Indian Self-Determination and Educational Assistance Act of 1975, and the American Indian Policy Review Commission of 1975.

10. The Indian Self-Determination and Educational Assistance Act authorized the Secretaries of Interior, Health, Education, and Welfare to enter into contracts

under which the tribes themselves would assume responsibility for the administration of federal Indian programs.

11. For a fuller discussion of this process, see H. Aram Veeser, *The New Historicism* (New York: Routledge, Chapman, and Hall, Inc., 1989).

12. Rudolf Kaiser, "Chief Seattle's Speech(es): American Origins and European Reception," in *Recovering the World: Essays on Native American Literature*, ed. Brian Swann and Arnold Krupat (Berkeley: University of California Press, 1987), 497–536. Kaiser provides a thorough analysis of the inauthenticity of Chief Seattle's speeches.

13. See Russell Thornton, "American Indian Studies as an Academic Discipline." *American Indian Culture and Research Journal* 2 (3–4): 10–19.

14. See John Greenway, "Will the Indians Get Whitey?" *National Review,* March 11, 1969.

15. Fergus M. Bordewich, *Killing the White Man's Indian: Reinventing Native Americans at the End of the Twentieth Century* (New York: Bantam Doubleday Dell Publishing Group, 1996).

16. The Indian Reorganization Act (also known as the Wheeler-Howard Act) ended the practice of allotment; extended indefinitely the trust period of existing trust lands; authorized the acquisition of land, the establishment of water rights, and the creation of new reservations; and launched an Indian credit program.

17. For example, see Adam Roberts's foreword in Daniel Patrick Moynihan, *Pandaemonium: Ethnicity in International Politics* (New York: Oxford University Press, 1993).

18. Moynihan, *Pandaemonium,* 172.

19. Beatrice Medicine, "The American Indian and American Indian Studies Programs," in Jeannette Henry, ed., *The American Indian Reader: Anthropology* (San Francisco: Indian Historian Press, 1972), 13–20.

20. In his *Interior Landscapes* (Minneapolis: University of Minnesota Press, 1990), Gerald Vizenor claims that the "American Indian Movement put my name on their enemies list; four trivial goons, two of whom had once been friends of mine, were told to make life miserable for me at an education conference at the University of Minnesota at Duluth. The goons arrived at the back of the auditorium in the middle of my lecture and blocked the exits. I raised a radical pose and turned over the microphone to the goon who could not resist a chance to rave at an audience" (240). Vizenor continues: "The confusion at the conference, my wild lunch invitation to the goons, and the unsolicited protection of the tribal students at the university, gave me time to leave down the back stairs and beat a retreat out of the city. . . . The American Indian Movement leaders became the new tribal totalitarians and the least tolerant of dissidence" (240).

21. See, for example, M. Annette Jaimes, "American Indian Studies: Toward an Indigenous Model." *American Indian Culture and Research Journal* 11 (3): 1–16.

22. William Willard and Mary Kay Downing, "American Indian Studies and Inter-Cultural Education" *Wicazo Sa Review* 7 (2): 1–8.

23. Vine Deloria Jr., "Indian Studies—The Orphan of Academia," in Deloria, *Indian Education in America* (Boulder, Colo.: American Indian Science and Engineering Society, 1991).

Whither the Asian American Subject?

LANE RYO HIRABAYASHI &
MARILYN CABALLERO ALQUIZOLA

IT IS WIDELY RECOGNIZED THAT THE PROVISIONS OF U.S. immigration reform, signed into effect by President Lyndon B. Johnson in 1965, have had a tremendous impact on individuals and populations of Asian descent in America. Now in a new millennium, population growth, hetero-geneity, and complexity are at a zenith, whether nationalities, class level, types of family formation, and sociocultural or political adaptations are consid-ered. More than ever before, Asians in America today have widely varying ties to their Asian roots as well as their placements in the United States, and their strategies for managing these complexities are as multifaceted.[1]

Not surprisingly, as a result of these changes, a growing number of pub-lications reflect the challenges regarding the "subject" of Asian American Studies (hereafter AAS). These challenges have been issued by theoreticians influenced by postmodernism in its various forms, by those in disciplinary fields whose work focuses on Asians in America, as well as by scholars from interdisciplinary enterprises that fall under the rubrics of American, cultural, and diasporic studies.[2] First, some scholars ask, for example, if there is really any such thing as an "Asian American" subject per se; that is, what makes this a distinctive and viable subject category? A corollary question is why some groups are included in the designation Asian American while other groups whose experiences seem to pertain to this generic category are left out. Second, the construction of an Asian American subject is predicated upon an inherent White-non-White dichotomy that tacitly fixes peoples of Asian descent in the United States into a subjugated, oppressed, and "othered" category—a population that coheres only in relation to the Euro-American majority. Some authors reject this premise as well as the seeming position of subordination that it creates.

Third, some scholars claim that the generalized amalgamation of the term Asian American results in essentialism and the elision of intragroup differences. Specifically, some have charged that an emphasis on "Asian Americanness" generates a myopia characterized by a failure to perceive how class, gender, sexuality, and even ethnicity come into play when persons are marginalized, silenced, or otherwise subject to victimization by their "own."[3] Fourth, other scholars argue that global economic restructuring, transnational migration, and electronic communication technologies have shattered the territorial bases and boundaries that lay at the foundation of the pre-1965 Asian American ethnic identities and communities.[4]

Finally, still other academics propose that postmodernist and poststructuralist perspectives can lead to new and innovative forms of anti-essentialist coalition building, which would revolve around "recognition of differences" rather than forced and narrow generalizations based on such similarities as "race" and ethnicity. This notion has effectively challenged male-dominant essentialism. If the "subject" invoked by Asian American Studies is put in doubt and permanently dissolved, however, it follows that construction of the key tropes of AAS —including Asian American history, community, political interests, and so on—can also be challenged. This has far-reaching implications, especially during a period when people of Asian descent are closer than ever to sustained levels of political participation and empowerment. In short, once priority is given to difference, and to difference alone and exclusively, it follows that the assertion of political unanimity between such a disparate set of peoples crumbles.[5]

While acknowledging that criticism is often a useful vehicle to heighten reflexivity about the limitations of any form of theoretical or methodological practice, we find ourselves struggling to correlate these points with the historical roots and political goals of the field of Asian American Studies.[6] We also note that critics, across the board, fail to draw a distinction between the discursive or rhetorical and the strategic practices that make up the overall education, cultural, and political domain of AAS. At least part of the problem is that it appears that critics have not done the archival, oral history, and the primary and secondary source work necessary to appreciate and thoroughly understand the roots of the very field that they aspire to deconstruct and ultimately dismiss. Nonetheless, because of rapid and profound demographic changes over the past three decades, Asian American Studies has had to rethink the definition of its subject, to determine whether the field is able to encompass the ethnic complexity of Asian American identities, including the political and cultural dimensions of the term.

Our thesis is that despite the complex controversies and polemical debates between subject areas and interest groups within the field—reflecting the pluralities of cultural nationalism, gender, sexuality, race, and ethnicity—there is actually a fair amount of continuity between the issues and methods of AAS, from the 1970s until now. A discussion of this continuity demonstrates that AAS is indeed a field rather than a mere conglomeration of focal areas with an "Asian American" subject matter. An examination of historical roots reminds us that the evolution of the field, its principles and goals, is vitally contingent on safe-guarding its autonomy. On this basis we sketch some of the field's key epistemological, theoretical, and methodological orientations to demonstrate how and why this is so. At the same time, when one considers the institutionalization of AAS in universities across the country, a disturbing tendency is evident: the reinforcement of old and the creation of new hierarchies. In our view discussion and analysis of this tendency is the key to eliminating or at least controlling the worst aspects of hierarchy, especially in regard to a field like AAS with such a strong commitment to social justice.

We also submit that AAS has generally failed to empower itself institutionally since its early development, which has resulted in significant limitations and constraints, simply because we have lost sight of the importance of self-determination in the necessary pursuit of new directions. As in all evolutionary processes, there is good and bad in this. At one end of the spectrum, a very male-dominated cultural nationalist stance in the initial discourses of AAS was badly in need of critique. Indeed, the initial discourses needed to be deconstructed. At the other end of the spectrum, postmodern applications of *différance* often have conflated the hierarchy of race, ethnic, class, and gender positions within the dominant society, almost ignoring relationships of power. There is a tug of war between these discourses, and in the future Ethnic Studies must negotiate these struggles to be truly effective and meaningful. Although seemingly a matter of academic debate, an analysis of contemporary challenges to "the Asian American subject" has profound implications for a wide range of educational and related policy issues, as well as for multicultural and diversity issues as a whole, which continue to divide American society in the twenty-first century.

Roots, Premises, and Propositions

Playing a dynamic role in the oppositional cultural and political climate of the 1960s, the movement to create what is now known as Ethnic Studies on campuses exploded onto the academic scene in 1968.[7] Asian American Studies was one of its constituent areas. The vision of the women and men who fought to build Ethnic Studies broke radically from that of the status quo in higher education. In part, this was because militant strikes and a series of protests were initially necessary to create institutional space for Ethnic Studies and AAS in an often rigid, traditional university setting. Furthermore, students and their supporters explicitly rejected the premise that the academy could generate viable, authoritative knowledge of Third World peoples and their experiences.[8] This realization was a result of pragmatic and basic deconstructions of existing knowledge production, fired by the spirit of the Civil Rights movement, the free speech movement, and the extreme dissatisfaction concerning U.S. involvement in Vietnam. Why was history only about Euro-Americans? Why did basic literature in the university only represent the English and the Anglo-American? Such simple and basic questions were asked about why the experiences of those who are not White, Euro-Americans were erased and relegated merely to singular chapters on the slavery of African Americans, a passing reference to Chinese workers on the railroads, a paragraph on the concentration camps where 110,000 Japanese Americans were imprisoned, euphemistically called "relocation centers," and no reference whatsoever to other people of color who helped build this nation. Where were our voices, our perspectives?[9]

In light of U.S. involvement in Vietnam, many student activists also realized that the front lines were constituted of men of color and of the working classes. Furthermore, Asian American soldiers that served in Vietnam were brutally confronted by the reality and the irony that Asians were used to kill Asians. With these and other realizations, a Third World consciousness was born; students and community activists agreed that the ability to grasp such experiences lay well beyond the ken of traditional academic institutions, the majority of faculty, as well as faculty's practices for generating knowledge.[10] To examine these assertions further, it is necessary to delineate broad issues of power and "knowledge production" in the context of the academy—the primary institutional structure charged with the responsibility of education.

Knowledge Production and Institutional Structures

Figure 1 presents a heuristic typology, delineating ideal types of educational production and reproduction in academic settings.[11] The first of the two key dimensions of the typology revolves around power over "educational resources," including whether such resources are rooted in one's own experiences or those that are exogenous. In the second dimension, simply speaking, the locus of "decision making and power" is dichotomized into situations, in which a given group either has or does not have self-determination. These dichotomies result in four cells that represent broad types of "educational production" that racialized minorities in the United States have had to deal with.[12]

FIGURE 1. The Matrix of Power within Processes of Educational Production and Reproduction in Asian American and Ethnic Studies

	DECISION MAKING AND POWER	
	OWN	OTHER
OWN (*Insider*)	Autonomous education	Alienated education
OTHER (*Outsider*)	Appropriated education	Imposed education

EDUCATIONAL RESOURCES

In its most destructive form educational production takes place in terms of a dominant "outsider's" perspectives on a minority group's history and experiences and subsequently determines images of the latter's roles and positions in the larger society. Similarly, inculcation in educational production occurs in institutional settings in which the "analyzed" group has no decision-making power with which to shape its own representations. This idea is worth exploring further in more detail. Although minority groups may "inform" by way of being the subject-object of surveys, ethnographies, creative literatures, and so on, they have had no real voice. Historically, before the creation of Ethnic Studies, minority groups did not have the academic privilege

174 / L.R. HIRABAYASHI & M.C. ALQUIZOLA

of defining the analyses of their production in whatever form it took. An informant, for instance, is used for gathering data while the scholar attempts to "make sense" of it. Even the racial-ethnic poet or novelist, although perhaps praised in the academy, is nevertheless often at the mercy of the literary critic who "interprets" within the traditional scholarly paradigm. This is not to say that there were no racial-ethnic scholars per se before Ethnic Studies, but rather that such scholars were constrained by the discourses that confined them in the first place. Thus an insider's perspective—which would include worldview and interests that are generated by positionalities of race, ethnicity, class, gender, and sexuality—traditionally did not figure in the formulation of the analyses.

Similarly, cultural differences and class positions often are not taken into account in traditional psychological analyses, mainstream feminist discourses, and so on. A discussion of individuation in psychology, for example, often does not take into account how cultural differences compound the tensions of generational difference, and the middle-class concern of professional women entering the work force completely ignores the particular oppressions of Asian American and other Third World women in sweatshops. To be fair, we also note that perspectives of gender and sexuality often are ignored in analyses that take only race and ethnicity into account. Early Asian American discourses on race issues, for example, paid attention to the oppression of male subjects because men disproportionately comprised the original communities of Asians in America, in Chinese and Filipino immigrant communities especially. Scholars must continue to struggle with and overcome this focus on male positionalities. Nonetheless, that traditional academic discourse is elitist in nature is a given. The discursive practice in which minority groups are the "analyzed" becomes the basis of an "*imposed* (and thus oppressive) education" that denies, alters, ignores, and devalues not only the ethnic group's histories and experiences as these are lived and perceived by members of that group, but also precludes these perspectives from informing and shaping alternative analyses.[13]

Within the same heuristic typology there are also forms of educational production that are mixed in nature and varied in terms of their possible freight. *Alienated education* entails a situation in which a group's own worldview is drawn from as a resource; however, in terms of the ultimate formulations and uses of that resource, the real decision making is simultaneously determined by some external educational entity. One can certainly identify cases that illustrate the negative dimensions of such alienated forms of education. For example, Asian Studies programs have resources and tools for the study of Asians in America that are based on in-depth historical and socio-cultural knowledge of the countries of origin. To this extent, they might claim to base their educational products on an insider's perspective, although their analyses or interpretations often are definitively not from the "inside." When peoples of Asian descent in America (whose experiences are described by the academy) are denied the power to shape, represent, and present these experiences, they are subjected to an alienating and negating process. Similarly, the application of postmodernist perspectives to Asian American writings, solely to demonstrate how Asian American literary production fits into a theoretical cubby hole, so to speak, is another example of a kind of alienated cultural production, because it deflects focus from the actual product and maintains the dominance of an external framework of aesthetic principles. *Appropriated education* represents another configuration of these elements. In this framework the views of "others"—which is to say, exogenous theoretical, analytic, and conceptual resources such as Marxism or feminism—are taken and applied to one's own history and experiences in an effort to illuminate or reexamine these from other vantage points and perspectives.

The movement to build Ethnic Studies, as an institutionalized educational alternative, can thus be viewed as an explicit reaction to "oppressive" forms of educational production and reproduction.[14] In its day this was a revolutionary vision insofar as it posited "ethnic education" as an autonomous educational enterprise, diametrically opposed to that generated by academicians working within the domain of "imposed education."[15] At this juncture it is useful to specify what Asian American Studies is all about in more detail. Doing so will ultimately enable us to see more readily the achievements as well as the challenges that face the field in the new millennium.

What Is Asian American Studies?

What specifically does the field of Asian American Studies entail? Asian American Studies is inherently a part of the larger field of Ethnic Studies. The student, community, and faculty activists who founded the field uniformly agreed that an alternative curriculum was imperative, given that "both implicit and explicit discriminatory attitudes and practices have and do exist in the academy and in our society."[16] Given this charge, AAS was and still remains a transformative enterprise, encompassing critique and practice to bring about constructive social change in pursuit of social justice, whenever and wherever necessary.[17] In terms of its day-to-day operations in the academy, AAS involves research, curriculum development, and teaching, all of which pertain to histories and experiences, identities, social and community formations, politics, and contemporary concerns of Asian Americans.[18] Although academic in nature, many Asian Americanists still are strongly committed to community-based issues and projects, at either ethnic-specific or "pan-Asian" levels. Others are committed to the extent that real-world politics informs their research directions and perspectives. Whether these scholars focus on a single community, the broader Asian American community, or take on such global pan-Asian issues as the problems of overseas domestic workers, political concerns are an integral part of their epistemology and methodology.[19]

In terms of institutional politics within the academy, AAS aims to make education more democratic—more "equitable, diverse, and inclusive"—through the examination of the experiences of racialized ethnic "minorities" in the United States, or populations whose sufferings and contributions have often been ignored and thus erased.[20] Democratic education would truly be democratized by these activities. Democratization of instruction and institutions, in turn, promotes a more meaningful and relevant educational experience that would effect wider sectors of the population at large. Because scholarship in Ethnic and Asian American Studies reveals that assumptions and biases are inherently a part of intellectual production, these studies provide a language and a standpoint from which people of color in the academy can raise critical discourse regarding the university's role in the production of knowledge, the inherent strengths and weaknesses of that knowledge, and the uses which that knowledge, as constructed by the university's faculty, is put to. Ultimately, the discourses of AAS and Ethnic Studies in general would only invigorate knowledge production that in itself is incomplete, being culturally based in its inception. These studies could only make existing discourses self-reflexive and critical of their own established assumptions. Perhaps because it does just that, there is institutional and public resistance to such an autonomous and self-defined Ethnic Studies.

The construction of ethnic-specific and pan-Asian subjects (in their early development as well as now) is strategy designed for specific rhetorical and political projects. On this basis AAS entails a coalition of like-minded students, professors, and activists who:

• Promote the analysis and critique of the "power-knowledge" matrix that is formulated and imposed by the academy.

- Critique, reject, and seek to dismantle assimilationist and Eurocentric and Euro-American-centered premises and biases.
- Promote the exploration of alternative, phenomenologically grounded ways to construct ethnic-specific as well as pan-Asian American "subjects."
- Promote self-determination over cultural resources, representations, and decision making.
- Reject the disarticulation of domestic and global links, because such links shape the perceptions and the very destinies of Asians in America.
- Seek ways to link Asian Americans, as Third World people, to other domestic and international struggles for equality and justice.
- Seek to connect the study of "race" and racialization to studies of other forms of social oppression, including those based on class, gender, and sexuality.[21]

Here we acknowledge that the term *American* in Asian American may be problematic for some, and with good reason because the very word *American*, in terms of its early historical usage, excluded all persons of color, including those with rightful, native birthright on this continent. Those who have experienced the painful realities of this apartheid history, may cringe at the implied identification with "America." Certainly, many people do not identify with the term, American. The term need not carry the connotation of idealism or the desire of assimilation, however. It is merely a practical term that asserts that all Asians, whether immigrant or United States-born, deserve and demand full and equal participation in a country where the economic and judicial systems have oppressed (and continue to oppress) them, both domestically and in the global arena. In this sense Asian Americans who identify as such believe that they should have fair and equal treatment in all facets of life in the United States, and that this treatment does not of necessity require them to "assimilate" by obliterating what they wish to retain of their diverse ethnic heritages. This also entails taking a critical perspective of the Euro-American culture in the United States, simply because of its dominance and its ability to define or absorb other cultures.

In short, the immediate and long-term goals of AAS were oriented toward a shift in thinking about society and intellectual traditions and ultimately toward personal agency and social change, which obviously includes conceptual changes. The field of AAS thus offers students a set of alternative and potentially oppositional intellectual perspectives and resources—simultaneously psychological, cultural, social, political, and aesthetic. These can be used for reviewing, re-visioning, and reconstructing their individual and collective destinies. The subject category of "Asian American" is therefore a convenient designation that can be used to identify those persons of Asian descent in the United States who are interested in maintaining their diverse ethnic heritages and willing to struggle to shape their boundaries and directions.[22] Obviously, there are complex differences between individuals of Asian descent that are based on issues of ethnicity, class, sexuality, and gender, not to mention the separate histories and contemporary experiences that are shaped in part by distinct combinations of these various categories. Nevertheless, the goals and political projects of AAS may always affect, assist, and invigorate those individuals in different ways and at different times. Furthermore, the erasure or disempowerment of AAS would indeed create a vacuum in the lives of these individuals whether they are conscious of it or not.

Implications for Educational Production

As discussed, the initial vision of AAS revolved around a strident analysis of institutional power. To counteract the academy's hegemony, students and faculty wanted to create a curriculum that assumed that "the thought, meaning, and understanding of Third World people must be based on the perceptions and conceptualizations of those who experience those lives."[23] This vision was initially nonessentialist; that is, it involved the construction of a subject, in effect a politicized reconstruction of self, politically informed about relationships of power and willing to engage at some level in alternative or oppositional thoughts and acts. It is also an evolving cultural construction. Practitioners of AAS often identify primarily as ethnic-specific, but they can also become "pan-Asian American" if and when strategically necessary. Even within these "pan-ethnic" moments, however, each distinct ethnic group could simultaneously keep their priorities and needs distinct. For example, the anti-immigration initiatives of contemporary times threaten some sectors of the Asian American communities more than they do others. This is true of the Filipino American, Chinese American, and Korean American communities (to name but a few); however, this issue does not affect these three populations in exactly the same way; nor does it affect the Japanese American community as much.

A commonality with the Chicano/a and Latino/a communities can also be found in this particular example, and thus anti-immigration politics becomes an Ethnic Studies issue. Although the anti-affirmative action amendment concerning education in California is said (according to media statistics) to affect the Chicano/a and African American communities more than the Asian American communities, whose voting trends have unfortunately shown a move toward conservatism, the passage of this proposition remains an Asian American Studies issue for the following reasons: (1) many Asian Americans still need affirmative action in other areas, such as to counteract the glass-ceiling syndrome; (2) some of the ethnic-specific Asian American communities may still need and benefit from affirmative action in education; and (3) as an ultimate strategy, community-specific issues should always be supported, at one level or another, on a pan-ethnic basis because the establishment has always used a "divide, conquer, and rule" strategy to its benefit. Therefore, identification is always political and strategically fluctuating.

Knowledge and "meaning" in Asian American Studies revolved around the assumption that interested students and faculty would take an active and central role in determining the content of their own education. What kind of research and pedagogical outcomes initially followed from this? On some campuses AAS became an institutional vehicle to authorize "community-based" orientations as the key criterion to determine the focuses, contents, and methodologies (including the pedagogies) of the studies. In retrospect, this agenda was implicitly and explicitly tied to both ethnic-specific cultural nationalism and the "internal colonial" model.[24] For example, student and community activist turned professor George K. Woo uses such tropes as "Asian American," "the community," and so forth: "The question of control becomes the central issue. . . . It is imperative that people, whether they are teachers, students, parents, etc., who involve themselves in Asian American Studies be involved and be part of the community the Studies are supposed to serve. Isn't community control the prime reason we had the strike? Isn't community control the reason we want Asian American Studies?"[25]

This type of vocabulary used by Woo and others in the 1970s may be viewed as rhetorical today. At the time, however, it provided a convenient way to identify and seek solidarity around common needs and interests. The stance of "community control" also allowed for what were in fact both a foundational principle and the modus operandi of the studies: ethnic-specific self-determination. In our opinion this foundational principle of self-determination, an integral part and basis for the field, has been effectively disregarded and muted in the name of an institutional professionalism that seeks a nonpolitical and nonthreatening route in the academy and a pseudo-intellectual posture that would dismiss political discourse as a nostalgic trope. In establishing a self-determined and self-defined curriculum, however, responsibility and accountability in research, teaching, and organizing were fostered. Students

a move away

It must be harder than ever in today's climate —

and faculty worked in conjunction with community-based political and service organizations to ameliorate and attempt to correct injustices throughout the larger political and socioeconomic order in such sectors as the educational system, the social service system, the justice system, and so forth.[26]

In one of its initial versions AAS thus entailed phenomenological and pragmatic epistemologies, both of which were rooted in a specific community base and practice to ensure accountability. Quite naturally, the key methodological approaches practitioners emphasized followed from these premises and included the development of ethnic-specific "insiders'" histories, oral history projects, literary compilations, "participatory action research" projects that were designed to address concrete and specific needs and advocacy.[27] Other concerns, however, were added to this agenda from the very beginning. First, some AAS programs paid more attention to developing an explicit class analysis of Asians in America. For example, early statements on the evolution of Berkeley's curriculum reflect an explicitly Marxist orientation.[28] Consideration of this point exemplifies how and why "appropriated education" has been part-and-parcel of the Asian American Studies enterprise. Retrospectively, it is worth noting that this was not a simple and mechanical application of Marx to the experiences of Asian Americans; rather, it was one informed by the specific needs of a given community. Early formulations were therefore provisional and directed toward a careful examination of how the conceptual tools of Marxist and neo-Marxist thought might be effectively appropriated, given that the trajectories of populations of Asian descent in the United States had their own characteristics and particular histories.

A central feature that helps account for the appropriation of the Marxist paradigm by members of the Berkeley and UCLA programs, for example, was its seeming utility as a "science" for the critique of capitalism on one hand and the implementation of revolutionary social change on the other. The Marxist paradigm also prioritizes the role of ordinary members of the working class in the struggle. Skeptical readers should not discount the tremendous impact that socialist ideologies had on people of color in the United States during the 1960s and 1970s, when challenges were being put to Western colonial and neocolonial rule throughout Asia, Africa, and Latin America by leaders under the influence of socialist ideologies; nor should readers forget social critic Noam Chomsky's thesis that the United States and northern Europe went to great lengths to ensure that no country advocating an "alternative path to capitalism" would be allowed to succeed.[29] For the record it should also be noted that this orientation brought certain AAS programs into direct articulation with explicitly revolutionary organizers and organizations, especially in California, an expression that sometimes resulted in periods of intense and open political struggle, especially in competition over the "hearts and minds" of students.[30]

Another type of internal struggle within the field of AAS (besides the struggle of Marxism) has to do with a complex set of dynamics that have yet to be analyzed. Some Asian American and Ethnic Studies programs have been the site of controversies having to do with the impact, and in fact the centrality, of gender and sexuality on the dynamics of "race and class" and vice versa.[31] Although some scholars view these struggles as divisive, they in fact promote reflexivity about the biases entailed in the often unexamined, implicitly male-oriented cultural nationalist assumptions that many—women and men alike—held in the early days of AAS. In this fashion if Asian Americanists should take seriously the study of gender and sexual biases and not merely dismiss them as divisive, bourgeois enterprises, the long-term impact of these struggles will very likely energize and strengthen the field. Suffice it to say, then, that some practitioners of AAS have been able to take from mainstream intellectual frameworks, specifically political economy and feminism, and shape them into viable, critical, and useful tools for the development of Asian American and Ethnic Studies.

Issues, Methodological, and Theoretical Orientations

This section identifies broad issues that in turn entail analytical and methodological orientations, each of which serve to unite past concerns with present concerns. One ongoing issue in AAS may be characterized as digging up "the buried past."[32] At one level this pursuit is akin to revisionist history insofar as new sources, creatively used, provide the basis to describe dimensions of U.S. history that have never been adequately captured by mainstream scholarship. Following in the footsteps of such pioneers as Yuji Ichioka and Him Mark Lai, the best of this scholarship combines "movement" sensibilities with the extensive examination of Asian-language resources.[33] Also developed along these lines is the work of such scholars as Marlon K. Hom, Jane Singh, Ben Kobashigawa, and Mitziko Sawada, as are the research agendas developed by Steffi San Buenaventura and Hyung-ju Ahn.[34] Ethnic Studies scholars Ronald Takaki, Sucheng Chan, and Gary Y. Okihiro have worked a variant methodology, examining primarily English-language archival holdings and re-reading these works in terms of their individual and collective standpoints.[35]

Similarly, from 1970 until now, other scholars have prioritized oral histories in giving "voice" to heretofore subaltern and silenced individuals, allowing the latter "pride of place" in terms of envisioning the historicization and conceptualization of their own experiences. Early on, books like Victor and Brett de Barry Nees's *Longtime Californ'* and Bong Youn Choy's study of the early Korean American experience exemplified the potential power of such work.[36] Such contemporary scholars as Arthur Hansen, Valerie Matsumoto, and Karen I. Leonard, among others, have made extensive use of oral history methodologies along these lines.[37]

Interestingly enough, however, much of Asian American literary production, ostensibly fictional, is closely linked to these approaches to scholarship. On the one hand, it is clear that authors often engage in extensive substantive research, collecting oral histories and generally digging up the buried past, to seek perspectives and factual grounding for their writing.[38] On the other hand, once produced, poetry, plays, novels, and short stories have also been used in Asian American Studies courses to generate discussion on subjectivities—perhaps because the passage of time blocks direct access to those who came before us.[39] Also, in terms of an Asian American literary aesthetic development, many creative writers have pushed the boundaries of fiction by blurring the lines between fiction and imaginary biographies.

Agendas revolving around restoring "the buried past" and "giving voice" segue easily into the prioritization of the meaning and role of gender and sexuality in ethnic-specific and pan-Asian American historical topics as well as in contemporary settings.[40] It is worth noting here that, as part of Ethnic Studies, work in AAS has always given preeminence to "race," or more precisely, to processes and dynamics of racialization and racial formation. This emphasis, however, as feminist and Ethnic Studies scholar Johnnella E. Butler has pointed out, has allowed scholars to subsume the importance of other systemic forms of oppression, including ethnicity, class, gender, and sexuality. She argues that the privileging of race as the main issue has resulted in a lack of attention to another important consideration: precisely how the links between these forms of oppression may best be conceptualized. Although research on sexuality has admittedly been a shortcoming in terms of both AAS research production and political organizing, a focus on gender and exploration of why gender biases were all-too-often elided have been ongoing topics in AAS from its earliest days.[41]

In terms of corollary work, which resembles early multidisciplinary classics such as the University of California-Berkeley's anthology *Asian Women*, there is a much wider set of resources to draw from, including pan-Asian volumes such as Asian Women United's *Making Waves* and Kitty Tsui's *Breathless—Erotica*, which anthologizes Asian American lesbian women's writing about sexuality, to "ethnic-specific" offerings. For example, one such pioneering anthology, *Our Feet Walk the Sky*, was produced by a South Asian women's collective.[42] Similarly, Asian American women activist-scholars, such as Bok-Lim Kim, Jacqueline R. Agtuca, and Mila Glodava, should be credited for continuing to bring the issue of domestic violence among Asian American and interracial couples to light.[43]

The literature of "community studies," an early genre of Asian American Studies, is also extant today, although in somewhat altered forms.[44] Some contemporary studies, such as those by David Mas Matsumoto and Wendy L. Ng, simultaneously describe the people, networks, and institutions that knit geographically delimited ethnic enclaves into a whole, at the same time giving voice to individuals and through these voices resuscitating forgotten histories.[45] Researchers whose projects continue this emphasis today include Timothy P. Fong's fascinating study of a newly emergent "suburban Chinatown" formation found in Monterey Park, California, as well as Madhulika Khandelwal's study of the transnationally framed adaptations of South Asians in the United States.[46] Both of these researchers have also paid special attention to the economic and class dimensions of racialization within their examination of network and community formations.

Other authors follow an earlier link between community studies on the one hand and such activist research methodologies as "participatory action research" on the other hand. Early on, scholar-activists like Peggy Li and Lillian Galledo and their colleagues, as well as Ramsay Shu and Adele Salamasina Satele, studied the pressing needs of specific communities: the rights of garment workers in Los Angeles, the impact of so-called urban development on the housing and community needs of elderly Filipino Americans in Sacramento, and the impact of both poverty and the lack of culturally and linguistically sensitive social services for Samoan Americans in Carson, California, respectively.[47] There is a strong affiliation between this kind of methodology and today's action-oriented contributions of, for example, such scholar-activists as Miriam Ching Louie or Edward T. Chang.[48] Another example can be found in Peter Nien-Chu Kiang's contributions. Kiang focuses primarily on new Asian immigrants, specifically Vietnamese and other Southeast Asian refugees, highlighting their experiences with racialization in elementary and high school educational settings.[49]

Similarly, many Asian American Studies faculty have always engaged in social advocacy. For example, the areas of health, mental health services, immigration, and media have long been subject to critical analysis and evaluation, on behalf of peoples of Asian descent in the United States, but not always with an emphasis on the latter's direct involvement in and feedback on a given project.[50] This tradition continues, as is evident from the cosponsored publications of the Leadership Education for Asian Pacifics (LEAP) organization and UCLA's Asian American Studies Center.[51] Since 1992, marked by the April uprising in Los Angeles, advocacy work has also manifested itself in terms of a wide and fascinating range of "minority coalition building" projects as well as theoretical speculation about viable premises that would allow coalition building that is grounded in operational bases (in terms of community formations) and practices.[52]

The study and application of class analysis and political economy constitutes an increasingly important activity for AAS as a whole, if only because the 1965 Immigration Act and the movement of peoples from war-torn Southeast Asia have resulted in increasingly heterogeneous populations of Asian descent. Some of the earliest participants in AAS who advocated the importance of class analysis are still very active on the research and community-organizing scene today. This fact has given their work and contributions a continuity that is perhaps less overtly evident as compared with other orientations described thus far. Among others, class-oriented scholars Edna Bonacich and Lucie Cheng represent this tradition on the West Coast, as does Peter Kwong on the East Coast.[53] These scholars are notable in that they have lent their theoretical and analytical talents to community-based organizers and activists; thus their research styles, as assessed relative to particular projects they have been involved in over the years, manifest links to the participatory action research and advocacy traditions previously mentioned.[54] The productivity and consistency of argumentation in such work by Bonacich and Kwong have given rise to interesting debates within AAS. Clearly, both authors challenge the preeminence of race as the key concept in Asian American and Ethnic Studies, arguing at various points that it can and should be supplanted by class, in the sense that racialization responds to both the domestic and international dynamics of global capitalism.[55]

Finally, this account should clarify the reasons behind our position that Asian American Studies should be an integrated area of study in which the constituent disciplinary areas can and should inform each other. By definition, AAS would be unable to survive intact if its constituent areas were to be meted out into traditional disciplinary areas. For the continued progressive and successful evolution of Asian American Studies, people involved in the field should do their best to check the academy for politically gutting and dismembering the field before it has had a chance to develop fully and mature.

Shifting Terrains

Having demonstrated that there is a fair amount of continuity within the research literature, what can be said about the institutionalization, so to speak, of Asian American Studies? Any attempt to understand recent developments in the later 1980s and throughout the 1990s must begin with changes in patterns of enrollment on the part of Asian American students in the sphere of higher education. On the one hand, because of their excellent grade point averages and college-entry test scores, students of Asian descent are entering Ivy League institutions in increasing numbers, considering the overall percentage of Asian Americans in the United States in 1990. For example, reports indicate that although Asian Americans constituted less than 3 percent of the total population in 1990, Stanford University's first-year class was some 24 percent Asian American, Harvard's was 20 percent, Yale's was 15 percent, and most other Ivy League schools have had on the order of 10 percent Asian American enrollment throughout the 1980s. Also "for the first time in history, Asian American freshman outnumbered Whites in both UC Berkeley and UCLA."[56] Similarly, UC Berkeley Ethnic Studies scholar Ling-Chi Wang reported that "by 1990, even the top elite liberal arts colleges were enrolling anywhere from 7 percent to 17 percent."[57] These trends are replicated at the junior and community colleges in large cities on the two coasts, where Asian Americans are demographically concentrated, although it must be acknowledged that the educational issues facing students at these institutions are distinct from those in the Ivy Leagues.

Tied to this is the fact that campuses from community colleges to the universities are increasingly requiring students to take one or more courses that reflect the multicultural diversities and realities of contemporary North American society. This means that courses with Asian American and/or Ethnic Studies content are in growing demand by students seeking to fulfill "general education" or graduation requirements.[58] In California, Asian American and Ethnic Studies curricula initially was not designed for non-Asians and nonethnics, primarily because this would, as delineated in the previous discussion of knowledge production and institutional structures, entail a paradigmatic shift in language, worldview, and orientation. Remember that AAS and Ethnic Studies courses in California were initially designed to "complete" the education of students of color and thus empower them, rather than to instruct a general public. A host of attendant issues and problems are raised by the changing requirements of higher education.

Needless to say, rising Asian American enrollments have generated twin dynamics. Increasingly, especially at campuses "east of California," students are demanding Asian American Studies courses as well as full-fledged AAS programs. Simultaneously, however, these challenges and demands have often been met with a climate of institutional resistance. Universities and the public at large, using such rhetorical terms as "overrepresentation" and "quality" have responded with a policy of de facto and de jure quotas, as they actively attempt to deny the value and validity of Asian American and Ethnic Studies.[59] At a broader sociopolitical level, it is therefore clear that these contexts are affected, to one extent or another, by a backlash against the changing demographics of higher education and against multicultural educational philosophies and approaches. Also, although postmodern thought has been useful in countering a rigid essentialism, scholars must be conscious that these strategic deployments do not subsume, dismiss, or eliminate the necessary considerations of the "everyday structures of racism" that continue to be the experience of many people of color in the United States.[60]

Emerging Hierarchies

Earlier in this chapter we proposed that there is a basic coherence to Asian American Studies: in terms of its premises and methodology as well as in terms of the themes and approaches that characterize its scholarship. A convincing case can be made, however, that for the past three decades AAS has struggled with a plethora of changes and challenges that have evolved along with, if not always as a result of, the tremendous increases in higher education in the numbers of students of Asian descent.[61] This is most evident when the patterns and consequences of the institutionalization of AAS are examined. Of special concern are five persistent manifestations of hierarchy that generate tensions and even divisions within AAS as it continues to evolve within the academy.

First, a clear hierarchy has emerged among the older, well-established programs and the newer, well-funded ones (typically found on the West and East Coasts) versus the smaller, underfunded, understaffed programs that struggle for their very existence on a year-to-year basis. To some extent this hierarchy mirrors the status and prestige of universities themselves as first-, second-, or third-tier institutions.[62] Concomitantly, the larger and better funded programs disproportionately influence the field as a whole, if only because affiliated faculty are in a better position to carry out and disseminate research or to find, sponsor, and fund graduate students.[63]

Second, it has often been noted that Chinese American and Japanese American scholars predominate in today's departmental and program leadership. According to the 1998 *Directory of Asian American Studies Programs,* for example, as far as we know, one Korean American, two South Asian Americans, one Filipino American, and one Euro-American run programs, but again these tend to be smaller or newer enterprises.[64] The composition of AAS faculty at many institutions is also predominantly Chinese American and Japanese American. In addition, these populations tend to be put at the center of AAS in terms of course offerings and the curriculum. Although colleagues have repeatedly stressed the value and importance of inclusion, both substantively and theoretically, of South Asians and Southeast Asians, it is all too easy to highlight populations with East Asian roots, perhaps because initially there was more information readily available about these populations.[65]

Third, AAS practitioners must continue to pay close attention to when and how gender and sexuality are included or elided when considering institutional manifestations of AAS. For example, although Professor of Urban Planning Shirley Hune and Professor of Psychology Kenyon S. Chan reported an overall increase in 1997 in Asian-Pacific American (APA) women faculty across the board in the academy, their findings indicated that "APA women still lag well behind their male counterparts."[66] More fine-grained research on the educational experiences and trajectories of women of Asian descent confirms the general picture: whether as undergraduates, graduates, or junior faculty, Asian American women face a special set of challenges because of their gender and "race," some of which are all the more demoralizing because their manifestations are subtle and covert.[67] Although comparable data concerning sexuality is lacking, it is reasonable to assume that a similar kind of marginalization affects Asian American gays and lesbians in the academy. As a result, AAS practitioners should be careful not merely to give "lip service" to gender and sexual diversity.[68] Our commitments need to be measured against our practices, and our indexes of inclusion—pertaining to such areas as workforce composition, curriculum, and publications—should be critically assessed from time to time so that we are honest with ourselves about the reality.[69]

A fourth manifestation of hierarchy appears when one considers the interests and needs of senior versus junior scholars in the field. For example, the current leadership of the Association for Asian American Studies (AAAS), the leading professional organization for college- and university-level professors of AAS, has recently been debating whether the organization should get involved in individual tenure cases. Such cases are understandably complex and in some instances entail protracted struggles. The association's caucuses "East of California," however, which is made up primarily of tenure-track professors, many of whom teach on campuses in relative isolation from their Ethnic Studies colleagues, have responded by asking AAAS to reconsider its apparent preference for "little-to-no" involvement. Clearly, the association's active participation in tenure cases would be of great value to junior professors who are concerned, with good cause, that their AAS-oriented publications and other contributions may be undervalued or even misunderstood by mainstream academic colleagues.

Hierarchy—on the part of senior AAS professors being less than fully supportive of junior AAS professors—may entail subtle considerations, so it is useful to analyze what may be going on below the surface, if only in a provisional fashion. Some AAS programs, even large ones, do not have much autonomy in hiring their own faculty. For example, there are many cases in which supposedly "senior" AAS scholars are rejected because the closest mainstream department to the scholar's training or orientation refuses to accept the scholar's pedigrees or publications. In many hiring situations academic departments are more interested in a candidate's mainstream credentials or contributions than in his or her scholarship, experience in, or commitment to Asian American or Ethnic Studies.[70]

Although Asian American Studies has always been an interdisciplinary and even multidisciplinary enterprise, AAS today has many practitioners based in such disciplinary fields as psychology, history, English, and so on. This is because the locus of control in the university setting rests primarily within departmental units. These practitioners have their own interests, caucuses, and even publications that reflect more of an academic specialist's orientation as opposed to a larger sensibility of the field's origins and aims as a whole—at least as these goals were originally conceived. Our concern is not to try to distinguish the "real" from the "fake" practitioners but merely to point out that within the context of the academy, disciplinary pursuits and publications are often more generously supported and rewarded than multidisciplinary ones.[71] Similarly, some scholars who write about Asian American issues, but whose primary commitments are within mainstream disciplinary departments, are able to use their positions to propose new directions for A A S, even as they do little to advance the field's autonomy within the academy, let alone engage in community-based struggles. In this light a senior A A S scholar who has pursued historical, community-oriented, or multidisciplinary kinds of research may find it difficult to write a letter endorsing the scholarship of a junior faculty person who writes about Asian American literature in terms of such theorists as Mikhail Bakhtin or even Homi K. Bhabha.

A new, fifth hierarchy may thus be emerging that pits multidisciplinary, practice-oriented A A S faculty against scholars at elite institutions who write about Asian American issues from a solely theoretical angle, positioned in the institutional spaces of mainstream academic departments. Although the meaning and outcome of this division is not yet clear, it is profound enough to label as a fifth dimension of hierarchy. The realities of institutional positioning have generated a related debate, which involves the oft-cited drift away from political commitments and engagement in A A S.[72] It has become fashionable in some circles to discuss culture, transnationalism, global class structures, and the dynamics of political economy without necessarily bringing the analysis back down to "the ground." The gap between theory and practice is a contentious topic among practitioners precisely because such a link was supposed to distinguish A A S from traditional fields of academic endeavor. In any case, whatever one's ultimate position, tying this debate back to the question of "sides"—in relation to hierarchy and how and why stratification emerges in the institutionalization of A A S—seems vital.

In summary, the development of Asian American Studies as a field offered an epistemology and a methodology regarding self-determination, knowledge production, and progressive political practice in U.S. institutional structures, including the academy. Returning to A A S's historical roots to refashion the field for today's challenges is imperative because the "subject category" of A A S revolved, and still revolves, around a political vision, as opposed to a culturally or psychologically grounded essence.

Notes

We would like to thank Johnnella E. Butler, James A. Hirabayashi, and Evelyn Hu-DeHart for their comments on a preliminary draft of this chapter. Naturally, however, we are responsible for its contents.

1. A concise overview of these trends is available in William P. O'Hare and Judy C. Felt, *Asian Americans: America's Fastest Growing Minority Group*, Population Trends and Public Policy, No. 19 (Washington, D.C.: Population Reference

Bureau, 1991). For a fascinating treatment of how these complexities are affecting the cultural landscape of Asian America, see Jinqi Ling, *Narrating Nationalisms: Ideology and Form in Asian American Literature* (New York: Oxford University Press, 1998).

2. The overall shape of the debate can be seen in the various contributions to a special issue of *Amerasia Journal* 21 (1995) titled *Thinking Theory in Asian American Studies*. The points that follow are largely synthesized from this source. The range of perspectives represented in this issue illustrate the topic's complexity as well as the contributors' underlying political projects. From postmodern to empirical and community to academic, these stances, also informed by the particular disciplines of individual authors, illustrate the broad interest of this topic.

3. Similar questions have been raised about the concepts of nation, nationality, and its derivations, including cultural nationalism. In terms of this critique, all manifestations of "identity politics" that revolve around "nation" are considered essentialist. Because of the current shape of global capitalism, transnational links frame the diasporas of many emigrants from Asia and are more characteristic of the lived experiences of Asians overseas than so-called immigrant models would suggest. Thus any notion of fixed boundaries that frame and separate "emigrant" and "immigrant" mentalities, networks, and resources must, perforce, mislead. See Lisa Lowe, *Immigrant Acts: On Asian American Cultural Politics* (Durham, N.C.: Duke University Press, 1976).

4. In a series of seminal publications the historian Arif Dirlik has effectively interrogated this position; see Dirlik, "Asians on the Rim: Transnational Capital and Local Community in the Making of Contemporary Asian America," *Amerasia Journal* 22 (1996): 1–24. A corollary perspective is presented by Evelyn Hu-DeHart in the introduction to her recent anthology, *Across the Pacific: Asian Americans and Globalization* (Philadelphia: Temple University Press, 1999).

5. Inspired by sources ranging from Jurgen Habermas to Michel Foucault to Ernesto Laclau, critics also challenge explicit and implicit formulations of power and "liberation" as presented in many Asian American Studies (as well as progressive feminist and social science) discourses, pedagogies, and research projects.

6. Glenn Omatsu provides a cogent overview of the sociopolitical climate that undergirded the formation of Asian American and Ethnic Studies; see Omatsu, "The 'Four Prisons' and the Movement of Liberation: Asian American Activism from the 1960s to the 1990s," in Karin Aguilar-San Juan, ed., *The State of Asian America: Race and Resistance in the 1990s* (Boston: South End Press, 1974).

7. Karen Umemoto documents the Asian American dimension of the Third World Liberation Front in her article "On Strike! San Francisco State College Strike, 1968–69: The Role of Asian American Students," *Amerasia Journal* 15 (1989): 3–41.

8. See George Kagiwada et al., eds., *Proceedings of the National Asian American Studies Conference II: A Tool of Change or A Tool of Control?* (Davis: Asian American Studies, Department of Applied Behavioral Sciences, University of California, Davis, 1973). Papers presented at this July 6–8, 1973, conference demonstrate that this was a position held by influential Asian American Studies personnel throughout California as well as at one of the key programs in New York. We have specified our own positions in our article, Lane Ryo Hirabayashi and Marilyn Caballero Alquizola, "Asian American Studies: Reevaluating for the 1990s," in Aguilar-San Juan, *State of Asian America*, 351–64.

9. These concerns help explain why early formulations of pedagogy in African American, Asian American, and Ethnic Studies often deployed the work of Brazilian education and literacy theorist Paulo Freire.

10. Similarly, parallel developments—such as the strikes of farmworkers of color, including Filipinos in California, the redress/reparations movement, the demonstrations in support of the International Hotel in San Francisco, the anti-Marcos movement, and the ongoing interest and growth of the Asian American literature and arts scene—have all been propelled and certainly informed and assisted by Asian American Studies (AAS), and vice versa, in contrast to most of the rest of the academy.

11. Although we arrived inductively at the elements in Figure 1, the setup of this typology was also influenced by the work of the late Guillermo Bonfil Batalla, presented in a series of articles published during the 1980s. For one example, see Bonfil Batalla, "La Teoría del Control Cultural en el Estudio de Procesos Étnicos," *Anuario Anthopologico* (Brazil) 86 (1988): 13–53.

12. Our use of the concept of "racialized" is drawn from "racial formation theory" as formulated by Michael Omi and Howard Winant; see Winant, *Racial Conditions: Politics, Theory, Comparisons* (Minneapolis: University of Minnesota Press, 1994). We also use the concept of "minority" in a technical rather than a numerical sense; see Richard T. Schaefer, *Racial and Ethnic Groups* (New York: HarperCollins, 1990), 4–9.

13. See James A. Hirabayashi, "Ethnic Education: Its Purposes and Prospects," *On Common Ground: A Journal of Ethnic Thought* 1 (1979): 1–3. This article was first presented as a paper at the Second Annual Conference on Emerging Programs, University of Washington, November 7–9, 1974.

14. For the record we acknowledge that all four of the types of educational production and reproduction presented in Figure 1 can result in knowledge production that is useful to Ethnic Studies, especially when the former are understood for what they are. Some Asian Americanists, for example, note the value of Mary Coolidge's and Bruno Lasker's pioneering work on the early histories of Chinese

and Filipino immigrants, respectively; see L. Ling-Chi Wang, "Asian American Studies," *American Quarterly* 33 (1981): 339–54. Thus Asian Americanists who work in the institutional context of American Studies and Cultural Studies programs can produce interesting and relevant work, even if they draw from outsiders' perspectives or if they do not consult with community-based activists and organizations in making decisions about interpretations or representations.

15. Over the years Ethnic Studies scholar James A. Banks and his colleagues have published a number of useful resources that have sought to draw from the original vision of Ethnic Studies and to translate its contributions into more standardized pedagogical forms; see, for example, James A. Banks and Cherry A. McGee Banks, eds., *Handbook of Research on Multicultural Education* (New York: Macmillan, 1995); and James A. Banks, ed., *Multicultural Education, Transformative Knowledge, and Action: Historical and Contemporary Perspectives* (New York: Teachers College Press, 1996).

16. Because the field is now thirty years old, a good amount of material is available on different aspects of Asian American Studies. It is particularly important to cite these publications, especially because the tendency of the "postmodern critics" to eschew all but the very latest citations by Asian Americanists elides a large and significant legacy. There are publications delineating:

How AAS was first started, including such works as Mike Ichiro Murase, "Ethnic Studies and Higher Education for Asian Americans," in Emma Gee et al., eds., *Counterpoint: Perspectives on Asian America* (Los Angeles: UCLA Asian American Studies Center, 1976).

The current state of the art, such as Michael Omi, "It Just Ain't the Sixties No More: The Contemporary Dilemmas of Asian American Studies," in Gary Y. Okihiro et al., eds., *Reflections on Shattered Windows: Promises and Prospects for Asian American Studies* (Pullman: Washington State University Press, 1988); Sucheng Chan and Ling-Chi Wang, "Racism and the Model Minority: Asian-Americans in Higher Education," in Philip G. Altbach and Kofi Lomotey, eds., *The Racial Crisis in American Higher Education* (New York: State University of New York Press, 1991).

Curriculum issues, including such works as Lowell Chun-Hoon, Lucie Hirata, and Alan Moriyama, "Curriculum Development in Asian American Studies: A Working Paper," in Kagiwada et al., eds., *Proceedings of the National Asian American Studies Conference II*; Sucheng Chan, "On the Ethnic Studies Requirement: Part I: Pedagogical Implications," *Amerasia Journal* 15 (1989): 267–80); Gary Y. Okihiro, "Education for Hegemony, Education for Liberation," in Okihiro, ed., *Ethnic Studies*, vol. 1 (New York: Markus Weiner, 1989).

The evolution of AAS programs in California and across the United States, such as Don Nakanishi and Russell Leong, "Toward the Second Decade: A

National Survey of Asian American Studies Programs in 1978," *Amerasia Journal* 5 (1978): 1–20; Raymond Lou, "'Unknown Jerome': Asian American Studies in the California State University System," in Okihiro et al., eds., *Reflections on Shattered Windows*; Peter Nien-chu Kiang, "The New Wave: Developing Asian American Studies on the East Coast," in Okihiro et al., *Reflections of Shattered Windows*; Peter Nien-chu Kiang, "Bringing It All Back Home: New Views of Asian American Studies and the Community," in Gail M. Nomura et al., eds., *Frontiers of Asian American Studies: Writing, Research, and Commentary* (Pullman: Washington State University Press, 1989); and Gary Y. Okihiro and Lee C. Lee, eds., *East of California: New Perspectives in Asian American Studies* (Ithaca, N.Y.: Asian American Studies Program, Cornell University, 1992).

Pedagogy, including such works as Dennis Fukumoto, Franklin Odo, and Bill Wong, "Course Design and Teaching Methods," in Kagiwada et al., *Proceedings of the National Asian American Studies Conference II*; Phil Nash, "Creating Critical Consciousness: Paulo Freire and the Mechanics of Teaching Asian American Studies," in Okihiro et al., *Reflections on Shattered Windows*; Glenn Omatsu, "New and Strange Political Animals: Asian Pacific American Neo-Conservatives," *Forward Motion* 11 (1992): 52–58; Lane Ryo Hirabayashi and Malcolm Collier, "Embracing Diversity: A Pedagogy for Teaching an Introductory Asian American Studies Course," in Wendy L. Ng et al., eds., *Revisioning Asian America: Locating Diversity* (Pullman: Washington State University Press, 1995); and Lane Ryo Hirabayashi, ed., *Teaching Asian America: Diversity and the Problem of Community* (Lanham, Md.: Rowman & Littlefield, 1997).

Assessments of policy issues, including such works as Dana Takagi, *The Retreat from Race: Asian-American Admissions and Racial Politics* (New Brunswick, N.J.: Rutgers University Press, 1992); Ling-Chi Wang, "Higher Education Policy," in *The State of Asian/Pacific America: Policy Issues to the Year 2020* (Los Angeles: LEAP Asian Pacific American Public Policy Institute and the UCLA Asian American Studies Center, 1992); and Don Nakanishi, "Another Quota Debate: Asian Pacific Applicants to Competitive Public and Private Colleges" in Linda A. Revilla et al., eds., *Bearing Dreams, Shaping Visions: Asian Pacific American Perspectives* (Pullman: Washington State University Press, 1993).

Asian Americans generally in the 1990s and beyond, including such works as Aguilar-San Juan, ed., *State of Asian America*; and LEAP Asian American Public Policy Institute and UCLA Asian American Studies Center, eds., *The State of Asian Pacific America: Policy Issues to the Year 2020* (Los Angeles: LEAP and UCLA Asian American Studies Center, 1993).

17. James A. Hirabayashi, "On the Relation between Asian American Studies and Asian Studies," paper presented at the session "Asian Americans in the Pro-

fession" at the Annual Meeting of the Association of Asian Studies, Boston, April 2, 1974; Hirabayashi, "Ethnic Education: Its Purposes and Prospects," *On Common Ground: A Journal of Ethnic Thought* 1 (1979). This article was first presented as a paper at the Second Annual Conference on Emerging Programs, University of Washington, November 7–9, 1974.

18. See three articles by Evelyn Hu-DeHart in this regard: Hu-DeHart, "Ethnic Studies in U.S. Higher Education: History, Development, and Goals," in Banks and McGee, eds., *Handbook of Research on Multicultural Education*; Hu-DeHart, "Reconceptualizing Liberal Education: The Importance of Ethnic Studies," *Educational Record* 76 (1995): 23–31; and her critique of how Ethnic Studies is marginalized in the mid-1990s, "The Undermining of Ethnic Studies," *Chronicle of Higher Education*, October 2, 1995, B1–B2, Section 2. Interested readers can also see ethnic-specific overviews, such as those presented by Russell L. Adams, "African-American Studies and the State of the Art," in Mario Azevedo, ed., *Africana Studies: A Survey of Africa and the African Diaspora* (Durham, N.C.: Carolina Academic Press, 1993); and Carlos Muñoz Jr., "The Development of Chicano Studies, 1968–1981," in Eugene E. Garcia et al., eds., *Chicano Studies: A Multidisciplinary Approach* (New York: Teachers College Press, 1984). Also available are overviews of the field as a whole, such as Johnnella E. Butler and John C. Walter, eds., *Transforming the Curriculum: Ethnic Studies and Women's Studies* (New York: State University of New York Press, 1991).

In terms of the evolution of the "pan-Asian" sensibility, see Yen Le Espritu, *Asian American Panethnicity* (Philadelphia: Temple University Press, 1992). Although Le Espritu's synthesis is admirable, in our view pan-Asian sentiments varied regionally, even within California, and they also waxed and waned over time in ways that have yet to be fully documented.

19. Shirley Hune, "Opening the American Mind and Body: The Role of Asian American Studies," *Change* (November-December 1989): 56–63.

20. See Shirley Hune, "Comments," in Nis A. Petersen, ed., *Asian Studies: Today's Educational Mandate: Integrating Asian Studies into the Undergraduate Curriculum.* Proceedings from the Asian Studies Academic Conference, Jersey City State College, New Jersey, October 18, 1991, pp. 25–31.

21. Given the publication and circulation of such anthologies as *Asian Women* (Berkeley: University of California, 1971), which were widely used as AAS textbooks in the 1970s, it is difficult to understand feminist anthropologists' charges that the construction of Asian American identity by the studies was "ideologically dominated by the history of male Chinese railroad workers," (749); see A. Ong, "Cultural Citizenship as Subject-Making: Immigrants Negotiate Racial and Cultural Boundaries in the United States," *Current Anthropology* 37 (1966): 749. This totally,

and erroneously, elides the published evidence of a dynamic and ongoing struggle over such biases. See also Judy Chu, "Asian American Women's Studies Courses: A Look Back on Our Beginnings," *Frontiers* 8 (1986): 96–101.

22. The criteria and priorities delineated on this list would provide one way to define the "our" that is referenced in Figure 1. To wit, our reading of early Asian American Studies materials from San Francisco State, as well as faculty meeting minutes which are available to us, indicates that as opposed to positing a "fixed essence," the aim was to enable a holistic, process approach to the constitution of a specifically political, or politicized, subject. Concomitantly, there are clear indications that differences among the constituent ethnic-specific groups that made up the original Asian American Studies planning groups—Chinese, Japanese, Filipino, and Korean—made for a working coalition that was fully aware of intra-group plurality at tacit and operational levels. See Lane Ryo Hirabayashi and Marilyn C. Alquizola, "Asian American Studies: Reevaluating for the 1990s," in Aguilar-San Juan, *State of Asian America*.

23. See James Hirabayashi, "Ethnic Education," 2. Also, James Hirabayashi, "On the Relation between Asian American Studies and Asian Studies."

24. See Oba Simba T'Shaka's commentary concerning the role of a "nationalist outlook" in his essay "The San Francisco State Strike: A Study of the First Black Studies Strike in the United States," University Archives, San Francisco State University, n.d. John Liu's article on cultural nationalism provides a good discussion of this kind of approach from an Asian American Studies perspective; see Liu, "Toward an Understanding of the Internal Colonial Model," in Gee, *Counterpoint*.

25. See George K. Woo, "Service and Action," in Kagiwada et al., *Proceedings of the National Asian American Studies Conference II*, 29–30, 56, and throughout.

26. During our high school and college years in the San Francisco Bay Area, we remember the evolution of a plethora of counterinstitutional service programs revolving around such issues as health (e.g., the Asian Women's Health Collective), youth (e.g., Leways), the elderly (e.g., the Korean Community Service Center), education (e.g., the Japanese Bilingual/Bicultural Program), and the justice system (e.g., the Asian Law Caucus). Similar programs sprang up across the United States, wherever there was a strong enough demographic base to support such organizing. Many of these organizations were either started or staffed by students. For a recent anthology that discusses, among other things, the importance of student-community ties regarding Asian American Studies in the contemporary academy, see Lane Ryo Hirabayashi, *Teaching Asian America*.

27. Examples of efforts along these lines include revisionist histories of Chinese in the San Francisco Bay Area and in California in general, such as Thomas W. Chinn et al., eds., *A History of the Chinese in California: A Syllabus* (San Francisco:

Chinese Historical Society of America, 1969); such oral history projects as Roberto V. Vallangca, ed., *Pinoy: The First Wave (1898–1941)* (San Francisco: Strawberry Hill Press, 1977), and Fred Cordova, ed., *Filipinos: Forgotten Asian Americans* (Seattle, Wash.: Demonstration Project for Asian Americans, 1983); and such literary compilations as *Third World Women* (San Francisco: Third World Communications, 1972), and Emily Cachapero et al., eds., *Liwanag: Literary and Graphic Expression by Filipinos in America* (San Francisco: Liwanag Publications, 1973). Action research and advocacy efforts have been largely undocumented but included links to community-based organizations such as those described in note 26. Roots were laid during the same period for what would emerge during the 1980s as a host of historical societies and museums.

28. Initial issues of a University of California-Berkeley, Asian American Studies publication, *Asian American Review*, include a number of articles that support this interpretation. See, particularly, "Curriculum Committee Report," *Asian American Review* 2 (1975): 6–15; "Yes, You Can Major in Asian American Studies," *Asian American Review* 2 (1975): 15–25; and Ling-Chi Wang, "The ABCs of Asian American Studies," *Asian American Review* 2 (1975): 26–43; as well as articles in a subsequent issue, published in 1976, which has no volume or number identification.

29. See Noam Chomsky, *Deterring Democracy* (New York: Hill and Wang, 1992).

30. One indication of this long-term struggle can be gleaned from "Asian American Studies: Ending Innovation," *The Berkeley Graduate*, January 1982.

31. In other words we ask why the prolonged struggles having to do with gender and sexuality, such as the Merle Woo case—when controversial radical feminist Woo was let go from her lecturer's position—at the University of California-Berkeley's AAS program rather than, say, at San Francisco State. See Merle Woo, "What Have We Accomplished? From the Third World Strike through the Conservative Eighties," *Amerasia Journal* 15 (1989): 81–89.

32. The phrase "the buried past" derives from a survey of Japanese-language sources pertaining to the early Japanese experience in America; see Yuji Ichioka et al., eds., *The Buried Past: An Annotated Bibliography of the Japanese American Research Project* (Berkeley: University of California Press, 1974).

33. See Yuji Ichioka, *The Issei: The World of the First Generation Japanese Immigrants, 1885–1924* (New York: Free Press, 1988); and Him Mark Lai et al., *Island: Poetry and History of Chinese Immigrants on Angel Island, 1910–1940* (San Francisco: Hoc Doi, 1980; reprint, Seattle: University of Washington Press, 1991).

34. See Marlon K. Hom, *Songs of Gold Mountain: Cantonese Rhymes from San Francisco Chinatown* (Berkeley: University of California Press, 1987); Jane Singh,

ed., *South Asians in North America* (Berkeley: Center for South and Southeast Asian Studies, 1988); Paul Kochi, *Imin no Aiwa: An Immigrant's Sad Tale*, trans. Ben Kobashigawa (Los Angeles: Dick Kobashigawa, 1978); and Mitziko Sawada, *Tokyo Life, New York Dreams: Urban Japanese Visions of America, 1890–1924* (Berkeley: University of California Press, 1996).

35. Ronald Takaki, *Pau Hana: Plantation Life and Labor in Hawaii, 1835–1920* (Honolulu: University of Hawai'i Press, 1983); Sucheng Chan, *This Bittersweet Soil: The Chinese in California Agriculture* (Berkeley: University of California Press, 1986); Gary Y. Okihiro, *Cane Fires: The Anti-Japanese Movement in Hawaii, 1865–1945* (Philadelphia: Temple University Press, 1991). Lane Ryo Hirabayashi has also carried out work along these lines in terms of resuscitating Issei perspectives on mass incarceration; see Hirabayashi, ed., *Inside an American Concentration Camp: Japanese American Resistance at Poston, Arizona* (Tucson: University of Arizona Press, 1995).

36. Victor and Brett de Barry Nee, *Longtime Californ'* (New York: Pantheon, 1973); and Bong Youn Choy, *Koreans in America* (Chicago: Nelson-Hall, 1979).

37. Arthur Hansen, "A Riot of Voices: Variables in Interactive Oral History Interviewing," in Eva M. McMahan and Kim Lacy Rogers, eds., *Interactive Oral History Interviewing* (Hillsdale, N.J.: Lawrence Erlbaum, 1994); Valerie Matsumoto, *Farming the Home Place: A Japanese American Community in California, 1919–1982* (Ithaca, N.Y.: Cornell University Press, 1993); and Karen I. Leonard, *Making Ethnic Choices: California Punjabi Mexican Americans* (Philadelphia: Temple University Press, 1992).

38. Many Asian American authors carry out their work in this fashion; for examples, see the work of playwright Philip Kan Gotanda, *The Wash* (Portsmouth, N.H.: Heinemann, 1992), and his recent anthology, *Fish Head Soup and Other Plays* (Seattle: University of Washington Press, 1995). Similarly, author Genny Lim has drawn from historical research for a number of her pieces; see an interview and the text of her play *Bitter Cane* in Velina Hasu Houston, ed., *The Politics of Life: Four Plays by Asian American Women* (Philadelphia: Temple University Press, 1993), 153–204. For a corollary treatment of how Asian American video documentaries have been based on very similar techniques, see Jun Xing's discussion "Teaching the Asian American Experience through Film," in Lane Ryo Hirabayashi, *Teaching Asian America*.

39. Many teachers of Asian American history surveys thus make use of literature to stimulate insights into the conditions that faced pre-World War II immigrants from Asia and their children in the United States. Such works have included, for example, short stories by the writer Hisaye Yamamoto in her *Seventeen Syllables and Other Stories* (Latham, N.Y.: Kitchen Table: Women of Color Press, 1988); or

the novel of author Carlos Bulosan, *America Is in the Heart* (Seattle: University of Washington Press, 1973). As Marilyn Caballero Alquizola has noted, however, teachers must use such materials carefully, for they may entail narrative techniques that go far beyond the aims of social history per se. This same analysis, by the way, provides a good example of how a failed application of both traditional aesthetic and traditional historicist principles can lead to a misreading and ultimate misunderstanding of the text. See Alquizola, "The Fictive Narrator of *America Is in the Heart*," in Nomura et al., *Frontiers of Asian American Studies.*

For interested readers, a comprehensive treatment of Asian American authors and critical evaluation of their work is available in Sau-ling Cynthia Wong, *Reading Asian American Literature: From Necessity to Extravagance* (Princeton, N.J.: Princeton University Press, 1993); and King-Kok Cheung, ed., *An Interethnic Companion to Asian American Literature* (New York: Cambridge University Press, 1997). Also useful is Chung Hsing, *Asian America through the Lens: History, Representations, and Identity* (Walnut Creek, Calif.: AltaMira Press, 1998).

40. In addition to such early anthologies as UC Berkeley's *Asian Women*, see the detailed regional study by Susie Ling, "The Mountain Movers: Asian American Women's Movement in Los Angeles," *Amerasia Journal* 15 (1989): 51–68, which probably represents similar developments in large metropolitan areas like San Francisco, Seattle, New York, and so forth. Also see David Eng and Alice Hom, eds., *Q and A: Queer in Asian America* (Philadelphia: Temple University Press, 1998).

41. See Johnnella E. Butler, "The Difficult Dialogue of Curriculum Transformation: Ethnic Studies and Women's Studies," in Butler and Walter, *Transforming the Curriculum.*

42. See, for example, Asian Women United, *Making Waves: An Anthology of Writings by and about Asian American Women* (Boston: Beacon Press, 1989); Kitty Tsui, ed., *Breathless—Erotica* (Firebrand Books, 1995); and Women of South Asian Descent Collective, ed., *Our Feet Walk the Sky: Women of the South Asian Diaspora* (San Francisco: Aunt Lute Books, 1993).

43. Bok-Lim Kim, *Women in Shadows: A Handbook for Service Providers Working with Asian Wives of U.S. Military Personnel* (La Jolla, Calif.: National Committee Concerned with Asian Wives of U.S. Servicemen, 1981); Jacqueline R. Agtuca, *A Community Secret: For the Filipina in an Abusive Relationship* (1992; reprint, Seattle: Seal Press, 1994); and Mila Glodava and Richard Onizuka, *Mail Order Brides: Women for Sale* (Fort Collins, Colo.: Alaken, 1994).

44. See my review, Lane Ryo Hirabayashi, "Back to the Future: Re-Framing Community-Based Research," *Amerasia Journal* 21 (1995): 103–18.

45. David Mas Masumoto, *Country Voices* (Del Ray, Calif.: Inaka Publications, 1989); and Wendy L. Ng, "The Collective Memories of Commun-

ities," in Shirley Hune et al., eds., *Asian Americans: Comparative and Global Perspectives* (Pullman: Washington State University Press, 1991).

46. Timothy P. Fong, *The First Suburban Chinatown: The Remaking of Monterey Park, California* (Philadelphia: Temple University Press, 1994); and Madhulika Khandelwal, "Indian Networks in the United States: Class and Transnational Identities," in Harriet Orcutt Duleep and Phanindra V. Wunnava, eds., *Immigrants and Immigration Policy: Individual Skills, Family Ties, and Group Identities* (Greenwich, Conn.: JAI Press, 1996).

47. Peggy Li et al., *The Garment Industry in Los Angeles Chinatown, 1973–1974* (Los Angeles: UCLA Asian American Studies Center, 1974); Lillian Galledo et al., *Roadblocks to Community Building: A Case Study of the Stockton Filipino Community Project* (Davis: Asian American Studies Division, Department of Applied Behavioral Sciences, University of California, 1970); and Ramsay Shu and Adele Salamasina Satele, *The Samoan Community in Southern California: Conditions and Needs* (Chicago: Pacific/Asian American Mental Health Research Center, 1977).

These studies directly inspired Lane Ryo Hirabayashi's own efforts to carry out community-based research in and around Los Angeles. See, for example, Lane Ryo Hirabayashi with George Tanaka, *The Early Gardena Valley and the Issei* (Gardena, Calif.: Gardena Pioneer Project, 1986); Hirabayashi with George Tanaka, "The Issei Community in Moneta and the Gardena Valley, 1900–1920," *Southern California Quarterly* 70 (1988): 127–58; Hirabayashi, "Community Lost? Notes on the Significance of a Contemporary Japanese American Community in Southern California," in Malcolm Collier, ed., *Asians in America: A Reader* (Dubuque, Iowa: Kendall-Hunt, 1993); and Hirabayashi, "Community Destroyed? Assessing the Impact of the 'Loss of Community' on Japanese Americans during World War Two," in Josephine Lee, Imogene Lim, and Yuko Matsukawa, eds., *Re/Collecting Early Asian America: Readings in Cultural History* (Philadelphia: Temple University Press, 2000).

48. Miriam Ching Louie, "Immigrant Asian Women in Bay Area Garment Sweatshops: 'After Sewing, Laundry, Cleaning, and Cooking, I Have No Breath Left to Sing,'" *Amerasia Journal* 18: 1–26. *Los Angeles—Struggles toward Multiethnic Community*, ed. Edward T. Chang, *Amerasia Journal* 19.

49. Peter N. Kiang, "Where Do We Stand? Views of Racial Conflict by Vietnamese American High-School Students in a Black-and-White Context," *Urban Review* 26 (1994): 95–119; and Kiang, "When Know-Nothings Speak English Only: Analyzing Irish and Cambodian Struggles for Community Development and Educational Equity," in Aguilar-San Juan, *State of Asian America*.

50. An example of such advocacy work in mental health services, immigration, media, and so on appears in a U.S. Commission on Civil Rights publication

from the late 1980s, *Voices across America: Roundtable Discussions of Asian Civil Rights Issues* (Washington, D.C.: U.S. Government Printing Office, n.d.). Ethnic-specific studies that come to mind include, for example, Chuong Chung, "Death and Dying: A Vietnamese Cultural Perspective," in Joan Parry, ed., *Social Work Practice with the Terminally Ill: The Transcultural Perspective* (Springfield, Ill.: Charles Thomas, 1990).

51. LEAP Asian Pacific American Public Policy Institute and the UCLA Asian American Studies Center, *The State of Asian Pacific America.* Also noteworthy are the grass-roots organizing efforts of groups like New York's Committee Against Anti-Asian Violence (CAAAV); see their newsletter, *The CAAAV Voice: Newsletter of the Committee Against Anti-Asian Violence.*

52. See the innovative and resourceful study written by a group of experienced community organizers known as the MultiCultural Collaborative, *Race, Power, and Promise in Los Angeles: An Assessment of Responses to Human Relations Conflict* (Los Angeles: MultiCultural Collaborative, 1996).

53. See Edna Bonacich, "Class Approaches to Ethnicity and Race," *Insurgent Sociologist* 10 (1980): 116–30. Bonacich has subsequently collaborated with John Modell, Lucie Cheng, and Ivan Light in applying her framework to Japanese Americans, pre-World War II Asian immigrants, and Korean Americans in Los Angeles, respectively. Peter Kwong, *Chinatown, New York: Labor and Politics, 1930–1950* (New York: Monthly Review Press, 1979); and Kwong, *Forbidden Workers: Illegal Chinese Immigrants and American Labor* (New York: New Press, 1997.)

54. Some of Bonacich's most recent work, research on new immigrant garment workers, is presented in Paul Ong et al., eds., *The New Asian Immigration in Los Angeles and Global Restructuring* (Philadelphia: Temple University Press, 1994). For such a productive scholar, Bonacich has been very active in Los Angeles metropolitan area community organizations and unions.

55. For one example, see Peter Kwong, "Asian American Studies Needs Class Analysis," in Gary Y. Okihiro et al., eds., *Privileging Positions: The Sites of Asian American Studies* (Pullman: Washington State University Press, 1995). Also see E. San Juan Jr., *Racial Formations/Critical Transformations: Articulations of Power in Ethnic and Racial Studies in the United States* (Atlantic Highlands, N.J.: Humanities Press, 1992).

56. Wang, "Higher Education Policy," 52–53.

57. Ibid., 57.

58. Professor Sucheng Chan is one of the few scholars who has systematically analyzed the impact of a broad Ethnic Studies requirement on pedagogy in her University of California-Santa Barbara courses; see Chan, "On the Ethnic Studies Requirement. Part 1: Pedagogical Implications," *Amerasia Journal* 15 (1989): 267–80.

We also note a corollary concern: that even if and when Ethnic Studies or Asian American Studies content has achieved greater circulation within the academy in the form of readings and classes, to simply include such content in the classroom, stripped of the principles and perspectives needed to generate it, is hardly enough. Indeed, in the days of Proposition 209 and federal cutbacks, it is too little too late.

59. See Carlos F. Díaz, "Resistance to Multicultural Education: Concerns and Responses," in *Multicultural Education for the Twenty-First Century* (Washington, D.C.: National Education Associations, 1992); Chan and Wang, "Racism and the Model Minority"; and Don T. Nakanishi, "Another Quota Debate: Asian Pacific Applicants to Competitive Public and Private Colleges," in Revilla et al., *Bearing Dreams, Shaping Visions.*

60. For example, a press release in our possession, compiled by "RESist: National Movement for Race and Ethnic Studies," delineates a series of vigils, demonstrations, and strikes at Ivy League colleges and universities in 1996, among them, Brown, Columbia, Northwestern, Princeton, Smith, and Yale. Fifteen other campuses across the country are also listed as "supporters" of the movement. A full-length article on an influential 1995 hunger strike at Northwestern to call attention to these issues appeared in the *Chicago Tribune,* 17 April 1995.

61. See a more extended discussion of these issues in Lane Ryo Hirabayashi, "Asian American Studies and Institutional Politics," in Thomas K. Nakayama and Carlton F. Yoshioka, eds., *Asian Americans in the Southwest* (Tempe: Arizona State University, 1997).

62. Sheng-Mei Ma offers a passionate commentary on this tendency; see Ma, "Second-Rate or Second-Rank: The Human Pyramid of Academe," in Renée Curry and Terry L. Allison, eds., *States of Rage: Emotional Eruption, Violence, and Social Change* (New York: New York University Press, 1996).

63. For example, over the past thirty years the faculty at UC Berkeley and UCLA and their graduate students have exerted an enormous influence on the field. In fact, we count ourselves as the products of these two institutions.

64. See the listings presented in the *Directory of Asian American Studies Programs* (Ithaca, N.Y.: Asian American Studies Program, Cornell University, 1998).

In some light, the crux of the *Blu's Hanging* controversy, in which author Lois-Ann Yamanaka's literary award was rescinded, goes well beyond arguments for or against literary censorship. The most judicious of these criticisms does not call for censorship of the novel. It simply protests the act of bestowing an Association of Asian American Studies (AAAS) literary award on a work that strongly offends the sensibilities of a significant part of a constituent minority group and is hurtful to members of this group on various levels. By ignoring a minority protest for two years, and by institutionally silencing the voices of this protest by systematically overruling them, the AAAS basically and ironically ignored its own explicit mandate to promote understanding and solidarity between its constituent members. Even if there may be extenuating circumstances, the resignations of all but one of the AAAS's executive board and regional representatives at the association's 1998 business meeting in Hawaii were the end result of the AAAS ignoring the essence of this extended minority protest. Yamanaka, through *Blu's Hanging* (New York: Farrar, Straus, and Girous, 1997) and other works, unwittingly has provided an effective site for this struggle, although the AAAS (and its action and inaction) remains the main target of criticism.

65. The controversy over Yamanaka's novel *Blu's Hanging* appears to have as much to do with hierarchies within AAS—where Filipino Americans are positioned within these hierarchies—as with interethnic stereotypes. See David Cordero, Mary L.Codero, Alfred Evangelista, Candace Fujikane, Linda Revilla, and Darlene Rodriguez, "Locals Must Listen to Locals: Filipino Community Responds to Review of Yamanaka's Book," *Hawaii Herald*, April 2, 1999, p. A6.

66. Shirley Hune and Kenyon S. Chan, "Special Focus: Asian Pacific American Demographic and Educational Trends," in D. Carter and R. Wilson, eds., *Minorities in Education* (Washington, D.C.: American Council on Education, 1997).

67. See, for example, Shirley Hune, *Asian Pacific American Women in Higher Education: Claiming Visibility and Voice* (Washington, D.C.: Program on the Status and Education of Women, 1998).

68. In his essay about his teaching experiences at UCLA, then staff person and activist Eric Wat offers a trenchant commentary about the need for links between theory and practice in regard to AAS's support for gay and lesbian issues; see Wat, "Beyond the Missionary Position: Reflections on Teaching Student Activism from the Bottom Up," in Lane Ryo Hirabayashi, *Teaching Asian America*.

69. Brown University doctoral student Jennifer Ting offers an insightful analysis of how homophobia colors perspectives in Asian American Studies; see Ting, "Bachelor Society: Deviant Homosexuality and Asian American Historiography," in Okihiro et al., *Privileging Positions*.

70. This and many other relevant points are discussed in Mitchell J. Chang's recent case study account, "Expansion and Its Discontents: The Formation of Asian American Studies Programs in the 1990s," *Journal of Asian American Studies* 2 (1999): 181–206.

71. Ibid.

72. Omatsu, "The 'Four Prisons' and the Movements of Liberation."

Thirty Years of Chicano and Chicana Studies

LAURO H. FLORES

MOST SCHOLARS WHO HAVE WRITTEN ON THIS SUBJECT generally agree that Chicano/a Studies, as a formal and academically sanctioned field of inquiry and pedagogy, came into existence as a direct result of the Chicano/a movement.[1] With institutionalized beginnings traceable to the late 1960s, the discipline's birth is clearly rooted in the competing "ideologies" that nurtured and energized the civil rights struggle that Mexican American people waged during those crucial years and continue to wage today.[2]

Yet, as with other Ethnic Studies fields, Chicano/a Studies existed before the term was coined. As ethnographer Susana L. Gallardo has pointed out in her eulogy discussion of the pre-*movimiento* activities of the late scholar Américo Paredes: "[he] was doing Chicano Studies before there ever was such a thing. He was doing cultural studies before there ever was such a thing. He insisted on respecting the basic dignity of Mexican peoples at a time when such dignity was a luxury for people of color."[3] Remarkably, Paredes accomplished these objectives within academia, during more than three decades at the University of Texas-Austin, "a campus that had never been particularly welcoming to Mexican-American students or scholars."[4] In addition to Paredes, the list of precursors usually included in this context are Arthur Campa, Carlos Castañeda, Aurelio M. Espinosa, Jovita González, George I.

Sánchez, and other academics who were active during the three decades preceding the Chicano/a movement proper.[5] One notable name that perhaps
should be added is Ernesto Galarza, whose seminal work on agribusiness and
the Bracero program in California was fundamental in raising the national
consciousness about an important segment of the Mexican-Chicano population in the United States. His work also established a meaningful trend of
inquiry in the field of a Chicano/a labor history.[6]

As historian Ignacio M. García has noted, this previous generation of
Mexican American intellectuals laid the foundation for the various endeavors tackled more recently by Chicano/a Studies scholars. These scholars also
inherited and were influenced by the labors of those who preceded them as
trailblazers in U.S. folklore studies as well as those involved in the embry-
onic forms of the struggle for civil rights.[7] It could be further argued that individuals like José de la Luz Sáenz, who wrote earlier in the 1920s and 1930s
about their experiences as Mexican Americans through autobiographical
accounts and other narratives, also contributed to laying the groundwork for
the future development of Chicano/a Studies, even if they did so unwittingly.[8]

A question that remains to be answered is where other, non-Chicano/a
academics fit into the equation. Most histories and analyses tend to focus exclusively on Chicano/a scholars when discussing Chicano Studies. But where does
Carey McWilliams's body of scholarship fit, for example, which, even before
Galarza's work, was so influential in subsequent studies on the life of Mexicans
in the United States?[9] This question begs still another one: Is the study of
Chicanos/as the exclusive realm of Chicano/a scholars or are others welcome
to take part in the academic dialogue? This is a particularly poignant issue
because the first blueprint for Chicano/a Studies, as expressed in 1969 in the
"Plan de Santa Bárbara" (details about this event are detailed later in this chapter) was in theory originally limited to meeting the Chicano/a community's
needs, and was thus fashioned as a recruitment vehicle intended to correct
the anomalous condition that prevailed at the time: namely, the conspicuous absence or very limited presence of Chicanos/as, both faculty and students, in most colleges and universities around the country. For whatever
reason, parallel and alternative structural formations that have sometimes subsumed Chicano/a Studies (Ethnic Studies, border studies, cultural studies,
and so on) seem to be more open and welcoming for other Latinos/as and
nonminorities into the faculty ranks. In some measure this factor fans the
flames of distrust among the more zealous advocates of "true," more mili-

tant *Chicanismo*, when proposals arise for subsuming Chicano/a Studies within other units such as Ethnic Studies.[10]

This is an important point because the insistence on preserving Chicano/a Studies as distinct, often separate units and specifically focused programs represents efforts by some Chicanos/as to defend the gains made over the previous three decades—gains that made it possible to define the particularities of Chicano/a history, culture, and current conditions in the midst of the larger and complex mosaic of racialized ethnic groups in the United States. Central to this thinking is the long-fought-for right to self-definition and the acquisition of an identity that would restore a sense of dignity and pride to a group of people that for many years have been victims of neglect, stereotyping, and institutional discrimination. From this perspective, for example, any attempt to dilute specific identity by amalgamating Chicanos/as under the officially fabricated and actively promoted label of "Hispanics" is thus perceived as an attack, as it threatens to undermine specific identity, history, culture, and any sense of autonomy or self-determination.[11] The question of naming is a crucial and hotly debated issue. For this reason I extensively quote the arguments presented by economists Refugio I. Rochín and Adela de la Torre:

During the 1980s, "Chicanos" faded from federal records as "Mexican-origin" Americans and were subsumed into the "Hispanic" classification, a concept fabricated by the U.S. Bureau of the Census. . . . As a result of the collapsing of "Chicanos" into the catch-all category "Hispanics," Chicanos lost a particular avenue for requesting that government meet their specific needs. In the quest for complete ethnic solidarity across all Hispanic subpopulations, Chicanos gave up the richness of their own identity as well as the ability to target specific "Chicano" public-policy issues. . . . Culturally and ideologically, the label creates a misleading image of the historically evolved cultures of the different aggregates to which it is applied, giving a European veneer to a widespread "culture-of-poverty" interpretation of the social problems afflicting a large proportion of this population. . . . In response to criticism that "Hispanic" does not capture the indigenous roots or mestizaje of Chicanos, the term "Latino/a" is sometimes used as a substitute for "Hispanic," in order to lessen the implied European bias of the latter. Those who use the term "Chicano" do so for political reasons to illustrate the need for further differentiation of the Mexican-origin population.[12]

As political scientist John A. García has put it: "Multiple identities do exist and extend beyond Chicanismo, and 'Hispanicity.' Yet Chicanos/as still think of themselves as Mexican-origin people with a long-standing quest for equity and empowerment in American society."[13]

El Movimiento, El Plan de Santa Bárbara, and the Birth of Chicano/a Studies

The social inequalities affecting Chicanos/as came to national attention in 1965, with the struggle to unionize the California farm laborers led by César Chávez. Another concern of the era was the disproportionate ratio of Chicanos/as and other Latinos/as who were dying in the Vietnam War (already close to nine thousand by 1970), which contrasted sharply with the minuscule number of Chicanos/as enrolled in colleges and universities and with the lack of Chicano/a faculty at these institutions. Such ingredients made for an explosive mix that resulted in numerous spontaneous actions that eventually were channeled into what is now known as the contemporary Chicano/a movement.

Educational reform in general, in higher education in particular, was a significant part of the dynamic. Students and other youths, an important force within the *movimiento*, demanded courses that were relevant to the recognition and understanding of the Mexican American experience in the United States. Naturally, the creation and offering of those courses necessitated the presence of Chicano/a faculty, both in the high schools and at university campuses, and the recruitment of a meaningful number of minority college students. The historian Guadalupe San Miguel has described the process in these terms: "Mexican American youth, especially high school students, voiced their opposition to discrimination and their support for significant changes in the schools by conducting school boycotts. College students protested the lack of minority recruitment by universities and supported the establishment of Chicano/a Studies programs. Militant strikes and protest actions at times were the primary means for bringing about change in higher education."[14] These at times militant activities resulted in changes within the educational system and brought in more Chicano/a students, which in turn led to larger organizing efforts.

The birth of Chicano/a Studies came about as an important aspect of the contemporary Chicano/a movement, and a painful birth it was. It is no accident that the first department of Mexican American Studies was established at California State College in Los Angeles in 1968.[15] The high school blowouts that took place in that city in 1967 and 1968 signaled the lighting of a fire that spread rapidly throughout California. In 1969 the Chicano Coordinating Committee on Higher Education organized a conference at the University of California-Santa Barbara campus. Attended by more than a hundred students, faculty, staff, and administrators from all over California, collectively representing nearly thirty institutions, the central purpose of the conference was to develop a master plan for the full participation and activity of Chicanos/as in higher education. Based on the "ideology" of *Chicanismo*, "El Plan de Santa Bárbara," the historical document that came out of the gathering, set some general guidelines for the recruitment of Chicano/a students, for the hiring and retention of more Chicano/a faculty, and for the creation of programs specifically designated to help Chicano/a students.[16]

El Plan de Santa Bárbara spelled out in general terms curriculum issues as well as the roles of students and the community in the development and governance of Chicano/a Studies programs. Also central to the proposals in the plan was the creation of a Chicano/a student organization, the Movimiento Estudiantil Chicano de Aztlán (better known today by the acronym MECHA), and of Chicano/a Studies as an academic field specifically focusing on the history, culture, political life, and general experiences of *la raza*. Beginning in 1969, El Plan de Santa Bárbara provided the impetus for the subsequent creation of Chicano/a Studies programs in a multiplicity of campuses throughout the country. The plan addressed accountability in the broadest terms, with only minimal effort given to the adoption of any one pedagogical model. In practice, each campus was left to create and evolve its own program, depending on the context and abilities of the locale to meet the Chicano/a community's needs. This freedom within the movement enabled it to spread throughout the Southwest and the North, to such areas as Washington and Oregon, which for some reason have rarely received due attention in the scholarship documenting the movement and Chicano/a history, as well as the Midwest. In the summer of 1970, for example, Chicanos/as in Minnesota organized a conference intended to delve into the plausibility of setting up a Chicano/a Studies program in the Midwest. Reportedly, 180 people from Illinois, Indiana, Iowa, Kansas, Michigan, Nebraska, Ohio, South Dakota, and Wisconsin attended the meeting and, after a weeklong discussion, reached unanimous agreement that the new unit should be housed in the University of Minnesota, that it should have full departmental status, and that it should be dedicated "to study Mexicans in their struggle to settle in the Midwest." The Minnesota experiment paid regional dividends, and such neighboring institutions as Wayne State University in Detroit and Northwest Indiana State

University eventually followed suit, creating "programs uniquely suited to the Latino populations of their areas."[17]

Although the Chicano/a Studies mission was originally limited in theory to meeting the Chicano/a community's needs, it initially served as a specific vehicle for college and university recruitment. Only later did institutional pressure force the articulation of the scholarly mission of these programs. Today Chicano/a Studies has become a rigorous, legitimate field of academic inquiry and research on some campuses. However, painful as it is to admit, in most places Chicano/a Studies units generally remain hampered by the inherent conflict between traditional academic standards and expectations and the field's inherited sense of mission to the community. Among the schools with better Chicano/a Studies programs are several within the University of California system, some of the California state universities, some private universities in California, the University of Arizona, Arizona State University, the University of Texas-El Paso, the University of Texas-Austin, the University of New Mexico, and the University of Michigan-Ann Arbor. Most programs are marginalized, and many are housed in units such as Ethnic Studies, cultural studies, Latino/a Studies, and so on.

Ideological Origins and the Positioning of Chicano/a Studies in the Academy

Throughout the 1960s and early 1970s the main dispute regarding the positioning of Chicano/a Studies within the academy was between the nationalistic views of various brands (with cultural nationalism being the predominant current) and several internationalist perspectives among which Marxism was the primary orientation. But even Marxist positions differed substantially in their multiple interpretations of "the Chicano/a question" and the solutions they advanced.[18] However diverse the various positions, most scholars agree that at its inception Chicano/a Studies was conceived as an oppositional and contesting undertaking intended to challenge the status quo of traditional academic structures as well as the generally disparaging and openly derogatory views of Mexican Americans that prevailed in this country at this time. Accordingly, the idea of Chicano/a Studies was initially cemented by the notion that it should help bring about social and political change, thereby advancing the collective interests of *la raza*. Chicano/a Studies, it was felt, should aid *la gente* (the people) to develop a new sense of identity and cultural value.

In other words, what later evolved as an essentially academic, scholarly endeavor of various sorts—often circumscribed to college campuses and increasingly removed from the extramural, nonacademic community and its real-life struggles—was first conceived precisely as an instrument or a force that would help to correct the anomalous situation of marginality and exclusion that the Chicano/a community suffered. Some Chicanos/as believed that this was a utopian project from the very beginning because it constituted an attempt to create an academic field out of an activist "utilitarian" purpose and perspective. This project by its very nature was thus inimical and in opposition to the privilege, individualistic competition, and elitist exclusivity that academia symbolized. Riddled as it was with these inherent and fundamental contradictions, the dream of a democratic, revolutionary Chicano/a Studies could not possibly survive and prosper.

In a punctually dialectical form, the contradictory, opposing, and often antagonistic ideologies that animated the debates that initially helped shape and propel forward the Chicano/a movement and Chicano/a Studies eventually became fetters to the process. Internal fragmentation along differing ideological lines—often only a mask for personal, dogmatic, and sectarian posturing—added to the movement's lack of a clear direction, and the failure to delineate a coherent and generally accepted paradigm in scholarly activities prevented any truly significant consolidation of the gains the student activists and their faculty supporters thought they had made.[19] Born out of strife, often permitted to be created only grudgingly by administrators and a largely conservative faculty, Chicano/a Studies has always thus carried a stigma that in the long run has become one of the serious challenges for achieving academic respect. The traces of this past are reflected in the discourse that some Chicano/a Studies centers use to define themselves. For example, in 1999 the University of Minnesota's Web site stated: "Crucial to the success of Minnesota's Chicano/a Studies department is that the unit was established not as a conciliatory gesture aimed at mending past racial grievances, but as a bona-fide department whose mission was to engage in research, teaching, and service to the community."[20]

In an attempt to place the department on a firm academic foundation, this statement tends to dilute, if not to negate, the activist origins that gave birth to the field as a whole. After thirty years of existence, and at the dawn of the new millennium, Chicano/a Studies is an interdisciplinary field at a crossroads.[21] More than three decades later most Chicano/a Studies programs in the United States remain precarious and marginalized and are perceived by many as academia's illegitimate children. Neglected, underfunded, and intellectually suspicious, these programs still occupy a position peripheral to the central research and educational missions voiced by the institutions that house them. Plagued from the beginning by internal divisiveness on one side and institutional and external hostility on the other, any real chances for Chicano/a Studies units to prosper and attain a healthy development have thus been hampered from the outset. In the best cases Chicano/a Studies programs institutionally have been the victims of benign neglect, tolerated only insofar as the faculty associated with them are willing to play the elitist game of academia and behave as "true" and "serious" scholars rather than as social or political activists. Lacking resources, and living with the threat of attrition through budget reductions or worse—total disappearance—these programs have failed for the most part to attain any significant level of academic recognition, credibility, or respect. Consequently, many scholars, old and new, shy away from Chicano/a Studies and seek appointments in such traditional departments as history, sociology, English, anthropology, or Spanish. In the best cases these faculty accept joint appointments.[22]

A similar pattern of avoidance may be discerned regarding the students. The militancy and unabashedly confrontational action of their late 1960s and 1970s counterparts provided the main force behind the original creation of Chicano/a Studies, pushing administrators and other bureaucrats to yield and concede that times were changing and that the creation of these programs was inevitable, if not desirable. But in more recent decades students have maintained a certain degree of complacency and even apathy, as documented by Ignacio García:

By the early 1980s, there also began a steady decline in the number of students taking Chicano Studies courses. The heightened activism of the late 1960s and 1970s had generated a great interest in these courses, but growing conservatism and a more narcissistic attitude on the part of students led to a steady decline in enrollment. Finding a job and getting a "useful" degree became of greater importance than becoming culturally aware for most students. In addition . . . many Chicano Studies programs began to move away from activist scholarship, which decreased their attractiveness. In these particular programs, it also meant the disfranchising of students: fewer and fewer students participated in decision making, in evaluating programs, or in the hiring process. The "militant" or "radical chic" faculty saw no need for student input as they felt they represented Chicano intellectualism, and conservative Chicano faculty and Anglo administrators saw the students as a threat to order and discipline in the academy.[23]

This lack of commitment in recent years, characterized by a dearth of activism or even moderate participation in campus politics, has had profound effects for Chicano/a Studies. Some scholars maintain that this lack of continued pressure from the students, among other factors, has resulted in a dwindling down of departments and programs.[24] On a larger scale, however, generational change and conflict plays an important part.

As historians have noted, the salient feature of the Chicano/a movement of the 1960s was its radical departure from the positions previously upheld by the so-called Mexican-American Generation, which (at times too quickly and simplistically) have been discarded as mere assimilationist and accommodationist postures of a middle-class group well-disposed to "selling out their heritage."[25] This view has been revised and rigorously corrected by historian Mario T. García, who has mapped out that period's full complexity in his study *Mexican Americans: Leadership, Ideology, and Identity, 1930–1960.*[26] This notwithstanding, however, the dramatic rupture between the two generations that Muñoz, San Miguel, and other scholars have highlighted is definite and historically accurate. Mario García himself admits that the "Chicano Generation moved to rectify the failures of the past and to break through the ideological handicaps of the Mexican-American Generation. For the Chicano Generation, reforms were not enough. National liberation—Chicano Power—or some form of it was now demanded. Similarities with other Americans were of no importance. Differences were now valued. Rather than just being a minority, Chicanos were now to be regarded as a conquered people suffering 'internal colonialism' but struggling to achieve their national independence."[27]

Therein lies an important piece of the rationale behind the initial push to create Chicano/a Studies as autonomous units within U.S. institutions of higher learning. The other fundamental aspects were to force recognition of the rights of Chicanos/as to have equal access to educational opportunities. After all, education had always been and continues to be a cornerstone of Mexican and Chicano/a cultures as one of the only viable means for individual improvement and upward social mobility, a goal that in itself was not fundamentally different from the aspirations that had also inspired the thinking and activities of the previous generation.[28] But now the goal was not to simply assimilate into pluralistic America. Rather, the aim was to reclaim an exclusive terrain that most Chicanos/as felt was somehow lost to aggressive U.S. imperialism. *Juntos, pero no revueltos* (together but not mingled), or as Mario García has said: "Similarities with other Americans were of no importance. Differences were now valued."[29]

The political and academic backlash that began with the Reagan and Bush administrations seems to be in full swing today, as corroborated by the continuous attacks on busing and bilingual education, the English-only movement, the anti-immigrant legislation in California and elsewhere, and the current campaign to dismantle affirmative action throughout the country. In this climate Chicano/a Studies, which did not adequately prosper under the more auspicious circumstances of the late 1960s and the 1970s, surely faces a more difficult experience today. New conservative forces have emerged that are out to quash anything that smells of liberalism, let alone what they perceive to be radicalism.

This is not to say that all is lost, however. Just as tactics have changed over the years to cope with new realities, adjustments will have to be made again to adequately confront the new challenges. After all, it is no longer the 1960s. Demographics have changed and the forces that attempt to turn back the clock do so at their own (or our collective) peril. A friend of mine, an old African American communist, used to say that it is easy to take candy away from a child that has never tasted candy. But try to take it away from one that has and that child is going to yell like hell. This is to say that once people have experienced a certain amount of success in gaining their civil or human rights, they will fight before relinquishing their gains.

If the Chicano Generation marked a divide with the previous so-called Mexican-American Generation and through its militancy and radical actions forced a change in the status quo, bringing about social and educational reforms that included the creation of Chicano/a Studies, the so-called Hispanic Generation that followed them in the 1980s responded to a different set of conditions. Many scholars believe this generation has adopted an accommodationist posture that undermines or at least ignores the spirit of Chicanismo that was the main philosophy during the previous decades. For example, San Miguel has written: "[The] new set of leaders [in the 1980s] replaced the Chicano/a ideology with an all-encompassing Hispanic model. More specifically, the identity of Chicanismo, or cultural identity was based not on *mestizaje*, or the indigenous past, but on the Hispanic or White-European heritage of Spain. The goal of radical social change, and its implicit call for a critical view of American institutions and ideals, was replaced by one of moderate social change based on the lack of a critical perspective toward governmental authority. Street politics was also frowned upon and replaced by the politics of persuasion and negotiation. The 'Hispanic generation' had arrived."[30]

Naturally, the decline in student activism that characterized the 1970s and 1980s was largely due, according to San Miguel, "to the increasing conservatism among the students and the dismantling of federal and state educational programs," a trend that accelerated during the 1990s and continues in the twenty-first century.[31] Yet, as previously discussed, San Miguel himself is quick to recognize that political activism and student involvement did not entirely die out in the 1980s. He therefore disagrees with scholars who have proposed otherwise: "The new political environment, as well as the emergence of the Hispanic generation, had a significant impact on the struggle against discrimination and assimilation in education. It either slowed, redirected, or diluted this struggle and its programs, but it did not halt the *movimiento*, as several scholars argue."[32]

Such developments as the protracted struggle at UCLA, beginning in 1989 and continuing through 1994–95, to attain departmental status for the Chicano/a Studies program—which ultimately resulted in a compromise and a partial victory that made possible the establishment of the César Chávez Research Center for Interdisciplinary Instruction in Chicana and Chicano Studies in the mid-1990s—as well as the 1999 fight "to save" Ethnic Studies at the University of California-Berkeley corroborate San Miguel's view about the false perception of the lack of activism in recent times. In both cases the events involved student hunger strikes. Interestingly, it appears that in the Berkeley case all of the students involved in the hunger strike were female, and a Chicana professor also took part in the fasting.

Chicano/a Studies was born during a period characterized by confrontation and controversy. With very few exceptions the various units established in universities and colleges throughout the United States have remained as programs and centers, never attaining departmental status. The ultimately successful struggle to create a department of Chicana and Chicano Studies lasted from 1989 until 1995. Even the aforementioned UCLA experience shows the degree of the university administration's resistance to altering the status quo. As small, underfunded, unwelcome but tolerated stepchildren of the academy, Chicano/a Studies programs remain precarious, stagnant units on most campuses today. Regardless of the structure or status, most of these programs do not offer graduate degrees, certainly not doctoral degrees, although the University of Arizona offers a master's program in Mexican American Studies not through a department but through the Mexican American Studies and Research Center. As Ignacio García has noted, however, the center "offers only three courses—two at the entry level—and has no real mechanism for influencing the content of courses offered by other departments."[33] Pragmatic considerations have compelled some individuals toward accepting, and even pushing for, the amalgamation of Chicano/a Studies with other programs, in the hope of strengthening their chronically weak position within the academy and achieving departmental status. Such institutional maneuvering has met with resistance and criticism from the more nationalistic advocates of Chicano/a Studies and Chicanismo, as espoused in the original Plan de Santa Bárbara. The content, form, and placement of Chicano/a Studies thus remains problematic and contentious, even after more than thirty years.

A Case Study: The University of Washington

As it developed at many other institutions, Chicano/a Studies (and other Ethnic Studies programs) came into existence at the University of Washington chiefly as a result of students' demands and activism. With the assistance and collaboration of a few sympathetic faculty members, students applied pressure, and finally in 1971 a small Chicano/a Studies program was established within the College of Arts and Sciences.[34] In 1975, after students confronted the university administration and occupied the office of the dean of Arts and Sciences over a controversial matter involving the aborted hiring of a Chicano professor, the program was removed from Arts and Sciences, transformed into El Centro de Estudios Chicanos, and put "floating" under the jurisdiction of a Board of Deans. Chicano/a Studies continued to exist as a center with insufficient personnel and meager resources: three full-time equivalent positions (distributed into one full-time lecturer, who was later promoted to assistant professor and put on a tenure track, one half-time director, and several part-time instructors) and one secretary.

Confronted with the financial crisis that shook up the university in the early 1980s, the campus administration was compelled to adopt a three-pronged approach to solving the budgetary problem: total elimination, reduction, and reorganization of units. Among the programs initially identified for possible elimination were various traditional departments (children's drama, kinesiology, Near Eastern languages and literature, textile arts, and so on). Unspoken, I believe, was the need to do something with the units that many considered "less legitimate," such as the Center for Chicano Studies and the other programs (Afro-American Studies, Asian American Studies, and Indian Studies, which remained housed in the College of Arts and Sciences). Eradicating these units would not have saved much money; reducing them, even less. And the political repercussions that any of these actions would have brought about were many and were clearly very serious. The only viable alternative, then, was reorganization. First a Committee and then a Task Force for the Reorganization of Ethnic Studies at the university was put together, and in 1985, after two years of negotiations (not without the proverbial student and community opposition and protests), a Department of American Ethnic Studies was born.[35] The new department encompassed Afro-American Studies, Asian American Studies, and Chicano/a Studies. American Indian Studies chose to continue as a program and to be housed in the Department of Anthropology, where it remains today.[36]

Negotiations were protracted and intense. Naturally, the main concerns revolved around the specter of total disappearance versus the survival and, if possible, the strengthening of the three units. In light of the circumstances in which it emerged, reorganization was perceived with suspicion; it was clearly a tricky and dangerous venture that involved bargaining and granting concessions. In the end the trade-off was the compromising of the relative autonomy each unit had enjoyed until then in order to collectively attain firmer ground within the institution. Two primary concerns guided the discussions: first, how best to preserve each program's integrity and original identity, and second, how best to incorporate provisions into the new department's constitution that would diminish internal competition and preserve democracy precisely by respecting each group's individual identity.

It is fair to say that neither Chicano/a Studies nor any of the other programs would have achieved departmental status at the University of Washington on its own. With the creation of the new department, however, instead of housing only one assistant professor and several part-timers, Chicano/a Studies enjoyed four tenure-line positions: two historians, one political scientist, and one economist. The University of Washington case illustrates the situation that most Chicano/a Studies programs have faced over the years as well as the difficult and complex choices they are often compelled to make.

A Generative Foundation for the Future

Despite its precarious positioning and the vicissitudes it has continuously confronted within academia, Chicano/a Studies prospered as a field of study, particularly between 1973 and 1983, an era that is now dubbed the "golden age" of Chicano/a Studies. An important aspect of this growth was the creation of the National Association for Chicano Studies (NACS) on May 18, 1973, at a conference organized and attended by scholars from around the country who were interested in establishing a common agenda to provide direction and help advance the field on a national basis.[37] Strongly influenced by and centered around the social sciences, NACS's program, according to Carlos Muñoz, called for a research model that was "problem-oriented, interdisciplinary, was critical of American institutions, and emphasized the relationship between class, race, and culture in determining the Chicano historical experience" in the United States.[38] By all measures the association thrived. It grew rapidly, holding annual meetings and publishing conference proceedings. At its peak, according to Ignacio García, "in the mid-1980s, the membership hovered around one thousand members."[39] In recent times, however, the NACS has confronted grave challenges, including a sharp internal dissension, which many see as undermining the organization's credibility and seriously threatening its very existence.[40]

Remaining challenges include the reconciliation of the academic and community missions of Chicano/a Studies, as well as the identification of exactly who comprises the Chicano/a community. For example, what is the relationship of Chicano/a Studies to other Latino/a Studies, to middle-class and upper-class Chicanos/as and Latinos/as? Can Chicano/a Studies embrace the self-reflexivity necessary to encompass the Chicana feminist analysis of what such scholars see as a "Chicana perspective fueled by the combined effects of class, race/ethnicity, and gender on Chicanas' life chances"?[41] Can Chicano/a Studies reconcile the conflicts inherent in the current academic context of emphasizing diversity; that is, can the field reconcile difference to the exclusion of power relationships? Can the field sustain itself with the ambivalences resulting from faculty in joint appointments, with conflicting demands from Chicano/a Studies and discipline-based departments? And finally, will students (Chicano/a and others) continue to demand the Chicano/a Studies scholarship and teaching as part of their education?

Such challenges are on the agenda of Chicano/a scholars. Stimulated by activities sponsored by the NACS and the Chicana feminist association Mujeres Activas en Letras y Cambio Social (MALCS), a significant amount of serious Chicano/a Studies scholarship has been produced during the past three decades. Chicano/a Studies scholars are also making incursions into traditional disciplines and into innovative interdisciplinary arenas. Undoubtedly, the most salient contributions have emerged in the fields of history, political science, Women's and Feminist Studies, border studies, and culture studies, including literature. The overall body of literature and the extensive bibliographies related to individual areas and disciplines bespeak of the achievements that have been made to date. It can thus be stated with certainty that, regardless of the name the endeavor may bear in the future and despite the form it may assume, Chicano/a Studies is a fruitful field of intellectual inquiry that will continue to produce valuable scholarly contributions as the field reckons with its many challenges and possibilities.

Selected Bibliography

Acuña, Rodolfo. *Occupied America: A History of Chicanos*, 3d ed. New York: Harper and Row, 1988.

Blea, Irene I. *Toward a Chicano Social Science*. New York: Praeger, 1988.

Córdova, Teresa, et al., ed. *Chicana Voices: Intersections of Class, Race, and Gender*. Austin, Tex.: Center for Mexican American Studies, 1986.

García, John A., Theresa [Teresa] Córdova, and Juan R. García, eds. National Association for Chicano Studies. *The Chicano Struggle: Analyses of Past and Present Efforts*. Binghamton, N.Y.: Bilingual Press/Editorial Bilingüe, 1984.

Mindiola Jr., Tatcho, and Emilio Zamora, eds. *Chicano Discourse*. Houston, Tex.: Mexican American Studies Program, 1992.

Romero, Mary, and Cordelia Candelaria, eds. *Community Empowerment and Chicano Scholarship*. Berkeley, Calif.: National Association for Chicano Studies, 1992. Sánchez, Rosaura, and Rosa Martínez Cruz, eds. *Essays on La Mujer*. Los Angeles: UCLA Chicano Studies Center, 1977.

Southwest Network of the Study Commission on Undergraduate Education and the Education of Teachers. *Parameters of Institutional Change: Chicano Experiences in Education*. Hayward, Calif.: World Publications, 1974.

Notes

1. Among these scholars are Carlos Muñoz Jr., *Youth, Identity, Power: The Chicano Movement* (London: Verso, 1989); Juan Gómez-Quiñones, "To Leave to Hope or Chance: Propositions on Chicano Studies, 1974," in *Parameters of Institutional Change: Chicano Experiences in Education* (Hayward, Calif.: Southwest Network, 1975); *Mexican Students por la Raza: The Chicano Student Movement in Southern California* (Santa Barbara, Calif.: Editorial La Causa, 1978), and *Chicano Politics: Realities and Promise* (Albuquerque: University of New Mexico, 1990); Alfredo Sánchez, "Chicano Student Movement at San José State," in *Parameters of Institutional Change*, 22–32; Eliezer Risco, "Before Universidad de Aztlán: Ethnic Studies at Fresno State College" in *Parameters of Institutional Change*, 41–47; Mario

Barrera, "The Struggle for Third College at UC San Diego" in *Parameters of Institutional Change*, 62–68; José Rivera and Luis Ramón Burrola, "Chicano Studies Programs in Higher Education: Scenarios for Further Research," *Aztlán* 15 (1985): 277–94; Refugio I. Rochín, "The Current Status and Future of Chicano Studies Programs: Are They Academically Sound?" Paper presented at the Fourteenth Annual Conference of NACS, El Paso, Texas, 10–12 April, 1986; Mario T. García, *Mexican Americans: Leadership, Ideology, and Identity, 1930–1960* (New Haven, Conn.: Yale University Press, 1989); René Núñez and Raúl Contreras, "Principles and Foundations of Chicano Studies: Chicano Organization on University Campuses in California," in *Chicano Discourse*, Tatcho Mindiola Jr. and Emilio Zamora, eds. (Houston, Tex." Mexican American Studies Program, 1992), 32–39; Guadalupe San Miguel, "Actors Not Victims: Chicanas/os and the Struggle for Educational Equality," in David R. Maciel and Isidro D. Ortiz, eds., *Chicanas/Chicanos at the Crossroads: Social, Economic, and Political Change* (Tucson: University of Arizona Press, 1996), 159–80; and Ignacio M. García, "Juncture in the Road: Chicano Studies since 'El Plan de Santa Bárbara,'" Maciel and Ortiz, eds., *Chicanas/Chicanos at the Crossroads*, 181–203.

Because San Miguel's "Actors Not Victims" and Ignacio García's "Chicano Studies since 'El Plan de Santa Bárbara'" were recently published and thus enjoy the benefit of the added perspective that chronological distance tends to provide, these works are useful and of much interest to this discussion. Both pieces are cogently argued and extremely well documented. I am particularly indebted to San Miguel and García. I am also grateful to the historian Vincent C. de Baca, one of the participants in the 1969 Plan de Santa Bárbara Conference, for his generosity in sharing his personal insights regarding the origins and development of Chicano/a Studies.

2. The term *ideology* appears here in quotation marks because it is employed in a "vulgar" sense (i.e., as a loose set of ideas), not in the strict Lukacsian signification, which defines it as false consciousness.

3. Susana L. Gallardo, "Con su pluma en su mano . . . a few words about don Américo Paredes," available on Gallardo's Chicana feminist Web site at http://www.chicanas.com.

4. Joe Holley, "Américo Paredes, 83, Pioneer in Chicano Studies," *New York Times* on-line news service, May 6, 1999. Holley also remarks that Paredes "returned to Texas in 1950 and enrolled at the University of Texas at Austin. The first Mexican-American ever to receive a Ph.D. at the University of Texas, he taught at the University from 1958 until his retirement in 1984."

5. See Ignacio M. García, "Juncture in the Road," 182; and Mario García, *Mexican Americans*, 273–74.

6. See Ernesto Galarza, *Merchants of Labor: The Mexican American Bracero Story—An Account of Managed Migration of Mexican Farm Workers in California, 1942–1960* (Charlotte, Calif.: McNally and Loftin, 1964); as well as Galarza's report, *Strangers in Our Fields* (Washington, D.C., 1956). One could argue that these books, like Julián Samora's *Los Mojados: The Wetback Story* (Notre Dame: University of Notre Dame Press, 1971), focus on Mexican immigrant labor, not specifically on Chicanos/as. But that is a more complex matter that does not allow such clear-cut distinctions, as discussed later in this chapter. Many scholars would agree that these phenomena in fact constituted an important basis for the establishment of Mexican American communities throughout the Southwest, the Midwest, and other regions, like the Pacific Northwest. For a lucid analysis of the latter, see Erasmo Gamboa, *Mexican Labor and World War II: Braceros in the Pacific Northwest, 1942–1947* (Austin, Tex.: University of Texas Press, 1990). Although Samora wrote his thesis, *Minority Leadership in a Bicultural Community,* in 1953, most of his published research is from the late 1960s and 1970s.

7. Ignacio García, "Juncture in the Road."

8. A true example of a Gramscian organic intellectual, José de la Luz Sáenz was an educator in the Texas public school system most of his life. He participated actively in the politics and organizing of the League of United Latin American Citizens (LULAC) in the early 1930s. He left a published book *Los Mexicoamericanos en la gran guerra (y su contingente en pró de la humanidad, la democracia y la justicia)* (San Antonio, Tex: Artes Gráficas, 1933), and an unpublished autobiography provisionally titled "Yo: Omnia mea mecum porto" (1944).

9. Carey McWilliams, *North from Mexico: The Spanish-Speaking People of the United States* (Philadelphia, Pa.: J. B. Lippincott Co., 1949); McWilliams, *Ill Fares the Land: Migrants and Migratory Labor in the United States* (Boston: Little, Brown and Company, 1942); and McWilliams, *Factories in the Field: The Story of Migratory Farm Labor in California* (Boston: Little, Brown and Company, 1939).

10. This issue seems implicit in such arguments advanced by Ignacio García, in "Juncture in the Road," who identifies one of the current challenges for the survival of Chicano/a Studies as such in the influx of non-Chicano/a academics: "Many centers find themselves challenged by non-Chicano Latino scholars who want to promote their scholarly interests. They argue that all Latino groups have a common experience with racism and poverty in American society. Also, programs that emphasize the inclusive Hispanic approach are more likely to gain research and support funds more easily. Because immigration has been a major area of study for Chicano Studies and because the immigrant groups are now more diverse among numerous Latino groups, there is an intellectual challenge to Chicano Studies to become inclusive or else to be seen as shallow and exclusionary" (189).

And, as García himself observes in a footnote, when presented as a forced issue, this challenge creates a more accentuated and militant nationalism: "At the national MECHA [Movimiento Estudiantil Chicano de Aztlán] conference in spring 1993, the students voted to refer to themselves as Chicanos and not admit anyone to the national organization who did not use the term" (202).

11. As has occurred within other U.S. ethnic groups, the nomenclature involved is complex and problematic. Before the late 1960s and the emergence of the Chicano/a movement, the official label bestowed upon this group was *Mexican-Americans*. The term was unsatisfactory on various grounds, however. First, it was not a self-given or self-chosen name, but rather one imposed on the people by the powers that be. Second, the term was embraced by the previous generation, which many considered to be an "accommodationist" generation whose political and social views and strategies had been defined and later rejected as favoring assimilation into mainstream America and therefore reneging on the more authentic and original cultural values cherished by the newer generations. Finally, although the hyphenated name could be taken to imply that the group was both Mexican and American, it also meant that the people were neither and that what best defined the condition was not the words but rather the nothingness, the limbo embodied by the hyphen itself.

Under these conditions the term *Chicano* (at times spelled "Xicano" to better approximate the original pronunciation of "Mexicanos" or "Meshicanos") was adopted as a term of cultural and political self-definition. After all, we were the descendants of the Aztecs who left the legendary Aztlán and migrated south to found one of the greatest Mesoamerican civilizations. Thus we were out to reclaim the original lands of our ancestors. All of the above notwithstanding, the terms Chicano and Mexican American are frequently used interchangeably as synonyms, and the same was true institutionally in defining academic units: Mexican American Studies or Chicano/a Studies.

12. Refugio I. Rochín and Adela de la Torre, "Chicanas/os in the Economy since 1970," in Maciel and Ortiz, *Chicanas/Chicanos at the Crossroads*, 52–80, 62–63.

13. John A. García, "The Chicano Movement: Its Legacy for Politics and Policy," in Maciel and Ortiz, *Chicanas/Chicanos at the Crossroads*, 83–107, 93.

14. San Miguel, "Actors Not Victims," 162.

15. Muñoz, *Youth, Identity, Power*, 130.

16. Although Chicanismo was loosely defined and meant different things to different folks, the essence of the concept is expressed in the "Manifesto" of El Plan de Santa Bárbara. Succinctly, the term refers to a cultural-nationalist position that attempted to instill pride among Chicanos/as by emphasizing the indigenous heritage, often mythicized and glorified, or the concept of *mestizaje* in which the

indigenous ingredient was predominant. Working-class culture, the fundamental experience of the majority of Chicanos/as, was also seen as one of the central features of this Chicanismo. Based on the *hermandad* or *carnalismo* (brotherhood) of *la raza*, the mandate of Chicanismo was the attainment of Chicano/a liberation, or self-determination, through political action. From El Plan de Santa Bárbara: "Culturally, the word Chicano, in the past a pejorative and class-bound adjective, has now become the root idea of a new cultural identity for our people. It also reveals a growing solidarity and the development of a common social praxis. The widespread use of the term Chicano today signals a rebirth of pride and confidence. Chicanismo simply embodies an ancient truth: that a person is never closer to his/her true self as when he/she is close to his/her community."

17. See the Web site of the University of Minnesota's Chicano Studies program at http://cla.umn.edu/chicano.

18. Historian Antonio Ríos Bustamante presents a concise and helpful outline of the most salient assertions in his booklet *Mexicans in the United States and the National Question: Current Polemics and Organizational Positions* (Santa Barbara, Calif.: Editorial La Causa, 1978). See also Richard Santillán, "The Dialectics of Chicano Political Development: A Political Economy Perspective," *Appeal to Reason* 5 (4, winter 1979–80): 51–63.

19. For an interesting discussion of this process in Southern California's Chicano/a student movement, see Gómez-Quiñones, *Mexican Students por la Raza* (1978).

20. From the University of Minnesota's Web site, http://cla.umn.edu/chicano; accessed on August 2, 1999.

21. This notion is conveyed by the wording of the themes of various conferences of such organizations as the National Association for Chicana and Chicano Studies (NACCS) as well as in book and article titles in such anthologies as that edited by Maciel and Ortiz, *Chicanas/Chicanos at the Crossroads* (1996).

22. For a lucid discussion of the dilemmas Chicano/a scholars confront in this regard, see Ignacio García, "Juncture in the Road," especially 188.

23. Ibid., 186–87. García cites Refugio I. Rochín's paper cited in note 1 above to support these allegations.

24. Among other scholars, however, San Miguel holds a different opinion: "Student involvement at the college level, unlike that at the secondary grades . . . continued during the 1970s. It did not die, collapse, or fade away as most historians have argued. University students continued to struggle for equality and cultural recognition after 1973, but they abandoned their militant tactics. Their actions, sometimes supported by faculty, and sometimes opposed by them, led to efforts to increase Mexican American access to higher education, strengthen Chicano Studies

programs, expand Chicano Studies classes to include gender issues, and to develop a critical and conscientious Mexican American literary and intellectual tradition in higher education." See San Miguel, "Actors Not Victims," 164.

25. Referring to the central tenets of the Plan de Santa Bárbara as they reflected the student movement, historian Carlos Muñoz Jr. wrote: "Key to that movement were pride in Mexican identity and Mexican cultural traditions and in the working class legacy of Mexican Americans, and active involvement in struggles for social and political change. The student movement thus reflected an unequivocal break from the assimilationist, middle class ideology of the Mexican American Generation." See Muñoz, *Youth, Identity, Power,* 139.

26. Mario García, *Mexican Americans,* 17–22; Santillán, on the other hand, in "Dialectics of Chicano Political Development," offers a more complex and in my opinion more accurate analysis about the coexistence of diverse political postures at every stage of the Chicano/a social development.

27. Mario García, *Mexican Americans,* 300.

28. San Miguel, "Actors Not Victims," 160.

29. Mario García, *Mexican Americans,* 300.

30. San Miguel, "Actors Not Victims," 165.

31. Ibid.

32. Ibid.

33. Ignacio García, "Juncture in the Road," 187.

34. Curiously, Joseph Sommers, one of the main faculty sponsors of these endeavors, was not Chicano/a. As at other campuses Chicano/a professors were rare commodities in the late 1960s and early 1970s.

35. Having been appointed as the half-time director of the Center for Chicano Studies in 1981, one year after my arrival at the University of Washington as assistant professor of Romance languages and literature, I was a member of both the Committee and the Task Force for the Reorganization of Ethnic Studies. When the Department of American Ethnic Studies was inaugurated, I returned to my full-time appointment in my original unit.

36. In addition to American Indian Studies, the position that each of the other programs adopted varied: Asian American Studies almost immediately accepted the notion of reorganization; Afro-American Studies was fundamentally opposed to it; and Chicano/a Studies stated that "while not opposed in principle" to the idea, the good faith and the earnest commitment of the administration to preserve and enhance the programs was a prerequisite for considering the move seriously. The term *amalgamation* was frequently thrown around, particularly by the harsher opponents to the measure, and the administration was always quick to clarify that the proposal on the table was for *reorganization*, not amalgamation.

37. According to Ignacio García, the conference was attended by "thirty-six individuals, of whom eight were women." See in García, "Juncture in the Road," 185.

38. Muñoz, *Youth, Identity, Power*, 150–51; quoted in Ignacio García, "Juncture in the Road," 185.

39. Ignacio García, "Juncture in the Road," 185.

40. For a frank and lucid discussion of these problems, see Ignacio García, "Juncture in the Road," especially 189–93.

41. Beatriz M. Pesquera and Denise A. Segura, "With Quill and Torch: A Chicana Perspective on the American Women's Movement," in *Chicanas/Chicanos at the Crossroads*, 231–47.

CHANGING
AND
EMERGING
PARADIGMS

Asian American Studies and Asian Studies: Boundaries and Borderlands of Ethnic Studies and Area Studies

SHIRLEY HUNE

FROM THE INCEPTION OF ASIAN AMERICAN STUDIES IN THE late 1960s, Asian Americanists have sought to establish their own programs in higher education. They have identified Ethnic Studies, with its particular perspectives, methodologies, and scholarship, as their rightful home. Nonetheless, on the many occasions that I have advised colleges and universities anxious to respond to student demands for Asian American Studies, I have been asked the same questions over and over again by presidents, provosts, department chairs, and faculty: Why can't we just put Asian American Studies in Asian Studies? Can't one of the Asian Studies faculty teach Asian American history and culture? Why do you want separate programs or your own department? Why do you want your own faculty?[1]

After more than three decades of Ethnic Studies in academe, these questions suggest that confusion remains in the minds of higher education leadership about the distinctions between Asian American Studies, which concerns itself with peoples of Asian and Pacific descent in the United States, and Asian Studies, an area of studies centered on the Asian region. Such a response also demonstrates the insensitivity of the leadership in higher education to the origin, intellectual mission, scholarship, and research interests of Asian American Studies in contrast to those of Asian Studies. This is a unique issue in Ethnic Studies: for example, rarely do academicians propose combining

African American Studies with African Studies or Puerto Rican and Chicano Studies with Latin American Studies. Educational leaders are able to distinguish the differences in those areas, but many have yet to fully comprehend what Asian American Studies represents as a scholarly field and how it contributes as an Ethnic Studies program.

Asian Studies generally focuses on the peoples, cultures, and developments within the Asian region and has given scant attention to Asians overseas. In contrast, Asian American Studies centers on Asian Americans as an integral part of U.S. civilization and regards Asia, especially historical and contemporary relations between the United States and Asia, with interest but from the perspective of how these aspects contribute to the making of Asian American history, culture, and identity. The intellectual and theoretical differences between these two fields, which are considered in greater detail throughout this chapter, have led Asian Americanists to argue that locating Asian American Studies within Asian Studies is problematic. In their view, by doing so, the interests and approaches of Asian American Studies would thus be subordinated within Asian Studies, making such an arrangement more of an administrative convenience imposed by a college or university rather than being their ideal intellectual home.[2] Thus over the years Asian American Studies has been protective of itself in building its specialty and warily eyes the influence of Asian Studies as an institutional organization, not as an intellectual terrain, on its legitimacy in the academy. This chapter explores the boundaries of Asian Studies and Asian American Studies, the emerging borderlands of their overlapping interests, and the continuing efforts of Asian Americanists to define for themselves the academic domain and institutional structure of Asian American Studies.

Racializing Asian Americans and Asian American Studies

Before discussing these two fields in academe, I offer some general comments on how race matters here. On a public level misconstruing Asian American Studies and Asian Studies illustrates the "ideological process" of racialization in America, as identified by sociologists Michael Omi and Howard Winant. In their words racialization signifies "the extension of racial meaning to a previously racially unclassified relationship, social practice or group."[3] For example, the notion of cultural citizenship in the United States is racialized. European Americans have historically been considered the norm, even as newcomers to the United States, while Asian Americans, including indigenous

Hawaiians and the descendants of several generations of American-born families, are frequently treated as permanent foreigners in the land of their birth.[4]

The racialization of cultural citizenship is also appropriated in academe. If Asian Americans are considered to be foreigners rather than Americans, concomitantly their history, culture, and identity are often mistakenly thought to be best explained by their racial connection to persons in Asia and the Pacific Rim; thus these studies, it follows, are more properly located within Asian Studies. The experiences of Asian Americans, which are primarily influenced by American history and culture and whose location is largely within the United States, are thus rendered invisible. Asian Americans are typically not seen as a racial-ethnic group that has actively participated in and contributed to the making of U.S. society or one that is identified with historical and contemporary struggles for survival, social equality, and community that comprise much of the rich texture of Ethnic Studies. Asian Americans are thus denied their claim to America and their place in U.S. history and culture. Academic fields and practices are therefore also embedded with racial meaning by notions of subsuming Asian American Studies within Asian Studies.

Boundaries

Asian Studies and Asian American Studies are both interdisciplinary fields whose faculty generally has been trained in traditional disciplines, but they are distinctly different in their origins, academic missions, and research interests. These differences serve as intellectual, ideological, and structural boundaries. Asian Studies made its first appearance in the late eighteenth century. Following the intellectual traditions of Europe, Americans expressed interest in the languages, ancient texts, philosophies, and religions of India and China. Like their European counterparts, they too "orientalized" Asia, its cultures and peoples, and they viewed the region not on Asia's own terms but through Western eyes as a passive object and often an exotic "other." Western superiority and civility were contrasted with Asian inferiority and barbarism to justify the West's interpretation of Asian culture and its management of Asian affairs. "Orientals," it was argued, were considered unfit for such important roles.[5]

These early Asianists (known as Orientalists) were joined later by missionaries eager to expand Western religion and diplomats and businessmen looking to trade in Asia and ensure America's foothold in the region. By the

1920s the field of Asian Studies was becoming professionalized, and the nation's foremost private and public research institutions began offering courses, especially on Chinese and Japanese history. Throughout World War II and the Cold War, Asian Studies on American campuses became interlocked with state interests as U.S. government funding supported the training of its scholars and helped to shape its programs. Like other area Studies, Asian Studies was in some regard part of a colonial project to better understand the colonies, the "natives," and the non-Western world to be able to achieve Western objectives. Many experts would be trained to interpret Asia from the perspective of U.S. interests. American elites studied Asian elites with an emphasis on assessing their politics and ideologies.[6]

In contrast to the development of Asian Studies, Asian American Studies is a comparatively smaller and much younger field in the academy. Until recently and for the most part it has limited its frame of analysis to within U.S. borders. Its intellectual mission focuses on the production of new knowledge and innovative theoretical perspectives on Asian Americans from the perspective of its subjects, who are viewed as active participants, not as objects, in the making of their own history, culture, and identity as well as that of the United States. Scholars of Asian American Studies also seek to reclaim omissions and to correct distortions in Asian American contributions to society in general, to center race in social analysis, to develop new paradigms of social relations that challenge biases of Western privileged males, and to ensure that Asian Americans are included in U.S. history and culture from an Asian American perspective. Recent scholarship also reflects fresh theoretical perspectives on race, gender, sexuality, and culture and the changing demographics of the Asian American population with, for example, studies of new ethnic communities, Asian American women, class differences, diaspora, gay and lesbian dimensions, and cultural representations.

Asian American Studies was initiated by nonelites. As part of the civil rights and antiwar movements of the late 1960s and early 1970s, students and community activists organized so-called Third World strikes on West Coast and other campuses. They demanded that higher education institutions be more responsive to racial and social injustices at home and abroad by providing curricula inclusive of racial minorities and increasing the numbers of diverse (i.e., non-White) students and faculty.[7] Asian American Studies was also part of an anti-internal colonialism project of Asian Americans and other marginalized groups. If Asian Studies was more closely identified with state interests and the status quo, Asian American Studies related (and continues to do so) to the disempowered population and seeks social change. Among its goals is a commitment to provide an intellectual space of resistance and support for marginalized students, especially Asian American students and other students of color, and to train specialists interested in community issues. Asian American Studies has encouraged the study of nonelites, especially working-class and first-generation Asian Americans, who are too often neglected in scholarship. Furthermore, the field has often criticized the role of the state and its agencies in their treatment of Asian Americans.[8] Asianists have not been distracted by the establishment of Asian American Studies and have generally disregarded its existence. Nonetheless, the antiwar movement of the 1960s and 1970s also led to a reexamination of the mission and research agenda of Asian Studies. Consequently, Asian Studies has given more attention to nonelites, looking at the concerns of women, peasants, laborers, and ethnic minorities, reviewing development issues from an Asian perspective, and critiquing U.S. involvement in Asian affairs.[9]

Asian Studies and Asian American Studies also differ in their presence and standing in higher education institutions. Of the approximately three thousand colleges and universities in the country, most offer Asian Studies in some form and the majority of its faculty are non-Asian males. In contrast, very few institutions have Asian American Studies programs, but the number of campuses offering courses continues to grow. Most Asian American Studies programs are on West Coast campuses of large public higher education systems. The presence of such programs in private elite institutions is still limited and often times resisted, although it increased throughout the 1990s primarily as an outcome of student sit-ins, rallies, and hunger strikes. A 1998 compilation of Asian American Studies programs noted seventeen free-standing entities and thirteen Asian American Studies programs within Ethnic Studies or American Studies units.[10] A number of other campuses offer one or two courses on an irregular and nonpermanent basis often taught by graduate students or visiting or part-time faculty, which is an institution's typical first response to student demands for Asian American Studies.

Since its inception, most administration and faculty at higher education institutions have held Asian Studies in high esteem, and the field has been long supported by the federal government and by private foundations with research, travel, and training grants. Until budget cuts to area studies came about after the end of the Cold War, graduate students, especially those in the most prestigious programs, typically had their entire graduate education funded.[11] In contrast, the academic legitimacy of Asian American Studies, like other Ethnic Studies programs, continues to be questioned. This seriously affects the field's efforts to establish and expand permanent programs and to hire and tenure its faculty. Asian American Studies also lacks external grant opportunities and is frequently omitted from funding targeted for Ethnic Studies programs and students. Although scholars of many backgrounds contribute to the study of Asian American history and culture, faculty in Asian American Studies programs are mostly Asian Americans and are well represented by women. Furthermore, training in Asian American Studies is almost exclusively at the undergraduate level.

Asian American Studies and Asian Studies are clearly demarcated in origin, intellectual mission (especially theoretical perspectives and research interests), number of programs in higher education institutions, perceived academic value, external funding, faculty and student composition, recruitment and retention of faculty, and other areas. Given that Asian Studies has given little attention to the activities of Asians outside of Asia and the Pacific Rim, eliding Asian American Studies within Asian Studies subordinates Asian American Studies. It denies Asian American Studies its distinctiveness as an intellectual endeavor and hinders its development as a field in its own right. Furthermore, such an academic arrangement often meets with resistance from faculty and students in both fields. Nonetheless, although intellectual, ideological, and structural boundaries exist between the two fields, there are some overlapping interests, and some scholars in Asian American Studies and Asian Studies are finding a common discourse.

Borderlands

The world continues to experience a global social and economic transformation in conjunction with the political changes that have occurred since the end of the Cold War. These changes are marked by multiple processes, including the redrawing of national borders; the creation of new political entities; the resurgence of nationalisms, ethnic national identities, religions, and interstate and intrastate conflicts; the growing use of new capital and labor formations; the development of innovative technologies; and an increase in regional and global population movements and resettlements. The terms *globalism* and *globalization* as well as descriptions of new economic restructuring that links the local with the global and a new international division of labor are frequently bandied about to encapsulate these vast changes. More relevant to this chapter, there is a new Asia in the world economy as well as a different type of Asian American in the United States. Migration to America from Asia and the Pacific Rim since 1965 has been more diverse in language, religion, nationality, education, and social class than older Asian American communities, and this diversity is changing the United States. The majority of Asian Americans in the 1990s were first generation—newcomers with fresh memories of homelands who often maintain strong connections to families and institutions in Asia and the Pacific Rim.[12]

This global transformation has had an impact on the academy's intellectual life and is generating a new frontier of inquiry for many scholars in area studies and Ethnic Studies. Innovative theoretical paradigms are emerging as diaspora, postcolonial, and transnational studies and seek to better interpret these global changes than do the existing frameworks. These new studies invoke disciplinary border crossings that are energizing fields of study and expanding, bridging, and occasionally blurring intellectual boundaries between and among fields. In her pioneering work *Borderlands/La Frontera*, scholar Gloria Anzaldúa developed the concept of a new consciousness that has emerged from the collision of cultures, the dismantling of paradigms, and the search for a revised synthesis in the negotiation of two or more cultures.[13] The borderlands concept is an appropriate metaphor for the intersecting and overlapping concerns of Asian Americanists and Asianists involved in diaspora, postcolonial, and transnational studies.[14] A glance at recent publications, such as the new journals *Diaspora* and *Positions*, reveals the interests of scholars with expertise in Asia and Asian Americans in these areas.[15] Also important is the distinction between intellectual border crossings that represent a new epistemological and ontological space of inquiry, and institutional boundaries between Asian American Studies and Asian Studies as structural organizations that remain generally intact.

Asian Studies and other area studies are now being encouraged to rethink "area" as a concept. For example, the 1996 Ford Foundation initiative "Crossing Borders: Revitalizing Area Studies" proposed that area studies explore reorganizing research and teaching around new themes, such as links between "local" and "global" processes, diasporas, and race, gender, ethnicity, class, and identity, which are also the concerns of scholars in other fields, particularly Ethnic Studies.[16] Such a direction could involve Asian Studies paying more attention to Asian peoples outside of Asia and the Pacific Rim. Asian American Studies, however, has always embraced international and national dimensions, such as in its attention to immigration. In negotiating these two terrains, Asian Americanists have historically emphasized

234 / SHIRLEY HUNE

reclaiming the place and role of Asian Americans in the United States. The new globalization brings more attention to international perspectives, namely, incorporating Asia and Pacific Rim developments in explaining Asian American history, culture, communities, and identities. Thus diaspora, post-colonial, and transnational studies as borderlands can also provide Asian American Studies with new opportunities to reappropriate intellectual terrain that has historically been defined within the confines of Asian Studies and to reinterpret it within an Asian American framework. Interest in these new areas is driven in large part, but not exclusively, by scholars raised in Asia or with close ties to their regional homelands, whose worldviews, education, cultures, and identities are more likely to be bi-, multi- or transnational. These scholars often differ from their second-, third-, and fourth-generation Asian American colleagues, whose life experiences, scholarly interests, and critiques have been centered largely in the United States.[17]

Diaspora, postcolonial, and transnational inquiries are not without critique, however. It has been noted that each new generation rewrites history in its own image. Some scholars question whether the focus on transnational and postcolonial experiences in the diaspora are a phenomenon of the first generation, generally a transition group, and whether it will taper off with succeeding generations who are more firmly settled in and focused on their new homelands and have less connection to their countries of origin. Given the long history of human migration and acculturation in different territories, other scholars do not regard these phenomena as being particularly new. They consider important many notions of diaspora, postcoloniality, and transnationality but find these concepts to be clearly intensified by this extraordinary period of global economic restructuring, which, these scholars believe, will eventually stabilize. Attention will then be drawn back to national and local terrains of analysis.[18]

Class also matters. Some scholars question to what extent the conditions, state of mind, and discourse of postcoloniality or transnationalism are simply the possibility, choice, and making of those of a certain class or status, namely capitalists and the intelligentsia, and differ dramatically from the less privileged of their homelands that comprise the vast majority of those in the United States and elsewhere in the diaspora.[19] Conjecture on the direction that the new studies and their critique will take for Asian Studies I leave for other colleagues. My concern here is with the implications of the borderlands of diaspora, postcolonial, and transnational studies on the intellectual focus of Asian American Studies.

Recent discourse in Asian American Studies calls for an expansion of the dominant national narrative to take into greater account its global dimensions and transnational processes in their multiplicity—such as flows of capital, labor, and culture and new family and other institutional formations—on the making of Asian Americans, their communities, identities, and commitments. But there is also a note of caution among the most carefully thought-out analyses that questions whether a transnational emphasis in a global context detracts from the national perspective of Asian American Studies to the extent that Asian Americans seek solutions to their concerns and identify their lives outside the United States, such as with those in their historical homelands, rather than with each other and in coalition with other marginalized groups in America and elsewhere.[20] In earlier studies I drew attention to the international dimension of U.S. immigration and have argued for comparative studies of Asians in the diaspora (sizable Asian communities can be found in Africa, Australia, Canada, the Caribbean, Great Britain, South America, and now in the Middle East) to further understanding of the complexity of being Asian outside of Asia, to join the efforts of Asian Americans for new and just lives with other groups likewise voluntarily and involuntarily dislocated and resettled, and to free Asian American Studies and studies on the United States in general from a paradigm of American exceptionalism.[21]

Using global dimensions in explaining human events is not a new framework. But it is their privileging and potential displacement of the historical location and standpoint of Asian American Studies that gives pause. In my mind the issue is not an either-or binary reasoning of the global or the national dimension as the center of Asian American Studies. Instead, drawing on the social theory of Edward W. Soja, I see a "both and also" logic with the international dimension as a trajectory of Asian American Studies within a new and enlarged terrain of analysis, whereby the national and international dimensions of Asian American experiences are recombined to rethink and reconceptualize the complexities of the contemporary world where the locations of Asian American lives—real, perceived, and conceived—are interrelated and experienced simultaneously.[22]

Any recentering of Asian American Studies within a global analysis must be grounded where people are: for the most part, in a national and sometimes local context. In this case it is the United States for Asian Americans, albeit a reconceived social space that is both real and imagined and territorialized and deterritorialized. To do otherwise would leave Asian Americans at sea, figuratively speaking, traversing the Pacific Ocean, unattached, unprotected, and belonging nowhere, which only further marginalizes Asian Americans nationally and globally.[23] Thus the primary intellectual focus of Asian American Studies remains in Ethnic Studies. The intellectual border crossings of diaspora, postcolonial, and transnational studies are infusing new energy among scholars and enriching theoretical perspectives and research agendas, but they do not fundamentally alter the intellectual, ideological, and structural boundaries of Asian Studies and Asian American Studies. There is still no intellectual rationale for combining these two distinct fields. In addition, Asian Studies—being the older, generally larger, and academically more established field on campus—would likely subordinate the academic mission and intellectual concerns of Asian American Studies. Asian American Studies is not Asian Studies, and Ethnic Studies is not area studies. Asian American Studies, like other Ethnic Studies programs, has therefore by necessity been preoccupied with building its own specialty. The paradigm of race relations in the United States has yet to shift fully from a vertical racial subordinate-white dominant standard, namely a Black-White duality, to a multiplicity of simultaneous racial group dynamics that include horizontal subordinate-subordinate or minority-minority relations between and among racial-ethnic groups in America that require fresh theoretical frameworks and innovative analyses.[24]

Ethnic Studies is also a borderlands. Asian American Studies can explore border crossings with other Ethnic Studies programs, intersectional studies that incorporate race, class, gender, generation, sexuality, age, and other features to better reflect the new complexities of social relations. Asian American Studies can also delve into comparative studies with racial-ethnic groups within the United States and with Asian communities outside the United States. This intellectual frontier beckons and awaits Asian American Studies in the new millennium.

Notes

1. These questions are most often asked by individuals at higher education institutions located east of California, where the Asian American population (which had been modest until recently) has grown significantly over the past two decades. Asian Americans today comprise as much as 40 percent of the undergraduates at some large public institutions in California and nearly 20 percent at such private institutions as Harvard and Northwestern Universities.

2. This chapter is concerned with the problematic of subsuming Asian American Studies within Asian Studies from an intellectual rationale. Institutions may also propose a fiscal rationale for combining Asian Studies and Asian American Studies. As a cost-saving measure that makes little academic sense, institutions often administratively house departments and programs together where they retain their intellectual autonomy. Such an administrative practice needs to be distinguished from that of combining programs with different intellectual traditions within a single administrative unit. This can result in uneasy governance, sometimes irreconcilable differences, and even power struggles in which one group seeks to dominate others.

3. Michael Omi and Howard Winant, *Racial Formation in the United States* (New York: Routledge & Kegan Paul, 1986), 64.

4. The following comment by a Brown University student expresses a commonplace experience of Asian Americans: "People ask you, where are you from? They mean in Asia—not America. Sometimes they actually ask, when are you going back? Even though you've spent your entire life in America." Cited in Charlotte Bruce Harvey, "To Be Asian-American," *Brown Alumni Monthly*, November 1989, p. 26.

5. Edward Said, *Orientalism* (New York: Vintage, 1978).

6. Sucheta Mazumdar, "Asian American Studies and Asian Studies: Rethinking Roots," in Shirley Hune, Hyung-chan Kim, Stephen S. Fugita, and Amy Ling, eds., *Asian Americans: Comparative and Global Perspectives* (Pullman: Washington State University Press, 1991), 32–36.

7. On the origins and early development of Asian American Studies, see the Commemorative Issue, "Salute to the 60s and 70s: Legacy of the San Francisco State Strike," *Amerasia Journal* 15 (1); and William Wei, *The Asian American Movement* (Philadelphia, Pa.: Temple University Press, 1993), especially chapter 5.

8. Shirley Hune, "Opening the American Mind and Body: The Role of Asian American Studies," *Change* (November-December 1989): 56–63; and Amy Ling, "Creating Asian America: The Ongoing Revolution," in Jenn-Yun Tein and Thomas K. Nakayama, eds., *Asian Americans: The Year 2000 and Beyond* (Tempe: Arizona State University, 1996), 87–95.

9. Mazumdar, "Asian American Studies and Asian Studies."

10. Asian American Program Compiler, *Directory of Asian American Studies Programs* (Ithaca, N.Y.: Asian American Studies Program, Cornell University, 1998).

11. Mazumdar, "Asian American Studies and Asian Studies."

12. The 1990 Census of the United States found that 63.1 percent of Asian Americans were born in a country other than the United States, in contrast to 36

percent of Hispanics and 3.3 percent of Whites. Language spoken at home is also revealing of first-generation status: for example, 13.8 percent of the general U.S. population speaks a language other than English, compared with 73.3 percent of Asian Americans. For a detailed discussion of Asian American demographic trends and social characteristics, see Shirley Hune and Kenyon S. Chan, "Special Focus: Asian Pacific American Demographic and Educational Trends," in Deborah J. Carter and Reginald Wilson, eds., *Fifteenth Annual Status Report on Minorities in Higher Education* (Washington, D.C.: American Council on Education, 1997), 5–8, 39–67, 103–7.

13. Gloria Anzaldúa, *Borderlands/La Frontera: The New Mestiza* (San Francisco: Aunt Lute Books, 1987).

14. I draw on Leonie Sandercock's use of borderlands as a metaphor here; see Sandercock, "Voices from the Borderlands: A Meditation on a Metaphor," *Journal of Planning Education and Research* 15 (1995): 77–88.

15. See, for example, special issue of *positions* on Asian American Studies 5 (2). Recent works include Linda Basch, Nina Glick Schiller, and Christina Szanton Blanc, *Nations Unbound: Transnational Projects, Postcolonial Predicaments, and Deterritorialized Nation-States* (Luxembourg: Gordon and Breach Publishers, 1994); Inderpal Grewal, "The Postcolonial, Ethnic Studies, and the Diaspora," *Socialist Review* 24 (4): 45–74; Aihwa Ong and Donald M. Nonini, eds., *Ungrounded Empires: The Cultural Politics of Modern Chinese Transnationalism* (New York: Routledge, 1997); and Peter van de Veer, ed., *Nation and Migration: The Politics of Space in the South Asian Diaspora* (Philadelphia: University of Pennsylvania Press, 1995). It should be noted that diaspora and transnational studies have the attention of scholars of many national and ethnic backgrounds, while postcolonial studies is of particular interest to South Asians and South Asianists.

16. Joye Mercer, "The Ford Foundation Shifts Its Focus and Structure," *Chronicle of Higher Education*, August 15, 1997, pp. A29–30.

17. The evolving discourse on the global versus the domestic dimension of the Asian American experience can be gleaned in articles in the following special issues of *Amerasia Journal*, "Asians in the Americas," 15 (2); "Thinking Theory in Asian American Studies," 21 (1 and 2); and "Transnationalism, Media, and Asian Americans," 22 (3). See also Hune et al., eds., *Asian Americans*.

18. These issues are based on discussions held at the Social Science Research Council Conference, "Becoming American/America Becoming: International Migration to the United States," January 18–21, 1996, Sanibel Island, Florida. For papers presented at this conference, see *International Migration Review* 31 (winter 1997).

19. Ibid. The writings of anthropologist Aihwa Ong on overseas Chinese (her-

self born into a Straits Chinese family in colonial Malaya and living half of her life in the United States) also explore and represent a number of these facets. See, for example, Ong, *Flexible Citizenship: The Cultural Logics of Transnationality* (Durham, N.C.: Duke University Press, 1999). Ong examines how racial and cultural hierarchy in the United States differentiates Asian immigrants by their class. Cosmopolitan Hong Kong Chinese have flexible citizenship because their capital investments enable them to live, work, and educate their children in a number of global sites, thus becoming "Whitened" in the United States. In contrast, Khmers have fewer choices because of their limited education and identification with welfare, thus becoming "Blackened" in America. It is interesting to note Ong's own first-generation transition, which she terms a "passage into American society." She concludes this particular work with a personal commentary on her "moral predicament" of becoming a legal citizen after twenty years in the United States only after the birth of her first child. Ong remains ambivalent about the term *Asian American* and concludes that for non-White Americans the future reconfiguration of citizenship in the West needs to consider "domestic, racial terms" along with "transnational, class ones" (752). I thank Shu-mei Shih for bringing Ong's works to my attention.

20. See, in particular, Arif Dirlik, "Asians on the Rim: Transnational Capital and Local Community in the Making of Contemporary Asian America," *Amerasia Journal* 22 (3): 1–24; Madhulika S. Kandelwal, "Thinking Inclusion in Asian America: Perspectives on Race and Ethnicity," in Tein and Nakayama, eds., Asian Americans (1996), 73–85; and Sau-ling C. Wong, "Denationalization Reconsidered: Asian American Cultural Criticism at a Theoretical Crossroads," *Amerasia Journal* 21 (1 and 2): 1–27.

21. I raised the neglect of the international dimension of Asian immigration to the United States and the need for Asian diaspora studies in an early critique of research on Asian Americans in Shirley Hune, *Pacific Migration to the United States: Trends and Themes in Historical and Sociological Literature* (Washington, D.C.: Research Institute on Immigration and Ethnic Studies, Smithsonian Institution, 1977), 59–60; and "Expanding the International Dimension of Asian American Studies," *Amerasia Journal* 15 (2): xix-xxiv.

22. Edward W. Soja, *Thirdspace: Journeys to Los Angeles and Other Real-and-Imagined Places* (Cambridge, Mass.: Blackwell Publishers, 1996).

23. I want to thank Russell Leong, the editor of *Amerasia Journal*, for helping me clarify my thoughts on this matter.

24. Shirley Hune, "Rethinking Race: Paradigms and Policy Formation," *Amerasia Journal* 21 (1 and 2): 29–40.

Reimagining Borders: A Hemispheric Approach to Latin American and U.S. Latino and Latina Studies

EDNA ACOSTA-BELÉN

THIS CHAPTER CAPTURES A FEW OF THE CHALLENGES CON-
fronting Latin American and Caribbean Studies and U.S. Latino/a Studies in
the twenty-first century. It outlines some of the conditions that call for more
integrated hemispheric approaches and reconceptualization of these fields.
Historically, the close of the nineteenth century provided an excuse for intellectuals to embrace a sort of fin de siècle malaise, a disquieting feeling of crisis and urgency through which intellectuals pondered certain human values
thought to be perilous and defined those values they hoped to advance. Now,
at the onset of the twenty-first century, I use this fin de siècle precedent as a
justifiable motivation to engage in my own ruminations about the current
tensions as well as the future directions and possibilities that stem from the
academic endeavors of area studies, Ethnic Studies, and Women's and Gender Studies. Humans are experiencing a time of what scholar Eric Hobsbawm
has described as unprecedented "global disequilibrium."[1] In this contentious
historical moment, scholars and educators must continue to play an activist
role in articulating the problems, contradictions, and possibilities of an increasingly and inevitably diverse U.S. society and interconnected transnational
world.

   In this postmodern era of contested boundaries, border transgressions,
building bridges, remapped geography, and unbounded nations, scholars are

240

focusing on conjunctures, disjunctures, intersections, and interconnections. Noticeably enough, most of the academic discourse in recent decades is rarely devoid of such theoretical jargon. Yet although the postmodern era witnesses claims to the collapse of the West's totalizing grand narratives and practices of ethnocentric representation, the world is subject to an ever-expanding web of economic, commercial, and cultural networks and forces that continue to propagate homogenizing images and values. The concept of a triumphant capitalist "New World Order" is still defined by the leading Western countries. Consequently, scholars are becoming increasingly engaged in analyzing the compelling realities resulting from the hemispheric integration and globalization processes. This is dramatized by the continuing international labor migration flows from the developing countries to the leading capitalist nations, by the expanding presence and projected demographic growth of the U.S. Latino/a population within the twenty-first century, and by the complex economic, social, and cultural dimensions and fluidity of the different forms of transnationalism that is taking place both within the Americas and on a global scale.

According to some immigration researchers, the global diffusion of consumption patterns, values, lifestyles, perceived opportunities, and material aspirations within the industrialized Western societies, coupled with the limited possibilities to see these ideas fulfilled in the immigrants' respective countries of origin, account for a large portion of present-day international migration flows.[2] More recent international labor migration patterns between the leading capitalist nations and the developing countries, particularly between the United States and the rest of the Western hemisphere, as well as the shifting demographic composition of U.S. society are changing and expanding the scope of Latin American and Caribbean Studies, American Studies, and those ethnic and Women's and Gender Studies programs that focus on U.S. Latino/a experiences. I refer here primarily to Chicano/a and Puerto Rican Studies, which emerged in the late 1960s and early 1970s, followed by Cuban, and more recently, Dominican Studies. It is also possible that other programs may emerge focusing on individual groups or the collective U.S. Latino/a experiences.

Without question, the incessant intersections between the local, the national, and the transnational are producing new forms of interaction and socioeconomic relations and structures that influence the nature of social and political movements and the construction and reconfiguration of cultures and identities in the Western hemisphere. Some of these new forms include the convergence in recent decades of views, strategies, and goals as articulated by various movements aimed at producing social and political change that have flourished in both Western and non-Western societies. Among the most conspicuous examples of these new forms of interaction are those that reflect the spread of what Mexican political leader Cuauhtémoc Cárdenas has called "ideals without boundaries."[3] Cárdenas primarily refers to those movements that promote human, women's, and ethnic rights as well as environmental and health concerns. These particular movements reflect the worldwide struggles for fundamental freedoms and rights, exposing uneven power relations and conflicts that exist among the persistent inequalities based on ethnic, racial, gender, and class differences.

This context provides a general framework for the chapter's main objective: to outline and foster a hemispheric approach to the study of Latinos/as in the American hemisphere. The perspectives introduced herein stem from the ongoing interconnections and dynamics that Latinos/as are developing within the United States as well as between the United States and their respective countries of origin. More rapidly than ever before, the Latino/a worlds of the North and the South are transcending spurious geographic, cultural, and linguistic borders, particularly in view of current U.S. demographic trends. The U.S. Census projects that, if current growth rates continue, Latinos/as will become the largest minority group in the country by 2050. With a current population of about 31 million (the equivalent of the combined population of several Latin American countries), one of every ten individuals living in the United States is of Hispanic origin, but by the middle of the twenty-first century this proportion could increase to one in five (see Tables 1 and 2).[4] Continuous migratory movements between the two Americas as well as the irrepressible current and projected growth in the U.S. Latino/a population are sustaining what anthropologist Constance Sutton has described as a "transnational sociocultural system" that increasingly and reciprocally influences cultural experiences both within the United States and within the Latin American and Caribbean countries of origin.[5] Within this system (im)migrants maintain multistranded relations that link together their host societies (in this case, the United States) and their homelands. While (im)migrants from Latin America and the Caribbean contribute to the "Latinamericanization" or "Caribbeanization" of particular U.S. communities, their current commuter patterns and persistent interactions with their countries of origin in turn influence the diffusion of U.S. values and ways of life. These patterns also significantly affect the cultural, political, and socioeconomic structures of the immigrants' countries.

TABLE 1. **Hispanic Population Distribution by Group, 1997**

Origin	Number (in millions)	Percent
Mexican	18,795	63.2
Puerto Rican	3,152	10.4
Cuban	1,258	4.2
Central and South American	4,292	14.4
Other Hispanic	2,206	7.4
Total Hispanic Population	29,703	100.0

Note: Population figures for nondecennial U.S. Census years are based on sample survey estimates or a relatively small number of cases, which often results in an undercount of particular population groups.

Source: U.S. Department of Commerce, Bureau of the Census, "The Hispanic Population of the United States (Washington, D.C.: U.S. Census Bureau, 1997). Table 10.1.

TABLE 2. **Hispanic Population Growth Projections**

Year	Total (in millions)	Increase (percent)	Percentage of Total U.S. Population
1970	9.1	n/a	4.5
1980	14.6	60.4	6.4
1990	22.4	53.4	9.0
2000	31.3	39.7	11.4
2010	41.1	31.3	13.8
2020	52.6	28.0	16.3
2030	65.5	24.5	18.9

Sources: Figures for years 2000–30 are based on *Current Population Reports*, Series P25–1130, "Population Projections of the United States by Age, Sex, Race, and Hispanic Origin: 1995–2050" (Washington, D.C.: Bureau of the Census, 1996). See also U.S. Department of Commerce, Bureau of Census, *Hispanic Americans Today* (Washington, D.C.: U.S. Government Printing Office, 1993).

Unequivocally, the transnational processes currently taking place in the Western hemisphere are leading scholars to engage in more integrated and broader approaches to the study of the cultural and socioeconomic conditions and interconnections among the peoples and nations of the Americas. Various scholars at the University at Albany, State University of New York (SUNY), including myself, have put forward some of these new perspectives in our research and teaching activities as well as within our publishing endeavor, the journal the *Latino/a Research Review* (formerly the *Latino Review of Books*). If there is one thing that has become quite clear to Latin Americanists, Caribbeanists, and other area, ethnic, and Women's and Gender Studies specialists in the past three decades, it is that these fields are no longer centered in the United States, as they once were. Rather, these studies involve more than ever the participation and contributions of scholars and activists from the countries and peoples under study. There is no doubt that the parochialism of the early years is being replaced, in the specific case of Latin American and Caribbean Studies and U.S. Latino/a Studies, by an expanding sense of hemispheric community in which scholars have come to rely on the scholarship, policy making, and activism of colleagues from these regions as much as they rely on the work being done by scholars in the United States and other parts of the world.

Multicultural Crossovers

No one can deny the increasing interdisciplinarity and cross-fertilization that have flourished in the academy, particularly within the past few decades. Such fields as Ethnic Studies, Women's and Gender Studies, cultural studies, diaspora studies, and Gay and Lesbian Studies provide new locations for scholars to pursue more inclusive analyses of the rapidly changing world. Now examined are the differences or particularities that shape human existence—social, racial, sexual, cultural, local, and transnational—from a critique of the traditional disciplines, from the interstices among disciplines, and from these new emerging fields. Worthy of notice is the fact that although these fields have emerged and introduced significant changes into the university curriculum in the United States and other Western countries, these areas of study are also making significant inroads throughout the rest of the world, including the developing countries of Latin America and the Caribbean.

Emerging from the transnational sociocultural system that characterizes the Americas are significant cultural and linguistic transformations and exciting hybrid cultural configurations, multicultural crossovers that are forcing scholars to rethink, redefine, and transgress the conventional boundaries of what we do in our respective academic disciplines. These crossovers represent more than the study of provocative sociocultural phenomena; they are changing the scope of some of the traditional disciplines, thrusting those fields into a transgression of rigid disciplinary demarcations. The traditional disciplines are opening their borders to paradigms that favor more connected or integrated approaches to the social realities, to paradigms that view societies as complex conglomerates of hybrid cultures, contested identities, and conflicting and uneven power relations. Some of the traditional disciplines are transforming themselves by exploring the interstices among disciplines, increasingly exposing their inherent biases and developing a better grasp of the social forces, power relations, and contradictions that shape disciplinary knowledge.

These knowledge transformations are quite evident within the realms of cultural, historical, and literary studies (my primary research interests), where the transnational interconnections, encounters, and crossovers taking place between the United States and Latin American and Caribbean countries are producing some provocative cultural configurations and discourses. One concrete example is how U.S. Latino/a writers increasingly are being studied and incorporated into the canons of U.S., Latin American, and Caribbean literatures. In turn, this is creating a Spanish-English publication market in which some of the largest U.S. publishing houses are releasing simultaneous editions in both languages of works by Latino/a writers.[6] Moreover, for many years the Latino/a and Latin American (im)migrant experience remained sharply segmented in most of the field's teaching and research endeavors. Many U.S. scholars in these programs felt their sphere of research began on the "other side of the Río Grande," while scholars in Latin America often viewed their Latino/a (im)migrants on the "other side of the Río Bravo" as an unappealing, illegitimate, or distorted (and therefore rejected) representation of their nationality.[7] In turn, scholars in American Studies typically focused on White America and for decades remained oblivious to issues of race, ethnicity, and gender as important components of the American experience. Thus the study of the U.S. Latino/a experience seemed always to belong elsewhere, with little attention paid to the group that had their feet in two societies, as feminist scholar Elsa Chaney pointed out back in 1979.[8] It is not surprising that until recently most textbooks used in introductory Latin American Studies courses or U.S. history courses practically ignored the U.S. Latino/a experience. The same holds true for textbooks used in Latin American and Caribbean countries.

Gay and Lesbian Studies is another crossover research area that is receiving increased attention after being considered an almost taboo subject in Latin American and Caribbean intellectual discourse. This relatively new field has already yielded several major Latino/a-focused studies in the past decade.[9] Most of these works are aimed at shattering prevalent myths and stereotypes and analyze the contingent nature of sexualities, how these identities are negotiated, and how constructions of masculinity and femininity are shaped by sociocultural and historical context.

The Local and the Global in the New World Order

Five hundred years ago Europe presumably "discovered" the New World. Accordingly, it can now be said that in the era of contemporary globalization, the world is beginning to discover itself as a more holistic system with as many commonalities of purpose and pressing problems as there are divergent interests and solutions. New technologies have created an increasing awareness of a global common destiny, and sustained efforts to bring down the barriers that have traditionally separated peoples and nations are becoming more apparent. There are many recent instances of what Puerto Rican scholar Frank Bonilla has labeled "the lingering unease" about economic integration initiatives.[10] In the Americas, for example, there is the increased hemispheric integration of markets impelled by NAFTA and the heated debates that arose before and after the act's approval by the U.S. Congress. In Mexico there is the growing Zapatista unrest, its influence on other indigenous movements in the hemisphere, the movements' unprecedented and remarkable use of the Internet in spreading their message and in garnering international support, and the subsequent Mexican economic crisis.

Such hemispheric events may also be considered within the framework of wider globalization processes that are forcing scholars in many fields to grapple with the implications of the new world order or, more accurately, the "disorder" brought about by the disintegration of the socialist bloc and the implementation of many structural adjustments in a world now dominated by internationalized capital. In this brave new world information and money can be exchanged in an instant, corporations keep moving and searching the planet for sources of low-wage labor, and goods can be transported more rapidly and efficiently than ever before. The processes of structural adjustment, privatization, and neoliberalization that the Latin American and Caribbean countries have experienced in the past decade and a half—which reflect some of the problems and inefficiencies that have afflicted their dependent economies—continue to exacerbate existing social tensions and inequalities. These processes also bring about major population displacements and considerable hardship for large sectors of the population, with only limited and not so obvious prospects for recovery and long-term prosperity.[11]

Most contemporary societies are confronting mass unemployment and poverty as well as increases in crime, violence, and homelessness even in the wealthiest countries. Clearly, "it is as if something has gone out of order with the New World Order," to quote the lyrics of Brazilian singer Caetano Veloso's popular song. These words poignantly capture the contradictions of a world characterized by growing inequalities and widening gaps between rich and poor, capital and labor, and between the status of men and women. In this new world order of transnational capital, women, immigrants, and the citizens of developing nations continue to be the major sources of low-wage labor. Nonetheless, to the mounting challenges implied in the homogenizing tendencies of contemporary globalization and the West's new world order, progressive forces continue to pose an array of social concerns—from human rights and environmental issues, to a rejection of patriarchal, sexist, heterosexist, and racist viewpoints and practices. Slogans such as "think globally, act locally" also permeate the collective consciousness, reminding scholars and activists of the potential threat of losing the subtleties, nuances, and particularities of each group or community as well as the empowering potential of specific subaltern constituencies.

Scholars Suzanne Jonas and Edward McCaughan have perceptively captured some of these dynamics, pointing out that "globalization is creating new regional centers of capital accumulation, and hence new alliances across states among segments of classes, transnational and local, that will benefit from new technologies and new forms of accumulation."[12] Within this new social map the authors stress the need for progressive cross-border coalitions, which may include labor, environmental, women's, and indigenous groups, particularly those in Canada, Mexico, and the United States—in other words the groups and areas that are most affected by the intemperate nature and undemocratic transgressions of transnational capital.

Current globalization processes also contribute to the notion of a new global citizenship. As part of his proposals for forging and advancing a sense of global citizenship, international law scholar Richard Falk has pointed to two types of globalization.[13] The first type is commonly identified with a new world order representing the interests of the G7 nations of the West, which Falk calls "globalization from above." This sort of globalization perpetuates an unbalanced new world order that, rather than being dominated by a single country, replaces the single-country hegemons of the past with geographic hegemonic blocs (e.g., North America, the European community, and the Pacific Rim).[14] More important, however, is the fact that this type of globalization reduces the world to "a homogenizing supermarket for those with the purchasing power."[15] The second, less widely spread form of globalization is "globalization from below," which represents a social vision reflecting "an array of transnational social forces animated by environmental concerns, human rights, hostility to patriarchy, and a vision of community based on the unity of diverse cultures seeking an end to poverty, oppression, humiliation, and collective violence."[16] This notion envisions a one-world community where human solidarity is based on democratic participation and principles that empower ordinary individuals and communities to have more control over the resources and conditions that influence their lives. This latter form of globalization best challenges the homogenizing tendencies and current contradictions inherent in the practices of globalization from above.

In the 1993 book *Global Visions: Beyond the New World Order,* editors Jeremy Brecher, John Brown Childs, and Jill Cutler introduce what they call a "multifesto" (rather than a manifesto) for promoting globalization from below, based on a vision of a world in which diversity is acknowledged but a convergence of goals is also sought.[17] Labor union expert Denis McShane offers the key to this convergence of goals in his proposal to move toward a global solidarity by fostering and forging complementary coalitions based on what he has identified as "the four E's"—economy, ethnicity, equality, and ecology.[18]

Some scholars claim that the stage of transition humans are experiencing in the current world economy is comparable in significance to the nineteenth-century Industrial Revolution, necessitating by implication the use of more global approaches in analyzing contemporary realities. Interestingly, in 1995 a group of British sociologists from the University of Manchester launched a new sociology of business journal, *Competition and Change: The Journal of Global Business and Political Economy*, to explore the implications of the current global economy. With an editorial board that includes scholars from Africa, Asia, Latin America, and the United States, the journal examines scholarly discussions about an emerging field of global studies in which researchers and policy makers in business and in the social sciences come together to address major issues and questions raised by globalization processes. These issues include the nature of competition today among nations and corporations; the effects of global competition among different forms of capitalism; the local ramifications of the global economy; the role of the nation-state in a world in which labor and capital are increasingly mobile; the relationship between interdependence and increasing social inequalities within and across nations; and the question of who can and should regulate businesses or corporations that have sites throughout the world. Other obvious questions of particular relevance to Latinos/as that arise from these hemispheric and global processes and interactions include ways in which U.S. employment and investment needs are linked to immigration, foreign trade, political regimes, the environment, and human rights concerns; the exacerbated social and political tensions and contradictions created by the widening cleavages between capital and labor and between highly industrialized North American nations and developing Latin American and Caribbean nations; and the influence of innovative information and media technologies on consumption patterns, values, and aspirations, as well as on the contemporary construction of Latino/a identities in the American hemisphere.

Rather than attempting to tackle these questions here, since most are beyond the scope of this chapter, instead I refer interested readers to the recent academic developments described above as examples of how globalization processes are confronting scholars with new challenges and with the need to articulate innovative responses. Needless to say, the voices and participation of Latin Americanists, Caribbeanists, and U.S. Latino/a Studies specialists are essential in delving into some of the manifold implications of hemispheric integration and globalization. The transnational encounters and crossovers taking place between the North and the South are not exclusive of the American hemisphere. Similar events also occur in other regions of the world, which means that the cross-border coalitions previously mentioned have the potential of developing into more far-reaching, international movements aimed at counteracting more effectively the inequities, excesses, and overall undemocratic tendencies of transnational capital, as well as the alarming spread of right-wing activism, especially in the industrialized Western nations.

The Restructuring of Knowledge

The global restructuring of the economy, briefly outlined earlier, implies a concomitant restructuring of knowledge production. World systems scholar Immanuel Wallerstein has pointed to this in his 1995 article about the state of African Studies, in which he noted that the field reflected "the uncertain path of redefinition, even of reassertion," as such constructs as Ethnic Studies, cultural studies, diaspora studies, and other movements influenced by poststructuralist theories were introduced into the academic enterprise.[19] He goes as far as predicting that "the whole disciplinary taxonomy is about to crumble," as part of a more encompassing general process of restructuring knowledge production, which Wallerstein compares in magnitude to the process that occurred in the nineteenth century.[20]

Other scholars, such as Nathan Glazer, have recently thrown in the towel, so to speak. Glazer has taken a step beyond his 1963 *Beyond the Melting Pot* (coauthored with Daniel P. Moynihan), when he begrudgingly proclaimed in the title of his most recent book that "we are all multiculturalists now."[21] The new book acknowledges that the multiculturalists have won the so-called U.S. culture wars due, to a large extent, to the country's failure to assimilate African Americans and other racial minorities. Glazer's main conclusion is that, like it or not, multiculturalism is here to stay, and only a dramatic change in the bipolar Black and White divisions of U.S. society would make it just another passing phase in the making of the nation. Historians Michael Greyer and Charles Bright announced in a 1995 article the revival of world history as an academic discipline, now that most Eurocentric biases and concepts are being exposed. They claimed that "the reimagining of the world as history is under way," stressing how the field once again has become one of the fastest growing areas of teaching.[22]

Considering the particular evolution of Latin American Studies (or, for that matter, of other area studies fields such as African Studies), these fields were initially influenced by Cold War and other foreign policy imperatives, such as the U.S. government's parallel push to "modernize" these geographic regions and to increase its knowledge and policy-making base regarding what were then considered the extremely poor, undeveloped, and politically unstable peripheral regions of the world. These were fields primarily represented by North American White male academics, with scant involvement of scholars from the targeted regions and little interest in looking at the presence of groups of Latin American or African origin in the United States or at gender issues. This situation, of course, has changed significantly over the years, particularly since the late 1960s, due in part to the efforts of professional area studies associations, major foundations, and research centers and programs in trying to be more inclusive of the work of Latin American and Caribbean scholars and providing travel and other collaborative opportunities and exchanges for scholars from these regions. A further development that is forcing the current reconceptualization of area studies is the increased academic legitimacy and institutionalization of Women's Studies and Latino/a Ethnic Studies (e.g., Chicano/a, Puerto Rican, Cuban, and more recently, Dominican Studies) as well as the scholarship that has emerged from these fields. The affinities and alliances that U.S. Latino/a and feminist scholars have forged with their Latin American and Caribbean counterparts have also contributed to this end. Without the infusion of gender perspectives into area studies by some feminist scholar pioneers, exactly how the lives of women are affected by modernization, development, and the international division of labor would probably not be understood today. Other contributions by feminist scholars have included documenting the uncounted or discounted hidden aspects of women's labor, examining women's significant role in the 1980s democratization process and in articulating and advancing social and human rights struggles in various countries; and increasing international awareness about environmental and health concerns.

During the past few decades scholars and others have expanded our knowledge about the pluralistic nature of feminism and of the many differences among women. The many forms that feminism assumes within specific communities, social sectors, and nations as well as among races or particular regions of the world have also been examined. Scholars and activists alike have recognized the need to make Women's and Gender Studies a more inclusive space for women of color in the United States, in the Third World, as well as in other Western countries. Despite continuing struggles and the high degree of consolidation and institutionalization of some academic programs, the fields of Ethnic Studies and Women's Studies themselves are at a critical juncture in their development, as they are affected by budgetary reductions and the educational and economic downsizing and restructuring occurring throughout the United States and the world. But perhaps the most threatening phenomenon at the beginning of the twenty-first century is found in the renewed life that right-wing demagoguery has gained, with all of its xenophobic, homophobic, sexist, and racist implications and backlashes. More alarming is that these xenophobic attitudes are turning into mass ideologies that are no longer country-specific or localized problems; many of these ideologies have acquired a global dimension. The global upheaval of the twentieth century has been, according to Hobsbawm, "spectacular and world-changing, but also unexpected and unpredicted."[23] Neither past experiences nor past ideologies and theories seem to fit the situation of the past three decades.

As scholars and activists today confront these dramatic changes in the world scene, they are still far from developing broad-based multicultural and gender-inclusive teaching and learning about the differences and commonalities within and across feminist or women's movements in various parts of the globe. For example, do scholars adequately understand the variety of Western feminisms and other non-Western discourses? What are some of the major differences in the development of women's movements in North America and Western Europe, in Western and Eastern Europe, in Latin America and Africa? Or, for that matter, in Germany and Australia, the United States and Japan, Cuba and Puerto Rico? What are some of the issues and conditions that transcend national borders, and what are the issues specific to a country or local community? Why is it that some women's movements do not (while others do) regard the state as the major instrument for improving their status? Why is it that in some countries women's movements are more grass-roots oriented than in others? What are some of the reasons that made Women's and Gender Studies flourish in academic settings in the United States and other Western nations, but primarily only at independent centers and institutes in most Third World countries? If feminism is viewed as a historically continuous and fluid movement, what are the factors that produce periods of expansion and stagnation in particular countries? If there is an international or global women's movement, what are the factors that bind it together? And if some of the present social and economic conditions are global and general, how can scholars and activists bring about articulated forms of global action around specific issues? Which are the issues that could make transnational and border coalitions possible?

The answers to these questions are far from obvious. I pose them to capture some of the challenges and complexities of women's conditions. Nonetheless, scholars have achieved some clarity about the fact that Western feminisms should not continue to be portrayed as one movement or as a master discourse that transcends cultures and national boundaries. In this sense feminisms cannot simply be exported just like any commodity or development program to "modernize" developing countries. This, of course, does not mean that we should stop searching for commonalities and convergences across feminist and women's movements. On the contrary, it is in emphasizing these commonalities and in learning about the singularities and pluralistic nature of women's struggles around the world, and the theoretical frameworks that emerge from less privileged settings, that we begin to build cross-border solidarities and coalitions around pressing issues that concern and affect large numbers of women. Promoting comparative and cross-cultural research can be quite valuable in increasing scholars' understanding about those specific historical, socioeconomic, political, or cultural factors that inform ideological strategies and visions of those women's and feminist movements that have been most effective in producing social change or in achieving particular goals.

Constructing Latino and Latina Identities

The past decade has witnessed a proliferation of scholarship on U.S. Latinos/as, especially works that acknowledge their heterogeneity, the significant racial, social, national, and generational differences among individual groups. At the same time, however, these works recognize the presence of "a Latino imaginary,"[24] "a Hispanic condition,"[25] or the forging of "a Hispanic nation"[26] within the United States. This chapter does not address the appropriateness of these concepts or the adequacy or shortcomings of the widely used Hispanic-Latino/a labels. Scholar Suzanne Oboler has already done this quite effectively in her 1995 book *Ethnic Label, Latino Lives.*[27] Determining which labels are the most appropriate or accurate has been a contested issue over the years; even after more than a century of using the term *América Latina* (Latin America), the name is perhaps more contested now than ever before. Since its early mid-nineteenth century origins, the term implied a separation between the ostensibly "Anglo" world to the North and the "Latin" world to the South. It can easily be argued in both cases, however, that this dichotomized view is far from reflecting the true character of the nations that comprise both regions.

Understanding the historicity of the Anglo-Latin, North-South hemispheric separation, as well as the interconnections between the two parts of the Americas, allows scholars to grasp the different character and functions of contemporary concepts of pan- or trans-Latino/a identities.[28] For more than a century a power-based differentiation has been made between the nations to the north and south, one essentially based on the notion of "Anglo" superiority over an undemocratic, politically unstable, socially impoverished, and economically dependent "Latin" world. In turn, the nations south of the border view the United States as the hemispheric hegemon whose world supremacy is based on imperialist and neocolonial practices of military intervention and economic exploitation in the developing countries. This counter-positioning is best captured in José Enrique Rodó's *Ariel*, published in 1900, which represents the gateway to twentieth-century Latin American thought.[29] This book introduced the characters Próspero and Calibán, from Shakespeare's *The Tempest,* into the process of constructing a pan-national Latin American identity and collective consciousness conceived in relation to the United States.

In Rodó's *Ariel*, Próspero's enlightened view of Western civilization is transmitted to his devoted disciple, Ariel, who from Rodó's perspective represents the essence of the Latin American soul, its spirituality and higher moral ground. In contrast, Calibán is still Shakespeare's barbaric monster, this time symbolizing the irrepressible flow of utilitarianism and materialist modernity embodied by the United States at the turn of the century. More than seven decades after the publication of *Ariel*, the Cuban intellectual Roberto Fernández Retamar gave new meaning to the Próspero-Calibán civilization-barbarism dichotomies in his efforts to dismantle Eurocentric colonialist thought in the Americas.[30] He went beyond Rodó's Latin-Anglo dynamic, which counterposed the figures of Próspero and Calibán and subverted the traditional meaning of these widespread symbols. In Fernández Retamar's work, Ariel was still the receiver of a body of knowledge that had laid hegemonic claims to civilization over the rest of the world. But the West imposed its civilization on the New World through conquest and the subsequent destruction and subjugation of the many colonized others. Thus the vision of a civilized Europe, incarnated by Próspero and Ariel, was far from revealing the story of enslavement, rapacious destruction, and the subsequent "creolization" experienced in the New World colonies by displaced indigenous peoples and transplanted Africans. Rather than reiterating the notion of a barbaric Calibán situated at the margins of a civilized world, Fernández Retamar subverts the symbols: the new Calibán "implies rethinking our history from the *other* side, from the viewpoint of the *other* protagonist."[31] It is in the rebellious nature of the enslaved Calibán that the story of subjugation, accommodation, resistance, and subversion against colonialist forces is finally revealed. Hence Calibán is a more accurate symbol of the historical experiences of the colonized peoples of the American hemisphere.

The increasing presence of Latinos/as in the United States has created a new context in which some of these old identity paradigms are replicated, while at the same time novel paradigms are created. Moreover, scholars are becoming more cognizant of the fact that contemporary globalization processes compel them more than ever before to look at the cultural, economic, and political interactions between the North and South. A stage has been reached in which the artificial boundaries that traditionally have separated the study of the Latin American and Caribbean regions from their counterpart (im)migrant populations in the United States are being transgressed, underscoring the need for wider hemispheric approaches to the study of different aspects of the Latino/a experience on both sides of the border. For too long scholars have associated the U.S. immigrant experience with a permanent rupture or separation from the countries of origin, rather than looking at the multistranded social, economic, and political interactions and networks that link these countries with the host societies (in this case, the United States). These interactions and networks represent some of the most obvious areas of common ground for salvaging the great divide that has traditionally separated Latin American Studies and Latino/a-focused Ethnic Studies programs, such as Chicano/a and Puerto Rican Studies—programs that emerged from the U.S. Civil Rights, antiwar, and ethnic revitalization movements of the 1960s and 1970s.

Area Studies, Ethnic Studies, and Women's and Gender Studies: Conjunctures and Disjunctures

Although it is true that some of the processes previously described are making the boundaries and scope of both area and Ethnic Studies fields more permeable, there are important distinctions to make and pitfalls to avoid. First, scholars should be mindful that the historical origins and fundamental approaches of both fields are quite different and these differences should continue to be stressed. Ethnic Studies programs were projects formulated out of oppositional social movements and shared a commitment to contestation. They have not only expanded the boundaries but also generated significant paradigm shifts within the traditional disciplines regarding the study of race, ethnicity, class, and gender, while struggling against the forces that constantly try to reduce Ethnic Studies to just another locus for identity politics or political correctness. Second, the specificities of major focus of these programs on social and racial inequalities and unresolved related problems that plague U.S. society should not get lost in the name of the larger problems confronted by other nations in the American hemisphere or throughout the world.

Today faculty that move with relative ease between area studies and Ethnic Studies are frequently caught in the bind of being delegitimized as real scholars in either field, precisely because they ventured out of the conventional demarcations of narrowly conceived disciplines and fields, exposing some of their biases and shortcomings and focusing on the intersecting nature of gender, racial, and ethnic constructs. Early in the development of Ethnic Studies Latin Americanists or Caribbeanists in the United States who were of Latin American or Caribbean origin, and who were drawn into Chicano/a and Puerto Rican Studies at a time when the pool of academics with doctoral training was much smaller than today, often saw their work being undermined or ignored because it was viewed as an extension of their genetic makeup rather than as a reflection of their intellectual preferences and professional expertise. While Anglo and European scholars studied the Latin American or African "others" using essentially faulty or limited approaches, the "others" were ostensibly considered to lack the "objectivity" to study themselves. Although it was perfectly legitimate for American Studies to glorify the *e pluribus unum* or melting-pot view of U.S. society, Ethnic Studies scholars continued to have to push their way in, with some degree of persuasion, perseverance, and success, if one considers the proliferation of scholarship in recent decades reflecting the influence of these fields. The entire process of making significant intellectual and educational inroads may be summarized in the words of the Chicano performing artist Guillermo Gómez-Peña as a practice in "creative appropriation, expropriation, and subversion of dominant cultural forms."[32]

During the early years Women's Studies was also dominated by the perspectives of White middle-class women in the United States and in the Western European nations. There was a prevalent tendency to view Third World women as the passive victims of oppression rather than as agents of change and as participants in the articulation of feminist theories. While women in Latin America and the Caribbean were keeping abreast of the work of women in the Western countries, Western White, middle-class feminists still knew very little about the different realities and responses articulated by less privileged women of different races, classes, and nationalities. In this regard U.S. feminist scholars in both the area studies and Ethnic Studies have been quite instrumental in bringing a multicultural and international dimension into Women's Studies and in influencing the proliferation of Women's Studies programs in Latin American and Caribbean institutions of higher education.

U.S. women of color were similarly absent in the emerging fields of Ethnic Studies and Women's Studies, as most programs initially focused on the collective subordination and disenfranchisement from the Western intellectual tradition of what were commonly portrayed as undifferentiated colonized peoples. These programs began to expose the lack of knowledge about these groups and the need to reconceptualize received knowledge about them by deconstructing the canonical practices of the disciplines. The years of precarious existence faced by many Ethnic Studies and Women's Studies programs and their struggles for institutional survival and intellectual legitimacy often relegated to another day discussions about commonalities and differences between the fields. After all, neither gender nor racial oppression were the great equalizers for women and minorities. Thus both fields had to make some inroads in each other's direction; these inroads continue to evolve.

These examples illustrate that the prevalent cross-fertilization among interdisciplinary fields is not only unavoidable within prevailing global-transnational contexts, but it is also desirable both in intellectual and practical terms. After more than three decades of existence, and even after generating some of the most provocative and influential scholarship, Women's Studies and Ethnic Studies programs are still viewed in some institutions as marginal to the academic enterprise. Thus the increased collaborations and alliances among the more established area studies programs and these other interdisciplinary fields should be pursued; in some cases this may be a productive way of sharing faculty and other resources and engaging in collaborations, rather than always competing for a shrinking pool of resources. In this collaboration, however, scholars must remain alert to the shortsightedness and prejudices of many faculty and university administrators.

The ongoing downsizing in recent years in U.S. higher education institutions, particularly in public university systems, has led some institutions to propose merging all kinds of interdisciplinary programs, under the misguided assumption that programs carrying the word *studies* and housing more than one woman or faculty member of color is not central to the curriculum. In these unfortunate scenarios little regard is given to the history or intellectual paradigms that are salient to each field. Thus the danger of being swallowed by broader "studies" categories is as palpable as is the racist optic that all of these programs are marginal to the academic enterprise, or that all subalterns should share the same umbrella.

New *Encuentros*

In a 1993 article I emphasized the importance of having such interdisciplinary fields as area, ethnic, and Women's and Gender Studies further explore their commonalities and differences by engaging in cross-cultural comparative research and approaches, both at the national and international levels.[33] This process would take each field beyond its shared purpose to decolonize knowledge about women and other subaltern groups into the potential formulation of alternative models of inquiry stemming from intercultural and intracultural, racial, and gender dialogues around the issues central to each field.[34] Contemporary postmodern, postcolonial, and feminist theories—with their guiding principles of decentering and deconstructing hegemonic models and their focus on the relations between elite and popular consciousness and practice, on transnational crossovers and changing identities, and on discourse and representation—have proven to be quite useful in dealing with the issues of borders and bridges and the constant back-and-forth commuting between the intertwining Latino/a worlds.

These ongoing dialogues, coupled with the tremendous increase in the U.S. Latino/a population of groups other than Mexicans or Puerto Ricans, are pushing some of the existing Chicano/a and Puerto Rican Studies programs, which emerged from the concerns of the U.S. Civil Rights and anti-war movements, to expand their research and teaching efforts and to incorporate comparative approaches that address a wide range of differences within and among U.S. Latino/a groups themselves. A similar process is beginning to take hold within Latin American and Caribbean Studies programs, which, after many years of neglect and exclusion, are now paying more attention to the experiences of Latin American and Caribbean (im)migrant populations in the United States as part of a contextual continuum with the countries of origin. More surprising is the fact that institutions and faculty both in Puerto Rico and Mexico have finally "discovered" Puerto Rican and Chicano/a Studies, and these new *encuentros* (or meeting of minds) are now leading to more meaningful, reciprocal collaborations. Considering that immigration has become one of the most contested issues within the current U.S. political discourse, particularly as it affects some of the most populated states (such as California, Florida, New York, and Texas), the immigrant experience still has not received the attention it deserves in Latin American and Caribbean area studies research and teaching.

Perhaps this benign indifference explains, at least in part, why the academic community currently is not playing a central role in shaping the ongoing public debates about immigration, and the prevalent discourses instead are dominated by a xenophobic immigrant-bashing, in which U.S. Latino/a communities are becoming scapegoats for many of the hardships and uncertainties caused by downsizing and economic restructuring throughout the United States. The passing of new restrictive laws to curb both legal and undocumented immigration, the various attempts to deny immigrant families access to educational and social services, and the discrediting and dismantling of affirmative action and bilingual education programs are symptomatic of this immigration backlash. The U.S. public discourse is plagued with fears about balkanization and the obligatory reference to the culture wars—in other words, sound bites that give new life to old myths and stereotypes about Latinos/as, that obfuscate the benefits and highlight the detrimental effects of immigration. It is both perplexing and ironic that as the world moves to increasing interdependence and dismantling of borders (at least for the movement of capital), there is such a concerted political effort in the United States to close its borders to immigrants.

Although the immigration debate was partly shaped by the political histrionics of most recent presidential and congressional elections, most Latin Americanists, Caribbeanists, and U.S. Latino/a Studies specialists cannot help but wonder how far this immigrant backlash will go before a much needed sense of balance is inserted into the debate. Those who advocate the building of a wall or the digging of a ditch across the U.S.-Mexico border (tasks that would probably employ immigrant labor) implicitly underscore the need for well-articulated counter-responses to the widely spread xenophobic and racist attitudes of recent years toward immigration. These attitudes must be counteracted by not losing sight, in the process of defining our research, teaching, and public policy agendas, of the pursuit of democratic values, social justice, and antiracist and antisexist societies. Considering the effects of increased immigration on the continuing and projected demographic changes in the racial and ethnic composition of U.S. society, migration is undoubtedly a pressing topic of future research in area, ethnic, and Women's and Gender Studies. And as transnational migrants commute between the United States and their Latin American and Caribbean countries of origin, one cannot help but wonder about the impact these migrants have on their homeland economies and the social structures of their communities. In turn, how are those communities responding to these changes? One key issue worthy of further study is the extent to which this transnational movement creates similar backlashes against those individuals who left, continue to circulate, or have returned permanently to their native countries.

Although Latin Americanists and Caribbeanists have paid some attention to the migratory movements within the regions themselves, particularly population displacements from rural to urban areas, until recently their interest in Latin American and Caribbean migrants within the United States had been less noticeable. Most immigration specialists tend to be demographers using data generated from the U.S. Bureau of the Census; few are area studies specialists who through fieldwork may address those aspects of immigration that cannot be explained by Census data. In a 1996 article in the *LASA Forum* (the Latin American Studies Association), former LASA president Wayne Cornelius observed that it may be already too late for scholarship to catch up with the anti-immigration backlash and to influence policy making so that it is based on the true costs and benefits that the presence of Latino/a groups has on specific states, cities, and localities.[35]

Another factor influencing the future of Latin American and Caribbean area Studies, or for that matter higher education in general, is the new technological advances that have made a reality of Marshall McLuhan's futuristic view of the world as a "global village."[36] Computers, satellites, and information systems and networks allow instant communication and the ability to witness "live" the conflicts, struggles, and accomplishments of global neighbors, be it from the industrial nations' metropolitan centers or the planet's most remote areas. Providing computer literacy and access to the World Wide Web for students is no longer a luxury but a necessity. Technology upgrades and the development of new software programs, databases, and other information sources are developed before we have learned how to use the earlier versions. Finally, the financial resources necessary to keep up with the changing pace are not easily available, creating additional disparities among peoples and nations.

At the same time, there is the risk of letting technology take over our lives, as we produce digital libraries, make our journals available online, develop interactive classrooms, buy satellite link-ups for distance learning, and essentially plunge into the uncharted electronic territory of cyberspace, running the risk of getting lost in space and of diminishing the human contact, interpersonal exchange, critical thinking, and mentoring that is such an important part of effective classroom learning and in training professionals and the new professorate. As we often contemplate in awe how the technology can facilitate research and teaching, how it can provide easier access to information, we must resist the creation of "Blockbuster universities," where the introduction of virtual reality takes the virtue away from human contact and some of our most treasured human values. Pursuing that delicate balance between the humanistic endeavors and the scientific and technological pursuits, and articulating ways of making technology accessible to the most disadvantaged sectors of society, rather than creating more segmentation and inequalities, remain major challenges for the future.

Another primary challenge for the twenty-first century is how to continue acknowledging and incorporating into teaching and learning experiences the increasing human diversity. This diversity has become a recognizable force not only within the United States but also within the increasingly global society. Demographic projections have revealed that by the middle of this century, Latinos/as will constitute the largest minority group in U.S. society and that almost half (47 percent) of the total U.S. population will be composed of groups of color (Latinos/as, Asians, African Americans, Native Americans). Of that figure, Latinos/as will constitute 40 percent of the combined population of these groups.[37] Scholars hold a major responsibility for preparing students to be active, informed, and productive participants in a multicultural U.S. society and an interdependent world. Perhaps more than ever before, these changes will continue to keep area studies and other interdisciplinary programs in business, but they also provide an opportunity to reassess how scholars will face this rapidly changing, undiscovered country of the future.

I conclude this chapter by reiterating the centrality of Latin American, Caribbean, and U.S. Latino/a Studies programs in facing the challenges of theorizing and analyzing hemispheric and global changes. U.S. Latinos/as are increasingly positioning themselves to participate in bringing about changes in the Americas from within the United States, while at the same time governments within Latin America and the Caribbean are showing increased interest in their respective U.S. Latino/a communities.[38] U.S. Latinos/as are thus playing a more proactive role in influencing the formulation of U.S. policy domestically as well as hemispherically. Moreover, scholars face a formidable challenge in training students to be critically informed and engaged global citizens. Alternative visions and approaches must continue to be defined by all kinds of constituencies, not only international agencies, governments, or political and cultural elites. Globalization and transnationalism clearly have introduced an important dimension in scholarly efforts to understand differences and commonalities within and among cultural groups. But only if scholars continue to see these differences and commonalities comparatively, while measuring the local as well as the regional and global dimensions, can they continue to yield fresh and provocative possibilities.

Selected Bibliography

Fernández Retamar, Roberto. *Calibán and Other Essays.* Trans. Edward Baker. Minneapolis: University of Minnesota Press, 1989.

Heilbrunn, Jacob. "The News from Everywhere: Does Global Thinking Threaten Local Knowledge?" *Lingua Franca* (1996): 49–56.

Sutton, Constance, and Elsa Chaney, eds. *Caribbean Life in New York City: Sociocultural Dimensions.* New York: Center for Migration Studies, 1987.

Notes

1. Eric Hobsbawm, "The Crisis of Today's Ideologies," *New Left Review* (March–April 1992): 192:55–64.

2. Alejandro Portes and Rubén Rumbaut, *Immigrant America: A Portrait* (Berkeley: University of California Press, 1990).

3. Cuauhtémoc Cárdenas, "Moving Peoples and Nations," in Jeremy Brecher, John Brown Childs, and Jill Cutler, eds., *Global Visions: Beyond the New World Order* (Boston: South End Press, 1993), 273–78.

4. U.S. Department of Commerce, Bureau of the Census, "The Hispanic Population of the United States" (Washington, D.C.: U.S. Bureau of the Census, 1994).

5. Constance Sutton, "The Caribbeanization of New York City and the Emergence of a Transnational Sociocultural System," in Constance Sutton and Elsa Chaney, eds., *Caribbean Life in New York City: Sociocultural Dimensions* (New York: Center for Migration Studies, 1987), 15–30.

6. A specific example of such a publishing house is Vintage Books and its division Vintage en Español. Some of the Spanish translations Vintage has published include Cristina García's *Dreaming in Cuban* (1992)/*Soñando en Cubano* (1993); Esmeralda Santiago's *America's Dream* (1996)/*El sueño de América* (1996); and Junot Díaz's *Drown* (Riverhead Books, 1996) and *Negocios* (1997).

7. Both names (the Río Grande and the Río Bravo) refer to the same river as it is known in English and Spanish.

8. Elsa Chaney, *Supermadre: Women in Politics in Latin America* (Austin: University of Texas Press for the Institute of Latin American Studies, 1979).

9. Among the most recent publications in Latin American/U.S. Latino/a Gay and Lesbian Studies are: Elena M. Martínez, ed., *Lesbian Voices from Latin America: Breaking Ground* (New York: Garland Publishing, 1996); Sylvia Molloy, ed., *Hispanisms and Homosexualities* (Durham, N.C.: Duke University Press; Alfredo Mirandé, *Hombres y Machos: Masculinity and Latino Culture* (Boulder, Colo.: Westview Press, 1997); Daniel Balderston and Donna J. Guy, eds., *Sex and Sexuality in Latin America* (New York: New York University Press, 1997); Matthew C. Gutmann, *The Meanings of Macho* (Berkeley: University of California Press, 1996); Ian Lumsden, *Machos, Maricones, and Gays: Cuba and Homosexuality* (Philadelphia: Temple University Press, 1996); Emilie L. Bergmann and Paul Julian Smith, eds., *Entiendes? Queer Readings, Hispanic Writings* (Durham, N.C.: Duke University Press, 1995); Marit Melhuus and Kristi Anne Stolen, eds., *Machos, Mistresses, Madonnas: Contesting the Power of Latin American Gender Imagery* (London: Verso,

1996). See also Juanita Ramos, ed., *Compañeras: Latina Lesbians* (New York: Latina Lesbian History Project, 1987).

10. Frank Bonilla, "Changing the Americas from within the United States," *Latino Review of Books* 2 (1): 2–4.

11. Edna Acosta-Belén and Carlos E. Santiago, "Merging Borders: The Remapping of America," *Latino Review of Books* 1 (1): 2–12.

12. Suzanne Jonas and Edward J. McCaughan, eds., Latin America Faces the Twenty-First Century: Reconstructing a Social Justice Agenda (Boulder, Colo.: Westview, 1994), 2.

13. Richard Falk, "The Making of Global Citizenship," in Brecher, Childs, and Cutler, *Global Visions*, 39–50.

14. Cárdenas, "Moving Peoples and Nations."

15. Falk, "Making of Global Citizenship," 50.

16. Ibid.

17. Brecher, Childs, and Cutler, *Global Visions*.

18. Denis MacShane, "Labor Standards and Double Standards in the New World Order," in *Global Visions: Beyond the New World Order*, ed. Jeremy Brecher, John Brown Childs, and Jill Cutler (Boston: South End Press, 1993), 204.

19. Immanuel Wallerstein, "Africa in the Shuffle," *Issue* 23 (1): 22–23.

20. Ibid., 23.

21. Nathan Glazer and Daniel P. Moynihan, *Beyond the Melting Pot* (Cambridge: MIT Press, 1970, 2d ed.); and Nathan Glazer, *We Are All Multiculturalists Now* (Cambridge: Harvard University Press, 1997).

22. Michael Greyer and Charles Bright, "World History in a Global Age," *American Historical Review* 100 (4): 1034–60, 1037.

23. Hobsbawm, "Crisis of Today's Ideologies," 15.

24. Juan Flores, "Pan-Latino/Trans-Latino: Puerto Ricans in the 'New Nueva York,'" *Centro Bulletin* 8 (1–2): 170–86.

25. Ilán Stavans, *The Hispanic Condition* (New York: Harper Collins, 1995).

26. Geoffrey Fox, *Hispanic Nation: Culture, Politics, and the Constructing of Identity* (Secaucus, N.J.: Birch Lane Press, 1996).

27. Suzanne Oboler, *Ethnic Labels, Latino Lives: Identity and the Politics of (Re)Presentation in the United States* (Minneapolis: University of Minnesota Press, 1995).

28. The term *pan-Latino* refers to a collective continental identity that transcends individual nationalities, while trans-Latino refers to a collective identity that is reciprocally shaped by the interconnections of Latinos with U.S. society and their countries of origin.

29. José Enrique Rodó, *Ariel* (Montevideo: Nornaleche y Rojas, 1900).

30. Roberto Fernández Retamar, *Calibán: Apuntes sobre la cultura en nuestra América* (México: Editorial Diógenes, 1972). In English as *Caliban and Other Essays,* trans. Edward Baker (Minneapolis: University of Minnesota Press, 1989).

31. Ibid., 16.

32. Guillermo Gómez-Peña, Warrior for Gringostroika (St. Paul, Minn.: Graywolf Press, 1993), 43.

33. Edna Acosta-Belén, "Defining a Common Ground: The Theoretical Meeting of Women's, Ethnic, and Area studies," in Edna Acosta-Belén and Christina E. Bose, eds., *Researching Women in Latin America and the Caribbean* (Boulder, Colo.: Westview Press, 1993), 175–86.

34. Johnnella E. Butler and John C. Walter, eds., *Transforming the Curriculum: Ethnic Studies and Women's Studies* (Albany: SUNY Press, 1991).

35. Wayne Cornelius, "The Latin American Presence in the United States: Can Scholarship Catch up with the Immigration Backlash?" *LASA Forum* (winter 1996): 4–6.

36. Marshall McLuhan, *The Global Village* (New York: Oxford University Press, 1989).

37. U.S. Department of Commerce, Bureau of the Census, *Current Population Reports*, Series P-25–1130, "Population Projections by Age, Sex, Race, and Hispanic Origin: 1995–2050" (Washington, D.C.: U.S. Bureau of the Census, 1996); and U.S. Department of Commerce, Bureau of the Census, "The Hispanic Population of the United States" (Washington, D.C.: U.S. Bureau of Census, 1997).

38. Bonilla, "Changing the Americas from within the United States."

Bridges to the Twenty-First Century:

Making Cultural Studies—and Making It Work

JUDITH NEWTON

ON A COOL OCTOBER MORNING, A WEEK PAST THE DEAD-line for this paper, I found myself still puzzling over how to begin. Feeling some guilt at inconveniencing the commentator and experiencing a twinge of incipient panic as well, I began to play with the panel—"Coalition or Collision: Difference, Territory, and the Institution"—and to sketch the different ways in which each term might be said have entered into the process of forming a cross-race, cross-gender coalition at the University of California-Davis. This coalition consisting of one department and five programs—African American and African, American, Asian American, Chicano/a, Native American, and Women's and Gender Studies—officially came into being in 1995. In the spirit of writing on this new formation, I conducted lengthy interviews with several colleagues. My efforts to begin writing that October morning were not made easier by the fact that I felt bound to touch upon the messy points of discord within the separate accounts of the entangled history of such a coalition.

Narrative One

If I began with the term *institution*, which as good materialists my colleagues and I are often wont to do, I could see that for most of us administrations appeared historically inclined both to ignore and to overemphasize the "differences" among our programs, and in so doing to threaten variously the continued existence of our *territories*. "Collision" in each case, we would agree, had been an outcome. In the early 1990s, for example, the Dean of the College of Letters and Sciences had floated the idea of gathering the four programs focused on race and ethnicity into an Ethnic Studies program and had suggested the possibility of housing the programs together under American Studies. At UC Davis my colleagues universally agreed this had spelled collision city, and the dean's proposal was voted down.

In 1995 a somewhat different administration had proposed to divide the College of Letters and Sciences into three divisions—Humanities and Arts, Social Sciences, and Math and Physical Sciences. Each of our programs was then told to decide, as a discrete unit, whether it would locate its own little territory within the newly created Kingdom of Social Sciences or within that of Humanities. When faculty from several interdisciplinary units protested that for us a choice between Social Sciences and Humanities did not make sense, we were informed, in a meeting with a top administrator, that we had best fall in line. From now on, we were strictly warned, small programs like our own would find themselves lacking resources unless we proved that we were able to produce (mainly by drawing large numbers of students into our classes) and implicitly "outproduce" each other. As small territories, we were advised, our best option might be to merge with larger landholders, such as English or sociology.

Narrative Two

It was in response to this second move by the institution, a move that emphasized our differences, encouraged further separation of our territories, and that threatened to set us on the road to permanent, competitive collision, that faculty from the future Hart Hall programs began to meet. It was in the course of these meetings, moreover, which initially focused on collision with the institution and on exerting control over how our differences and territories would be defined, that a different sort of narrative began to emerge. This narrative, while preserving difference, gave more emphasis to mutuality and while maintaining territory, spoke of crossing borders. Eventually this narrative would lead us toward coalition as an alternative to institutionally induced collision. It is this second narrative that dominates the notes I made during September 1995 and that, at the behest of my colleagues, I later turned into an informal history. The following is constructed from these notes.

September 15, 1995. I see that the idea of a separate division of "Ethnic and Women's Studies" was being floated, but what actually came out of our meeting was a proposal to group all the interdisciplinary programs and graduate groups on campus in a separate, fourth division, with our own dean. When one colleague proposed that there was a danger here of constituting ourselves as a ghetto, another colleague said she had less fear of being ghettoized than of being disappeared.

September 23, 1995. We met with administrator X with a petition to be made a separate division of "Interdisciplinary and Interethnic Programs." Our proposal did not win favor.

September 30, 1995. Another meeting, called by S, involving the faculty from the future Hart Hall programs, was held in the Chicano/a Studies conference room. This time the discussion focused on whether to propose a separate division of "Ethnic, Women's, and Cultural Studies," represented by a dean that understood our work. As a prelude to deciding what to do, we began to brainstorm about what we wanted as individual programs. Here is what we listed on the board:

1. To get support as research units; to be in relation as research units.
2. To do informed, politicized teaching; to turn out students that are human beings, that want to change the world, that have consciences and accountability to their respective and shared communities; to retain students, to ground students and faculty.
3. To do comparative work on multiculturalism; to do cross-cultural analysis; to have exchange and collectivity; to not be competitive with each other.
4. To create identity, to do public relations; to build our image; to define for the campus who we are; to take leadership; to participate at the root level; to be a vanguard.
5. To maintain autonomy and independent development; to develop separate graduate programs.
6. To choose our dean; to name ourselves; to have the full-time positions promised us as well as space, operating money, and a library.
7. To have an outreach system and summer institutes.
8. To benefit the campus through diversity, discourse enrichment, extramural funds, and visiting scholars.
9. To respond to California's demographics; to have a global perspective.
10. To have national and international leadership.

My notes report that on the basis of this list we decided to cast our lots together. The stray word "utopian" appears near the end of the page.

By October 10, 1995, the faculty of these programs had petitioned the administration and faculty committee in charge of college reorganization to become a separate division named Ethnic, Women's, and Cultural Studies. Our petition, to no one's surprise, was promptly denied, but our fallback position of becoming a named subsection of the Humanities Division, won approval. On October 21 we learned that we were an official subsection of the renamed Humanities, Arts, and Cultural Studies Division.

Our five directors and single chair, having begun to meet weekly over breakfast, eventually reached a consensus that African American and African, American, and Women's and Gender Studies should move into some newly vacated space in Hart Hall, where Asian American, Chicano/a, and Native American Studies were already housed. Having made this decision, however, we were informed by the administration that in line with a college-wide initiative, we, like all programs inhabiting the same buildings in Humanities and Social Sciences, would now have to reorganize our staff into a central unit.

This staff reorganization imposed by the administration initially involved some collision-bound proposals regarding space and personnel, which prompted a flurry of student e-mails announcing an institutional plot against our programs. In response to student concerns, a series of meetings followed in which the narratives of institution, difference, territory, and collision returned in full force. In the fall of 1996, nonetheless, despite many second thoughts and ambivalence all around, African American and African, American, and Women's and Gender Studies crossed historic borders and settled into Hart Hall. An executive council of our chair and directors was quickly formed, and we began a long and seemingly endless discussion of staff reorganization.

Conversations among Hart Hall programs nowadays, several years after our petition and historic move, include both the narratives of territory and of crossing borders, although as individuals and programs we do not give the same emphasis to these narratives or even produce them in the same way. As a White woman who worked to build a mixed-race Women's Studies program, I tend to regard the institution's decision to divide the college into three parts as having unwittingly provided a window of opportunity for the historic choice to cross old borders. For many of my colleagues in programs focused on race and ethnicity, however, it sometimes seems that it was the institution that chose and that forced us into shared territory. "Is this Ethnic

Studies?" one of the colleagues I interviewed for this paper mused. "Ethnic Studies without the name?"

While most of us in Hart Hall share a double vision of the move as at once the mutual creation of a larger and richer multicultural neighborhood, a neighborhood in which we get to know each other and develop trust—one colleague reported feeling "free and happy" since the move—we also feel to very different degrees, the ways in which the move has functioned as an invasion of the potential space for Asian American, Chicano/a, and Native American Studies' potential space. Thus along with the narrative of borders crossed, the narratives of territory and difference, collision has played itself out among us in multiple ways—in relation to office space, resources, and the all-consuming details of staff reorganization. For one colleague, at least, coalition proved an empty concept: "Nothing came of the coalition; people got involved in their own things" and "what began as an intellectual venture ended up in a discussion of how to run the kitchen." The same colleague reported that he liked some of his colleagues better "before the move."

Overall, however, my interviews with colleagues confirmed my sense that both narratives, that of territory and of border crossing, are still engaged and that while mixing together in complicated ways, each has come to dominate in different realms. On the level of our undergraduate programs, for example, the narrative of maintaining difference and territory, on our own terms rather than on those dictated to us by the institution or the state, seems most prominent. Overwhelmingly my colleagues in programs focused on race and ethnicity agreed that post Proposition 209, the pressing need at the university was for "each [program] to be strong individually." The need was to get students in, to retain them, and to employ a "constituency-based discourse." On the level of undergraduate programs, my colleagues felt that "fear gets us together" and that "that is not a way to think of coalition." Yet most of the colleagues in race and ethnicity programs wanted "nothing grander" at this point. As one colleague put it, the program has "sprouted"; the job now "is keeping the bud alive."

The narrative of crossing borders, however, has come to dominate my and my colleagues' thinking about our newly proposed graduate group in cultural studies. At UC Davis a graduate group is a gathering of faculty from different programs and departments who come together to offer interdisciplinary graduate degrees. Our proposed group, which was approved this year, involves some sixty faculty from two dozen different programs and departments. The Cultural Studies Master's and Doctorate Program, which was first proposed in the fall of 1995, has as one of its central goals the facilitation of comparative work on race, gender, sexuality, class, and national identities. Although the Cultural Studies Program is widely seen as an avenue to the creation of individual doctoral programs down the line, it has also become the focus of our border-crossing desires.

Colleagues interviewed described the Graduate Group in Cultural Studies as "our way to come together," saying that "borders be damned at times," that this will "break down the boundaries," and that "you make spaces where you can." Some colleagues spoke of their "hunger" to intellectually engage more with each other, a hunger that I share. Others spoke of "influencing a whole new generation of scholars," hoping that "graduate students of color will come" and of feeling that "this is the only way to get politicized Asian American students into the humanities." They believe that the Graduate Group will challenge students by "asking them to engage in practices that aren't in the world." At the same time students will "lead to the desire for greater change" "challeng[ing] their professors to come together." Still others commented that "we are overburdened in our programs; grads are not as stretched," and that this is "the fantasy opportunity to do collaborative teaching and research."

Narrative Three

This narrative of mutuality, crossing borders, and coalition—like that of institution, difference, territory, and collision—took me only part way in my attempt that October morning to shape a solid history of the changes at UC Davis. Awkwardly, both narratives seemed in some tension with my own hastily chosen but now official and printed title: "Bridges to the Twenty-First Century: Making Cultural Studies and Making It Work." *Bridging, making,* and *making it work* seemed stubbornly disconnected from the public and heroic-sounding narratives of territory and crossing borders. My intuitively chosen title seemed to evoke some homely, domestic narrative, a story having less to do with forging public compacts than with "working on the relationship." The latter, of course, is a form of labor much like housework in that it is invisible to those not directly engaged in it themselves.

Moreover, this narrative of working on the relationship appeared almost exclusively in the interviews of my female colleagues, where in its emphasis on labor, struggle, and even contest it signaled its difference from the more organic- and harmonious-sounding domestic metaphors of the past—the beloved community, la familia, sisterhood. When I asked my female colleagues, for example, what had made the Hart Hall Alliance or any such alliance possible, they answered: "friendship," "putting it out there," "knowing where you stand," "making an effort to understand," "respect," "passion," "tears," "eating," "good fights," "*confianza* that we could talk about it," and the "trust to say what you really feel together and apart." For the female feminists I interviewed, in particular "the difference was women." One said, "It [the executive council] could have been a problem if we had had different bodies."

Central to the bridging process, according to some had been the existence of Women's Studies faculty with departmental joint appointments focused on race and ethnicity as well as a commitment on the part of the program as a whole to the study of co-constructing categories—gender, race, sexuality, national identity, globalization, and class. What this meant is that women's links to each other were "not just about problems with men" but involved dealing with the "contested terrains of feminism." On the basis of these shared concerns and contests, such bridge building among feminists in different programs had been going on for at least nine years, consisting of showing up at each others' talks and demonstrations, checking in with each other, becoming engaged with each others' personal lives, talking out conflict, eating meals together, throwing parties, and the like.

I have come to think of these colleagues, these White women and women of color, along with a very few men, as having acted as a species of what the sociologist Belinda Robnett, in her 1997 book on Black women in the Civil Rights movement, has referred to as "bridge leaders."[1] These leaders, mainly African American women in this case, had worked behind the scenes during the Civil Rights movement, had listened to people's needs and had worked at meeting them, and had built face-to-face relations of friendship and trust. This "bridge work," Robnett argues, was critical to the success of the Civil Rights movement and, I would argue, that it is critical to the success of present-day coalitions. I am not the first scholar to argue that a lack of attention to people's hunger for community accounts for many failures or absences of coalitions on the Left, while the presence of them on the Christian Right has much to do with its current grass-roots appeal.

This third narrative of working on the relationship, I would argue, needs to become as visible and acknowledged as the narratives of maintaining territory or crossing borders. It needs to become the object of our conscious strategies, and it needs to be more fully shared. In a recent article on masculinity, I hazarded the claim that most of the bridge work in communities

I had been a part of had been done by very few men and by many women, overworked women, "women on Prozac."[2] And, like myself, my female colleagues also testified to the desire that more progressive men use their backs as bridges and perform the emotional work of alliance building: getting folks together, deflecting conflict, mending fences, building relationships of trust, hosting dinners, and maybe taking Prozac too. In academic subcultures in particular, where we are frequently beset by isolation, competition, lack of solidarity, and overwork, the successful enactment of border crossing sagas may rest upon this less visible but equally heroic narrative—a tale of bridging, of making the relationship, and of persisting in the sometimes hard emotional labor of making it work.

Notes

1. Belinda Robnett, *How Long? How Long? African-American Women in the Struggle for Civil Rights* (Oxford: Oxford University Press, 1997), 17.
2. Judith Newton, "White Guys," *Feminist Studies* 24 (3): 1–26.

Heavy Traffic at the Intersections:

Ethnic, American, Women's, Queer,

and Cultural Studies

T. V. REED

FOR SOME YEARS IT HAS BEEN APPARENT THAT THE VARIOUS interdisciplinary fields centered on analyzing history, culture, and power in the United States are being shaped not only by the intersection of disciplines (history, sociology, English, and so forth) but also by intersections with their related interdisciplines. Ethnic Studies, American Studies, Women's Studies, Lesbian/Gay/Queer Studies, and cultural studies are entering into increasingly complex relations with each other. Although many scholars sense this, there has not been much critical analysis of what this intersection means theoretically or practically regarding day-to-day collegial and institutional relations. Although there is a growing body of literature on what interdisciplinary scholarship is in general, as well as some good work on particular interdisciplines, we lack a sustained practical and theoretical comparison of what interdisciplinarity means in the different but related fields that are broadly concerned with race, class, gender, sexuality, dis/ability, and other modalities of socially constructed difference in a U.S. context.[1] What does it mean for American, Ethnic, Women's, Lesbian/Gay/Queer, and cultural Studies, which all claim to be interdisciplines concerned with the interrelations among these various modes of difference? And what does it mean that many scholars working in these fields feel increasingly that our work exists at a confluence of two or more of these related fields? Are these fields talking about

[handwritten marginal note: gerontology isn't seen as one of them —]

273

the same "difference"? Or do their interdisciplinary norms or their political assumptions differ significantly? Addressing such questions begins by acknowledging that the answers may be quite different at the theoretical and the institutional levels.

Intersections on Interdisciplines

As I explore later in this chapter, the various "studies" fields seem to be converging more and more in terms of theoretical orientation. Indeed, particularly among younger scholars I talk to, raising issues about the relations among these fields, or asking which label identifies their intellectual location makes no sense at all. Each of these fields is in effect doing postcolonial American, cultural, Ethnic, gender, sexuality Studies. But however much this convergence may be occurring at the level of theory and scholarly practice, real historical, generational, institutional, and structural differences mean that these fields are divergent "cultural formations," with some significant differences in their intellectual foundations, ideological orientations, and research agendas. In practice, overlapping political and scholarly agendas, combined with different institutional locations, mean that these fields are increasingly competing for the same limited resources.

One way to see the structural tensions among these interdisciplines is to look at some stereotypical ways in which the relations between and among them have been described. For example, on the one hand American Studies looks to some traditionalists in Ethnic and Women's Studies like it has stolen from and perhaps sought to colonize them, both in terms of scholarship and institutional space. By contrast, to some traditionalists in American Studies, it looks like the field has been fully taken over by Ethnic and Women's Studies perspectives and practitioners. From yet another angle American Studies, in the earlier scenario, the aggrandizing force par excellence, is seen merely as a rather parochial branch of a still greater imperial power called "cultural studies." To still other scholars, cultural studies and American Studies both seem watered down, mainstreamed versions of more radical critiques coming out of Lesbian/Gay/Queer, Gender, and Ethnic Studies.

Each of these stereotypes points to certain parts of the truth about complicated power relations among these fields. We need more open and frank discussion at conferences, in journals, and in the hallways about these power relations. We also need careful comparisons of the interdisciplines to try to understand more fully what differences and similarities exist on various ideological, structural-institutional, and methodological-epistemological levels. In my own experience talking with colleagues working with me in American Studies at Washington State University, but whose primary affiliation is with Ethnic or Women's Studies, it has become apparent that what at times appeared to be substantive ideological differences were, in part at least, different ways of articulating the common political trajectories of our respective interdisciplines. This is not, I hasten to add, predicated on the assumption that all people within a given interdiscipline share the same understanding of the interdiscipline, the same ideology or the same methods. Nor does this assume that most scholars identify exclusively with only one of these labels that I am using here as a shorthand for the complicated, internally diverse fields with fluid borders. Nevertheless, by definition, interdisciplines (like all cultural formations) tend to have shared conceptual and experiential dimensions that differ significantly from other, even closely related, fields. Discussing the similarities and differences in the nuances of the ways these respective interdisciplines articulate their methods, their politics, and their research agendas provides a fruitful way to lay groundwork for cooperation among varied departments and programs.

The attempt to identify commonalities should not be made too quickly or glibly, however. For if one takes the position, articulated most forcefully by the French philosopher Michel Foucault, that all disciplinary formations are inherently limiting and inherently good at disguising their limitations, then having multiple interdisciplines approaching some of the same critical issues can be crucial to seeing and correcting some of the respective blind spots. Moreover, however much each of these fields now stresses what some call "intersectionality" (the complicated interweavings of race, ethnicity, class, gender, sexuality, and other forces), it seems likely that each interdiscipline will be particularly vigilant in paying attention to the force against which their field was founded (e.g., sexism and Women's Studies, racism and Ethnic Studies, heterosexism and Lesbian/Gay/Queer Studies). This is reason enough to make it imperative that the integrity of each field be protected, including the integrity of the separate ethnic-specific departments and programs within the terrain of Ethnic Studies. But the reality of cultural intersections also means that comparativist Ethnic Studies programs, as well as broadly focused American and cultural studies formations, each have a role to play.

The positioning of American and cultural studies in this story is complicated, however. To pose the arguments I want to make, I position myself by putting on two masks. The first mask is that of an American Studies practitioner. Because I direct an American Studies program and consider the American Studies Association my professional home, it is a mask that fits well enough. But that mask represents only one of my professional identities. Even as I assume this position within American Studies, I assert that the field's borders, as well as the borders of the other related "studies" fields, are very much in flux these days, for both good and bad reasons. I wear the American Studies mask because my argument is particularly focused on the political responsibilities of that field. My analysis has prime implications, however, for scholars who position themselves within other interdisciplinary fields, or who, like myself, often find themselves in some borderlands between fields.

The second, scarier mask I wear is that of the notorious creature known as the straight White male. Although in other contexts I might challenge the essentialist nature of that mask (or masking), for the purposes of this chapter it is important that I speak from inside this mask. I have particular things to say to those folks who share the privileges that this mask allows. I say this not to do the usual positioning of self that can as often be self-aggrandizing as it is politically self-aware; rather, I use this technique as a way of pointing toward one of this chapter's themes. Partly because of its relations to Ethnic, Women's, and Lesbian/Gay/Queer Studies, American Studies has been historically and institutionally structured as, if not straight, White, male, and middle-class, then at least as *straighter, Whiter, maler*, and *middle-classier* than these other related fields. I say this emphatically not to erase the presence of women, scholars of color of all genders, and gay/queer scholars in American Studies, but for quite the opposite reason: to underscore a continuing structural problem of the field itself that makes it difficult to recognize the growing presence of variously marginalized folks at the center of American Studies. In other words, unless we acknowledge and discuss the historically and institutionally structured Whiteness, maleness, and straightness of American Studies, we are not able to see fully the ways in which the field is increasingly female (and feminist), queer (and anti-heterosexist), of color (and antiracist).

A similar argument can be made regarding the structural positioning of the emerging field of cultural studies, which (reductively but I think not wholly unfairly) has been seen by some as a new and perhaps more effective route by which straight White males have found a way back into a sense of themselves as politically engaged critics of racial, gender, sexual, class, and other social hierarchies. I say this not to denigrate my own social positioning or the serious scholarly work done under the label "cultural studies" (including much work by scholars also identified with Ethnic, Women's, and Lesbian/Gay/Queer Studies); rather, I call attention to one of the reasons why the current constellation and institutionalization of the various interdisciplinary "studies" fields make it difficult to do the progressive coalitional work that many of us would like to do.

Partly because its legacy stretches back before the anticolonial, antiracist, feminist, and lesbian and gay liberation movements, and partly because many of its practitioners are from privileged social groups (embodied in my mask) that have been relatively insulated from the oppressions driving these movements, American Studies remains unevenly committed to progressive scholarship (although I do not assume that there is an easy mapping of political beliefs onto ascribed categories in any of these fields). As American Studies Association past president Mary Helen Washington has reminded scholars, the interdiscipline remains haunted by "ghosts" of its past that have very real, material effects on the present.[2]

Alternatively, cultural studies is haunted in a sense by its lack of a past. Because it arrived in the United States in the 1990s, without a history of connection to U.S. social movements, and because it too has a high percentage of practitioners from privileged groups with less clear stakes in the politics of race, gender, class, sexuality, and nationality, cultural studies is often seen as unevenly committed to or glibly appropriative of positions born in intense communal, political struggles.[3] These characterizations in no way do justice to the complexity of any of these fields, but if scholars do not acknowledge and analyze the ways in which the very forces of race, class, gender, sexuality, nationalism, and empire now at the center of our work have shaped the various interdisciplinary histories, then potentially useful alliances among fields will prove impossible.

Institutional Instability

It is a great irony, one all too familiar to students of American history, that at a time when there are more reasons than ever for political and scholarly coalition, in many colleges and universities relations among the various "studies" programs and departments are being set on collision courses. This is primarily because they are being sized up and carved up as potentially redundant territories in what administrators and corporate overlords portray as a zero-sum game of resources. Each of the studies fields has in fact experienced at least modest growth overall in recent years, but this growth has been unevenly distributed within each of the fields (some programs are dying even as others are born). This overall growth has only intensified the perception of redundancy among many administrators.

In this context perhaps the fundamental question that American Studies scholars need to ask is, Should American Studies continue to exist at all as an institutionalized academic site? My short answer is no. No, because American Studies is not necessarily an indispensable site in any particular institution. It may not be in any given educational site the place where the vital knowledge about race, ethnicity, gender, sexuality, nationality, and empire as the shaping forces of U.S. experience is disseminated. While this knowledge is at the heart of American Studies, it is also at the center of other locations. If that educational work is being done as well or better in an Ethnic, Women's, Lesbian/Gay/Queer, cultural, or other related Studies department or program, the existence of a parallel American Studies program may not be a wise use of diminishing resources.

My longer answer, however, is yes. Yes, American Studies should continue to exist in those institutions at which it has been the primary place where critical work on American cultures is done, where in fact it has often provided a haven for scholars of race, ethnicity, gender, and sexuality who have felt marginalized in their own departments. But I add that this haven is often also a prison. The legitimacy that the words *American* or *cultural* often convey versus the words *women's* or *ethnic* or *gay/lesbian/bi/trans* can come at a cost to the programs bearing these latter names. Any argument legitimating American (or cultural) Studies today must continually emphasize that Ethnic, Women's, and Lesbian/Gay/Queer Studies are intellectually on the cutting edge of current scholarship. Furthermore, it is largely because of the work done by scholars in Ethnic, Lesbian/Gay/Queer, Women's, and postcolonial Studies that "we" in American Studies can now see the illegitimate, limited, and distorted nature of much scholarly work done in the name of a falsely inclusive-sounding "American" Studies of the past.

Because institutional conditions vary immensely around the country and within different educational sites, clearly no single paradigm of how or whether to continue to champion American Studies departments and programs can work for all. Despite and because of its ambiguous legacies as a field, American Studies continues to offer unique and important insights. But I do not think that a laissez faire or a "let a thousand flowers bloom" approach follows from this. Rather, certain priorities should pertain, and I phrase them crudely in this way: to the extent that American Studies (and cultural studies in most of its incarnations) remains a site more congenial to Whiteness, maleness, straightness, and middle-classness than are Ethnic, Women's, or Lesbian/Gay/Queer Studies, the burden of legitimation in any struggle over decreasing resources falls more heavily on American and cultural studies. In other words, priority (especially in the context of ongoing and increasing attacks on affirmative action) should go in most institutional settings to those units whose structures foreground the need to hire women, scholars of color, gay/lesbian/queer scholars, and scholars with disabilities, to those units that have a proven history of serving marginalized communities, and to those units with the strongest tradition of high quality scholarship on race, class, gender, sexuality, and their intersections. In some locations those units may well be American Studies or cultural studies, but more often they will be Ethnic, Women's, and Queer Studies departments or programs. The relative autonomy of Ethnic, Women's, and Gay/Queer Studies has been and remains crucial to their evolution. Because critical interdisciplinary studies will continue to be attacked as "politicizing" putatively value-free scholarship, it is imperative that we point again and again to the ways in which all the disciplines, as well as such traditional interdisciplines as American Studies, have been profoundly transformed by scholarship emerging from or inspired by Ethnic, Women's, and Gay/Lesbian/Queer Studies. It is imperative to remind our critics that it is the high quality of this scholarship that has forced reassessments within traditional fields, and that the "mainstreaming" and "assimilation" of this scholarship has diminished but certainly not eliminated the need for ongoing critique of the racist, sexist, and hetero-normative biases that continue to dominate much scholarship.

Ethnic and Women's Studies, to name the most established sites, continue to have a highly developed sense of relating to marginalized communities within and outside the university. Although scholars in American and cultural studies who have not been constructed as members of oppressed communities may feel similar obligations, they have been historically and are currently more insulated from and less engaged with embattled communities. (Again, this is not an assumption that all scholars in Ethnic, Women's, and Queer Studies are members of the groups they focus on, nor is this an attempt to erase the presence of members of these groups who work in American or cultural studies as a field.) But if one's gender, race, class, sexuality, nation of origin, and physical ability has been defined as normative, even if one has devoted much of one's life directly and indirectly to supporting movements for social justice, privilege is reflected in myriad ways in one's everyday academic career. These privileges reinforce structural differences between Ethnic, Lesbian/Gay, and Women's Studies on the one hand and more generally, not to say imperially, constituted American and cultural studies terrains on the other hand.

One of the prime ways in which different group and field histories are manifested is in the far greater amount of direct forms of community and "role modeling" work demanded of many Ethnic, Women's, Queer, and Disability Studies scholars. For example, scholars of color, women scholars of all racializations, lesbian/gay/queer scholars, and disabled scholars more often also work as mentors for students who share their ascribed positioning. By contrast, as the director of an American Studies program, I have yet to be asked to stand up and model "Americanness," nor has the local community of "Americans" put any special demands on my time. At the same time the rise of "multiculturalism" in its moderate administrative form means that Women's, Ethnic, and other socially "marked" Studies programs are increasingly being asked to serve ever larger general campus communities, while seldom being offered greater resources.

In practical terms of day-to-day interaction this means that those who identify with American or cultural studies are often greeted with a certain amount of justifiable suspicion by those in the trenches of Ethnic and Women's Studies or more recently emerging and equally "trenchy" fields like Lesbian/Gay or Disability Studies. And those who are serious about coalition building, as opposed to collision, need to recognize that even relatively marginalized American Studies programs (which are in fact far fewer in number than Ethnic or Women's Studies programs) are often in positions of privilege that they need to wield quite self-consciously and wisely if they are to benefit still more marginalized locations. Building the trust that enables alliances can take many forms. In extreme cases it might entail, as suggested above, the full-scale dissolution of some programs in favor of Ethnic, Women's, or Queer Studies. More often it will entail less drastic actions like authorizing a major shift of resources to start or strengthen Ethnic, Women's, or Gay/Lesbian Studies departments at the cost of American or cultural Studies program growth; or helping to create university tenure guidelines that acknowledge so-called service work as of equal importance with teaching and scholarship; or rearranging curricula to minimize competition; or targeting American Studies teaching assistantships for Women's or Ethnic Studies departments; or working to lessen the academic load carried by faculty serving two or more of these departments or programs. But whatever form it takes, this work must take the form of "walking the walk," not just "talking the talk."

Although these struggles no doubt often mean making difficult compromises, one must also keep in mind that the current state of institutional instability in most if not all colleges, universities, and other learning institutions is a potential resource as well as a liability. The current popularity of the terms *interdisciplinary* and *multicultural* among administrators provide some room to maneuver. Although some administrative talk about "interdisciplinarity" is really a ruse for "downsizing" (throwing departments together), and much talk about "multiculturalism" or "diversity" is superficial at best, the language is pervasive and can be used strategically to expand the terrain of established interdisciplinary fields that do real social justice work. Scholars need not and should not take only defensive stances. And legitimation should not be the sole goal. Sometimes the most effective work is done not within sites of institutional legitimation but between them, in the interstices, in places where the inevitable constraints that come with officially sanctioned discourse are less present. In practical terms sometimes an informal coalition or a committee of faculty and students can enact a more profound effect than a department or program, especially when that group speaks for a larger constituency on and off campus. Because institutionalization can be as much a trap as a power base, one must look carefully at local conditions rather than always extolling the virtues of greater institutional legitimacy. The strongest political position is probably one that continues to tack between legitimacy and insurgency.

But a different answer to the question about the ongoing viability of American Studies at the institutional level arises if the institution in question is the American Studies Association. The ASA, founded in 1951, has become a very interesting scholarly organization. The association has a long, though imperfect, history of encouraging Ethnic and Women's Studies scholarship and was the initial home for many scholars doing feminist and antiracist scholarship before the rise of Ethnic and Women's Studies departments and programs. The ASA also has strong formal ties with the Asian American Studies Association, and with African American, Native American, and Chicano/a and Latino/a Studies associations. The national ASA convention has become the conference of choice for many Ethnic Studies and Women's Studies scholars. Membership is predominantly female, and apart from the various Ethnic Studies associations, the ASA has the highest percentage of scholars of color of any major scholarly association. The association has also taken the strongest

possible stand in support of affirmative action and immigrant rights, including a conference boycott of California in the wake of Propositions 187 (immigrant rights restrictions) and 209 (anti-affirmative action), and Washington
in the wake of Initiative 200 (anti-affirmative action). Moreover, the great
majority of scholarship presented at the ASA is consistently centered in the
analysis of race and ethnicity, class, gender, sexuality, colonialism, and their
intersections. In this context the 1997 election of feminist African Americanist
Mary Helen Washington as president of the ASA was of more than symbolic
significance. Washington's election rightly acknowledges that the majority
of American Studies practitioners are committed to a continued process of
actively "divesting" themselves of the ways in which the field remains implicated in racial, gender, class, and national privileges.

Interculturalisms and Their Limits

Having suggested earlier that each interdiscipline is a cultural formation, if
not a subculture, unto itself, I add that the current intersection of interdisciplines is at once a product of and a contributor to changes in the larger national
and global cultures. I call this process and the theories that analyze it the rise
of "interculturalisms." Interculturalism is not one trend but rather several overlapping, related ones. It would include a variety of ways of articulating the
intersections of key "marginal" groups (including not only multiple identities but also liminal identities that fit no existing categories), challenges to U.S.
borders, and work that uses these kinds of complications to dissect the fiction
of "mainstream" hegemonic cultures. This latter mode is in part a reaction to
the ways in which weak versions of "multiculturalism" have too little to say
about the power relations between dominant and subordinate groups.[4]

Most of these intercultural approaches are critical of the notion that
cultures or even subcultures are whole, independent, essential, or natural
entities. By contrast, these approaches stress hybridity, fluidity, mestizaje
processes, borderlands, and interdependent relations among groups. Often
these approaches argue the mutually constitutive or co-constructed nature
of racial, gendered, sexual, regional, and other cultural binaries. Interculturalism would include various attempts to question the borders between
gender categories, sexualities, and U.S. ethnic and racial categories, as well
as approaches that focus not on one discrete national culture but rather on
a system of interrelations designated by terms like *border studies, comparative American Studies, transnational studies,* and *postnational studies.*

If the work of Ethnic, Women's, Gay/Lesbian, and "critical" American Studies can be defined broadly as the attempt to uncover, rediscover, invent, and elaborate on previously marginalized cultural strands in the United States, interculturalism includes attempts to show how those so-called marginal cultures have in fact profoundly shaped the so-called cultural center.[5] As a concept and a practice, interculturalism is certainly not entirely new. Indeed, one could no doubt show that it has been an element in American cultural analysis from the beginning of the studies interdisciplines, if not from the beginning of "America" itself. What is new today is the extent to which questions about the relations between, among, and within multiple American cultures have come to the foreground, and the extent to which that work challenges the notion that there is some "mainstream" in America that is relatively untouched by such allegedly "tributary" streams as those identified with, for example, African Americans, American Indians, women, or homosexuals.

The story of the rise of interculturalist perspectives has been told in a number of ways. Because origin stories matter a good deal, it matters how this one is told. Often the narrative focuses on or around a set of "post-er" boys (and some girls), especially poststructuralist, postmodern, and postcolonial theorists. These theorists are, of course, of real importance. But versions of the story that label these as *the* Theorists, with a capital T, often underplay or ignore the work of social movements as theorizing forces. They do not think enough about what feminist theorist Katie King has called the political question of "what counts as theory" and who is accounted a theorist.[6] It is no accident that many of the most powerful intercultural theorists—such figures as Gloria Anzaldúa, Audre Lorde, Cherríe Moraga, and Chela Sandoval, among many others—work their academic theoretical knowledges through lives lived as multiply marginalized subjects. My thumbnail genealogy thus claims that these interculturalist modelings of America and "Americanness" emerged primarily through ongoing social movement activity by feminists, antiracists, and gay liberationists that in turn informed scholarship and theory. Even the important contributions made by continental poststructuralist and other postmodern theorists have found their most useful forms only when reworked by scholars identified with marginalized communities and committed to scholarship that is shaped by movement desires.

This newer work was enabled by earlier generations of Ethnic and Women's Studies scholarship that is sometimes dismissed by some of the glossier strands of the "new" work. This enabling earlier work grew under pressure from movements within and outside the university that brought changes in the student body and professorate structures that in turn largely enabled vast innovative areas of research, much of it through the then emerging fields of Ethnic and Women's Studies. Because their objects of knowledge had to be legitimated, and because of pressure from nationalist dimensions in movements by various peoples of color coupled with a strong separatist element within first the women's movement and later the gay and lesbian liberation movement, this early scholarship tended to focus almost exclusively on singular objects/subjects of knowledge. This phase included immense efforts of recovery (of lost texts, individuals, movements) and invention (of new subjects and objects). Out of this phase emerged a brilliant, varied, expansive body of work that immeasurably extended knowledge of the working classes, women, African Americans, Latinos/as, Chicanos/as, Asian and Pacific Americans, Native Americans, gays, lesbians, bisexuals, and a host of other "others." A significantly different picture of America emerged from this scholarship, a picture of not one but many cultures existing simultaneously within (and in some cases across) the territorial boundaries of the American colonies and the United States.

Much of the strength of this scholarship lies in the particularity and intensity of its focus on complex efforts at group cultural survival and development despite intense oppression, repression, and efforts at assimilation and co-optation. But a certain limitation flows from the necessary effort to define and refine relatively autonomous elements of these various American cultures. That limitation is the decreased ability to talk about the influence of those cultures on the so-called "mainstream," or to analyze the interacting influence of marginalized cultures on each other. This limitation grew naturally out of the profoundly difficult task of (re)constructing group experiences that have been long buried, closeted, erased, ignored, and distorted. To do this for one group at a time seemed daunting enough. To do it for several groups simultaneously was for a time unimaginable. To discuss these cultures as shapers of the dominant Anglo or European American cultures would have seemed to cede too much attention to the dominators who had monopolized the historical and historiographic stage for many generations.

In my version of the story, however, a new stage evolves out of and within this powerful moment, a phase paralleled and shaped by social movement activity. The very effort to do isolated histories, literary and cultural studies, ethnographies, and so on further revealed (with the help of much shouting from the streets) that there was a great deal more internal diversity within marginalized cultures than most scholars knew or acknowledged. Although this drove some scholars toward greater defensive emphasis on group solidarity (and to various neonationalisms and neoseparatisms), it led others toward more inclusive and complex work emphasizing gender, class, sexual, and other differences as existing within as well as cutting across marginalized communities.[7] This work challenged the maleness of much of Ethnic Studies, the Whiteness of much of Women's Studies, and the straightness of both Ethnic Studies and Women's Studies. Complicated, often bitter continuing struggles within and outside of the academy shook up existing cultural solidarities but also created new solidarities that link folks in networks within and across older community lines.

At the same time, out of this process a second dimension, a new envisioning of the so-called mainstream, began to emerge. Visible in a number of areas by the late 1980s and early 1990s, this stage includes a radical refusal of continuing forms of marginalization within versions of mulitculturalism. Think, for example, of the way the term *multicultural student* continues to function as a barely disguised instantiation of the term and status "minority" that it ostensibly replaces. A *multicultural student* means anyone but the White students, who somehow remain merely cultural, "unmultied" and unmelted. Against these new forms of marginalization, intercultural studies articulate difference as relational, interactive, and thus always caught up in multilayered questions of power.

Although some scholars from embattled groups within and outside the university greet intercultural positions as a loss of focus if not identity or as a form of weakened "mainstreaming," these positions in fact represent a stronger claim that the "mainstream" is a kind of hegemonic fantasy, at least in the pure form it claimed for itself. Interculturalism instead rests on the premise that a certain kind of Ethnic, Women's, gay, and "multicultural" studies was claiming too little, rather than the "too much" decried by conservatives. In particular, some scholars began to notice that "race" often meant only "non-Whites," and "gender" often meant only "women," leaving Whiteness the privilege of being "unraced" and maleness "ungendered." The new studies, at their best, maintain a sense of the accomplishments of rich, semiautonomous traditions of so-called minority or marginalized cultures, while at the same time making the far stronger claim that there is no pure American cultural center apart from those other cultures. In effect this approach takes the conservative claim that emphasizing diversity or multiculturalism is divisive and balkanizing, and turns that claim on its head by suggesting that the "national culture"—much vaunted by the Right—exists because of, not despite, these so-called marginal cultures.

When done well—with political grounding and with knowledge of and respect for the earlier scholarship that has enabled the newer work—these various "interculturalist" strands have produced some of the most important and exciting work in current scholarship.[8] But within this context of the intersection (if not collision) of interdisciplines, I offer the caveat that some "interculturalist" visions seem too quickly or cavalierly to subvert strategically useful nationalisms and community identities along with the hegemonic forms of nationhood and cultural identity that is their prime target. This is apparent in relation to continuing trends in Ethnic Studies in which older and new versions of ethnic cultural nationalism play a significant role. It is also present in the debates around "queer" versus "gay and lesbian" identities, in the debates around essentialism within Women's and Gender Studies, and in debates about national liberation struggles within postcolonial studies.[9]

Moving toward coalitions means that even those scholars that feel highly critical of the limitations of so-called identity politics need to understand and respect cultural nationalisms and related cultural identities as historically and currently important sites of survival for those in marginalized communities. Although many interculturalists are willing to entertain notions of "strategic essentialism," fewer seem as willing to notice that "anti-essentialism" is also a strategy, not a truth or an absolute method.[10] The point is not to lock anyone in an essential identity, privileged or marginal, but rather to reiterate a position many critics have made who have experienced marginalization: it is far easier to celebrate the fluidity or disappearance of identities when your identity group has not been enslaved, lynched, raped, battered, deported, bashed, maimed, killed, or silenced by academic elites.

I suggest that critical interculturalism will respect strategic cultural essentialisms and work to specify not only the limitations of relatively stabilized identities but also illuminate more fully those points where such strategic stabilization forms a crucial stage in much political work. The way to a more profound interculturalism has to pass through, not around, continuing cultural nationalisms and the messy terrain of seemingly essentialized politico-cultural identities. Those scholars who have gone only to Paris, or to Birmingham, as it were, to learn their theory need to read and acknowledge the work of activists and scholar-activists in Ethnic and Women's Studies who deconstructed elements of the power-knowledge nexus long before they read (and learned some useful things from) Derrida, Foucault, Deleuze, Bahktin, Kristeva, or Raymond Williams. More collisions between interculturalisms and "identity" nationalisms of various kinds are necessary. And if these collisions occur in a spirit of mutually respectful contestation, scholars will identify some underlying political commonalities that will lead to stronger coalitions as well as to clarification of those points where principled differences remain to be argued.

Social Movement Interventions

As those familiar with my work know, I have long advocated a closer relationship between social movements and the academy.[11] Such a relationship is more crucial now than ever before, and the intersection of interdisciplines is a key place to rethink and rework that relationship. As previously discussed, nearly all of the scholarship at the heart of these interdisciplines has been deeply shaped by the wave of so-called "new" social movements that began in the late 1950s and early 1960s and that continues today, despite challenges and disruptions. Although this relationship between movements and academic critique is generally better known and understood in Women's, Lesbian/Gay, and Ethnic Studies than it is in American and cultural studies, this relationship is nowhere as strong as it needs to be. Scholars have a responsibility to retell those histories, to rearticulate those links, not nostalgically as old war stories but strategically as resources for future action. Ethnic and Women's Studies grew directly out of the Civil Rights, ethnic nationalist, and women's movements. Lesbian/Gay/Queer Studies grew as much out of Stonewall, lavender menaces, and ACT-UP, as the field does today from the rich imaginations of queer theorists. Despite Michael Denning's convincing argument rooting American Studies in what he has called the "Popular Front social movement" of the 1930s, the general field of American Studies does not sense as strong a connection to a social movement legacy.[12] And, as Ellen Rooney has argued, the "political subject" of cultural studies has never been as clear as the political subjects represented by Women's Studies and by various ethnic-specific Ethnic Studies departments.[13] This different sense of connection to a social movement is often one source of significant tension between American Studies and cultural studies on the one hand and Ethnic and Women's Studies on the other hand, which is often exacerbated by a certain glib fluency among scholars who learned their politics at considerable distance from the struggles that have cost lives, careers, and a host of other pains.

But even as scholars historicize the social movement roots of the inter-disciplines, they must not let backward glances, to the 1960s (or to the 1930s), blind them to the particular conditions faced by the current generation of students, who face unresolved questions first raised by the labor, women's, and racial justice movements and who raise new questions themselves about current modes of racialization, genderization, sexualization, and national iden-tity formation. Those students find on most campuses that Ethnic, women's, gay/lesbian/bi/trans/queer Studies programs are still the crucial sites from which to work, sites of important generational struggle that link the insights of earlier struggles to the particularities of current conditions.

"Walking the walk" thus includes walking out to what some of us (nos-talgically?) still call "the streets." As this chapter has argued, different insti-tutional histories mean that campus politics, even narrowly construed, are real sites of struggle. Campus politics can also be a trap, however, a divide and conquer strategy, from which all parties can lose. Without other sources of leverage, the zero-sum game of resources portrayed by the managers of the "education business" works against everyone. The best way to avoid these traps is to link campus politics to wider issues of social justice that are cur-rents on, as well as off, the campus. Social movement struggles always already exist within our campuses and in our scholarship, even as they point outward to larger circles of contestation, collision, and coalition. If we wish our scholarship to be more than brilliant critiques of failed opportunities, we need to build stronger links to unions, to community-based struggles, and to public policy debates—to sites of struggle that can focus, critique, chal-lenge, and enlarge academic critique. Not because the university and "the real world" are, as is often alleged, separated, but precisely because the two realms are not.

I do not pretend to know where the most fruitful alliances will be created—again that depends to a large degree on local conditions. The issues range from tribal sovereignty to urban employment, from affirmative action to immigration restrictions. But I want to end by mentioning one area that provides a particularly rich intersection: issues around work. The so-called new labor movement has belatedly acknowledged that issues of race, ethnicity, national origin, gender, and to some extent even sexuality are very much labor and class issues. With education going the way of other corporations by "downsizing" (the elimination of departments) and "outsourcing" (the hir-ing of part-timers), labor issues among tenure-line professors, adjuncts, and graduate student employees have never been more crucial. Raising issues about the conditions of our own academic employment and the employment of our colleagues and students, while linking these issues to affirmative action and to other labor issues on campus and in the surrounding communities, is crucial to the survival of not only our programs but of a viable critical culture. Doing this work makes it clear that local struggles are increasingly connected to national and transnational forces. Caught in the same globalizing economy are First Nation peoples dying of cancer from jobs in the nuclear industry; South American and South Asian immigrants working in the garment industry sweatshops of San Diego, Los Angeles, and San Francisco; Malaysian, Mexican, and Taiwanese workers going blind staring into microscopes that examine the chips that go into U.S. computers; lesbian and gay workers who have lost jobs by coming out or being found out; underpaid and overworked African American men and women who make up the majority of the service and maintenance workers at Yale University and many institutions like it; and yes, even academic workers in these same universities experiencing speed-ups, or part-time underemployment, if they have found jobs at all. Resistance to these abuses requires both global and local points of solidarity, the kind of connection forged during the "battle of Seattle" demonstration against the World Trade Organization as the twentieth century came to a close.

Projects such as the AFL-CIO's "Union Summer" campaign, which linked labor historians and other academics to union and community activists in preparing students to take part in labor-organizing drives, suggest one of many possible routes to create stronger links. The graduate student struggles at Yale, the City University of New York, and elsewhere, deeply tied as they are to the struggle of campus service and maintenance personnel, suggests another path, and the Students Against Sweatshops movement suggests a third.[14] Many other routes are possible. These struggles around work could provide a practical focal point for not simply analyzing but materially redirecting academic labors at the intersections of transnationalism, gender, race, class, and sexuality.

By weaving the words *collision* and *coalition* throughout this chapter, I have suggested that these two words are in opposition. But in fact, as most scholars know, and as hinted throughout the essay, that is not really the case. In my closing thoughts, I remind scholars that the kind of work described herein requires that we acknowledge and work through serious collisions of interests, backgrounds, desires, experiences, and ideologies. As the great teacher, musician, and scholar-activist Bernice Johnson Reagon has reminded us, coalition is painful.[15] It is about leaving behind the comfort of home—whether that home be an identity, an ideology, or an interdiscipline—and risking new connections. The various coalitions sketched in this chapter will not emerge without painful interactions. Being nice to one another, avoiding difficult questions, repressing differences, will not do it. In other words, "no collisions, no coalitions."

Notes

1. For useful overviews that include some gestures toward comparison, see two books by Julie Thompson Klein, *Interdisciplinarity: History, Theory, and Practice* (Detroit, Mich.: Wayne State University Press, 1990), and *Crossing Boundaries: Knowledge, Disciplinarities, and Interdisciplinarities* (Charlottesville: University Press of Virginia, 1996). For some of the best work beginning this process of comparative studies of interdisciplines, see Johnnella E. Butler and John C. Walter, eds. *Transforming the Curriculum: Ethnic Studies and Women's Studies* (Albany: State University of New York Press, 1991). Elizabeth Weed and Naomi Schor, eds., *Feminism Meets Queer Studies* (Bloomington: Indiana University Press, 1997) furthers this project.

2. Mary Helen Washington, " What Happens to American Studies If We Put African American Studies at the Center?" *American Quarterly* 50 (March 1998): 1–23.

3. Stuart Hall, often portrayed as one of the founders of cultural studies, makes points along this line in discussing the rapid movement of what is often called "British cultural studies" into an American and global context. He notes that the history of struggle around issues of gender and race within the Birmingham school is often occluded in the importation process. Hall notes that the dazzling "theoretical fluency" of the younger practitioners of cultural studies makes him sometimes feel uneasy about the depth of their understanding of the political stakes of the work. See Hall, "Cultural Studies and Its Theoretical Legacies," in David Morley and Kuan-Hsing Chen, eds., *Stuart Hall: Critical Dialogues in Cultural Studies* (London: Routledge, 1996), 262–75.

4. *Multiculturalism* is, of course, a very contested term that exists in conservative, moderate, liberal, and progressive forms. The term is worth struggling over because it has become a key one in the "culture wars," particularly the debates around public education at all levels. But most uses of the term seem aimed at "managing" or "celebrating" diversity, not liberating those groups labeled as "diverse" from oppressive structures. For an extended discussion of these issues, see David Theo Goldberg, ed., *Multiculturalism: A Critical Reader* (London: Blackwell, 1994), especially the essays by Peter McLaren, Lauren Berlant and Michael

Warner, and the Chicago Cultural Studies Group; also see Avery F. Gordon and
Christopher Newfield, eds., *Mapping Multiculturalism* (Minneapolis: University
of Minnesota Press, 1996), especially the essays in part 1.

5. For example, the important early anthology, Russell Fergussen et al., eds.,
Out There: Marginalization and Contemporary Cultures (Cambridge: MIT Press,
1988), takes this process as the core of its theoretical task.

6. See Katie King, *Theory in Its Feminist Travels* (Bloomington: Indiana University Press, 1994).

7. This emphasis on group solidarity has generated a complex intellectual
and political argument that perhaps too easily can be named the essentialist versus
the social constructionist debate. For a succinct summary of how this debate has
played itself similarly and differently among African Americans, women, and gays
and lesbians, see Diana Fuss, *Essentially Speaking* (London: Routledge, 1989).

8. The list of exemplary work in this field is long indeed. My eclectic shortlist
of important figures includes Thomas Almaguer, Gloria Anzaldúa, H. L. Gates,
Paul Gilroy, Donna Haraway, George Lipsitz, Audre Lorde, Lisa Lowe, Toni Morrison, Peggy Pascoe, José David Saldívar, George Sanchez, Chela Sandoval, Joan
Scott, Eve Kosofsky Sedgwick, Leslie Marmon Silko, Hortense Spillers, Gerald
Vizenor, Michael Warner, Robert Warrior, Richard White, among many others.

9. Feminist Naomi Schor, for example, has examined charges of "mainstreaming" exemplified by the emergence of "Gender Studies" within and to
some extent against "Women's Studies." She has suggested that in part a generational transition accounts for this tension. This is indeed one factor and may be
generalized to include shifts in Ethnic Studies and the shift from Gay and Lesbian
to Queer Studies in a younger generational cohort. But certainly one also sees
many from an earlier generation of scholars following, and in some cases, leading
this transition. Debates continue to rage about the benefits and losses associated
with each positioning. See Schor, "Feminist and Gender Studies," in Joseph Gibaldi,
ed., *Introduction to Scholarship in Modern Languages and Literatures*, 2d ed. (New
York: Modern Language Association, 1992). See also Joan Scott, ed., "Women's
Studies on the Edge," special issue, *differences 9* (fall 1997). Thomas J. La Belle and
Christopher R. Ward also address some of these tensions in their comparative
study *Ethnic Studies and Multiculturalism* (New York: New York University Press,
1996). With regard to postcolonial theory, see critiques by Ahmad Aijaz, *In Theory:
Classes, Nations, Literatures* (London: Verso, 1992); and E. San Juan Jr., *Beyond
Postcolonial Theory* (New York: St. Martins, 1998).

10. This point is elaborated incisively by the writer Noel Sturgeon in relation
to the essentialist moments in some environmental feminisms in her book *Ecofeminist Natures* (New York: Routledge, 1997).

11. See, for example, T. V. Reed, *Fifteen Jugglers, Five Believers: Literary Politics and the Poetics of American Social Movements* (Berkeley: University of California Press, 1992).

12. Michael Denning makes this argument in his book *The Cultural Front* (London: Verso, 1996), especially in the concluding chapter. It is congruent with the fact that many spoke from the beginning of the American studies "movement," a term not generally applied to sociology or English. But this does not invalidate earlier work, by Denning and others, showing that the American studies movement was significantly interrupted by McCarthyism's dampening of dissent and by Cold War co-optation of some American studies practitioners and programs.

13. This point is made by Ellen Rooney in an essay entitled, "Discipline and Vanish: Feminism, the Resistance to Theory, and the Politics of Cultural Studies," in John Storey, ed., *What Is Cultural Studies?* (New York: Arnold, 1996), 208–20. Originally presented in 1988, Rooney's argument seems even more relevant today, as cultural studies has become increasingly "disciplined" and for some, like India for nineteenth-century British imperialists, a "career" (careerism is, of course, not unknown in the other studies fields).

14. Two recent collections offer useful analyses of the current trends in academic and other labor circles. See Cary Nelson, ed., *Will Teach for Food: Academic Labor in Crisis* (Minneapolis: University of Minnesota Press, 1997), and "Academic Labor," a special issue of *Social Text* 51 (summer 1997). One of the key clearinghouses for these struggles is the Center for Campus Organizing, which can be reached by mail at Box 748, Cambridge, Mass., 02142, by telephone at 617–354–9363.

15. See Bernice Johnson Reagon's celebrated essay, "Coalition Politics," in Barbara Smith, ed., *Home Girls: A Black Feminist Anthology* (New York: Kitchen Table: Women of Color Press, 1983).

Contributors

EDNA ACOSTA-BELÉN is Distinguished Service Professor of Latin American and Caribbean Studies, and Women's Studies at the University at Albany, State University of New York, where she also serves as director of the Center for Latino, Latin American, and Caribbean Studies (CELAC). Her areas of research are Hispanic Caribbean and U.S. Latino literary and cultural history as well as Women's Studies. Publications include *Women in the Latin American Development Process* (with Christine E. Bose, 1995), *Researching Women in Latin America and the Caribbean* (with Christine E. Bose, 1993), *The Hispanic Experience in the United States* (with B. R. Sjostrom, 1988), and *The Puerto Rican Woman: Perspectives on Culture, History, and Society* (1979, 1986). Acosta-Belén is one of the founding editors of the *Latino Review of Books*, a journal that focuses on the U.S. Latino experience and the transnational connections between Latino groups and their Latin American and Caribbean countries of origin.

MARILYN CABALLERO ALQUIZOLA has taught Asian American literature at the University of California-Los Angeles, at Colorado College, and at San Francisco State University. She is currently a faculty member in the Department of Ethnic Studies at the University of Colorado-Boulder and a doctoral candidate in Ethnic Studies at the University of California-Berkeley. Her articles on Filipino American literature appear in *Frontiers of Asian American Studies: Writing, Research, and Commentary* (1989) and in *Asian Americans: Comparative and Global Perspectives* (1991). She has also published on Asian American Studies in *The State of Asian America: Activism and Resistance in the 1990's* (1994). She was co-editor of *Privileging Positions: The Sites of Asian American Studies* (1995).

JOHNNELLA E. BUTLER is Associate Dean of the Graduate School, Professor in the Department of American Ethnic Studies, and adjunct professor of Women's Studies and English at the University of Washington-Seattle. A nationally recognized consultant on higher education curriculum and diversity, she is the co-editor with John C. Walter of *Transforming the Curriculum: Ethnic Studies and Women's Studies* (1991), co-editor with Carol Severino and Juan Guerra, *Writing in Multicultural Settings,* and the author of "*Mumbo Jumbo:* African American Literary Theory and Wholeness" (in *Aesthetics in a Multicultural Age,* edited by Emory Elliott, Oxford University Press, 2001). Her collaborative work has become a model in the field of curriculum transformation. In 1992–93 she was named Liberal Arts Professor by the University of Washington. Butler was the Carruthers Distinguished Lecturer at the University of New Mexico in 1993.

ELIZABETH COOK-LYNN, a member of the Crow Creek Sioux Tribe, is Professor Emerita of English and Native American Studies at Eastern Washington University. She has also been visiting professor in Native Studies at the University of California-Davis and Arizona State University-Tempe. A poet, writer, editor, and consultant in Native American Studies, Cook-Lynn was one of the founders of the journal *Wicazo Sa Review.* Her books include *From the River's Edge* (1990), *The Power of Horses and Other Stories* (1991), *The Politics of Hallowed Ground* (1998), *Aurelia: A Crow Creek Trilogy* (1999), and a collection of essays, *Why I Can't Read Wallace Stegner and Other Essays: A Tribal Voice* (1996).

LAURO H. FLORES is Associate Professor of Chicano and Latin American literatures and cultures in the Spanish and Portuguese Division of the Department of Romance Languages, and Professor of Ethnic Studies at the University of Washington-Seattle. During his tenure at the university, he has been the Director of the Center for Chicano Studies, Chair of the Latin American Studies Program at the Jackson School of International Studies, and Special Assistant to the Provost. He is the senior editor of *The Americas Review,* his anthology *The Floating Borderlands: Twenty-Five Years of U.S. Hispanic Literature* (1998) won an American Book Award in 1999, and he has published a critical edition of Luis Pérez's autobiography, *El Coyote, The Rebel* (2000). Flores has also been a visiting professor at Stanford University (1989–90) and at the University of California-Los Angeles (1990–91) as well as a member and chair of the Committee on the Literatures and Languages of America of the Modern Language Association. He is currently the regional liaison for the Ford Foundation Fellows.

LANE RYO HIRABAYASHI is a professor in the Department of Ethnic Studies at the University of Colorado-Boulder, where he is also the coordinator of Asian American Studies and a graduate faculty member of the Department of Anthropology. He is author of *Cultural Capital: Mountain Zapotec Migrant Associations in Mexico City* (1993) and *Politics of Fieldwork: Research in an American Concentration Camp* (1999). Hirabayashi is the editor of *Inside an American Concentration Camp: Japanese American Resistance at Poston, Arizona* (1995) and *Teaching Asian America: Diversity and the Problem of Community* (1998).

CRAIG HOWE, a member of the Oglala Sioux Tribe, has served as Director of the D'Arcy McNickle Center for American Indian History at the Newberry Library in Chicago and Deputy Assistant Director for Cultural Resources at the Smithsonian National Museum of the American Indian. He has taught American Indian Studies courses at universities in the United States and Canada.

EVELYN HU-DEHART was born in Chunking, China, raised in California, and attended Stanford University (B.A. in political science) and the University of Texas-Austin (Ph.D., history), where she pursued Latin American and Caribbean history. During the past decade she has moved into the forefront of the evolving field of comparative race and Ethnic Studies, serving as Director of the Center for Studies of Ethnicity and Race in America (CSERA) and as Chair of the Department of Ethnic Studies at the University of Colorado-Boulder. Her major publications have been on the Yaqui Indians of Sonora (Mexico) and Arizona and on the Asian diasporas (primarily Chinese, Japanese, and South Asian) in Latin America and the Caribbean.

SHIRLEY HUNE is Associate Dean in the Graduate Division at the University of California-Los Angeles, where she is also Professor of Urban Planning. Her recent publications on race and gender include *Asian Pacific American Women in Higher Education: Claiming Visibility and Voice* (1998), *Teaching Asian American Women's History* (1997), "Higher Education as Gendered Space: Asian American Women and Everyday Inequities, in Everyday Sexism in the Third Millennium" (1997), and "Rethinking Race: Paradigms and Policy Formation" (in *Amerasia Journal* 21 [1 and 2]: 29–40).

RHETT S. JONES is Professor of History and Afro-American Studies at Brown University, where he chaired the Afro-American Studies Program for twelve years and directed the Center for the Study of Race and Ethnicity from 1991 to 1995. The author of nearly three hundred scholarly articles, reviews, and essays, he has received grants from the American Council of Learned Societies, the Coolidge Research Colloquium, The Ford Foundation, the National Endowment of the

Humanities, the Rockefeller Foundation, the Trotter Institute, and the Southern Fellowships Fund. Jones was the recipient of the 1992 Rhode Island Black Heritage Society award for outstanding service to the Rhode Island Black community, and the 1996 Ochillo Award for the best article published in the *Griot*, the journal of the Southern Conference on Afro-American Studies. He also serves on the editorial boards of *Explorations in Ethnic Studies, Plantation Societies in the Americas*, and the *Western Journal of Black Studies*.

MANNING MARABLE is Professor of History and Political Science and Director of the Institute for Research in African-American Studies at Columbia University. He is the author of many books on African-American politics and history, including *W.E.B. DuBois: Black Radical Democrat (1986), Race Reform and Rebellion* (1991), *Beyond Black and White* (1995), and *Speaking Truth to Power* (1996). He also is the editor of *Dispatches from the Ebony Tower: Intellectuals Confront the African American Experience* (Columbia University Press, 2000).

JUDITH NEWTON is Professor and Director of Women and Gender Studies at the University of California-Davis. She is the author of *Starting Over: Feminism and the Politics of Cultural Critique* (1994) and is finishing a book entitled *Born— Again! From Panthers to Promise Keepers with the "New Men"* (Rowman and Littlefield, 2001).

T. V. REED is Director of American Studies at Washington State University. He is the author of *Fifteen Jugglers, Five Believers: Literary Politics and the Poetics of American Social Movements* (1992). His articles have appeared in the journals *Representations* and *American Literary History*, and his widely used essay "Theory and Method in American/Cultural Studies" is now available on the Internet at http://www.wsu.edu:8080/~amerstu/tm/bib.html. Reed's next works include a book on the 1930s radical novelist Robert Cantwell and another book on the role of various art forms in social movements from the Civil Rights era to the present.

RONALD TAKAKI is one of the foremost nationally recognized scholars of multicultural studies. The grandson of Japanese immigrant plantation laborers in Hawaii, he holds a Ph.D. in American history from the University of California-Berkeley, where he has been Professor of Ethnic Studies for more than two decades. The Berkeley faculty has honored him with a Distinguished Teaching Award, and Cornell University appointed him as Messenger Lecturer for 1993. He is the author of the critically acclaimed *Iron Cages: Race and Culture in Nineteenth-Century America* (1990), the prize-winning *Strangers from a Different Shore: A History of Asian Americans* (1989), which the *New York Times Book Review* selected in 1989 as one of the year's Notable Books, and the classic *A Different Mirror: A History of Multicultural America* (1993).

JOHN C. WALTER is Professor in the Department of American Ethnic Studies and a member of the Graduate Faculty of the Department of History at the University of Washington-Seattle. A past president of the New England Region of the National Council for Black Studies and of the National Association for Ethnic Studies, he has chaired African American Studies departments and programs at John Jay College of Criminal Justice of the City University of New York, Bowdoin College, Smith College, and the University of Cincinnati. At the University of Washington, Walter has also served as Director of the African American Studies Program and chaired the Department of American Ethnic Studies. His book *The Harlem Fox: J. Raymond Jones and Tammany, 1920–1970* won an American Book Award in 1990.

Index

Academic discourse, elitist nature of, 174
Achebe, Chinua: and *Things Fall Apart*, 9
Addams, Jane: and NAACP, 77
Affirmative action: rollback of, 19; and Asian Americans, 179
African American history, 65–97 passim; and the African American experience, 67
African American Museum Association (AAMA), 137–38 passim
African Americans, xix, 122, 141; legal treatment of, xx; and World War I, 80–81; and the Great Migration, 81–83; and African diaspora, 73; and Black Studies, 104; and Whites, 119; in academia, 142–45; relationship with Ethnic Studies 143; and Afrocentricity, 144–45; and racism, 144–45; and different picture of America, 284
African American Studies, xix; and borderlands, xii; majors in, 35; beginnings and development of, 118, 141; and Ethnic Studies, 118–19; and recruitment of Black scholars, 130; and other disciplines, 138; periodicals in, 139–42. *See also* Africana Studies; Black Studies
Africana Studies, 118, 124–29; early responses to, 114; and racism, 115, 124; ideologies in, 124–25; and Christianity, 135; periodicals from, 139–41; and Black middle class, 141; and bipolar racial model, 141; and Ethnic Studies departments, 144
African diaspora, 129; and Marcus Garvey, 73; and globalization of Black Studies, 114
African Studies: and globalization, 249
Afro-American Studies. *See* African American Studies; Africana Studies; Black Studies
Afrocentricity: and Ethnic Studies, 27; and Molefe Kete Asante, 131; and National Council for Black Studies, 131

Afrocentrism, 19; rise of, in America, 126; and NCBS, 131; defined, 144; as model for Black Studies, 145

Agtuca, Jacqueline R., 183

Ahn, Hyung-ju, 181

Aldridge, Delores, 129

Allen, Robert, 46

American Indian Movement (AIM), 50

American Indians/Native Americans: legal treatment of, xx

American Indian Studies, 159, 160; and Native American Studies, xx; and place in the academy, 30–31, 35, 122, 150; and indigenous model, 106; and ethnicity, 151; and First Nation status, 151–52, 154, 163; and colonial race laws, 151; and forced citizenship, 151; and colonialism, 152; intellectual paradigm in, 153–57; and studies of sovereignty and autonomy, 155, 156, 158, 160, 163; and Nixon policy, 154, 166; and termination and relocation policies, 154; and organization of tribal knowledge, 155; and deconstruction, 156; epistemology in, 156–57; and oral tradition, 157; curriculum, 161; and post-colonial studies, 163; and tribal nationhood, 163; and national identity, 163; termination policy, 166. *See also* Native American Studies

American Studies, 19, 274–82 passim; race theory in, 26; and Ethic Studies, 35, 274, 275; and progressive scholarship, 277; and research on American culture, 278; as Popular Front social movement, 287; and labor struggles, 288–89

American Studies Association, xvii, 277, 282; and Ethnic Studies, xiv; and scholars of color, 281

Anderson, Talmadge, 127–28

Anzaldúa, Gloria, 37; and *Borderlands/La Frontera*, 233. *See also* Borderlands; Mestiza consciousness

Area Studies, in academia, 250

Asante, Molefi Kete, 47, 131

Asian Americans, xx, 284; and political identity, 179

Asian American Studies, 171, 185, 228; and borderlands, xiii, 233–36; and *Aiiieeeee!*, 23; place of, in academy, 30–31, 53; majors in, 35; as subject category, 169, 177–78; and postmodernism, 169; essentialism in, 170; postmodernist perspective in, 170, 175; and erasure of class, gender and sexuality, 170; and post-structuralism, 170; and Civil Rights Movement, 172; power and knowledge in, 172; heuristic typology in, 173; and traditional scholarly paradigm, 174; Marxism in, 175, 180; feminism in; 175; importance of community-based project in, 175, 184–85; goals of, 176–77; personal agency in, 177; experience as key to understanding, 178; methodological approaches in, 180–86; and internal struggles, 180–81; and feminism, 181; and oral histories, 182; and role of gender, 182; and racialization, 182, 228; community studies in, 183; class in, 184, 234; as required course, 185; predominance of Chinese and Japanese in, 186; hiring practices in, 186; and Asian Studies, 227; as interdisciplinary field, 229; as participant in history, culture, identity, 229, 230, 231; and migration to America, 233; and diaspora, postcolonial and transnational studies in, 233–36; and American exceptionalism, 235

Asian American Studies Association, xvii, 277, 282; and Ethnic Studies, xiv; and scholars of color, 281

Asian diaspora, 104

Asian Studies, 228, 230

Raab, Earl, 13
Race: defined, 44, 56; and ethnicity,
    45; political economy approach, 46;
    within North American context, 57;
    as challenge to historians, 75; white-
    oriented bipolar model of, 118; as
    Whiteness, 285; contrasted with
    unraced, 285
Racial essentialism: and Afrocentrism,
    47; and cultural amalgamation, 56
Racial formation, 42–43, 228; and im-
    migration, 58. See also Omi, Michael;
    Winnant, Howard
Racialization: of European immigrants,
    xix; in Ethnic Studies, 22, 56
Racism, xxi; as challenge to historians,
    75; and ideal of individualistic
    achievement, 120; and slavery, 120;
    Marxist attacks on, 125; as force in
    America, 129; origins of, 135; apogee
    of, in U. S., 144; roots in traditional
    disciplines, 144; woven into fabric of
    American life, 145; justification for,
    145; in academy, 162; everyday struc-
    tures of, 186; rigid essentialism in,
    186; and right wing demagoguery,
    251. See also Africana Studies;
    Essentialism
Randolph, A. Phillip, 88
Ravitch, Diane, 6, 7
Reagan, Ronald, 67, 212
Reagon, Bernice Johnson, 289
Rebellodo, Tey Diana, 35
Reconstruction: as defining subject
    in Black history, 69; as historical
    period, 86; included in history texts,
    95; treatment of, in history texts, 96
Reed, T. V., xxiii
Relational pluralism, 33–34. See also
    Ethnic Studies
Re-memory, xxiv. See also Ethnic
    Studies
Retamar, Roberto Fernández, 4, 254
Rice, Norm, xiv

Ringer, Benjamin: and "We the People"
    and Others, 7
Rivlin, Harry N., 34
Robinson, William ("Smokey"), 95
Robnett, Belinda, 271
Rock 'n' roll: role in Civil Rights, 70;
    and social change, 75; treatment
    in American history texts, 94–95
Rodó, José Enrique: and Ariel, 253–54
Roediger, David R., 30, 43. See also
    Whiteness
Rogin, Michael, 4
The Rolling Stones, 94
Rooney, Ellen, 287
Roosevelt, Franklin: and Executive
    Order 8802, 88
Roosevelt, Theodore: and Brownsville
    Riot, 96
Ross, Diana, and the Supremes, 95
Rudwick, Elliott: and Black History
    and the Historical Profession, 65; and
    From Plantation to Ghetto, 67, and
    Journal of Southern History, 67;
    and Civil Rights Act of 1964, 88
Rush, Bobby, 74
Russell, Joseph, 129
Russia, 3, 7
Rustin, Bayard, 88, 115

Sáenz, Jóse de la Luz, 204
Sambo thesis. See Slavery
Salamasina, Adele, 183
San Miguel, Guadalupe, 206
Sánchez, George T., 203–4
Santería: and Catholicism, 136
Sawada, Mitziko, 181
Schlesinger, Arthur, Jr., 13, 47; and The
    Disuniting of America, 7; and The
    Age of Jackson, 8; and cult of ethnic-
    ity, 8; and Ethnic Studies, 109
Scott, Patricia Bell, 32
Second Reconstruction: and Civil
    Rights Movement, 49
Segregation: as Southern institution, 48;